"Within a period of about seventy-five years, a s̲. Jesus became a major religious movement that thrived within its c̲.̲.̲.̲ context. Edwards looks at the many factors that contributed to this radical transformation. He convincingly shows that this period—often seen as a hazy and undefined period—was the most dynamic that Christianity has ever seen. This volume will be enlightening reading for anyone interested in Jesus, Paul, and what became the Christian church."

—**Stanley E. Porter**, McMaster Divinity College, Ontario, Canada

"Edwards is an adept guide to the tectonic shifts that gave rise to the now-familiar features of Christian faith; he makes a compelling case for the striking metamorphosis the early church underwent in its infancy. Yet while this book's domain is the past, its stakes are in the future. At the same time that he undoes assumptions about the given forms of Christian faith, Edwards witnesses to the surprising power of the gospel to take seed and bear new fruit. Written at the cusp of a post-Christendom, postmodern, and post-Covid era of great change, *From Christ to Christianity* is a welcome and instructive reminder of the enduring changelessness of the gospel through the vicissitudes of time."

—**Amy J. Erickson**, St. Marks National Theological Centre, Barton, Australia

"Scholars have thoroughly worked the ground of the apostolic period, almost turning it into fine dust. That same thoroughness predominates once we arrive at the end of the second century. But the post-apostolic period has suffered relative scholarly neglect. It seems a strange world, as evidenced, for example, by the writings of Ignatius. Edwards's book fills in the empty space as no other has done. He traces the dramatic changes that occurred in the Christian movement from the close of the apostolic period to the year 140 or so: from Jewish to Gentile, from Hebrew to Greek, from rural to urban, from scroll to codex, from Sabbath to Sunday, and so much more. And yet, in spite of these dramatic changes, he shows the continuity that prevailed, too. It is clearly the same faith. The fruit looks much riper; but it is still the same fruit. Edwards knows the literature, writes with precision, and makes the story come alive. He is a master of writing engaging narrative without sacrificing accuracy and good judgment."

—**Gerald L. Sittser**, Whitworth University (emeritus); author of *Resilient Faith: How the Early Christian "Third Way" Changed the World*

"In this absorbing work, Edwards, in mastery of a wealth of ancient materials, traces how the small, rural movement of followers of Jesus in Galilee became, in less than a century, an expansive network of churches throughout the great urban centers of the Roman Empire and in regions far beyond. Edwards's work demonstrates both meticulous historical research and judicious theological conclusions, singularly marked by an unwavering attendance to the truth that it was the proclamation and exaltation of Jesus as Lord, and a Christology in correspondence to that witness and worship, that remained at the center of the church amid all ensuing changes. In writing on the New Testament and the Apostolic Fathers, Edwards demonstrates that which J. B. Lightfoot, his predecessor in this task, lifted up as the ideal for such work: 'The highest reason and the fullest faith.' This work embodies this ideal, and as such it will be a gift not only to students of the history of Christianity but also to the church at large."

—**Kimlyn J. Bender**, George W. Truett Theological Seminary, Baylor University

"For such a time as this. . . . As epochal changes in our world challenge the Christian movement to seek deeper transformation than it has experienced in centuries, Edwards invites us to learn from the amazing changes that took place in the movement's first seventy-five years of life. With careful scholarship and communicative skills honed by a lifetime in podium and pulpit, Edwards shows how the movement centered in the person and work of Jesus Christ adapted almost all of its forms while preserving its essential message."

—**Stanley D. Slade**, American Baptist International Ministries

"This study takes up the question of what transpired within the seventy-five-year period between the death of Jesus and the death of Ignatius to account for the strikingly creative transitions that shaped the church's evolving self-identity. Sharing an affinity with Lohmeyer's depiction of the church as marked by 'unchanging essence amid changing forms, adaptive to culture but not captive to culture,' Edward pinpoints and fleshes out fourteen facets of the emerging church in which that insight seems most clearly evident. Readers hungry for a thorough, rigorously well-researched, astutely analytical study that is meticulous in scholarly details while not overreaching about historical lacunas where literary evidence is scant will be amply rewarded. His writing style is both erudite and elegant."

—**Jeannine M. Graham**, George Fox University (emerita)

From Christ to Christianity

*How the Jesus Movement Became the Church
in Less Than a Century*

James R. Edwards

Baker Academic
a division of Baker Publishing Group
Grand Rapids, Michigan

© 2021 by James R. Edwards

Published by Baker Academic
a division of Baker Publishing Group
PO Box 6287, Grand Rapids, MI 49516-6287
www.bakeracademic.com

Printed in the United States of America

Library of Congress Cataloging-in-Publication Data
Names: Edwards, James R., author.
Title: From Christ to Christianity : how the Jesus movement became the church in less than a century / James R. Edwards.
Description: Grand Rapids, Michigan : Baker Academic, a division of Baker Publishing Group, 2021. | Includes bibliographical references and indexes.
Identifiers: LCCN 2020033253 | ISBN 9781540961402 (paperback) | ISBN 9781540964106 (casebound)
Subjects: LCSH: Church history—Primitive and early church, ca. 30–600.
Classification: LCC BR165 .F784 2021 | DDC 270.1—dc23
LC record available at https://lccn.loc.gov/2020033253

Unless otherwise indicated, translations of Scripture are the author's own.

Scripture quotations labeled ESV are from The Holy Bible, English Standard Version® (ESV®), copyright © 2001 by Crossway, a publishing ministry of Good News Publishers. Used by permission. All rights reserved. ESV Text Edition: 2016

Scripture quotations labeled NIV are from THE HOLY BIBLE, NEW INTERNATIONAL VERSION®, NIV® Copyright © 1973, 1978, 1984, 2011 by Biblica, Inc.® Used by permission. All rights reserved worldwide.

Scripture quotations labeled RSV are from the Revised Standard Version of the Bible, copyright 1946, 1952 [2nd edition, 1971] National Council of the Churches of Christ in the United States of America. Used by permission. All rights reserved worldwide.

21 22 23 24 25 26 27   7 6 5 4 3 2 1

In grateful memory of my teachers

David Dilworth
Bruce M. Metzger
Eduard Schweizer
Ralph P. Martin
Martin Hengel

Contents

Preface

The number and variety of resources for understanding the New Testament—commentaries, word studies, lexica of ancient languages, theological dictionaries, comparative studies of Judaism and Hellenism, and specialized studies in the history, sociology, culture, and archaeology of the first Christian century—make the study of the New Testament a veritable oasis for layperson and scholar alike. I have been privileged to spend the greater part of my professional and scholarly life in this oasis.

The New Testament lies at the epicenter of the present study and thus affords us the benefits of the trove of resources just mentioned. But the field of our inquiry—which is the development of the Jesus movement into an autonomous church, the move from Christ to Christianity—exceeds the circumference of the New Testament oasis and includes a body of literature known as the Apostolic Fathers, which lies on the periphery of the New Testament era. The Apostolic Fathers have not received the scholarly attention that the New Testament has, but they are essential for our historical investigation and, as I hope to demonstrate, their fruitfulness for our project is indispensable, for it is with them, and not within the oasis of the New Testament alone, that the movement begun by Christ becomes fully recognizable as Christianity.

———•———

In order to disrupt the flow of the narrative as little as possible, three or more biblical citations, and all extrabiblical citations, are given in footnotes. In addition to providing source citations, footnotes often supply further explanation or evidence on a given point. Readers who choose not to read the footnotes should be reassured that they will forgo only such supporting evidence and not the main point(s), which are made in the body of the text. With regard to nomenclature, I refer to the Jewish Scriptures, often called the "Hebrew Scriptures" today, according to the traditional designation "Old Testament." The latter continues to be acceptable in scholarly reference works and, especially for the purposes of this work, has the benefit of linking the old covenant organically to the new covenant (Jer. 31:31), to which the early church, in particular, testified in its commitment to the Greek Old Testament (LXX).

The writing of this book is indebted to more names than appear on its cover. I wish to thank Baker Academic, and especially its editor Robert Hosack, for welcoming this work. The thoroughness and technical expertise of Alexander DeMarco in editing the manuscript of this book have improved its published state in innumerable ways. I am indebted to friends, colleagues, and family who have read and critiqued earlier versions of this work, especially Gary Watts and Jerry Sittser, who read and critiqued drafts of the work in its entirety. Adam Neder, Josh Leim, and my wife, Jane, have also made important contributions to the writing of this book. All have improved my strengths, ameliorated my weaknesses, and helped eliminate my errors, making this a better book than it would have been without them.

It is a special pleasure for me to dedicate this book to the memory of my teachers, David Dilworth, Bruce M. Metzger, Eduard Schweizer, Ralph P. Martin, and Martin Hengel. Their lives were, and continue to be for me, a cloud of witnesses.

James R. Edwards

Abbreviations

General

AD	*anno Domini* (in the year of the Lord)	Gk.	Greek
		Hb.	Hebrew
Aram.	Aramaic	Lat.	Latin
BC	before Christ	*log.*	*logion*, saying
bk.	book	MT	Masoretic Text of the Hebrew Bible
c.	century		
ca.	circa	p(p).	page(s)
cf.	compare	pl.	plural
ch(s).	chapter(s)	r.	reigned
d.	died	rev.	revised
ed(s).	editor(s)	SBL	Society of Biblical Literature
e.g.	for example	trans.	translated by, translation
esp.	especially	UBS	United Bible Society
frag.	fragment	v(v).	verse(s)

Bibliographic

ABD	*The Anchor Bible Dictionary.* Edited by D. N. Freedman et al. 6 vols. New York: Doubleday, 1992
ANF	*The Ante-Nicene Fathers: Translations of the Writings of the Fathers down to A.D. 325.* Edited by Alexander Roberts and James Donaldson. 10 vols. 1885–87. Repr., Grand Rapids: Eerdmans, 1978
ATANT	Abhandlungen zur Theologie des Alten und Neuen Testaments
AYBRL	Anchor Yale Bible Reference Library
BAR	*Biblical Archaeology Review*
BDAG	*A Greek-English Lexicon of the New Testament and Other Early Christian Literature.* Edited by Frederick W. Danker, Walter Bauer, William F. Arndt, and F. Wilbur Gingrich. 3rd ed. Chicago: University of Chicago Press, 2000.
BHT	Beiträge zur historischen Theologie

BRev	Bible Review	IDB	Interpreter's Dictionary of the Bible. Edited by George A. Buttrick. 4 vols. New York: Abingdon, 1962
BZNW	Beihefte zur Zeitschrift für die neutestamentliche Wissenschaft		
CD	Barth, Karl. Church Dogmatics. Translated by Geoffrey Bromiley. Edited by T. F. Torrance. Vols. I–IV, in 13 parts. Edinburgh: T&T Clark, 1956–69	IVPNTC	IVP New Testament Commentary
		JBL	Journal of Biblical Literature
		JBTh	Jahrbuch für Biblische Theologie
CRINT	Compendia Rerum Iudaicarum ad Novum Testamentum	KEK	Kritisch-exegetischer Kommentar über das Neue Testament (Meyer-Kommentar)
EDEJ	The Eerdmans Dictionary of Early Judaism. Edited by J. J. Collins and D. C. Harlow. Grand Rapids: Eerdmans, 2010	LCL	Loeb Classical Library
		LNTS	Library of New Testament Studies
		LSJ	A Greek-English Lexicon. H. G. Liddell, R. Scott, and H. S. Jones. 9th ed. with rev. suppl. Oxford: Clarendon, 1977
EDNT	Exegetical Dictionary of the New Testament. Edited by Horst Balz and Gerhard Schneider. 3 vols. Grand Rapids: Eerdmans, 1990–93		
		LXX	Septuagint, Greek Old Testament
EEECAA	The Eerdmans Encyclopedia of Early Christian Art and Archaeology. Edited by Paul C. Finney. 3 vols. Grand Rapids: Eerdmans, 2017	NHL	The Nag Hammadi Library in English. Edited by James M. Robinson. San Francisco: Harper & Row, 1977
Enc. Jud.	Encyclopedia Judaica. 16 vols. Jerusalem: Keter, 1972	NIBCNT	New International Biblical Commentary on the New Testament
FRLANT	Forschungen zur Religion und Literatur des Alten und Neuen Testaments	NICNT	New International Commentary on the New Testament
GEDSH	Gorgias Encyclopedic Dictionary of the Syriac Heritage. Edited by Sebastian P. Brock, Aaron M. Burns, George Kiraz, and Lucas Van Rompay. Piscataway, NJ: Gorgias, 2011	NovT	Novum Testamentum
		NSHERK	The New Schaff-Herzog Encyclopedia of Religious Knowledge. Edited by Samuel M. Jackson. 15 vols. Grand Rapids: Baker, 1977
HALOT	The Hebrew and Aramaic Lexicon of the Old Testament. Edited by Ludwig Koehler, Walter Baumgartner, and Johann J. Stamm. 2 vols. Leiden: Brill, 2001	NTAbh	Neutestamentliche Abhandlungen
		NTApoc	New Testament Apocrypha. Edited by Edgar Hennecke and Wilhelm Schneemelcher. Translated and edited by R. McL. Wilson. 2 vols. Louisville: Westminster John Knox, 1991–92
HNT	Handbuch zum Neuen Testament		
HNTC	Harper's New Testament Commentaries	NTS	New Testament Studies

OTP	*Old Testament Pseudepigrapha*. Edited by James H. Charlesworth. 2 vols. New York: Doubleday, 1983–85		Strack and Paul Billerbeck. 6 vols. Munich: Beck, 1922–61
PG	Patrologia Graeca. Edited by J.-P. Migne. 161 vols. Paris, 1857–86	TBC	Torch Bible Commentary
		TDOT	*Theological Dictionary of the Old Testament*. Edited by G. Johannes Botterweck, Helmer Ringgren, and Heinz-Josef Fabry. 15 vols. Grand Rapids: Eerdmans, 1974–2006
PGL	*A Patristic Greek Lexicon*. Edited by G. W. H. Lampe. Oxford: Clarendon, 1961		
PNTC	Pillar New Testament Commentary	TWNT	*Theologisches Wörterbuch zum Neuen Testament*. Edited by Gerhard Kittel and Gerhard Friedrich. 9 vols. Stuttgart: Kohlhammer, 1932–79
SBT	Studies in Biblical Theology		
SJT	*Scottish Journal of Theology*		
Str-B	*Kommentar zum Neuen Testament aus Talmud und Midrasch*. Edited by Hermann L.	*TynBul*	*Tyndale Bulletin*
		WUNT	Wissenschaftliche Untersuchungen zum Neuen Testament

Old Testament

Gen.	Genesis	Song	Song of Songs
Exod.	Exodus	Isa.	Isaiah
Lev.	Leviticus	Jer.	Jeremiah
Num.	Numbers	Lam.	Lamentations
Deut.	Deuteronomy	Ezek.	Ezekiel
Josh.	Joshua	Dan.	Daniel
Judg.	Judges	Hosea	Hosea
Ruth	Ruth	Joel	Joel
1–2 Sam.	1–2 Samuel	Amos	Amos
1–2 Kings	1–2 Kings	Obad.	Obadiah
1–2 Chron.	1–2 Chronicles	Jon.	Jonah
Ezra	Ezra	Mic.	Micah
Neh.	Nehemiah	Nah.	Nahum
Esther	Esther	Hab.	Habakkuk
Job	Job	Zeph.	Zephaniah
Ps(s).	Psalm(s)	Hag.	Haggai
Prov.	Proverbs	Zech.	Zechariah
Eccles.	Ecclesiastes	Mal.	Malachi

New Testament

Matt.	Matthew	1–2 Cor.	1–2 Corinthians
Mark	Mark	Gal.	Galatians
Luke	Luke	Eph.	Ephesians
John	John	Phil.	Philippians
Acts	Acts	Col.	Colossians
Rom.	Romans	1–2 Thess.	1–2 Thessalonians

1–2 Tim.	1–2 Timothy	1–2 Pet.	1–2 Peter
Titus	Titus	1–3 John	1–3 John
Philem.	Philemon	Jude	Jude
Heb.	Hebrews	Rev.	Revelation
James	James		

Old Testament Apocrypha and Pseudepigrapha

1–4 Macc.	1–4 Maccabees	Pss. Sol.	Psalms of Solomon
Let. Aris.	Letter of Aristeas	Sib. Or.	Sibylline Oracles
Odes Sol.	Odes of Solomon		

New Testament Apocrypha

Acts Paul Thec.	Acts of Paul and Thecla	Gos. Thom.	Gospel of Thomas
Acts Pet.	Acts of Peter	Ps.-Clem.	Pseudo-Clementines
Acts Thom.	Acts of Thomas	*Hom.*	*Homilies*
Gos. Phil.	Gospel of Philip		

Dead Sea Scrolls

1QS	Rule of the Community	4QTest	Testimonia
1QSa	Rule of the Congregation (appendix a to 1QS)	11QMelch	Melchizedek
		CD	Damascus Document (from
4QFlor	Florilegium		Cairo Genizah)

Rabbinic Tractates

Tractates preceded by *b.* or *m.* are from the Babylonian Talmud or Mishnah, respectively.		Meg.	Megillah
		Miqv.	Miqva'ot
		Parah	Parah
Avot	Avot	Rosh Hash.	Rosh Hashanah
B. Bat.	Bava Batra	Sanh.	Sanhedrin
Ber.	Berakhot	Shabb.	Shabbat
Betzah	Betzah (= Yom Tob)	Sotah	Sotah
Eruv.	Eruvin	Ta'an.	Ta'anit
Git.	Gittin	Tehar.	Teharot
Hag.	Hagigah	Tem.	Temurah
Hul.	Hullin	Yad.	Yadayim
Kelim	Kelim	Yoma	Yoma
Ketub.	Ketubbot		

Apostolic Fathers

Apol.	Aristides, *Apology*	Diogn.	Epistle to Diognetus
Barn.	Epistle of Barnabas	Herm. Mand.	Shepherd of Hermas,
1–2 Clem.	1–2 Clement		Mandate(s)
Did.	Didache		

Herm. Sim.	Shepherd of Hermas, Similitude(s)	Ign. *Pol.*	Ignatius, *To Polycarp*
Herm. Vis.	Shepherd of Hermas, Vision(s)	Ign. *Rom.*	Ignatius, *To the Romans*
		Ign. *Smyrn.*	Ignatius, *To the Smyrnaeans*
Ign. *Eph.*	Ignatius, *To the Ephesians*	Ign. *Trall.*	Ignatius, *To the Trallians*
Ign. *Magn.*	Ignatius, *To the Magnesians*	Mart. Pol.	Martyrdom of Polycarp
Ign. *Phld.*	Ignatius, *To the Philadelphians*	Pap. *Frag.*	Fragments of Papias
		Pol. *Phil.*	Polycarp, *To the Philippians*

Classical, Jewish, and Patristic Writings

Ag. Ap.	Josephus, *Against Apion*	*Hist.*	Tacitus, *Histories*
Alleg. Interp.	Philo, *Allegorical Interpretation* 1, 2, 3	*Hist. eccl.*	Eusebius, *Ecclesiastical History*
Ann.	Tacitus, *Annals*	*Hist. rom.*	Dio Cassius, *Roman History*
Ant.	Josephus, *Jewish Antiquities*		
1 Apol.	Justin Martyr, *First Apology*	*Holy Theoph.*	Hippolytus, *Discourse on the Holy Theophany*
Apol.	Tertullian, *Apology*		
Aug.	Suetonius, *Divine Augustus*	*Hom. Matt.*	John Chrysostom, *Homiliae in Matthaeum*
Cels.	Origen, *Against Celsus*		
Civ.	Augustine, *De civitate Dei*	*J.W.*	Josephus, *Jewish War*
Claud.	Suetonius, *Divine Claudius*	*Nat.*	Tertullian, *To the Heathen*
Descr.	Pausanius, *Description of Greece*	*Nero*	Suetonius, *Nero*
		Pan.	Epiphanius, *Panarion*
Dial.	Justin Martyr, *Dialogue with Trypho*	*Pud.*	Tertullian, *Modesty*
		Sel. Ps.	Origen, *Selected Psalms*
Dom.	Suetonius, *Domitian*	*Strom.*	Clement of Alexandria, *Stromateis*
Embassy	Philo, *On the Embassy to Gaius*		
		Trad. ap.	Hippolytus, *The Apostolic Tradition*
Ep.	Gregory of Nyssa, *Epistles*		
Ep. Tra.	Pliny the Younger, *Epistle to Trajan*	*Vesp.*	Suetonius, *Vespasian*
		Vir. ill.	Jerome, *On Illustrious Men*
Haer.	Irenaeus, *Against Heresies*		
Hist.	Rufinus, *Eusebii Historia ecclesiastica a Rufino translata et continuata*	*Vita*	Josephus, *The Life*

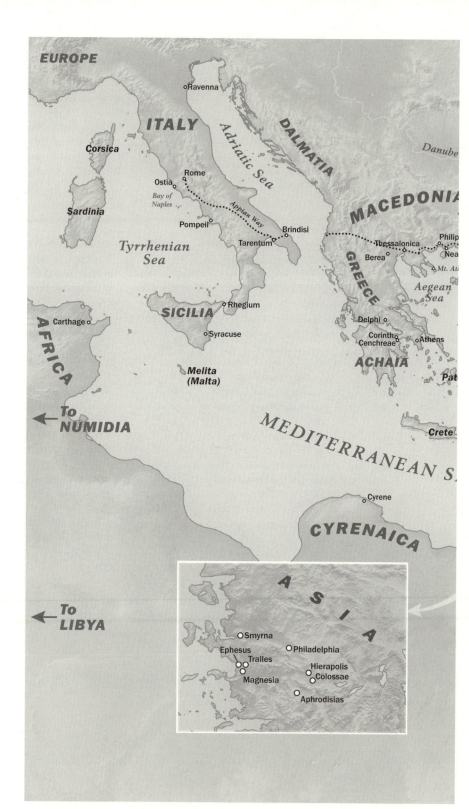

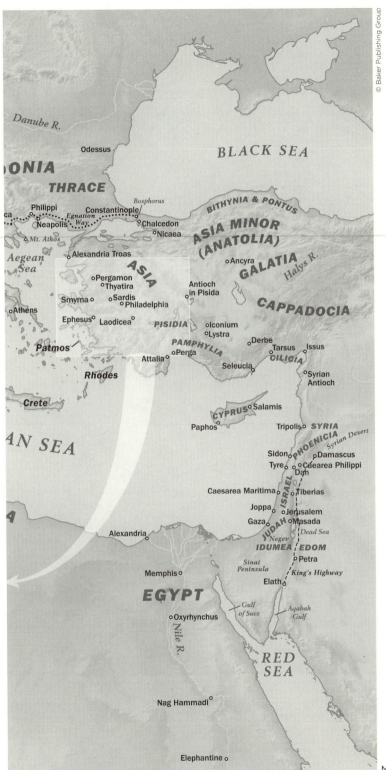

Map 1, Mediterranean Basin

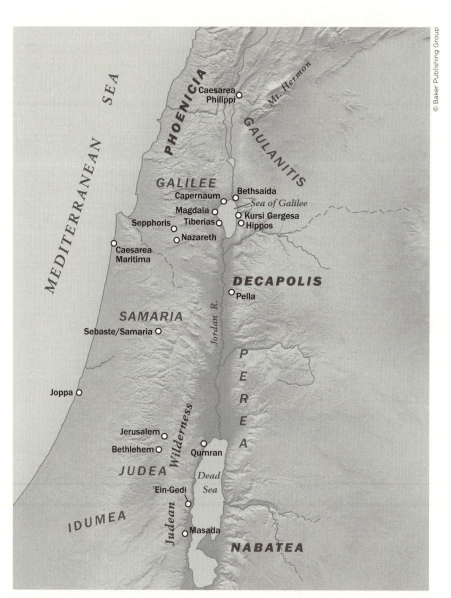

Map 2, Judean Wilderness

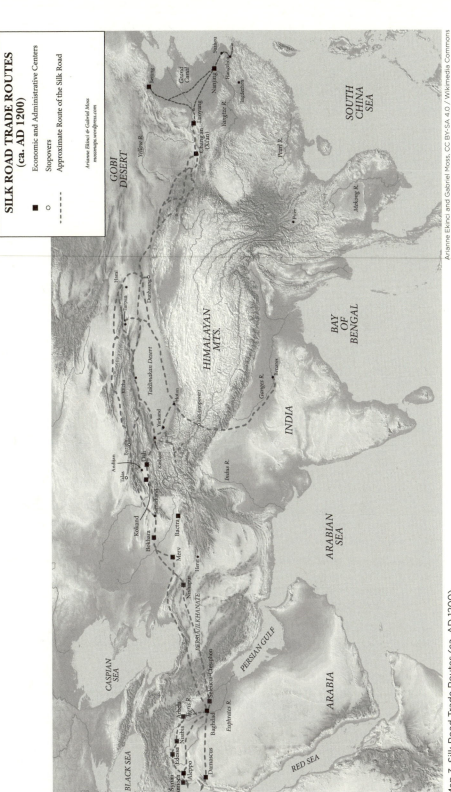

Map 3, Silk Road Trade Routes (ca. AD 1200)

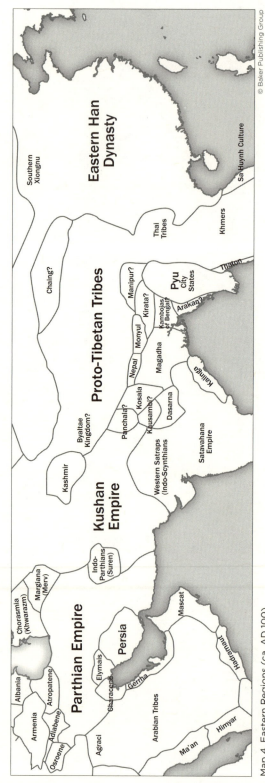

Map 4, Eastern Regions (ca. AD 100)

Introduction

Two Profiles of One Reality

If we were asked to list the basic characteristics of Jesus's ministry in the Four Gospels, we might come up with the following:

- It is an *itinerant* ministry.
- It is a *rural movement*.
- It is located in *Palestine*, mostly on the northwest quadrant of the Sea of Galilee.
- It is an ethnically *Jewish* movement.
- Its inner circle consists of *twelve men* accompanied by many *other men and women*.
- Its participants speak *Aramaic* in public but *Hebrew* when reading and discussing Scripture.
- Its participants worship in *synagogues* on the *Sabbath*.
- Its leader and his followers celebrate *Passover*.
- Its sacred texts are those of the synagogue, and they are written on *scrolls*.
- It is a movement with *no official name*.

Now suppose we were asked to come up with a second profile, this time of the church as it was at the time of Ignatius of Antioch (the end of the first century). We are, of course, much less familiar with Ignatius than we are with the Gospels. Nevertheless, we can read through all seven of his letters in less time than it takes to read through the Gospel of Mark, the shortest of the Gospels. From Ignatius's letters, we might make the following deductions about the church in that time:

- It is primarily *urban*.
- It exists mostly outside of Palestine, in the *Roman world*.
- Its life is centered no longer around synagogues but *churches*.
- Its members are predominately *gentile*.
- Its primary language is *Greek*.
- Its members worship by celebrating the *Eucharist*, and they do this on *Sunday*.
- It is superintended by *bishops*.
- Its Sacred Scripture is no longer limited to the Jewish Pentateuch, Writings, and Prophets; it now also includes specifically *Christian writings*.
- Its Scriptures are written in *codex*, or book, form.
- Its members are called *Christians*.

These are the two profiles: the first, of Jesus's ministry circa the year 30; the second, of the church in Ignatius's day, circa 100. We often fail to see the significance of things with which we have long been familiar. This phenomenon of familiarity may affect our judgment of the two profiles. We affirm that both are fair representations, and we regard both as equally "Christian." Otherwise, we may find neither surprising. Therein lies the beclouding potential of familiarity, of "seeing but not seeing" (Isa. 6:9)—*for not one item in the second profile is the same as in the first.* Within seventy-five years of the death of Jesus, the movement he founded conformed to virtually none of the forms of his ministry. A rural movement became acculturated to an urban environment; a Jewish movement became primarily gentile; a movement that spoke exclusively Aramaic and Hebrew transformed into one that wrote, preached, and evangelized in Greek; a movement born and bred in Palestine evolved into a thoroughly cosmopolitan, Greco-Roman movement that spread along the highly influential Jerusalem–Rome corridor. The seed of a movement planted in synagogues flowered in churches—churches that met no longer on Sabbath but on Sunday; that celebrated Eucharist rather than Passover; whose canon was no longer limited to the Torah, Prophets, and Writings of the Old Testament but was expanded to include Christian writings that were produced and disseminated no longer on scrolls but in codices.

One of these changes—the transition from Aramaic and Hebrew to Greek—was already complete at the time the New Testament was being written. All extant Christian writings of the first century are written in Greek rather than in Aramaic or Hebrew. Jesus and his followers spoke Aramaic and worshiped in Hebrew, yet *not one* first-century Christian document is extant in either language. The lingua franca of the early church—at least in written form—changed to Greek early and, in the West, entirely. Most of the changes listed in the profiles, however, were still in progress when the New Testament was being written. Descriptions of the Jesus movement as "the Way," "saints," or "brothers and sisters," for instance, were in the process of yielding to the name "Christian," first given in Antioch (Acts 11:26). Similarly, the transition in leadership—from the apostles, also known as "the Twelve," to the offices of elder, deacon, and especially bishop—was already underway in the New Testament. Other changes had only just begun in the New Testament era. It is unclear, for example, whether Jesus followers were worshiping on Sabbath or on Sunday (or perhaps on both). The single greatest change occurring in the early church was its separation from the Jewish synagogue—which took place sooner in some places, later in others, but eventually in all. And, finally, some changes had not yet begun. The formation of the New Testament canon, for one, lay in the future and is mentioned in neither the New Testament nor the Apostolic Fathers.

We devote individual chapters to each of the above changes, seeking to follow each transition from the Jesus era to the Ignatius era. Some of the transitions leave a rich trail of evidence, others a faint trail, and some almost no trail. A single and momentous reality emerges from them, however, and towers like Mount Rainier above Puget Sound: within a seventy-five-year period—the span of a single lifetime—the Jesus movement had become the Christian church. How exactly did the movement that was begun by Jesus become the church described by Ignatius? The answer to that question is the focus of this book.

Parsing the Profiles

Why is the quantum change from Jesus's ministry to the early church of Ignatius's time seldom recognized and explored? One reason is historical bias. Histories of early Christianity generally regard the time of the Apostolic Fathers as less worthy and rewarding of rigorous investigation than the preceding age (of the apostle Paul) and the following age (of Justin Martyr, Irenaeus, and Clement of Alexandria). Protestant scholarship, in particular, has tended to regard the Apostolic Fathers as something of a no-man's-land dividing the critical poles of the New Testament and the apologists. Various reasons account for this. The increased institutionalization and hierarchization of the church in the post–New Testament era, especially as exemplified in the office of bishop, have resulted in characterizations of the era as "early Catholicism," a time in which one sees the "routinization of charism." Such descriptions imply a calcifying of tradition.[1] There has also been a prevailing bias that Christianity came of age and warranted genuine historical inquiry only after it freed itself from the confines of Judaism and merged with the Greco-Roman ethos in the writings of the apologists in the mid-second century and following.

Our chief sources for understanding the Christianity of the post–New Testament era, the seventeen documents composing the Apostolic Fathers, are also judged to fall short of the literary quality and theological substance of the New Testament.[2] The very designation of the era as "postapostolic" and its writings as "the Apostolic Fathers" compares both unfavorably with the New Testament. Such comparisons extend to the authors as well as to the literature. The disparagements, again, are largely Protestant in origin rather than Orthodox or Catholic. Catholic and Orthodox scholars have traditionally regarded Ignatius as the greatest post–New Testament figure, to whom both traditions appeal as a shared authority. Adolf Harnack notes that the Orthodox regard Ignatius alone among the ante-Nicene Fathers with complete trust as the classical witness of the faith between the New Testament

---

1. Adolf Harnack, the outstanding twentieth-century historian of the early church, regarded Jesus's chief theological contribution to be his monotheism and his chief ethical contribution to be the Sermon on the Mount. The main failures of the early church, in his estimation, were its retention of the Old Testament, its allegiance to Judaism, and its high Christology—which, in his judgment, quenched the spirit of early Christianity. For Harnack's harsh and jaundiced judgment of Judaism, see *Mission and Expansion*, bk. 1, ch. 5. On his setting institutionalization in opposition to *charisma*, see Schröter, "Harnack Revisited." Max Weber, similarly, characterized the postapostolic era as "a routinization of charism" in which the free-flowing charism of Jesus as a religious founder hardened into institutional governance, order, and discipline. See the discussion of Weber in Freyne, *Jesus Movement and Its Expansion*, 8.

2. J. B. Lightfoot's mastery of the postapostolic era was unrivaled, but his judgment of their literary and theological quality was not uncritical. In *Apostolic Fathers*, he writes that the fathers are "too desultory in form and too vague in doctrine to satisfy the requirements of more literary circles and a more dogmatic age" (1:1). Further, "'The Apostolic Fathers,' it has been justly said 'are not great writers, but great characters.' Their style is loose; there is a want of arrangement in their topics and an absence of system in their teaching. On the one hand they present a marked contrast to the depth and clearness of conception with which the several Apostolic writers place before us different aspects of the Gospel. . . . They lack the scientific spirit which distinguished the fathers of the fourth and fifth centuries. . . . They are deficient in distinctness of conception and power of exposition." The fathers, Lightfoot concludes, "command for their writings a respect wholly disproportionate to their literary merits" (1:7).

and Athanasius.[3] Protestants, by contrast, often disparage the era for lacking a great missionary theologian like the apostle Paul. In this view, only with mid-second-century leaders such as Justin, Irenaeus, Clement, and Tertullian does Christianity free itself from the constraints of Judaism and contend for the faith according to the standards of Greek philosophy.

Not all these judgments are equally valid. With regard to the last, it is true that the postapostolic era lacked an apostle Paul. This fact is hardly a debarring factor, however, for *all* subsequent eras of Christianity have lacked an apostle Paul. No other figure in Christianity—not Origen or Augustine, not even Luther—equals the contribution and significance of the apostle Paul. Disparagements of postapostolic associations with Judaism likewise strike our post-Holocaust ears as ethnic biases rather than substantive critiques. Whatever the shortcomings of the postapostolic era, actual or perceived, the fact that the writings of the fathers were preserved testifies to their merits in the eyes of their contemporaries.[4]

The purpose of this book is not to debate the particular merits or demerits of the above judgments but to focus on our opening thesis: that the apostolic and postapostolic era was not a holding pattern, a delayed adolescence, or a devolution of Christianity. Whatever the deficiencies of its leaders and

3. Harnack, *Geschichte der altchristlichen Literatur*, vol. 1, part 1, xlii.

4. However moderns may judge the Apostolic Fathers, it is important to remember, as Harnack reminds us, that religious texts that failed to achieve canonical status (however determined) were almost inevitably doomed to eventual loss and extinction (*Geschichte der altchristliche Literatur*, vol. 1, part 1, xxviii). The early centuries were a life-and-death struggle for Christianity, a struggle to preserve the lives of both its members and its sacred texts from opponents such as Jews who did not follow Jesus, polytheists, Gnostics, Manichees, Arians, and schismatics of various kinds. "The relevant question to ask in this regard is not why this or that early Christian text perished, but why it was preserved," observes Martin Hengel (*Studien zum Urchristentum*, 298 [my trans.]).

We cannot say exactly what percentage of early Christian literature has perished. Hengel's estimation that "more than 90 percent has been lost" seems too high (*Studien zum Urchristentum*, 298). For example, the sources that Eusebius cites for the first 150 years of his history of the church are mostly extant today (including Josephus, Philo, Julius Africanus, Hippolytus, Clement of Alexandria, and fragments of Papias), with the exceptions being Hegesippus and a fuller version of Papias (*Hist. eccl.* 1.4). Similarly, in *Vir. ill.*, Jerome lists some one hundred written works that preceded Justin Martyr, roughly seventy of which, by my count, are extant (at least in part), and thirty of which have perished. Jerome is an important source in this regard, for *Vir. ill.* ostensibly lists all Christian literature known to him. The documentation of Eusebius and Jerome computes to a loss of roughly 40 percent of early Christian literature. Harnack's esteem of the early church in this regard is justly deserved, for it preserved—under the most difficult circumstances, and in the face of well-armed opponents—the Septuagint, the texts that would make up the New Testament (with the exception of the loss of the Epistle to Laodicea, Col. 4:16), and the texts of the Apostolic Fathers. Especially commendable was its preservation of the Apostolic Fathers, given their noncanonical status.

literature, it remains the most creative era in the entire history of Christianity.[5] The Christian movement, which at its birth was almost indistinguishable from Judaism, within seventy-five years assumed a set of identifiable characteristics that were distinct from Judaism and remained remarkably constant for the next two millennia. Martin Hengel describes Christianity as "a corner sect from rural Galilee that within two generations became a new religion that reached the distant parts of the *Imperium Romanum* and successfully evangelized its greatest cities."[6] Ramsay MacMullen sees the rise of Christianity as the most significant factor in the closing centuries of the ancient world.[7] This era is all the greater because of its democratic character. The lack of a Promethean figure, such as the apostle Paul, in the postapostolic era is reason to acclaim rather than to disparage it—for after Paul's death in the 60s of the first century, Christians achieved what their arguably greater forebears and successors did not achieve. The greatness of this most creative era in the history of Christianity is magnified not by top-down imposition but by grassroots achievement.[8]

The Unchanging Constant

A second and even greater fact of first-century Christianity was the constancy of the inner core of the Jesus movement amid drastic external changes in the church. The summary changes in the *forms* of the Jesus movement from Jesus to Ignatius did not alter the *content* of the movement, which remained rooted in, continuous with, and faithful to the character and ministry of Jesus. This unchanging constant was the DNA of Christianity through its changing forms of life. A century ago Ernst Lohmeyer summed up this explosive paradox:

> The history of early Christianity offers from its earliest beginnings an uncommon double drama. Rarely has any other religion "filled" other lands and

5. Thus Grant, *Roman Hellenism*, 160: "The first fifty years [of Christianity] were probably the most crucial."

6. Hengel, *Theologische, historische und biographische Skizzen*, 530 (my trans.).

7. See MacMullen, *Christianizing the Roman Empire*, viii: "The period 100–400 might fairly be given pride of place in the whole of Western history." On the same period, see also MacMullen and Lane, *Paganism and Christianity*, vii: "The emergence of Christianity from the tangled mass of older religious beliefs, eventually to a position of unchallenged superiority, is surely the most important single phenomenon that can be discerned in the closing centuries of the ancient world. In its impact on the way life was to be lived thereafter in the West, it outmatches even the decline of Rome itself."

8. First Clement, written in the late 90s, commends the achievement of faithful normalcy over superstardom in these words: "It is better for you to be found small but included in the flock of Christ than to have a preeminent reputation and yet be excluded from his hope" (57.2, Holmes trans.).

provinces with the gospel so rapidly, and none rooted itself in the human condition and circumstances so deeply, as early Christianity. . . . Yet scarcely has any other religion been less affected by the tempests of destiny and fate in which it came into existence and grew, holding so steadfastly to the course prescribed by its divine call that it remained largely undeterred by the burning questions of the time and surmounted the difficulties of each day and hour.[9]

Lohmeyer aptly captures the paradox of early Christianity's "double drama"—unchanging essence amid changing forms, adaptive to culture but not captive to culture. The changes in the forms of the Jesus movement that constitute the chapters of this book were not the result of strategizing or central planning. In the early church, most of them occurred at different times and places and in various ways. They were not random and arbitrary, however, or even, as evolutionary theory proposes, adaptations to environmental conditions. On the contrary, the transition from Christ to Christianity was the result of Jesus followers seeking to organize their corporate life of witness, worship, and mission according to the fundamental nature of Jesus's person and ministry. Christology was the veritable North Star of the entire phenomenon. Nearly every change charted in this book was the result of Jesus followers seeking to conform their corporate fellowship to something essential in the character and ministry of Christ.

This explains why the early church adopted forms and behaviors that Jesus himself did not prescribe. Sunday worship replaced Sabbath, for example, not because Jesus prescribed it or even set a precedent for it (he did neither), but because Sunday was the day of his resurrection from the dead. Again, without dominical instruction, the church—especially the gentile wing of the church—understood the promise to Abraham (Gen. 12:3), Jesus's ministry in the gentile Decapolis (Mark 7:24–8:9), and even in the temple itself (Mark 11:17) to presuppose inclusion of gentiles in the church. This same principle explains why the church resisted other doctrines or practices that, despite their pragmatic appeal, could not be theologically justified. For example, Marcion's maneuver to expunge the Old Testament from the Christian tradition in the second century was very tempting for a church whose Lord had been rejected by Jews and whose members were opposed by Jews. The church nevertheless rejected Marcion's logical appeal on *theological* grounds, for to reject the Old Testament was to reject Jesus as Israel's Messiah and the world's Savior. For

9. Lohmeyer, *Soziale Fragen im Urchristentum*, 129 (my trans.). In Lohmeyer's inaugural address as president of the University of Breslau in 1930, he articulated this idea similarly: "The unchangeable form and content of the gospel manifests itself in the changeable form of history" (quoted in Edwards, *Between the Swastika and the Sickle*, 89).

Jesus, "new wine" required "new wineskins" (Mark 2:22), and that metaphor illustrated the essence of an unchanging constant within changing forms.

Other Considerations before Embarking

Four additional words of explanation may aid in profitably reading this book. First, as already noted, the Apostolic Fathers represent the terminal point of our investigation.[10] The dates of the documents in the Fathers are only roughly determinable, so the terminal point of the corpus as a whole remains approximate rather than exact. Some of the documents can be dated fairly precisely (according to the standards of dating ancient texts) to the last decade of the first century (1 Clement, almost certainly) or to the last two decades of the first century (the Didache, probably). The majority, however, cannot be dated more precisely than the first half of the second century, and in the case of some, like the Epistle to Diognetus, even that time frame may be too specific.[11] The New Testament and the Apostolic Fathers thus determine the primary scope of our study—namely, the roughly one-hundred-year period between the writing of the first document in the New Testament (probably Galatians, in the late 40s) and the close of the era of the Apostolic Fathers (around 150).

I also augment the New Testament and the Apostolic Fathers with two smaller, non-Christian bodies of literature from the same period. From the Jewish quarter, I regularly cite Josephus and the Mishnah, and occasionally Philo. And from the Roman quarter, I cite Tacitus, Suetonius, and Pliny the Younger nearly as freely. These texts also can be assigned only approximate dates: the works of Josephus, around 80–100; the three Roman writers, around 110–20; and the rabbinic tradition of the first two centuries that was published in the Mishnah, around 200.

The final body of literature supporting this study is the array of secondary scholarly literature relevant to the development of early Christianity. In

10. The traditional corpus of Apostolic Fathers includes 1 Clement; 2 Clement; the seven letters of Ignatius; Polycarp, *To the Philippians*; the Martyrdom of Polycarp; the Didache; the Epistle of Barnabas; the Shepherd of Hermas; the Epistle to Diognetus; and the Fragments of Papias. Classic editions of these works appear in Theodor Zahn, *Ignatius von Antiochien*; J. B. Lightfoot, *The Apostolic Fathers*; and Adolf Harnack, *Geschichte der altchristlichen Literatur bis Eusebius*. Greek texts and modern translations appear in Kirsopp Lake, *The Apostolic Fathers*; and Michael W. Holmes, *The Apostolic Fathers*. Since the Apology of Aristides the Philosopher (*ANF* 10:257–79) can be dated to the era of the emperor Hadrian (r. 117–38), which lies within the time frame of the Apostolic Fathers, I also include it in the Apostolic Fathers.

11. On the naming, dating, and contents of the Apostolic Fathers, see Pratscher, *Apostolic Fathers*, 1–6.

the past two decades, Protestants have rediscovered the post–New Testament world, contributing to a wealth of literature. The modern scholars to whom I am most indebted are evident in the bibliography and footnotes of this work, but I refer to them as commentary on, rather than as replacements for, the primary sources.

Second, I am acutely aware of the problem of authorship as it pertains to many documents in the New Testament and Apostolic Fathers. Whether the apostle Paul wrote the Pastorals, Ephesians, Colossians, or 2 Thessalonians, for example; or whether any of the documents in the Apostolic Fathers, with the exception of the letters of Ignatius and Polycarp, can be definitely ascribed to their putative authors; or what to do with Diognetus, which eludes questions of either authorship or date—all these questions and others of a similar nature remain open. The scope of our study is too broad, and our sources too many, to entertain source criticism in any depth, and conclusions on such issues would rarely further our object. I have therefore confined my research to and based my conclusions on the texts *as received and preserved*, not as hypothetically reconstructed. It is the voice and content preserved in the texts rather than the particular speaker and occasion for speaking that carry conclusive weight for our study.

Third, there is no generally agreed-upon term for the early Christian movement prior to the development of the name "Christian" and prior to the separation of "Christians" from Jewish synagogues to form "churches." I refer to this movement as the "Jesus movement" and to these believers as "Jesus followers." There is, however, no evidence of early believers themselves using either designation. I intend them simply as functional descriptions and unbiased epithets for the earliest adherents to the gospel, whether they were associating with Jewish synagogues or separated into "churches," before "Christian" became an accepted epithet.

Fourth and finally, the transition from Christ to Christianity was of incalculable significance in world history. But it was not neat and tidy. It included multiple transitions that were inseparably intertwined with one another, occurring for the most part simultaneously. Readers must not imagine that the division of this book into its various chapters implies that the different transitions occurred separately and successively. They did not. The chapter divisions are solely practical, intended to allow for adequate consideration of each strand of a complex fabric, so that the intricacy of the whole weaving—the development of Christianity—might be better understood and appreciated.

From Rural to Urban

A Galilean Country Preacher

"Jesus went throughout the villages teaching" (Mark 6:6). So the Gospel of Mark summarizes the itinerant ministry of Jesus. His circuit-riding fame spread beyond Galilee to Syria in the north, Transjordan in the east, and Idumea in the south; but his ministry proper remained almost completely confined to Galilee. To a rather small part of Galilee, in fact. If you picture the Sea of Galilee as the face of a watch, nearly every episode in Jesus's Galilean ministry takes place between ten o'clock and one o'clock, and almost all near the shore of the sea. Only isolated episodes take place at three o'clock, on the eastern side of the sea, in the Decapolis—the healing of the Gerasene demoniac, for instance,[1] and the feeding of the four thousand.[2] Most surprisingly, not a single episode in the Gospels takes place between six o'clock and nine o'clock. Tiberias, the capital of Galilee and the largest city in Palestine outside Jerusalem, was positioned on the western shore of the sea, at nine o'clock sharp, visible from virtually any place on the sea, and only ten miles south of Capernaum, the home base of Jesus's ministry. There is, however, no record of Jesus or his disciples ever going there.

Tiberias was founded by Herod Antipas, who ruled Galilee as tetrarch for close to a half century—from the death of his father Herod the Great in 4 BC until his own banishment by Emperor Caligula in AD 39. Aspiring to

---

1. Matt. 8:28–34; Mark 5:1–20; Luke 8:26–39.
2. Matt. 15:32–39; Mark 8:1–9.

his father's genius for construction, Antipas broke virgin ground in the year 19 on the western shore of the Sea of Galilee in hopes of creating a capital city that would rival his father's spectacular building exploits. Located near a hot spring, Tiberias was named after Antipas's patron, the emperor Tiberius. Antipas built his urban showplace on the site of an ancient cemetery, which, according to Jewish teaching, rendered the city unclean.[3] This initially impeded Jewish occupancy of Tiberias, but Antipas compensated by luring unscrupulous settlers with gifts of free housing and land. He further populated the city by relocating people from other parts of Galilee.[4] By the middle of the first century, Tiberias was a burgeoning Jewish metropolis and its stigma of ritual pollution a fading memory. In fact, the city's unkosher conception may have aided it in the art of realpolitik, for during the First Jewish Revolt (66–70), in which all Galilee capitulated to Vespasian's Roman legions, Tiberias cast its lot with the Romans rather than with the surrounding cities and villages that fought against them. Unlike those other cities and villages, and especially Jerusalem to the south, Tiberias emerged from the devastation of the revolt unscathed and quickly became a center of renascent Judaism in Palestine. Jesus and his movement played no role in this renaissance, however, for as noted above, there is no record of him or his disciples going to Tiberias.

Even more surprising is the lack of any record of Jesus visiting Sepphoris, the other major city of Galilee. Perched on a hill—the name "Sepphoris" derives from the Hebrew *Zippori*, meaning "bird"—Sepphoris was a mere three miles from Jesus's hometown of Nazareth. Following the Roman annexation of Palestine by Pompey in 63 BC, Sepphoris was elevated to capital of Galilee, but the Hasmoneans, descendants of the Maccabees who had long been influential in Sepphoris, rebelled against the Roman client king Herod the Great in 38 BC. Herod retaliated with a vengeance, destroying Sepphoris and leaving it in ruins. After Herod's death, Antipas restored Sepphoris as "the ornament of all Galilee."[5] Few archaeological sites in Israel rival the grandeur of Sepphoris. Its mosaic floors are expansive and exquisite, one of which is now christened "the Mona Lisa of Galilee." According to the Gospel of Matthew, when Joseph returned with Mary and Jesus from Egypt and learned that the ruler of Judea was Archelaus—one of Herod the Great's sons whose reputation was as notorious as his father's—Joseph "departed to the district of Galilee" (Matt. 2:22–23). He settled in Nazareth, perhaps because Sepphoris, a forty-five-minute walk away, offered employment for artisans like him, and perhaps for Jesus and his brothers as well. After two

3. Num. 19:11–16; 2 Kings 23:13–14.
4. Josephus, *Ant.* 18.36–38.
5. Josephus, *Ant.* 18.27.

decades of construction at Sepphoris, however, Herod Antipas shifted his energies and resources away from Sepphoris in order to make Tiberias the new capital of Galilee. Antipas judged the western shore of the Sea of Galilee a more advantageous location for his capital than landlocked Sepphoris. He may have shared Josephus's high estimation of "the natural properties and beauty and fertile soil" skirting the Sea of Galilee.[6] We can also imagine that freedom from Jewish constraints on the new municipality played a role as well, for Tiberias quickly became the more Roman of the two cities in terms of layout and architectural features.

Both Sepphoris and Tiberias were flirtatiously accessible to Jesus, the first a forty-five-minute walk from his hometown in Nazareth and the second only a few hours from his ministry base in Capernaum. Not one reference in the Gospels reports Jesus setting foot in either city, however. That cannot have been by chance. Jesus's ministry on the northwest quadrant of the Sea of Galilee was intentionally and exclusively rural.

The Gospels refer to the places visited by Jesus as both "villages" (Gk. *kōmai*) and "cities" (Gk. *poleis*). In the Gospel of Mark the two terms are about equal in number, but Matthew, Luke, and John refer to them more frequently as "cities." Regardless of terminology, the locales were rural Galilean towns and settlements. Although the Gospels record no visits of Jesus to either Tiberias or Sepphoris, they do record journeys south to attend Jewish festivals, especially Passover, in Jerusalem. Jerusalem was the major city of Palestine, but it is important to note that, according to the first three Gospels, Jesus went to Jerusalem only once in his ministry, and then only because the all-important Passover festival required his presence as an observant and faithful Jew. It is probable that Jesus journeyed to Jerusalem for other festivals as well, especially Pentecost and the Feast of Booths, but in truth he showed little positive affiliation with Jerusalem. More often than not, in fact, Jerusalem was a place of opposition to him. The dozen episodes reported in Mark 11–15 depict the leaders in Jerusalem arrayed against Jesus in various forms and degrees of opposition. And not only against Jesus, but also against his followers, for at his trial before Caiaphas, bystanders identified—and dismissed—Peter's testimony because of his Galilean speech.[7] Ernst Lohmeyer saw Galilee and Jerusalem in opposition: Galilee as a place of blessing and receptivity for Jesus,

6. Josephus rhapsodizes over the clear, sweet water of the Sea of Galilee and its abundance of different species of fish (*J.W.* 3.506–9) and over the "luxuriant" walnut trees, palms, figs, and olives around the sea. Josephus concludes, "Nature had taken pride in assembling, by a *tour de force*, the most discordant species in a single spot . . . by a happy revelry . . . of the seasons" (*J.W.* 3.516–21 [LCL]).

7. Matt. 26:73; Mark 14:70; Luke 22:59.

and Jerusalem as a place of cursing and rejection.[8] That may be too categorical. Even in Galilee, Jesus followers attempted to restrain and deprogram him (Mark 3:20–21); there too, Jesus called down woes on Chorazin and Bethsaida (Matt. 11:21; Luke 10:13). And conversely, he declared a temple leader in Jerusalem "not far from the kingdom of God" (Mark 12:34). Lohmeyer was nevertheless right in detecting a juxtaposition in the Gospel narratives between Galilee and Jerusalem, for Jesus elected rural Galilee as a mission field in a way that he did not elect urban Jerusalem.

The Gospels present Jesus as purposefully attuned to rural Galilee. His ministry was woven on the warp and woof of open-air preaching; village synagogues; natural imagery (flowers of the field, sowing and reaping, storm clouds and rain, fishing and shepherding); and, above all, the Sea of Galilee itself. So rooted in Galilee was the ministry and message of Jesus and his followers that it is hard to imagine them successfully transplanted to an urban context. It is surprising, therefore, to find only a dearth of evidence in both Christian literature and the material culture of Galilee for a Christian presence in Galilee after the death of Jesus.[9] Given the lack of such evidence, the church in Galilee plays a very minor role in histories of early Christianity. Regarding material culture, Christian worship spaces do not appear to have been built in Galilee before the fourth century. We find no remains of church buildings, altars, and baptistries prior to that time. Other materials that may have attended the Christian presence in Galilee before that time have not survived the past two millennia. According to archaeological excavations, Jewish synagogues and Christian churches coexisted in lower Galilee in the Byzantine era. The single exception, not surprisingly, was the cluster of churches on the shore of the Sea of Galilee where Jesus ministered—in Capernaum, Kursi, Tabgha, Magdala, Philoteria, and Hippos. In upper Galilee, churches and synagogues were more clearly divided in this period, with Christians in western Galilee, primarily from Nazareth northward, and Jews in eastern Galilee, especially in Tiberias and northward. Eric Meyers states the contrast distinctly: "The Jewish sites were in eastern Galilee, the Christian sites were in western Galilee."[10] When Rome destroyed Jerusalem in the year 70, rabbinic scholars in Judea fled north to Galilee and founded major rabbinic academies in Sepphoris and Tiberias. The academies greatly fortified the Jewish presence in eastern Galilee and may have pushed Christians into western Galilee.

8. Lohmeyer, *Galiläa und Jerusalem*.

9. See Hengel, *Studien zum Urchristentum*, 344; Schröter, "Harnack Revisited," 489.

10. Meyers, "Side by Side in Galilee," 143. For more on Christian and Jewish material remains in Galilee, see Mordechai Aviam, "Galilee," *EEECAA* 1:557–59; and above all, Freyne, *Jesus Movement and Its Expansion*, esp. 242–72.

Despite the paucity of Christian material remains in Galilee from the first and second centuries, there are nevertheless clues of a Christian remnant there. The Gospels of Matthew and Mark record Jesus commanding his followers to rendezvous with him in Galilee after his resurrection.[11] We may suppose that his followers took that command seriously and returned to Galilee to raise up believers among their families and acquaintances. The book of Acts offers peripheral evidence of this when it speaks of churches "throughout Judea, *Galilee*, and Samaria" (Acts 9:31, emphasis added). In the late 60s, Pella, a city twenty miles south of Galilee on the eastern bank of the Jordan River, saw a major influx of Christians. According to both Eusebius and Epiphanius, at the beginning of the Jewish Revolt in 66, a divine revelation commanded Jesus followers to abandon Jerusalem and flee north to Pella.[12] The absence of artifacts, inscriptions, or wall paintings in the caves of Pella has caused some scholars to question this tradition,[13] but lack of material evidence is not conclusive in this instance, for Christians did not build churches or identify themselves with normative architectural symbols in the 60s. Despite the lack of material evidence, historical circumstances strongly favor the early Christian flight to Pella as recorded by Eusebius and Epiphanius. James, the brother of Jesus, was martyred in Jerusalem in 62: thrown down from the pinnacle of the temple, stoned, and then beaten to death.[14] In the lead-up to the Jewish Revolt four years later, the leading Jewish factions, including the Sicarii and the Zealots, singled out Christians in Jerusalem for harsh persecution. It is entirely reasonable to think that Christians would flee such circumstances for sanctuary in the caves of Pella to the north.[15]

Another clue of a remnant Christian presence in Galilee at the end of the first century also comes from Eusebius, who reports that the emperor Domitian (r. 81–96) questioned the grandsons of Judas the brother of Jesus (Mark 6:3) to determine if they, as relatives of Jesus and descendants of David, harbored intentions of insurrection against Rome. The grandsons admitted their lineage, but when the emperor saw their poverty and hardened hands "embossed with incessant work," and above all, their complete indifference to earthly power (for Domitian found that they awaited only the world to come), the emperor's suspicions were allayed, and he dismissed them as despised and

---

11. Matt. 26:32; 28:7, 10, 16; Mark 14:28; 16:7.

12. Eusebius, *Hist. eccl.* 3.5.3; Epiphanius, *Pan.* 29.7.7–8.

13. See Watson, "Christian Flight to Pella?"

14. Josephus, *Ant.* 20.200; Eusebius, *Hist. eccl.* 2.23. Eusebius attributes his account of the martyrdom of James to the second-century church historian Hegesippus (*Hist. eccl.* 2.23.18).

15. For positive assessments of the Pella tradition, see Robert H. Smith, "Pella," *ABD* 5:219–21; Freyne, *Jesus Movement and Its Expansion*, 232; and esp. Bourke, "True or Tale?"

harmless peasants.[16] Eusebius does not specifically name either the men or Galilee in his report, but their family history and rustic speech may associate them with rural Galilee.

To summarize thus far, evidence for Jesus's rural ministry in Galilee is rock solid. All four Gospels, each of which was written in the first century and indebted to apostolic memory, reflect Jesus's indifference to urban locales, including Tiberias, Sepphoris, and even Jerusalem itself, and his conscious preference for rural Galilee. Only a few years after Jesus's death, however, the record of his followers in Galilee diminishes, leaving only sporadic and tenuous traces of a Christian presence in Galilee.

Christianity Becomes Cosmopolitan

In startling contrast to their rural routine with Jesus in Galilee, his apostles, disciples, and family relocated to Jerusalem after his ascension. Jerusalem had been ground zero of opposition to Jesus, with both temple leaders and Roman authorities colluding to crucify him. Despite hostility in Jerusalem and the ipsissima verba of Jesus to return to Galilee,[17] the Twelve appear in Jerusalem—with the very temple as their operational base!—at the beginning of the book of Acts. This wholly unexpected event, for which no explanation is offered in the New Testament, illustrates the point of this chapter.[18] In Martin Hengel's words, "There are hardly any parallels in the sociology of religion to the astonishing fact that in the briefest period of time the Galilean Jesus movement, which to begin with was a purely rural phenomenon, became a predominantly urban community in Jerusalem."[19] Briefest period of time, indeed. The Twelve are anchored in the temple at Pentecost, forty days after Jesus's crucifixion.

Remarkable as this was, a precedent did exist for Jesus followers to locate in Jerusalem. Jerusalem was Israel's providential city par excellence, where the authority of the ark of the covenant and the temple combined with the political

16. *Hist. eccl.* 3.19–20.

17. Matt. 28:7; Mark 16:7.

18. Fredriksen, *When Christians Were Jews*, 14–22, attributes the surprising relocation of Jesus followers to Jerusalem following the crucifixion to their conviction that the eschatological salvation foretold in the Old Testament would unfurl in Jerusalem, on the "holy mountain" of Zion. That is possible, although it assumes a very mature eschatology at such an early date. Freyne, *Jesus Movement and Its Expansion*, 187, 201–5, is probably closer to the truth in attributing the relocation of Jesus followers to Jerusalem to the fact that Jerusalem was the place where Jesus was resurrected, where his status as the royal Davidic Messiah was validated and must be proclaimed—in Zion.

19. Hengel, *History of Earliest Christianity*, 99.

and military authority of the Davidic ruler to form the sacred alloy of Zionism. According to Isaiah, the cloud and fire symbolizing God's abiding presence over the tabernacle (Exod. 40:34–38) would come to rest on the Holy City as well (Isa. 4:2–6). It was perhaps for this reason that Jesus's apostles found their divine purpose and realization in Jerusalem. Even if this is the case, however, it does not explain why the Jesus movement that expanded outward from Jerusalem identified so fundamentally with cities rather than with the more numerous towns and villages, like the ones that birthed it. At the conclusion of this chapter, I will argue that the geographical expansion of the gospel did, in fact, include villages as well as cities. The fact remains, however, that in the early church's autobiography, the expansion of the gospel is distinguished by its focus on urban centers—the first being Jerusalem, of course, followed by Sebaste/Samaria after the martyrdom of Stephen (Acts 8:4–25), then Damascus and Caesarea Maritima (Acts 9:1–25; 10:1–11:18), and soon thereafter, in a revolutionary advance, to Antioch of Syria (Acts 11:19–30).

Antioch

Antioch of Syria was much larger and much more gentile than Jerusalem, and its church leadership was significantly independent of Jerusalem. It was in Antioch that Christian mission achieved the programmatic status necessary to reach Rome. "Antioch," in the words of Martin Hengel, "was the first great city of the ancient world in which Christianity gained a footing."[20] The city of Antioch boasts a continuous history of twenty-three hundred years, beginning in earnest with Seleucus, one of Alexander the Great's generals, who, following the death of Alexander in 323 BC, made Antioch the grandest and most beautiful of Hellenistic cities. In the words of Josephus, "Antioch, the capital of Syria, unquestionably ranks third among cities of the Roman world in extent and opulence."[21] The population of Antioch in the first century was perhaps a quarter of a million people, densely compacted on a north–south ribbon of land about half a mile wide that was sandwiched between sixteen-hundred-foot Mount Silpios to the east and the Orontes River to the west. The Orontes emptied into the Mediterranean fifteen miles from Antioch at the port of Seleucia Pieria. Located in the crosshairs of the north–south trade route between what is today Turkey and Egypt and the east–west trade route between Rome and Persia, Antioch was auspiciously positioned for both land and maritime transportation.

20. Hengel, *History of Earliest Christianity*, 99.
21. *J.W.* 3.29. The two cities more prominent than Antioch were Rome and Alexandria.

Rome invested handsomely in Antioch. Five emperors personally visited Rome's "navel of the East."[22] In 47 BC, Julius Caesar erected a basilica, amphitheater, and theater in Antioch. Augustus (r. 27 BC–AD 14) twice returned to Antioch to further projects begun by Caesar. In 37, Tiberius developed plans for Antioch's great colonnaded street, accentuated by a stone statue of Rome's famous she-wolf nursing Romulus and Remus. In 115–16, the emperor Trajan was nearly killed in a massive earthquake while he was personally overseeing beautifications of Antioch. His successor, Hadrian, continued Rome's investment in Antioch by vastly improving its water system. A showcase metropolis like Antioch attracted celebrities and ceremonial events. Antony and Cleopatra reputedly married in Antioch in 37 or 36 BC—at the same time that another paramour of Cleopatra, Herod the Great, was present in the city. In AD 43, the emperor Claudius launched his own Olympic Games in Antioch. By then early Jesus followers had already established Antioch as a mission base on the Jerusalem–Rome corridor (Acts 13–14), and Antiochians had perceptively renamed them "Christians" (Acts 11:26).

Rome's investment in Antioch was calculated on the city's strategic importance on the eastern frontier of the empire. Following the Roman invasion and annexation of Palestine in 63 BC, Antioch became Rome's staging point for military operations in the east, a status it retained for five centuries! Rome stationed as many as four legions in Antioch—totaling some forty thousand troops. From Antioch, Rome crushed the first-century Jewish Revolt, after which it built the theater at Daphne, a suburb south of Antioch, with spoils from the siege of Jerusalem. From Antioch, Rome defended the empire against the Parthian threat in the second century and from the Sassanid Persian Empire in the third century.

When Christians arrived in Antioch in the 30s, Tiberius had completed his Great Colonnade, which extended a full two miles from the Aleppo Gate in the north to the Daphne Gate in the south. Roman urbanism was on grand display on this roughly 120-foot-wide main street, each side of which was covered with porticos that housed vendors, shops, businesses, personal dwellings, and public spaces. From the spine of the Great Colonnade, byways branched like ribs eastward to the foothills of Mount Silpios and westward to the Orontes and the five bridges that spanned it. The splendid mosaics that have been uncovered at Antioch are exuberant and sensuous. John Chrysostom stated that 10 percent of the city was wealthy and 10 percent poor, with a hefty

22. This expression, often translated "capital of the East," is found on coins struck in Roman Antioch (Keener, Acts, 2:1834).

80 percent of the population in between.[23] If Chrysostom's fourth-century estimate is also representative of Antioch in the first century, Antioch was a good place to live. It was a heterogeneous and polyglot city of citizens, free persons, and slaves. Its residents spoke Greek, Latin, Hebrew, Aramaic, Syriac, Coptic, and Persian. Latin could be heard at Rome's administrative and military installations in the city, but otherwise, Greek predominated. As one ventured east of Antioch, however, Syriac eclipsed both Latin and Greek. Antioch's three Semitic languages—Hebrew, Aramaic, and Syriac—support the archaeological and literary record showing that Jews, especially hellenized Jews, had lived in Antioch since its early days and constituted an important subculture.[24]

Rome's administrative objective in the early empire was to maintain order and exact profits and taxes from subjects. At least initially, its objective did not include turning subjects into Roman citizens; indeed, it may have discouraged this, for Rome owed citizens more rights and privileges than it owed subjects.[25] The teeming diversity of cultures and languages that characterized Antioch could also be found, to varying degrees, in other major cities ruled by Rome. This diversity rendered a monolithic Roman culture not only impractical but also virtually impossible. Rome wisely permitted indigenous lifestyles within its urban centers and their environs, as long as the standards of Roman law were maintained. In Judea, Rome exempted Jews from military service and also established a surrogate political body, the Sanhedrin, to rule directly over the people. Rome was wise enough to know how seriously Jews took the Torah commandment not to allow a non-Israelite to rule over them (Deut. 17:15). Rome was politically pragmatic, compromising on means in order to achieve uncompromised ends. Such pragmatism was rather remarkable in Judea, for Judea bordered the unconquered regions to the east of the Roman Empire and was not a senatorial province (a secured region administered by a Roman proconsul or governor) but, rather, an imperial province (an insecure region ruled directly by the emperor). Judea was a volatile region, and Rome amassed a heavy concentration of troops there. At least until the Second Jewish Revolt (132–35), however, Rome intended neither to eradicate Jewish life nor to overburden it more than was necessary for Rome to establish hegemony in Palestine. Rome's military presence in Palestine and elsewhere in the empire

23. *Hom. Matt.* 66.

24. On Antioch and its relation to Christianity, see Kondoleon, *Antioch*, 3–11; Wilson, *Biblical Turkey*, 71–78; Keener, *Acts*, 2:1834–40.

25. The Roman emperor Caracalla first instituted universal citizenship throughout the empire in 212.

was, to be sure, mostly unchallenged; when challenged, however, it was brutal. But its cultural presence was less autocratic and more laissez-faire.[26]

Antioch was only 250 miles north of Jerusalem, but it was a world apart in terms of culture, ethnicity, and outlook. Ironically, between the two, it was Antioch that emerged as a hub for Jesus followers. In the words of Wayne Meeks: "Within a decade of the crucifixion of Jesus, the village culture of Palestine had been left behind, and the Greco-Roman city became the dominant environment of the Christian movement. . . . The movement had crossed the most fundamental division of the society of the Roman Empire, that between rural people and city dwellers, and the results were to prove momentous."[27]

The results were momentous both east and west of Antioch, although, as we will see in chapters 2 and 3, only the westward Christian mission left an accompanying literary record. From Antioch, the first Pauline Christian mission hopped to the island of Cyprus—to the cities of Salamis in the east and Paphos in the west—and then north to what is now west-central Turkey: to Perga, Pisidian Antioch, Iconium, Lystra, and Derbe. Two more Pauline missions, probably one by the apostle Peter, certainly one by the apostle John, and also one by the bishop Ignatius extended the Christian mission westward throughout the cities of Roman Asia—to Hierapolis, Colossae, Laodicea, Magnesia, Pergamon, Philadelphia, Sardis, Thyatira, Tralles, Ephesus, Smyrna, and Alexandria Troas. Paul, especially, extended the mission farther west, across the Aegean Sea and into Macedonia—to Neapolis, Philippi, Thessalonica, and Berea—and from there south to Achaia: to Athens, Cenchreae, and Corinth. Finally, as a prisoner in chains, Paul arrived in Rome itself.

The various missions to the above cities will be discussed more fully in the next chapter. Here I wish simply to note, first, that most of the foregoing cities are examples of a specific kind of Greco-Roman city, a *polis* (which we will discuss below), and, second, that the advance of the westward Christian mission is marked by the names of cities, with a conspicuous absence of named towns and villages. William Ramsay speaks to this absence: "[Paul] always sought out the great civilized centres. The towns which he visited for the sake of preaching were, as a rule, the centres of civilization and government in their respective districts—Ephesus, Athens, Corinth, Thessalonica, Philippi. He must have passed through several uncivilized Pisidian towns, such as Adada and Misthia and Vasada; but nothing is recorded about them. He preached, so far as we are informed, only in the centres of commerce and of

26. On Roman political theory and practice, see Maas, "People and Identity," 16.
27. Meeks, *First Urban Christians*, 11.

Roman life, and among these ranked Lystra Colonia and Claudio-Derbe."[28] I will cite evidence for early Christian rural mission at the close of this chapter, but Ramsay's overall point nevertheless stands: the absence of named rural settlements in the westward mission expansion shows the importance of the Greco-Roman *polis* as a metric of mission progress. The gospel was not only planted in the *polis*, but it also took root there, for there is record of a Christian presence a hundred years hence, in the mid-second century, in every city named above.[29]

Cities as Transmitters of Christianity

The transition from rural to urban, the "crossing of the most fundamental division of the society of the Roman Empire," in the words of Wayne Meeks,[30] was a momentous step for early Christianity because the qualities that made the Greco-Roman city effective for mediating the dominant values of Hellenism also made it effective for mediating Christianity.[31] The typical Greco-Roman *polis* was ruled by a legislative council consisting of as many as several hundred free men. It had stadiums for athletic and chariot races; theaters for dramatic performances, blood sports, and political gatherings; and gymnasia and baths for physical training, bathing, and displaying personal influence. All these monumental edifices were enclosed within city walls and serviced by aqueducts. Aqueducts alone changed the nature of a city, for they eliminated the massive expenditure of physical labor and resources required to haul water into a city from the outside. The availability of clean water made possible public baths and the commerce and human interchange that attended them, raised standards of living and general health, and produced a leisure class of citizens.

The focal point of the *polis* was the *agora*, the exhibition area at the city center that was surrounded by columns, to which city gates opened and arterial roads led, and over which architectural monuments presided. Regardless of how many people lived in a given *polis*, each *polis* functioned as a purveyor of Greco-Roman culture. Similar to "Hollywood" today, which signifies not only a suburb of Los Angeles but also a worldwide purveyor of American film,

28. Ramsay, *Church in the Roman Empire*, 56–57.
29. For evidence of a Christian presence in the above cities in the year 150, see Koch, *Geschichte des Urchristentums*, 421–22.
30. Meeks, *First Urban Christians*, 11.
31. Among the many discussions of the conditions in the Roman Empire conducive to the spread of Christianity, see Harnack, *Mission and Expansion*, 19–23; and, more recently, Sanneh, *Translating the Message*, 20–27.

the *polis* was not only a place but also a means of transmitting the influence of Rome to the world it dominated. The *polis* inculcated a more universal perception of humanity than any previous social structure. A human being was no longer a member of a small city-state, wherein nonmembers were considered aliens and barbarians, but a member of a universal empire that superseded tribal divisions and embraced all peoples. When Christianity made its way into the *polis*, it made its way into the dominant social influencer of the ancient world. The magnetism of the *polis* in attracting and shaping peoples is evident in the sixteenth chapter of Paul's Epistle to the Romans, in which he names over thirty individuals, many of whom he knew from previous mission locales, who in the intervening years had migrated to Rome.

Several of the foregoing cities are mentioned repeatedly in the early Christian record. Of the seven cities in Roman Asia (today western Turkey) addressed in Revelation 2–3 (Ephesus, Smyrna, Pergamon, Thyatira, Sardis, Philadelphia, and Laodicea), three were also recipients of letters from Ignatius in the early second century: Ephesus, Philadelphia, and Smyrna. Ignatius wrote letters to Magnesia, Tralles, and Rome as well. Smyrna figured in yet a third Christian epistle, the Martyrdom of Polycarp, as the city where the famous second-century bishop lived and was martyred. More popular still in early Christian epistles was Corinth, to which the apostle Paul wrote ostensibly four letters, and to which 1–2 Clement are also addressed—making a total of *six* epistles to this one locale.[32] No city along the Jerusalem–Rome corridor, however, was more important in early Christianity than Ephesus, which is mentioned more frequently in the New Testament than any city except Jerusalem.[33]

City Dwellers as Transmitters of Christianity

In the next chapter, we will discuss the importance of hellenized Jews in early Christianity; these were Jews who spoke Greek and lived in the diaspora. Hellenistic Jews not only dwelled in the *polis*, they were also products of it.[34] It was with such Jews that Christianity germinated in Antioch. But Hellenistic Jews were not the only purveyors of the gospel in cities. Cosmopolitan Romans were also groomed to transmit Christianity in a way that village dwellers and

32. First Corinthians 5:9 mentions a previous letter to Corinth. Following 1 Corinthians, Paul sent another letter to Corinth (which may be contained in whole or in part in 2 Cor. 10–13) by the hand of Titus (2 Cor. 7:13–14), after which he sent a fourth and final letter (2 Corinthians).

33. On the role of Ephesus in early Christianity, see Edwards, "Paul's Ephesus Riot."

34. Rodney Stark notes not only that "the Christian proportion of the population was substantially higher in cities than in the rural areas at this time" but also that its initial growth and strength began with Hellenistic Jews in urban settings. *Rise of Christianity*, 10, 57–59.

rural folk were not. The old rural traditions, often rooted in pagan agrarian cults, quickly lost appeal for and influence on those living in Roman cities.[35] Scores of ancient religious cults appealed to the forces of nature to sustain agriculture: Attis promised to renew nature; Artemis pledged success in the hunt and in the nurturing of life; Bacchus and Dionysus were gods of wine and fertility; Ceres and Demeter, goddesses of grain; Persephone and Hades, goddess and god, respectively, of summer and winter, of harvest and fallow; and Pan, lord of pastoral pursuits, serenaded them all with his happy flute.[36]

The mystery cults were closely bound to deities of earth and nature. Chief among them were the chthonic mysteries of Eleusis, which saw the death and rebirth of human life prefigured in the annual cycles of death and rebirth in nature. Such deities were normally venerated in remote and arboreal places—by streams of water, in caverns, among trees, and with animals present (especially those to be slain for sacrifice).[37] The word *pagan*, from the Latin *paganus* (meaning something like "country bumpkin"), was an urban put-down of rustic villagers. Mystery cults were in their heyday when the gospel was being proclaimed and planted in the Roman world, but their influence was minimal in comparison with Christianity, and for at least two reasons. First, and most obvious, mystery cults were exclusive. Their extravagant sacrifices—one of which involved sacrificing a bull—required of their devotees investments of time and money that were beyond the reach of most ancients. But second, and perhaps more important, the emphasis on the particular and provincial made mystery cults inaccessible and often irrelevant to the culture of the *polis*. Weaned from agrarian rural life, urban dwellers were influenced by commerce, diverse peoples, exposure to new ideas and travel, and above all to the homogenizing effect of the *polis*. Their world was no longer rural and provincial but urban and cosmopolitan. Even when the mysteries were transported to urban locales, they lost attractiveness for most urban dwellers.[38]

There were further reasons why the secularizing effects of Roman urbanization were conducive to the expansion of Christianity. Christianity did not have holy sites, such as those of the mystery cults or the many temples that abounded in Roman cities. Nor did it prescribe sacred rites of circumcision and Sabbath observance, as Judaism did, or bloody animal sacrifices, as the polytheistic cults did, or veneration of the emperor by formulas and libations.

35. Nock, *Conversion*, 227.
36. On the names and nature of rural and agricultural gods, goddesses, and cults, see G. W. Butterworth, "Appendix on the Greek Mysteries."
37. See Pausanias, *Descr.* 9.39, for a long description of the cult of the oracle of Trophonius.
38. On Paul's allusion to the cult of Cybele in Galatia, see Edwards, "Galatians 5:12"; and on John's treatment of the Apollo cult in Revelation, see Edwards, "Rider on the White Horse."

The Christian faith imposed fewer conditions on would-be recipients than did other cults, but the conditions it required were more life changing.[39] Christianity introduced the concept of humanity reconstituted in "the image of God" as manifested in Jesus Christ. This was accomplished by conversion rather than by external observances, and the concept of conversion was utterly new in the Roman understanding of religion.[40] Christianity called people to leave old loyalties behind and turn to something new—a transforming faith, a transforming community of believers, and the ethics of a transformed life.[41] The new world of the Greco-Roman *polis* helped to set a social stage congenial to the script of the gospel.

The Christian concept of *conversion* to one true faith was, with the exception of Judaism, novel in ancient religions. The ancients tended to be syncretistic in their religious allegiances. Like moderns approaching financial investment, they preferred diverse rather than uniform portfolios. Nevertheless, the novelty of Christian monotheism, which echoed some aspects of the dominant Stoic philosophy, was not unappealing to the Greco-Roman *polis*. Judaism was, of course, monotheistic like Christianity, but Judaism's insistence on circumcision, food laws, and separation from gentiles played poorly with the culture of the *polis*. Its moral standards attracted no small number of adherents among non-Jews, but circumcision and food laws ensured few full converts, and even full converts were not fully received by the Jewish community. Those who turned to Christianity were typically influenced by friends and by personal relationships with those who initiated new believers into networks of fellowship, belief, and practice. Exposure to persons practicing alternatives to the local cults was much more likely in cities than in isolated rural settings, and it was more effective with urban dwellers who, whether by necessity or choice, had weaned themselves from pagan cults.[42]

Conclusion

We have seen in this chapter how the Gospels identify Jesus's ministry almost exclusively with rural Galilee. Jesus consciously avoided the two showcase cities of Galilee: Sepphoris and Tiberias, both of which were within the orbit of his ministry. And had Jewish festivals not required Jesus's presence in Jeru-

39. See Sanneh, *Translating the Message*, 65–76.
40. See Beard, *SPQR*, 519: "Christianity was defined entirely by a process of spiritual conversion that was utterly new."
41. Nock, *Conversion*, 134–37.
42. See Stark, *Rise of Christianity*, 18–21; Fox, *Pagans and Christians*, 316; Brown, *Body and Society*, 90.

salem, he might have avoided the Holy City as well. Following Jesus's death, however, his followers identified with Jerusalem as decisively as he had with Galilee. Galilee receded drastically thereafter from the Christian narrative. The successful identification of the early Christian movement with the capital of the Jewish world, with Jerusalem, became an archetype, a firstfruit, of its ultimate identification with the capital of the gentile world, with Rome. A significant reason why the gospel gravitated to urban areas was that Jewish synagogues were more likely to be found in cities, and synagogues were the initial stepping-stones in early Christian missions. Acts 17:1, for example, describes Paul bypassing Amphipolis and Apollonia, where there were no synagogues, on his way to Thessalonica, "where there was a synagogue of the Jews." The synagogue was not the only or the final attraction of cities, however. The centripetal attraction of the Greco-Roman *polis*—drawing individuals from remote and diverse regions into close proximity, transforming a tribal consciousness into a more universal consciousness—established a unique social context in which early Christians declared that "there is no Greek and Jew, circumcision and uncirumcision, barbarian, Scythian, slave and free; rather, Christ is all and in all" (Col. 3:11). The list of cities along the Jerusalem–Rome corridor in which Christian churches were established within the thirty-five-year period chronicled in the book of Acts testifies to the success of the gospel in the Greco-Roman *polis*.

In conclusion, however, let us return to the starting point of our chapter. If the early Christian mission became urban, and *gentile urban* shortly thereafter, what became of its original rural emphasis? Since the 1980s the success of the Christian mission in, and its identification with, the urban ancient world has been ably and widely advocated. A great deal of literature on the subject leaves the impression, in fact, that the early Christian mission was *exclusively* urban.[43] Ramsay MacMullen speaks for many when he says,

> Everyone is agreed that the church started as an urban phenomenon and continued in that tendency throughout our period of study [100–400]. . . . Surviving

43. Wayne A. Meeks opened the gate on the urbanity of early Christianity in 1983 with *The First Urban Christians: The Social World of the Apostle Paul*. The torrent of literature that soon followed made it a floodgate. The present chapter obviously concurs with the essential position of Meeks and others. In concluding this chapter, however, I wish to contend that early Christianity was not *exclusively* urban but included rural regions as well, especially those surrounding urban areas. For a critique of a hyper-urban understanding of early Christianity, see Robinson, *First Urban Christians?*, who argues that if, as many sociologists of early Christianity maintain, Christians comprised 10 percent of the population of the Roman world (ca. 5–6 million people) by the 4th century, that would have constituted virtually the *entire* urban population of the Roman world (pp. 1–25). That is obviously impossible. Such statistics would require a (sizeable) rural Christian presence as well.

sources . . . show missionary impulses moving out from the centers to less populated areas, not the other way round. So everyone assumes, and surely they are right, that the countryside lagged far behind the cities in degree of Christianization. It is also agreed . . . that a great majority of the empire's total population lived outside the cities. . . . It follows from all this that . . . vast parts of the empire that lie outside our range of clear sight . . . must be counted as less vigorously evangelized.[44]

More briefly and concisely, Meeks writes, "Within a decade of the crucifixion of Jesus, the village culture of Palestine had been left behind, and the Greco-Roman city became the dominant environment of the Christian movement."[45] Other scholars have also joined the "left behind" chorus.[46]

The issue is not whether the early Christian mission was primarily an urban mission. It was. The issue is whether it was *exclusively* urban. It was not. A mélange of evidence in the coming chapters points to a mission that was both urban and rural. In a letter to the emperor Trajan around the year 113, Pliny the Younger, governor of Bithynia, writes that "this superstitious contagion [Christianity] is not confined to the cities only, but has spread through the villages and rural districts."[47] In his defense of Christianity to the emperor Antoninus Pius in Rome in about the year 150, Justin Martyr likewise describes Sunday worship services where "all who live in cities or in the country gather together to one place."[48] Christian mission in Syria "was not limited to cities, but from the beginning concerned itself with the evangelization of country-folks also."[49] All twelve Scillitan martyrs, though martyred in the city of Carthage, hailed from the village of Scilli, west of Carthage, indicating that "the new faith had taken root not only in cities but also in the countryside."[50] In his summary of the triumph of Christianity

44. MacMullen, *Christianizing the Roman Empire*, 83.

45. Meeks, *First Urban Christians*, 11.

46. See Lohmeyer, *Soziale Fragen im Urchristentum*, 129: "[Christianity] grew up in the free countryside, but it changed into a purely urban movement" (my trans.); Meyers, "Side by Side in Galilee," 143: "The impact of Christianity, which increased significantly in this period [the early centuries], did not extend to the rural population"; Holmes, *Apostolic Fathers*, 14: "Lack of evidence frustrates efforts to ascertain much about the social or economic circumstances and outlook of these congregations beyond the observation that Christianity remained overwhelmingly urban"; Stark, *Rise of Christianity*, 10: "There is an agreement among historians . . . that the Christian proportion of the population was substantially higher in cities than in the rural areas at this time."

47. Pliny, *Ep. Tra.* 10.96.

48. Justin, *1 Apol.* 67 (ANF 1:186).

49. Metzger, *Early Versions*, 7–8.

50. Merdinger, "Roman North Africa," 233–34. For the account of the martyrs, see Gwatkin, *Selections from Early Writers*, 78–83.

in the Roman Empire, Eusebius attests that "in every city and village arose churches crowded with thousands of men, like a teeming threshing floor."[51] These witnesses come from North Africa, Palestine, Mesopotamia, Bithynia, and Rome. With the exception of Spain, these regions constituted the footprint of the Roman Empire in the first century. All the quotations attest to a Christian presence in both urban and rural areas. We may conclude—and conclude rightly—that the early Christian mission was primarily urban, but not exclusively so, for the urban centers to which it spread invariably extended the gospel to surrounding regions.

51. Eusebius, *Hist. eccl.* 2.3.2 (LCL).

2

From Jerusalem to Rome

The Finish Line Becomes the Starting Line

"You will be my witnesses in Jerusalem and in all of Judea and Samaria and to the end of the earth" (Acts 1:8). This formulaic introduction to the book of Acts has become so well known that we forget how confounding it would have been to the Jesus followers who first heard it. They were Jewish, and the Old Testament narrative that informed their faith taught the reverse: Jerusalem—or Zion, the larger religious and geographical entity of which Jerusalem was the epicenter—was the terminus of the divine destiny of Israel. Abraham had been summoned from urbane Ur on the Euphrates River to journey to Canaan and establish an outpost that, in the promise and power of God, would become a great people blessed by God and great in name (Gen. 12:2). The fulfillment of this promise would entail the overcoming of many unforeseen obstacles. The descendants of Abraham relocated to Egypt, their geopolitically powerful neighbor to the south, to escape famine. There they were enslaved and needed to be liberated by divine signs and wonders in the exodus. Divine favor reestablished the outpost, by this time known as Israel, in the promised land—and this time with deeper roots, culminating in the establishment of the Israelite monarchy, with Jerusalem as its capital. A glorious temple was erected, and the nation flowered for a season as a power of consequence in the Levant. The kingdom divided, however, and both sides suffered decline and eventual destruction: the Northern Kingdom by Assyria in the eighth century BC and the Southern Kingdom by Babylon a century and a half later.

The promise to Abraham was revived, or a vestige of it, in the late sixth century, when the Israelites were allowed to return to Jerusalem. But the concept of Israel had been forever altered. The monarchy was destroyed, as was the temple and its priesthood. Israel no longer existed as a sovereign nation, and the remnant that constituted postexilic Judaism was barely recognizable as the nation's successor. Synagogues—mere community halls—replaced the glorious temple; a clerical class of scribes replaced the richly invested priesthood; and the divine will was communicated through a written narrative, Torah, rather than through prophets and priests. As for the land itself, except for a century-long interlude (168–63 BC), it would not be restored to Israel for the next two and a half millennia! Israel's pruning had grossly altered the promise to Abraham. Only one key element—more important than anything but Torah itself—remained constant: the Jews returned to the land, to Zion. In Jerusalem they reconstituted their remnant community, not into a new nation but into a new understanding of themselves as God's people. They defended their remnant revival from extermination during the Maccabean Revolt. And even with the Roman occupation of Palestine in the first century BC, all Jewish sects defined their stance vis-à-vis Rome in one way or another with reference to the land, *eretz Israel*.

This was the history and the religiopolitical landscape that confronted Jesus followers around the year AD 30. And with this we return to Acts 1:8: "You will be my witnesses in Jerusalem and in all of Judea and Samaria and to the end of the earth." In Israel's history, Jerusalem was the finish line, the fulfillment of divine destiny. In Acts 1:8, however, Jesus turns the finish line into a starting line. Jerusalem is not a terminus but a genesis. Few declarations of Jesus had greater consequence for Jews, and for what would become the Christian movement, than this one.

"... to the End of the Earth"

Acts 1:8 does not identify exactly what Jesus has in mind by "the end of the earth," but Luke clearly sets Rome as the geographical terminus and goal of Acts. His disciplined narrative charts the missionary witness of the early church as it progresses incrementally from Jerusalem to Judea and Samaria, to Roman Asia, to Macedonia and Achaia, and finally to Rome. The resultant Jerusalem–Rome corridor forms the narrative spine of the Acts of the Apostles.

Acts describes the first experimental form of the Jesus community in Jerusalem. Following the resurrection, Jesus's disciples relocate from Galilee to Jerusalem. There they participate publicly in the temple cult[1] while privately

---

1. Acts 2:1; 3:1; 5:12, 42.

observing the teaching and leadership of the apostles, joining in fellowship and group prayer and sharing both meals and goods in common.[2] The private gatherings are the more distinct of the two expressions of their communal life (5:13) and account for the first use of the word "church" (Gk. *ekklēsia*) in Luke's history.[3] In their public witness, believers proclaim the uniqueness of Jesus as "the author of life" (3:15), especially as attested by his resurrection from the dead.[4] And in accordance with Jesus's earthly ministry (10:38), they also perform "signs and wonders" in his name.[5] Jesus followers maintain their commitment to witness in the temple (5:20), despite the provocations their preaching and ministry cause temple authorities.[6] Their numbers increase exponentially: an initial 120 believers are soon augmented by 3,000 believers, and thereafter by another 5,000.[7] Their Judean Jewish converts include "a large number of priests" (6:7), but also Hellenistic Jews from the diaspora (6:1–5). We cannot say how long Jesus followers continued these two forms of observance—one public, in the temple, and one private, in believers' homes—but by the death of James the son of Zebedee at the hand of Herod Agrippa I in the early 40s (i.e., within a decade of the resurrection), the house church had become the identifiable form of the Jesus movement. By the time Luke reports that "Herod the king laid hostile hands on some members of the church" (12:1–2), the church clearly seems to have separated from the temple.

In addition to the binary of public and private gatherings, a second binary in the book of Acts is introduced with the "Hellenists" in chapter 6. This group profoundly influences the development of Christianity, for Hellenists (i.e., Jews whose primary cultural and ethnic references come from the Greek-speaking diaspora rather than from Judea or Jerusalem) take the baton from the first Judean Jesus followers and carry it beyond Jerusalem and Judea, and soon thereafter beyond Jewish ethnicity itself.[8] The Hellenists propel the Christian mission along the Jerusalem–Rome corridor, and along other axes as well, eventually distinguishing it uniquely from Judaism. The future of the Christian movement thus belongs not to the Christian Hebrews of the

2. Acts 2:42–47; 4:32–5:11.
3. Acts 5:11; 8:1–3.
4. Acts 4:2, 33; 5:31; 10:40.
5. Acts 4:30; 5:12; 6:8.
6. Acts 4:1–22; 5:17–40.
7. On the increase of numbers, see Acts 1:15; 2:41; 4:4; 5:14.
8. According to John Barclay, diaspora Jewish communities provided Paul with the most viable model for Christian communities: "If, in this respect, Diaspora communities constituted 'ethnic schools,' Pauline churches look most like Diaspora synagogues in their 'philosophical' mode, or most like a 'Judean school' whose membership was not characterized by an ethnic bond." *Pauline Churches*, 14–15.

first five chapters of Acts but to the Christian Hellenists of chapters 6 and following. Essential and enduring arteries flow between Christian Hebrews and Christian Hellenists, of course, including the indispensability of the Jesus tradition for salvation, prayer, and mission, as well as for the significance of baptism, the Lord's Supper, and works of mercy done in Jesus's name.

But not all characteristics of the first Jesus community in Jerusalem endure with the Christian Hellenists. Stephen's survey of God's saving purpose in Israel's history in Acts 7 is a *Hellenistic* survey, and it dispenses with the dominant jewel in Jerusalem: the temple. "The Most High does not dwell in [houses] built by human hands," he declares (Acts 7:48).[9] The destruction of the temple by the Romans in the year 70 made Stephen's dictum a historical reality. Nor will Christian Hellenists or any other early Christian communities that we know of continue the experiment in charitable communism attempted by the Jerusalem church. Christian Hellenists, moreover, introduce elements into the early church that were not practiced in the early Hebrew Jesus community in Jerusalem—including a missionary component and, above all, a full embrace of both Jews and gentiles in one universal church.

Stephen's martyrdom in Acts 7 forcibly breaks the early church loose from its Jerusalem-centeredness. The cause of Stephen's martyrdom was the radical nature of his sermon before the Sanhedrin. His lengthy defense shifts the locus of authority in Judaism from Moses to the prophet Jesus, who succeeded and superseded him (Acts 7:37). Indeed, as noted above, Stephen dispenses with the temple (7:48), for God's saving purpose is fulfilled in the very Jesus whom Stephen sees standing at the right hand of God in glory (7:56) and to whom he cries his martyr's prayer: "Lord Jesus, receive my spirit" (7:59). For Stephen and the Hellenists, Jesus supersedes the law of Moses as the revelation of God; as Messiah, Jesus fulfills the history of God's self-revelation in Israel.

From Acts 8 until the middle of Acts 11, the persecution following Stephen's death drives early Jesus followers out of Jerusalem and into Judea and Samaria. Philip journeys north to Samaria "to preach Christ" (8:5). This must be Philip the deacon, last mentioned in the list of Hellenists in Acts 6:5 (rather than Philip the apostle, who is named in Acts only in the apostolic list of 1:13).[10] He carries forth the vision declared by Stephen in his martyr testimony. So extraordinary is Philip's mission in Samaria that Peter and John, the two Jerusalem "pillars" (as Paul calls them in Gal. 2:9), journey north to observe and approve the mission there (Acts 8:4–25). Philip then travels to the coastal lowlands of Gaza and Azotus, where his witness results in the conversion

---

9. A point Paul repeats in his Areopagus speech in Athens (Acts 17:24).
10. Philip the deacon may also be the same Philip who is called an evangelist in Acts 21:8.

and baptism of an Ethiopian finance minister, a eunuch (8:26–40). Eunuchs were debarred from becoming full proselytes, according to the law of Moses (Deut. 23:1), but such barriers were not decisive for Hellenist Jesus followers.

Saul, the Pharisaic firebrand, is dramatically introduced in Acts 9, "fuming threats and murder against the disciples" (v. 1). He journeys north to Damascus, and surely not by accident, for the Jewish community there was large and influential.[11] Such a community would foreseeably be receptive to the Hellenist version of the gospel propagated by Stephen and Philip—a gospel less allied to Torah and temple than the one advocated by Jesus's Galilean disciples superintending the community in Jerusalem. Saul's plan to seize and arrest believers remains one of the great unfulfilled missions of history, for by divine intervention he becomes the supreme advocate of the faith he sought to destroy. Other church leaders also participate in the centrifugal expansion of the gospel following Stephen's martyrdom, including Peter, the superintendent of the church in Jerusalem. Peter journeys westward to Joppa, on the Mediterranean coast (9:32–43), and from there north to Caesarea Maritima, where his witness as lead apostle of the "Way" to the Roman centurion Cornelius results in a *gentile* conversion and baptism in the church (10:1–11:18). Acts 8:1–11:18 thus recounts the initial result of the persecution following Stephen's martyrdom: the extension of the gospel in Jerusalem and Judea and Samaria, and northward as far as Damascus.

Following the death of Stephen, a second wave of expansion pushes the gospel farther north along the Mediterranean coast, to Phoenicia and Antioch, and westward to the island of Cyprus. Once again, Hellenists are the driving force. The evangelists initially proclaim the gospel only to Jews (Acts 11:19). But evangelists from the island of Cyprus and from Cyrene, on the north coast of Africa, arrive in Antioch of Syria and "[proclaim] the good news of the Lord Jesus" also to "Hellenists" (11:20). Cyprus and Cyrene had large Jewish populations that had been thoroughly hellenized from the time of the Ptolemaic successors to Alexander the Great in the late fourth century BC. Luke refers to this population as "Hellenists," the same term he used earlier with reference to Greek-speaking Jews in Jerusalem who were Jesus followers (6:1). But in Acts 11:20 the term must be understood more broadly: as a reference to Greek-speaking *gentiles*. Had the missionary evangelists preached to Greek-speaking *Jews* in Antioch, as was customary, Luke would not have needed to assure readers that "the hand of the Lord was with them" (11:21), nor would church leaders in Jerusalem have dispatched an embassy from Jerusalem to examine the extraordinary occurrence (11:22).

11. Josephus, *J.W.* 2.559–61.

The "certain men from Cyprus and Cyrene" (Acts 11:20) are far more important than the prosaic reference to them implies. Although others before them had borne incidental witness to gentiles, most notably Philip to the Ethiopian eunuch (Acts 8:26–40) and Peter to Cornelius (Acts 10:1–11:18), the unnamed men from Cyprus and Cyrene breach the historically impenetrable ethnic barrier by a programmatic proclamation of the gospel to gentiles. Who were they? From whom did they hear the gospel and come to faith? Who sent them to Antioch? Our sources leave these burning questions unanswered. Prior to this point in Acts, only Barnabas has been identified as a Cypriot (4:36). We know that the Simon who carried Jesus's cross was from Cyrene,[12] even that "a synagogue of freedpersons from Cyrene and Alexandria" existed in Jerusalem (6:9). But the synagogue of freedpersons led the charge against Stephen and seems not to have been hospitable to Christians. Adolf Harnack and others suggest that the identities of the mystery evangelists of Acts 11:20 are given in 13:1 in the names of Simeon of Niger, Lucius the Cyrene, and Manaen.[13] Harnack may be partially right, but there must have been more individuals in view in 11:20, for none of the names in 13:1 is identified with Cyprus.[14] We are thus left with a famine of information about the influential individuals who shifted the center of gravity in early Christianity from Jerusalem to Antioch, and in so doing, began the shift of the center of gravity in Christianity from Jews to gentiles. How much more (if anything) Luke knew about them we cannot say. He is not interested in their histories. Like Apollos (18:24–19:1), they are significant for Luke's narrative only because of their role in advancing the gospel along the Jerusalem–Rome corridor. Luke was aware that the gospel followed many paths to different destinations in the first century, but in Acts he is interested only in those paths that led to Rome.

The Pauline Mission

As our review of Acts to this point makes clear, Hellenist Jesus followers capitalized on their commonalities with Jewish Hellenists in the diaspora in order to proclaim the gospel. It was among these diaspora Hellenists, according to

---

12. Matt. 27:32; Mark 15:21; Luke 23:26.

13. Harnack, *Mission and Expansion*, 52n1. Harnack crowns the three "the founders of the church, and consequently the first missionaries to the heathen." Indeed, for Harnack, "*Barnabas must be mentioned first of all among the originators of the Gentile mission*" (italics original). It is true, as Harnack notes, that Barnabas acted as an intermediary between Paul and the early apostles, but if Barnabas was indeed the pioneer of the gentile mission, it would seem strange for him to have sided with the Jerusalem apostles against that mission in the conflict of Gal. 2:11–14.

14. Barnabas was, of course, from Cyprus (Acts 4:36), but he arrived in Antioch only later with Paul.

Luke in the latter half of Acts 11, that Barnabas and Saul took up residence in Antioch. And by them, Barnabas and Saul were sent into mission in Acts 13.[15] Antioch in Syria became the major staging point for the gentile mission along the Jerusalem–Rome corridor, but equally—as we will see in the next chapter—for the expansion of the gospel to the far reaches of the East.[16] In Acts 13:1 Luke names five prophets and teachers in the church of Antioch, along with their places of origin, who by prayer, fasting, and the laying on of hands commission two of their number, Paul and Barnabas, into mission. In addition to Barnabas, a Levite from Cyprus (4:36), and Paul, born and raised in Tarsus but educated in Jerusalem (22:3), the mission circle in Antioch includes "Simeon called Niger," whose epithet in both Greek and Latin means "black" or "dark complexioned," and "Lucius, the Cyrene," whom we mentioned above. Both of these men evidently hailed from North Africa. The final and most surprising member of the circle is Manaen, whom Luke identifies in Greek as a *syntrophos* (companion or close friend) of Herod Antipas. The Jesus movement, ironically, found adherents in the innermost circle of Herod Antipas, whose capital, Sepphoris, was barely three miles from Jesus's hometown of Nazareth. Joanna, wife of Chuza, the manager of Herod's household, was one of several women who traveled with Jesus and supported him financially (Luke 8:3). Manaen may have been an acquaintance, a relative, or perhaps a son of Joanna. It could have been from Manaen that Luke learned of Antipas's obsession with Jesus and desire to meet him.[17] These five individuals form a remarkable community in Antioch: a Levite responsible for temple rituals, a Pharisaic confidant of the Sadducean high priest in Jerusalem, two North Africans (at least one of whom was a man of color), and a close associate of the tetrarch of Galilee who was infamously associated with Jesus's execution. The geographical, ethnic, racial, and social diversity of the Antioch mission society differs radically from the Twelve who followed Jesus fewer than twenty years earlier.

The third quarter of the book of Acts (chs. 13–21) narrates the expansion of the gospel along the Jerusalem–Rome corridor with almost military precision. Three successive mission journeys, each commencing from Syrian Antioch, advance the gospel incrementally westward. In the late 40s, the first journey takes Paul and Barnabas to the island of Cyprus, and from there north to the mainland, where they evangelize and establish churches in the Pisidian

---

15. On "Hellenists," see Bruce, *Peter, Stephen, James, and John*, 49–80; Hengel, *History of Earliest Christianity*, 71–80; Hengel, *Studien zum Urchristentum*, 54–62; Meyers and Chancey, *Alexander to Constantine*, 1–49.

16. On Syrian Antioch, see ch. 1, pp. 7–11.

17. Luke 9:7–9; 13:31–33; 23:7–15.

cities of Antioch (of Pisidia), Iconium, Lystra, and Derbe, all of which are in modern south-central Turkey. In the early 50s, a more ambitious journey takes Paul, Silas, and Timothy back through the above cities in Pisidia, and from there to Troas, on the northeast arc of the Aegean Sea, where they leave Roman Asia and sail north to evangelize the Macedonian cities of Philippi, Thessalonica, and Berea, followed by a mission to the south, in the Achaian cities of Athens and Corinth. Both journeys are monumental: the first occupying perhaps a year, and the second and longer journey perhaps four years (ca. 49–52), a full year and a half of which was spent in Corinth (18:1–17).

With barely a pause in Luke's narrative, Paul and Silas set out on a third mission journey, again visiting the cities in Pisidia evangelized on the two previous missions (Acts 18:22–23). From there they travel due west along the Meander River valley to Ephesus, a city equal in size to Antioch but, on the Jerusalem–Rome corridor, second in importance only to Rome itself. In Ephesus, Paul halts his metronomic mission itinerancy and establishes a residential ministry for two years (19:1–41). Then disturbances in the church of Corinth draw Paul back to both Macedonia and Achaia in order to teach, train, and undergird churches that he established on his previous journey. He celebrates his reconciliation with the church in Corinth by extending his stay there for three months (20:2–3), during which he probably pens his magisterial epistle to Rome. From Corinth, Paul virtually retraces the long and complex route over land and sea, returning at last to Jerusalem (Acts 21).

Few chronicles in ancient literature contain the riptide narrative force of the Pauline mission in the third quarter of the book of Acts. Tacitus's descriptions of the various Germanic campaigns of the Roman emperors and generals are turgid by comparison. Not even Alexander's long trek to the Himalayas or Xenophon's harrowing account, in the *Anabasis*, of his return with ten thousand Greek mercenaries from the battle with Artaxerxes II is as engaging. Luke provides enough detail to allow us to date events in his narrative with reasonable precision, and to infer the dates of other events as well. The transition in the governorship of Judea from Felix to Festus (Acts 24:27), for example, can be dated to within a five-year period (55–60).[18] The death of Herod Agrippa I in Acts 12, an event also reported by Josephus, can be dated to the year 44.[19] Paul's appearance before the proconsul Gallio's *bēma*—his speaker's platform at Corinth (still visible today)—can be dated to within a matter of months.[20]

---

18. See the full discussion of evidence on the matter in Keener, *Acts*, 4:3442–48.
19. Josephus, *Ant.* 19.343–53.
20. An inscription chiseled in minute precision on the retaining wall of the Temple of Apollo at Delphi reports that Gallio served as proconsul of Corinth from July 51 to July 52.

The third quarter of Acts comprises the ten-year period from the late 40s to the late 50s. Paul is the central figure, but he is rarely the only figure. Rather, he leads a company of named individuals committed to a common mission. The three companions who bear the brunt of the responsibility with him are Barnabas, on the first mission, and Silas and Timothy, on the second and third missions. Timothy's name, in particular, is omnipresent in the last two missions. Indeed, Timothy is mentioned as a fellow worker with Paul in every one of his epistles except for Galatians and Ephesians; and his name also appears in Hebrews. Most names are linked to specific localities. Epaphroditus is an emissary between Paul and the Philippians. He even exhausts himself to the point of death in laboring on their behalf.[21] Titus and a disciple whom Paul refers to only as "the brother" (because of protective anonymity?) render yeoman service in Corinth and are acknowledged by Paul for "their renown in the gospel and in all the churches" (2 Cor. 8:18–24). Epaphras is evidently dispatched as Paul's surrogate to evangelize Colossae while Paul remains in Ephesus.[22] Phoebe, a deaconess, is entrusted to carry Paul's Epistle to the Romans safely from Corinth to the capital (Rom. 16:1–3). Others attend to Paul's needs when he is imprisoned. Roman prisons made no provisions for feeding and clothing prisoners, so prisoners depended on family or friends to provide basic necessities. Paul names and honors such providers—Andronicus and his wife (or sister) Junia (Rom. 16:7), Aristarchus (Col. 4:10), and Epaphras again (Philem. 23)—as his "fellow-prisoners." Other individuals, such as the oft-mentioned Priscilla and Aquila,[23] or Apollos (Acts 18:24–28), work independently of Paul, although their missions frequently intersect. Some eighty individuals appear in the book of Acts and in the Pauline epistles in relation to the Pauline mission.[24] Paul's repeated references to these individuals—

---

21. Phil. 2:25–30; 4:18.

22. Col. 1:7; 4:12.

23. Acts 18:1–3; Rom. 16:3; 2 Tim. 4:19.

24. With the twenty-nine individuals (twenty-seven are named) in Rom. 16:1–16, and in addition to the numerous references to Timothy, Titus, and Silas/Silvanus, there are Apollos (Acts 18:24–28), Apphia (Philem. 1–2), Aquila (Acts 18:2; 2 Tim. 4:19; Rom. 16:3), Archippus (Philem. 1–2), Aristarchus (Acts 20:4; Col. 4:10; Philem. 24), Artemas (Titus 3:12), Barnabas/"Brother" (2 Cor. 8:18–24), Claudia (2 Tim. 4:21), Clement (Phil. 4:3), Demas (Col. 4:14; Philem. 24), Epaphras (Col. 1:7; 4:12; Philem. 23), Epaphroditus (Phil. 2:25; 4:18), Erastus (Rom. 16:23; 2 Tim. 4:20), Eubulus (2 Tim. 4:21), Euodia (Phil. 4:2), Gaius (Acts 20:4; Rom. 16:23), Jason (Rom. 16:21), Jesus Justus (Col. 4:11), Linus (2 Tim. 4:21), Lucius (Acts 13:1), Luke (Col. 4:14; Philem. 24), Manaen (Acts 13:1), Mark (Col. 4:10; Philem. 24), Mnason (Acts 21:16), Nympha (Col. 4:15), Onesimus (Philem. 10; Col. 4:9), Onesiphorus (2 Tim. 4:19), Philemon (Philem. 1–2), Philip and his four daughters (Acts 21:8–14), Phoebe (Rom. 16:1–3), Priscilla (Acts 18:2; 2 Tim. 4:19; Rom. 16:3), Pudens (2 Tim. 4:21), Quartus (Rom. 16:23), Secundus (Acts 20:4), Sopater/Sosipater (Acts 20:4), Sosthenes (Act 18:17; 1 Cor. 1:1), Symeon Niger (Acts 13:1), Syntyche (Phil. 4:2), Tertius (Rom. 16:22), Trophimus (Acts 20:4), Tychicus (Acts 20:4; Titus 3:12), and Zenas (Titus 3:13).

acknowledging their contributions as "sister," "brother," "fellow-worker," "fellow-servant," "fellow-prisoner," "fellow-kinsman," and the like—testify to a trusted community of mission along the Jerusalem–Rome corridor.

The gentile mission decentralized Jerusalem, qualifying the Holy City's importance in early Christian outreach. Antioch assumed a status second in importance to Jerusalem, and Ephesus and Alexandria may have assumed tertiary roles of more regional importance. Jerusalem remained important throughout first-century Christian mission, however, as both sender and receiver. Acts records either five or six instances of Paul, champion of the gentile mission, returning to Jerusalem to confer with leaders, especially James.[25] Additionally, Paul's fundraising in Macedonia for the impoverished church in Jerusalem[26] and his rehearsal of the role of the Jerusalem leaders as the font of the kerygmatic tradition (1 Cor. 15:1–11) testify to the enduring importance of Jerusalem in early Christian mission. The Jerusalem–Rome corridor was both artery and vein, a two-way lifeline in which the outward mission retained its integrity by repeated inward reference to its source.

For the book of Acts, Rome is the providential "end of the earth" to which the disciples must bear witness. The final quarter of Acts (chs. 22–28) presents readers with something of a conundrum, for the seemingly unstoppable Pauline mission is seemingly stopped with the arrest and imprisonment of the apostle. Luke seizes on the conundrum to accentuate a point that might otherwise have been overshadowed by Paul's prodigious mission momentum—namely, that the author and orchestrator of Christian mission is not Paul or Peter, or anyone else, but the Holy Spirit. With Paul rendered inoperative, the role of the Holy Spirit can be recognized more clearly for what it has always been. That the Holy Spirit is the prime mover of the church's mission is underscored by three assurances to Paul that he must bear witness before Caesar in Rome.[27] These assurances are crucial for the narrative of Acts, for they identify both the *terminus* of the mission—Rome—and the *means* of its completion: the agency of the Holy Spirit. Luke underscores the central importance of the Holy Spirit by ending his two-part history of the early church without mentioning the fate of Paul in Rome. Readers of Acts have historically regarded this ending as flawed, or even failed, but for Luke the completion of the Jerusalem–Rome corridor depends not on Paul's fate but on the arrival of the gospel in Rome.

25. Acts 9:26; 11:29–30; 12:25; 15:2; 18:22; 21:17; cf. Gal. 1:18–2:10. It is possible, however, that Acts 12:25 describes the same Jerusalem visit as 11:29–30.

26. Rom. 15:26; 1 Cor. 16:1–4; 2 Cor. 8–9.

27. Acts 19:21; 23:11; 27:24; see also Rom. 1:10.

Peter

The Jerusalem–Rome corridor was more than Luke's elective narrative scheme for the book of Acts. It was also an acknowledgment of a historical reality, for all other first-century witnesses to the expansion of the church attest to the same corridor. Clement, writing at the close of the first century, identifies "the limit of the west" as the apostle Paul's destiny.[28] Independently of both Acts and 1 Clement, moreover, we know that the essential missionary itinerary adopted by the apostles Peter and John, and by Ignatius, bishop of Antioch, also followed the Jerusalem–Rome corridor.

Let us first examine Peter, whose initial appearance on the corridor is his crucial meeting with the centurion Cornelius in Caesarea Maritima (Acts 10:1–11:18), which still lay within Roman Palestine. Luke concludes Peter's role in the book of Acts with his crucial testimony at the Council of Jerusalem, advocating for the full acceptance of gentile believers into the church (Acts 15).[29] The council must be dated to the late 40s. Peter is omitted from the narrative of Acts following the council not because his ministry ceased but because, like the unnamed missionaries from Cyprus and Cyrene that we noted in Acts 11:20, his ministry no longer contributed to the first advance of the gospel to Rome. Peter lived nearly twenty years after the Council of Jerusalem, however, and additional information in the New Testament augments Acts, giving us a fuller picture of his ministry.

Paul himself expands our picture of Peter's ministry and mission. Three years after Paul's conversion to the faith, he went from Damascus to Jerusalem, where for two weeks he met with Peter—or Cephas, as he usually calls him (Gal. 1:17–18).[30] Fourteen years later, he again visited Jerusalem—this time meeting with the "pillars" Peter, James, and John—where he agreed to an apportionment of ministry: Peter would be the "apostle to the circumcision" and Paul the "apostle to the gentiles" (Gal. 2:1–10). That apportionment was later sharply invoked by Paul in Antioch when he rebuked Peter publicly for expecting gentile converts to comply with Jewish regulations with which Peter, though a Jew, did not himself comply (Gal. 2:11–14). The evidence of Galatians 2 thus attests to Peter's apostolic authority and presence in Antioch.

Paul's letters also attest, although not with equal specificity, to Peter's presence in Corinth. Peter was known to the Corinthians as the first member of the Twelve to see the resurrected Jesus (1 Cor. 15:5), and he was the

28. 1 Clem. 5.7.
29. The council is discussed in ch. 9, pp. 158–60.
30. Paul refers to Peter eight times in 1 Corinthians and Galatians by his Aramaic name, Cephas, and twice in Galatians by his Greek name, Peter. Both names mean "Rock."

only one of the Twelve that Paul mentioned by name in his letter. A faction of Corinthian believers allied themselves with Peter, as other factions allied themselves with Apollos or Paul or even Christ.[31] Peter's example, along with James the brother of the Lord, of taking his wife on mission travels set a standard in the Corinthian mindset for what was acceptable for other missionaries, Paul included (1 Cor. 9:5). Most striking, perhaps, is Paul's appeal to Hebrew and Israelite standards as the epitome of apostolic authority in pagan Corinth: "Are they Hebrews? So am I. Are they Israelites? So am I. Are they descendants of Abraham? So am I. Are they servants of Christ? I am more so" (2 Cor. 11:22–23). Although we have no explicit testimony to Peter's presence in Corinth, it is hard to imagine that the figure of Peter would recur so frequently in Paul's Corinthian correspondence unless he were known personally to the Corinthians.

Peter's certain tenure in Antioch and probable tenure in Corinth provide plausible contexts for considering the reference in 1 Peter 1:1 to "the elect exiles in the diaspora of Pontus, Galatia, Cappadocia, Asia, and Bithynia." Eusebius and Jerome both mention Peter's name with reference to these same regions, and in the same order.[32] Pontus, Cappadocia, and Asia are also mentioned in Luke's account of Pentecost (Acts 2:9), which could plausibly indicate a relationship between Peter and residents of those regions dating back to Pentecost. Two further witnesses, Pseudo-Hippolytus in the third century and Epiphanius in the fourth, independently confirm that relationship.[33] The testimony of Pliny the Younger, the Roman governor of Bithynia, is also important in this regard. Writing in approximately 110 to the emperor Trajan, Pliny reports that Christians existed in Bithynia at least twenty years prior to the commencement of his governorship there.[34] We know of only one first-century Christian associated with Bithynia, and that is the apostle Peter (1 Pet. 1:1). Peter's association with the region could explain why, according to Acts 16:7, Paul refrained from mission activity there; for it was Paul's principle "not to build on the foundation laid by another" (Rom. 15:20).

The above evidence, admittedly, does not prove that Peter evangelized the coast of Turkey south of the Black Sea. It seems to indicate, however, that Peter did enjoy a relationship with residents of Pontus, Galatia, Cappadocia, Asia, and Bithynia. And in light of the foregoing, we might hazard the

31. See 1 Cor. 1:12; 3:22.

32. Eusebius, *Hist. eccl.* 3.4.2; Jerome, *Vir. ill.* 1.1. By his own admission, however, Eusebius's report is dependent on 1 Pet. 1:1, and Jerome's may be also. Neither citation therefore offers independent corroboration of 1 Pet. 1:1.

33. Pseudo-Hippolytus, *De Duodecim Apostolis* (PG 10:952); Epiphanius, *Pan.* 27.6.6.

34. Pliny, *Ep. Tra.* 10.96.

suggestion that Peter visited the above-named regions on his journey to Rome, perhaps to renew relationships he had formed at Pentecost (Acts 2:9), and that once in Rome, he wrote a follow-up letter, 1 Peter, back to churches in those regions (1 Pet. 1:1; 5:13). Forty years later, Ignatius followed precisely this procedure on his journey to Rome with respect to churches in Roman Asia. Peter's example may have provided both precedent and incentive for Ignatius to do the same.[35]

The tradition of Peter's death in Rome is universally upheld in Christian tradition.[36] In the fourth century, both Eusebius and Jerome report that Peter became bishop of Antioch, whence he journeyed to Rome, where he defended the gospel from attack by Simon Magus. Eusebius and Jerome further report that Peter remained in Rome as bishop until his martyrdom (along with Paul) under Nero in the year 64.[37] The tradition of Peter being crucified head downward—corresponding to Adam's headlong fall into sin, according to the Acts of Peter—is preserved in Eusebius and Jerome as well.[38] In sum, the references to Peter's activities in Corinth and Asia Minor in the Pauline letters, the peerless honor in which he was held in the early church, and the unquestioned tradition of his death in Rome are probable evidence—despite the silence of Acts on such matters—of Peter's extended missionary influence, either by personal participation or representatives, along the Jerusalem–Rome corridor.

Regarding the literature associated with the apostle Peter, the First Epistle of Peter has historically been credited to him, and a second epistle was attributed to him early in the tradition. The several apocryphal writings associated with Peter's name—including the Gospel of Peter, the Acts of Peter, the Preaching of Peter, and the Apocalypse of Peter—testify to the renown in which he was held in the early church.[39] The status accorded Peter in early Christianity is,

35. Bruce, *Peter, Stephen, James, and John*, 42–43, regards Peter's presence in Corinth as representative of a broader ministry that could have included the regions mentioned in 1 Pet. 1:1. Hengel, *Saint Peter*, 49, takes for granted that "Western communities knew the apostle [Peter] himself or learned about him from messengers." And Bockmuehl, *Simon Peter*, 30, finds "a Petrine mission to Pontus widely presupposed in subsequent Christian sources."

36. Jerome, *Vir. ill.* 1.2; Eusebius, *Hist. eccl.* 3.1.2; Acts Pet. 38–39. For the summary evidence of Peter's death in Rome, see Bruce, *Peter, Stephen, James, and John*, 44–47; and especially Bockmuehl, *Simon Peter*, 101–4.

37. Eusebius, *Hist. eccl.* 3.26.2; Jerome, *Vir. ill.* 1.1. The apocryphal Acts of Peter is devoted almost entirely to Peter's overthrow of Simon Magus in Rome. Eusebius is the earliest direct witness to the Acts of Peter, which was probably composed in the late second century.

38. Eusebius, *Hist. eccl.* 3.1.2; Jerome, *Vir. ill.* 1.2; Acts Pet. 38–39.

39. Eusebius, *Hist. eccl.* 3.3.1, reports that the authenticity of 1 Peter was "unquestioned" in the ancient church. See Bockmuehl, *Simon Peter*, 126 (esp. n. 40), for a positive assessment of the authenticity of 1 Peter. Both Eusebius, *Hist. eccl.* 3.3.1, and Jerome, *Vir. ill.* 1.3, however, doubt the authenticity of 2 Peter, although they recognize that many in the church find it useful. Regarding the apocryphal literature named for Peter, Eusebius emphasizes that "no orthodox

in the words of Martin Hengel, "incomparably greater than that of all the other disciples"—that is, of all the original Twelve.[40] Hengel further contends that Jesus's description of Peter as "the Rock" should not be predicated solely on the latter's confession at Caesarea Philippi (Matt. 16:18) but on the whole of his thirty-five-year witness and stature in early Christianity.[41] The reason for that greatness emerges from Peter's role in relation to Paul and James, two other pillars in first-century Christianity. To quote James D. G. Dunn, "Peter was actually more successful than either Paul or James in maintaining a mission both to fellow Jews and to Gentiles, more successful in promoting an expansion beyond the Jewish people which actually retained the Jewish character of the new faith more faithfully than either Paul or James. As the one who became known as *pontifex maximus*, was he in fact the most effective bridge-builder of his generation?"[42]

John

No point along the Jerusalem–Rome corridor rose to greater prominence in Christianity between roughly AD 75 and 125 than Ephesus. Like Rome, Ephesus was a huge metropolis of some 250,000 people, tied with Antioch for the distinction of third largest city in the Roman Empire. And also like Rome, Ephesus attracted now unknown and unnamed Christians who established a Christian presence there at an early though unspecified date. Luke first mentions Ephesus in Acts 18:18–22 as the convergence point of three independent, or perhaps loosely related, missionary companies: Paul, Priscilla and Aquila, and Apollos.[43] On his third mission journey, in the mid-50s, Paul established a two-year residential ministry in Ephesus that resulted in "all who dwelled in Asia hear[ing] the word of the Lord" (Acts 19:10). Paul's epistles to both Colossae and Laodicea were likely written from Ephesus (Col. 4:16).

Toward the end of the first century, Paul's tenure in Ephesus was succeeded by both the apostle John and Ignatius, bishop of Antioch. Regarding the first, the name of John (along with that of Mary, the mother of Jesus) is firmly anchored to Ephesus in Christian tradition. The Gospel and Epistles associated

---

writer of the ancient time" accepted the testimonies of the Gospel of Peter, the Acts of Peter, the Preaching of Peter, or the Revelation of Peter (*Hist. eccl.* 3.3.2–3).

40. Hengel, *Saint Peter*, 49.

41. Hengel, *Saint Peter*, 100.

42. Dunn, "Beyond the Jewish People," 201. Similarly, Bruce, *Peter, Stephen, James, and John*, 43: "*Peter was probably in fact and effect the bridge-man who did more than any other to hold together the diversity of first-century Christianity*" (italics original).

43. On the basis of Acts 18, presumably, Eusebius credits the apostle Paul with founding the church of Ephesus (*Hist. eccl.* 3.23.4).

with the name of John likely originated in Ephesus. The seven cities to which John addresses the book of Revelation are geographically situated in Roman Asia in the shape of a spearhead—from Ephesus north to Smyrna, from Smyrna north to the tip in Pergamon, then turning southeast from Pergamon to Thyatira, Sardis, Philadelphia, and Laodicea (Rev. 2–3). Within a decade of John's tenure in Asia, Ignatius, bishop of Antioch, wrote letters to some of these same churches, and to others in the same region along the Meander River valley—to Smyrna, Ephesus, Magnesia, Tralles, and Philadelphia. (He also wrote a letter to Christians in Rome and a personal letter to Polycarp.) This literary productivity and the presence of revered leaders—John and Mary (the mother of Jesus) in Ephesus, Philip and Papias in Hierapolis, and Ignatius throughout the region—distinguished Roman Asia as the most influential font of Christian leadership and literature at the end of the first Christian century.[44]

The memory of John in Ephesus is rooted in credible historical tradition, although apocryphal imagination certainly compensated for its sparsity of detail.[45] The earliest and most reliable historical witnesses regarding John's tenure in Ephesus are Papias and Irenaeus in the mid-second century, especially as they are delivered to us by Eusebius and Jerome in the fourth century. Fourteen years after Nero's death, according to Jerome, John was banished by the emperor Domitian to the island of Patmos, where he wrote the book of Revelation. Nero was assassinated in 68, so Jerome's testimony would date John's exile on Patmos to 82. At Domitian's death in 96, continues Jerome, John was allowed to return to Ephesus under the reign of the emperor Nerva (r. 96–98), where he lived into the reign of the emperor Trajan (r. 98–117).[46] The note that John *returned* to Ephesus implies that he had lived there prior to his exile. In the mid-second century, Papias, bishop of Hierapolis, reports that John wrote the Gospel attributed to him following his return to Ephesus, after which he was martyred.[47] The extant historical tradition is thus agreed in placing John in Roman Asia, primarily in Patmos and Ephesus, in the last quarter of the first century.

The most visible tokens of John's Ephesus sojourn are the remains of the Basilica of St. John the Divine in present-day Selçuk, Turkey, which, according to tradition, stand over the grave of the apostle. The original basilica

---

44. Zahn writes, "In the second century, this provincial church (in Asia Minor) was by all accounts the most significant, spiritually alive, and finally literarily productive of all the churches." *Skizzen*, 40 (my trans.).

45. See the Acts of John, which relates a variety of teachings and incidents ascribed to the apostle John in Ephesus (*NTApoc* 2:152–212).

46. Jerome, *Vir. ill.* 9.6–7; Irenaeus, *Haer.* 5.30.3; Eusebius, *Hist. eccl.* 3.17–18.

47. Pap. *Frag.* 6.1–2.

was constructed in several stages by the Byzantine emperors Constantine (4th c.), Theodosius II (5th c.), and Justinian (6th c.). Constantine's architects are known to have constructed churches associated with Jesus and the apostles on sites that claimed old and venerable historical tradition. The three most reputable evangelical sites in the eyes of Constantine's architects were Jesus's birthplace in Bethlehem, his crucifixion and burial site in Jerusalem, and John's grave in Ephesus. Modern archaeological investigations into the Church of the Nativity in Bethlehem, the Church of the Holy Sepulchre in Jerusalem, and the Basilica of St. John in Selçuk corroborate the historical veracity of all three sites.[48]

John's name is also associated with a circle of followers in Roman Asia. The Second and Third Epistles of John, for example, were sent by an individual who identifies himself as "the Elder."[49] The Elder is presumably a different individual than the apostle John (although no author's name appears in the Gospel and First Epistle of John). Papias, the mid-second-century bishop of Hierapolis who never tires of reminding readers of his personal acquaintance with John the apostle, distinguishes between John the apostle and John the Elder.[50] The relation of John the apostle and John the Elder to the Johannine corpus in the New Testament is not entirely clear. A united tradition makes a strong case for assigning the authorship of Revelation to the apostle John while he was in exile on the island of Patmos. A similarly strong case can be made for assigning the First Epistle of John to the apostle John. On the

48. See Bruce, *Peter, Stephen, James, and John*, 122–25, 151–52; Wilson, *Biblical Turkey*, 223–25.

49. See 2 John 1; 3 John 1.

50. Papias endeavored to preserve the most reliable traditions related to the apostles by inquiring "what Andrew or Peter or Philip or Thomas or James or John or Matthew or any other of the Lord's disciples had *said*, and what Aristion and the Elder John *say*" (Pap. *Frag.* 3.4; see also Eusebius, *Hist. eccl.* 339.4). The distinction in verb tenses between what John the apostle *said* and what John the Elder *says* implies that the apostle had died but that the elder was still alive when Papias wrote. Jerome follows Papias in this regard, saying that "the John who is listed among the apostles is not the same as the Elder John," further concluding that the elder was the author of the Second and Third Epistles of John (*Vir. ill.* 18.2–3 [Halton trans.]). Further allusions in the Johannine literature and the early church assume an extended group of disciples loyal to John the apostle. The concluding testimony in the Gospel, "We know that his witness is true" (John 21:24), presumably refers to such a group, as do "the elect lady and her children" (2 John 1); "Gaius, the beloved" (3 John 1); and "Demetrius" (3 John 12). By their own admissions, Papias and Polycarp belonged to this loyal group of disciples, as did the "many" followers of John alluded to by Irenaeus, *Haer.* 2.22.5; 3.3.4. On the Johannine circle in Asia, see Bruce, *Peter, Stephen, James, and John*, 141–45. Whether the disciples of John made up an actual "school"—a theologically defined and missionally intentional organization distinct from other early Christian groups—as many twentieth-century scholars have assumed, or whether they remained an informal but loyal cadre of followers and admirers of John the Apostle, remains an open question.

basis of internal evidence, the reference to "the Elder" (as noted above) makes an equally strong case for John the Elder's authorship of the Second and Third Epistles of John. With regard to the Fourth Gospel, tradition is united in attributing it to the apostle John, although internal evidence implies the transmission or editing of the apostle's witness via the hand of a third party.[51] Given the distinctive Greek style and vocabulary that characterize the Gospel and Epistles of John, it seems plausible that John the Elder, who identifies himself in Second and Third John, may have been the third party responsible for the final form of both the Gospel and the First Epistle.

To summarize the importance of the apostle John, he, like Peter, was held in high esteem along the Jerusalem–Rome corridor at the end of the first century and the beginning of the second. In Asia Minor, his reputation was unrivaled. The place of John's burial was commemorated by a basilica (the Basilica of St. John the Divine in Ephesus).[52] More New Testament documents bear the name of John than the name of any other apostle except for Paul. And the names of known individuals who composed the Johannine "school" are also second in number only to the followers of Paul.

Ignatius

The final first-century figure of importance for the Jerusalem–Rome corridor that we will consider is Ignatius, who was either the second or third bishop of Antioch.[53] The background, birth, and education of Ignatius are wholly unknown to us. His epistles suggest that he was raised in a non-Christian home and came to faith later in life, but these remain no more than hints.[54] Around the year 70, he ascended to the bishopric of Antioch, a post he proudly held until his martyrdom in Rome in approximately 110.[55] The circumstances that led to his condemnation are as mysterious as those of his early life. Indeed,

51. See John 19:35 and 21:24, where the author of the Fourth Gospel refers to the apostle John in third person. The description of John as "the beloved disciple" (13:23; 19:26; 20:2; 21:7; 21:20) also seems more plausible as a reference of a second party than as a self-reference of John.

52. Among those of the other apostles, only the burial sites of Philip (in Hierapolis) and of Peter and Paul (in Rome) were honored by the construction of basilicas. All three are historically reputable sites.

53. Eusebius, *Hist. eccl.* 3.36.2, has him as the second while Jerome, *Vir. ill.* 16.1, has him as the third. On the whole question, see Lightfoot, *Apostolic Fathers*, 1:29n1.

54. In Ign. *Rom.* 9.2, Ignatius confesses that he "is ashamed to be counted among [the faithful]," adding, in echo of Paul in 1 Cor. 15:8–9, "for I am not worthy, since I am the last of them and an untimely birth." For further references to himself as "last" among the faithful, see Ign. *Eph.* 21.2; Ign. *Trall.* 13.1; Ign. *Smyrn.* 11.1.

55. The rudiments of Ignatius's life are offered by Eusebius, *Hist. eccl.* 3.36, who is followed in the main by Jerome, *Vir. ill.* 16. Jerome dates Ignatius's martyrdom in the eleventh year (109)

we have no certain knowledge that he reached Rome or that he was martyred there, although we have no reason to doubt either outcome. Unlike the apostle Paul, who was sent to Rome to stand trial, Ignatius was sent to Rome already condemned to death.[56] Also unlike Paul, who, as a Roman citizen, could be beheaded by the sword but not thrown to the beasts in the arena, Ignatius was not a citizen and was thus subject to death by any means, whether "fire, sword, or wild beasts."[57]

Only as Ignatius is escorted by Roman soldiers from Antioch to Rome does this enigmatic figure emerge from the shadows of obscurity. Like a bolt of lightning that splits a night sky, the light of Ignatius shines for a few brief weeks in Roman Asia while en route to Rome, before being swallowed again by darkness. Ignatius is chained to "ten leopards" (i.e., to a company of Roman soldiers), who, in his words, "only get worse when they are well treated."[58] Even en route, Ignatius describes himself as "fighting with wild beasts" in preparation for the Roman arena. As the mortal pilgrimage proceeds westward through Asia, a northerly route is chosen through Philadelphia and Smyrna, bypassing the churches to the south in Tralles, Magnesia, and Ephesus, to which Ignatius sends letters via their messengers. He apparently asked these churches to send delegations to meet him in Smyrna. He also writes an epistle to Rome, informing believers there of his impending arrival.[59] From Smyrna, the guards conduct Ignatius to Troas, where he writes two more letters, to the two churches he had visited in Philadelphia and Smyrna, respectively, as well as a final letter to Polycarp, bishop of Smyrna.[60] Ignatius is then hustled from Troas to Neapolis and Philippi (via the same route taken by the apostle Paul a half century earlier), where he is received warmly. After Philippi, all trace of Ignatius vanishes.

Despite the brevity of his tenure in Asia, Ignatius, like Paul and John, ministered there via a community of loyal disciples; in Ignatius's case, these included bishops in Ephesus, Magnesia, Tralles, and Smyrna as well as deacons and friends. Twenty-three named individuals appear in his correspondence, three of whom are women (one is the head of her household). Most names are prefaced by encomiums such as "brother," "sister," "model of service," "wor-

---

of the emperor Trajan (*Vir. ill.* 16.10). For a full review of the sources relevant to the life of Ignatius, see Lightfoot, *Apostolic Fathers*, 1:20–40.

56. Ign. *Eph.* 12.1; Ign. *Trall.* 3.3; Ign. *Rom.* 4.1.

57. Ign. *Smyrn.* 4.2; Ign. *Rom.* 5.

58. Ign. *Rom.* 5.1.

59. Eusebius, *Hist. eccl.* 3.36.5–9.

60. Eusebius, *Hist. eccl.* 3.36.10. Both Eusebius and Jerome (*Vir. ill.* 16.2) list the letters of Ignatius to the churches in the same order: Ephesus, Magnesia, Tralles, Rome, Philadelphia, Smyrna, Polycarp.

thy of God," "fellow servant," and "godly counselor." The correspondence is replete with information about the churches in Asia at the end of the first century. Throughout this study, we will harvest information from Ignatius's letters, which refer to topics such as the unity of the church; the authority of the bishops; the necessity of contending for a right understanding of the gospel over against false teachers and their teachings; the need to imitate Jesus Christ; the significance of the physical incarnation of Christ; and the importance of a steadfast witness, especially in martyrdom. In the letters of Ignatius, the balance of orthodoxy and orthopraxy is especially noteworthy. Few persons who appeared on the stage of history so briefly have influenced the world as greatly as Ignatius did. All the more worthy, therefore, is Harnack's tribute: "In truth, there was only one author among the pre-Nicene Fathers to whom the Byzantine church ascribed unconditional trust, transmitted his works, and held him to be the classical witness between the New Testament and Athanasius, and that Father was Ignatius."[61]

"And So We Came to Rome"

The long and harrowing mission of the apostle Paul reaches its climax in Acts 28:14: "And so we came to Rome." Rome seems an obvious goal to Western readers, for whom Rome's influence has been so formative. There were many reasons, however, why Rome would not have been the obvious terminus of the Christian mission in the first century. Judaism set the precedent for early Christianity in many respects, and when Jews were driven from Palestine, they went south to Egypt or east to Babylon, but not to Rome. With the annexation of Palestine to the Roman Empire under Pompey in the first century BC, Jews began turning to Rome, but usually for redress of grievances or financial errands related to Rome's hegemony in the Mediterranean. These detours did not change the enduring cultural alliance of Palestine with Egypt and Babylon, which had withstood the dissolution of Alexander the Great's empire into the petty kingdoms of the Antigonids (Macedonia, Attica), Seleucids (Syria, Palestine, Mesopotamia), and Ptolemies (Cyprus, Egypt, Cyrene). Historically, Palestinian Jews were influenced by—in order of significance—the Seleucids, the Ptolemies, and the Antigonids. Rome rarely figured into the equation.

The ministry of Jesus was equally indifferent to Rome. Only one of the various Jewish parties, the Sadducees, formally allied with the Romans. Jesus seems to have been indifferent to the Sadducees: the Gospels preserve only

61. Harnack, *Geschichte der altchristlichen Literatur*, vol. 1, part 1, xlii (my trans.).

two instances—once at his trial and once in response to a question about the resurrection[62]—when Jesus talked exclusively to Sadducees, neither time at his initiative. Jesus bluntly disparaged Herod Antipas, Rome's puppet tetrarch in Galilee, as "that fox" (Luke 13:32), and he honored Caesar only conditionally (Mark 12:13–17). Pontius Pilate's role in the crucifixion of Jesus cast Rome in a profoundly pejorative light. Thirty years later, in 64, the emperor Nero (r. 54–68) systematically and sadistically murdered Christians in Rome. And by century's end, the emperor Domitian (r. 81–96) had kicked the emperor cult, and its threat to Christians, into high gear. Christians could hardly be blamed for being unsympathetic to the imperial capital.

It is quite surprising, therefore, that by the mid-first century the church had pioneered, both missionally and literarily, a well-beaten path to Rome that, as far as we know from written records, was without compare elsewhere in the empire or beyond. After the abdication of the Christian-persecuting emperor Diocletian (r. 284–305) and the accession of the Christian-professing emperor Constantine (r. 306–37), "the triumph of Christianity" was rightly celebrated. But long before Constantine, a plethora of Christian witnesses anticipated this triumph not in spite of the empire but because of it. The providential relationship that many early Christian writers saw between Christianity and Rome requires our attention here at the end of this chapter.

The Roman world was the heir, and in many respects the executor, of the Greek world before it. Many elements of the Roman Empire that were conducive to the germination of Christianity were pioneered by the Greeks, although they were often integrated more fully into Roman society than they had been in the Hellenistic world.[63] Chief among these elements was the prevalence of the Greek language, which in the first century was the common, unifying tongue of the Roman Empire. Greek offered Christian missionaries a medium of communication within the empire that was denied to missionaries traveling outside it, especially to the east. Nearly as important, the architecture and culture of the *polis*, which we discussed in the last chapter, promoted Hellenistic values throughout the empire. In general, the Roman Empire was as absorbent of Greek religious ideas and practices as it was of the Greek lan-

---

62. For the question about resurrection, see Matt. 22:23–33; Mark 12:18–27; Luke 20:27–40. For Jesus's trial before the Sanhedrin, see Matt. 26:57–68; Mark 14:53–65; Luke 22:54, 63–71; John 18:13–14, 19–24. In addition, Matt. 16:1–2 preserves a brief encounter with Jesus by both Pharisees and Sadducees.

63. Freyne writes, "It is important to emphasize that the arrival of Rome in the East in no way halted the promotion of Greek culture. If anything, there was an intensification of the process of Hellenization. 'Captured Greece conquered the arms of its capturers' is how one Roman poet described the fascination of the Romans with Greek culture in every sphere." *Jesus Movement and Its Expansion*, 53.

guage and *polis*. Rome's tolerance of cults and temples from Greece, Egypt, and Persia—as long as such cults did not jeopardize the traditional Roman rites on which Romans believed the welfare of the state rested—was unusual for the age. In principle, this tolerance opened a door to Christianity as well.[64] As we saw in the last chapter, the geographical extent of the empire and the shaping influence of the *polis* engendered a new understanding of what it meant to be a human being. The maturation of the concept of a human from a tribal creature to a member of a larger and integrated domain was also inherited by the Romans from the Greeks, particularly from Alexander the Great.[65] The stability, extent, and longevity of Roman governance of the ancient world and, above all, the universal application of Roman law to its citizens made this new understanding of humanity, one that transcended the bounds of one's native region and language, a permanent and defining element of the empire.[66]

With the exception of the Jewish War from AD 66 to 70, the Pax Romana was a window of unprecedented peace and security that prevailed from a hundred years before the birth of Jesus to two hundred years after his death. The *pax* (peace) produced social stability throughout the empire and structural stability within it. The development of the Roman Republic prior to Julius Caesar had revolutionized virtually every aspect of Roman life, but Caesar's introduction of imperial rule in the first century BC, which continued until the fall of the empire in the fifth century AD, produced not only a stability but also a virtual stasis in Roman politics and society. This long season of dependability in Roman life provided early Christianity with a reliable point of reference to which it established corresponding patterns of behavior that,

64. Note Nock's contention that the average citizen of the Roman Empire "was prepared to avail himself of new cults as additional means of ensuring protection against various dangers here and hereafter, and how this use of the novel did not, except in rare cases, mean any rejection of the familiar and any renunciation of a man's past." *Conversion*, 267.

65. Boatswain and Nicolson explain, "Alexander had changed the world. The Macedonian monarchy, influenced by its contacts with the oriental kingdoms, now infused the Greek mind not only with an alternative concept to the city as the only appropriate model for government, but also furnished the individual with a more universal perception of mankind: man was not merely a citizen of a small city-state while the rest of humanity was alien but he was part of a universal empire which embraced all mankind." *Traveller's History of Greece*, 93.

66. Harnack concludes his discussion of the conditions that favored Christian expansion in *Mission and Expansion*, 19–23, with the following paean: "The narrow world had become a wide world; the rent world had become a unity; the barbarian world had become Greek and Roman: *one* empire, *one* universal language, *one* civilization, a *common* development towards monotheism, and a *common yearning* for saviours" (22). This description is overly idealized and presupposes only those elements in the Roman Empire that were fulfilled in the Constantinian synthesis of the fourth century. Nevertheless, it succeeds in naming the new impulse of the empire that aided the spread of Christianity.

with occasional exceptions, fostered coexistence between itself and the Roman imperium.[67]

Already in the New Testament, we see nuanced affirmations of some aspects of the Roman Empire. Roman proconsuls or governors such as Sergius Paulus (Acts 13:4–12) and Gallio (Acts 18:12–17) play positive roles in relation to the advance of the gospel. More remarkable, repeated references to Roman tribunes and centurions in Luke-Acts are, without fail, favorable.[68] The story of the temple tax (Mark 12:13–17) and Paul's reflections on the state and its power to restrain evil (Rom. 13:1–7; perhaps also 2 Thess. 2:3–12) attest to the benefits of Roman stability, which Jesus followers could appreciate as long as those benefits did not conflict with the ultimate authority of God.[69]

It is helpful to remember that the Roman Empire was not ruled by a nation, as are modern states, but by a single city. Under the emperor Hadrian (r. 117–138), the empire reached its greatest extent, roughly equivalent to half the size of the contiguous United States.[70] As a city, Rome did not have—nor did it seek to have—the homogenizing effect on its far-flung territories that a modern nation has on the territories incorporated within its borders. Rome allowed its territories, whether conquered or annexed, to retain their respective cultures and languages as long as they paid taxes to Rome, submitted to military conscription, observed various Roman customs, and maintained peace. In this respect, Rome's hegemony over its territories was more colonial—like England's over India prior to 1947, for example—than it was total.

Nevertheless, Roman rule did lead to common systems and shared culture that afforded early Christian missionaries enviable advantages. Wherever they went in the empire, the transportation systems, legal practices and rights, and general cultural tolerances mirrored those of their native provinces. Nowhere

67. Note the judgment of Beard, SPQR, 335–36, on the significance of the Roman principate on the Pax Romana: "At the end of the first century BCE, for more than two hundred years there is no significant change at Rome. Autocracy represented, in a sense, an end of history. Of course, there were all kinds of events, battles, assassinations, political stand-offs, new initiatives and inventions; and the participants would have had all kinds of exciting stories to tell and disputes to argue. But unlike the story of the development of the Republic and the growth of imperial power, which revolutionized almost every aspect of the world of Rome, there was no fundamental change in the structure of Roman politics, empire or society between the end of the first century BCE and the end of the second century CE." Similarly, though less graphically expressed, see Harnack, Mission and Expansion, 20.

68. See Edwards, "'Public Theology.'"

69. See Goguel, Birth of Christianity, 445–46.

70. Grant, Roman Hellenism, 84, following Edward Gibbon's Decline and Fall of the Roman Empire, fixes the territorial extent of the Roman Empire at its greatest extent at 1.6 million square miles, approximately half the size of the contiguous United States, and its population, following the German historian Karl Julius Beloch, at approximately 54 million people.

in the empire were Christian witnesses as foreign as are modern missionaries, for example, who bring the gospel to a people whose culture and language are patently different from their own. The sense of cultural familiarity and identification throughout the Roman Empire fostered a freedom and boldness on the part of missionaries.

The transportation systems were especially important to this mission-conducive milieu. Thoroughfares extended from Rome, like spokes from the hub of a wheel, south to North Africa; west to Spain; north to Gaul (present-day France), Germania, and Britannia; and east to Palestine and Mesopotamia. The eastward spoke, our chief interest in this chapter, extended like a telescoping pole from Rome to Brindisi on the Via Appia, then across the Adriatic Sea to the Dalmatian coast, where the Via Egnatia continued east to Byzantium, and the Via Sebaste, the construction of which was begun by Augustus Caesar about the time of the birth of Jesus, extended the overland route from Byzantium into the interior of modern Turkey. Milestones rather than maps informed travelers of distances, and inns (though not always free of prostitutes, thieves, and bedbugs) afforded accommodations for travelers without tents or private lodgings provided by acquaintances or members of associations to which they belonged. Julius Caesar opened up one of the Roman world's chief means of travel by ridding the Mediterranean Sea of pirates in the late first century BC. Paul's list of travel dangers in 2 Corinthians 11:24–26 corroborates this, for he mentions (highway) robbers and shipwrecks but not pirates.

The New Testament attests to extensive travel in the first century.[71] The combined itineraries of the apostle Paul, which have been calculated to approximately ten thousand miles,[72] though far-flung, were not as unusual as we might suppose. The length of Origen's many itinerations almost certainly rivaled the length of the apostle Paul's. Harnack names nearly thirty Christian leaders in the first two centuries whose travels included personal trips to Rome.[73] An epitaph on a tomb in Hierapolis (modern west-central Turkey) boasts of a merchant whose trade in textiles required of him *seventy-two* trips to Italy.[74] Students traveled long distances, and in large numbers, to study in

71. Jesus itinerated widely throughout Galilee, and he journeyed to Jerusalem for Jewish festivals. Acts records extensive travels of many Christians throughout the Roman Empire, and passages such as James 4:13 and Revelation 18 attest to further travels of early Christians.

72. Hock, *Social Context*, 27.

73. Harnack, *Mission and Expansion*, 369–72.

74. "[Zeuxis], the merchant, rounded Cape Malea (tip of the Peloponnesian peninsula) seventy-two times on voyages to Italy." *Inscriptiones Graecae ad Res Romanas Pertinentes*, 4.841, quoted in Wilson, *Biblical Turkey*, 239.

Alexandria, Athens, Rome, and Antioch.[75] The exchange of letters by personal couriers was also widely employed by Christian leaders as a means of purveying the Christian message and fortifying Christian culture.[76]

Despite the ambiguity of early Christians to Roman rule, the empire in fact played an important role in the story of Jesus and his followers from the very beginning. Thirty years before the birth of Jesus, Rome installed Herod the Great as its client king to unite Palestine and defend it against threats from the east.[77] Thenceforth, Rome played an increasingly important role in the fate of Palestine. Herod and his son Antipas, and especially his later progeny Agrippa I (r. 41–44) and Agrippa II (r. 53–66), willingly accommodated Roman wishes during their respective reigns. All four of these rulers intersected with the beginnings of the Jesus movement—the first three negatively, but the fourth, Agrippa II, more positively in how he dealt with the apostle Paul.[78] Many Jewish elites found Rome's sense of election and destiny a compatible corollary to Judaism's.[79] Josephus (ca. 37–100), for example—who, like the Agrippas, was raised and education in Rome—identified with Rome as much or more than he did with Judaism. The primary stage for the New Testament drama was Jewish, but the secondary and larger stage was Roman.[80] This larger stage inevitably influenced Jews and, just as inevitably, Christians.

75. Zahn, *Skizzen*, 8–12.

76. Meeks, *First Urban Christians*, 16–23, offers a concise but informative review of travel in the first-century Roman Empire.

77. Josephus, *Ant.* 14.119–22, 158–62, 324–26, 370–89; *J.W.* 1.282–89.

78. For Herod the Great, see Matt. 2; Luke 1:5. For Antipas, see Matt. 14:1–6; Mark 6:14–22; Luke 3:19; 9:7–9; 13:31; 23:7–15; Acts 4:27. For Agrippa I, see Acts 12. For Agrippa II, see Acts 25:13–26:32.

79. Berthelot, "Paradoxical Similarities," 95–109, argues that "Rome threatened the Jews in a very particular way, and could be perceived as taking Israel's place in the world." Jewish writers often identified Romans with Esau and Edom, and the provocative rivalry between Jacob and Esau, as with Judea and Rome, resulted because each nation believed that it possessed divine election and a guaranteed destiny.

80. The Herodian dynasty was inextricably intertwined with both Judaism and Rome. Rome aborted the attempt of Archelaus to succeed his father, Herod the Great, in 4 BC (Josephus, *J.W.* 2.1–116; Matt. 2:22), installing Herod Antipas in his stead (Josephus, *Ant.* 17.224–27; *J.W.* 2.20–22; Luke 3:1). Agrippa I influenced the accession of Claudius as emperor in the year 41, thus sparing Rome a potential civil war following the assassination of Claudius's predecessor, Caligula, in the same year (Josephus, *J.W.* 2.204–213; Acts 12:1). Agrippa II advocated the case for Jews against Samaritans in Claudius's reign (Josephus, *J.W.* 2.245–46; Acts 25–26). Throughout the first century, Jews sent embassies to Rome to court the favor of Caesar. On the many Jewish embassies that were sent to Rome and their importance for the commonweal of Judea, see Goldsworthy, *Pax Romana*, 139–44. The prodigious temple constructed by Herod the Great attracted Romans to Jerusalem (Acts 2:10), but Roman power attracted Jews more strongly to the capital city (Acts 28:17–28).

Religion also played an important role in attracting Christianity to Rome. Jewish synagogues were virtual stepping-stones that accommodated Jewish-Christian missionaries on their way from Jerusalem to the heart of the empire.[81] Similar networks of synagogues almost certainly accommodated Jewish-Christian missionaries traveling in other directions—although, as we will see in the next chapter, we are less well informed of the advance of such missionaries outside the Jerusalem–Rome corridor. In their openness to new gods, even polytheistic cults played a role in drawing Christianity to the imperial capital. In the Greek pantheon, Rome found gods and goddesses equivalent to the ones in its own pantheon, and it renamed its own pantheon accordingly. Rome also welcomed cults that worshiped gods for which it had no native equivalents to assume places along the Tiber River—including the worshipers of Magna Mater (or Cybele), Mithraism, Orphism, and the cult of Isis and Serapis.[82] Given Rome's openness to different forms of religious devotion from across the empire, it is unsurprising that it should attract Christianity, and attract it early. The migration of Christianity to Rome may have begun already at Pentecost (Acts 2:10). Paul's Letter to the Romans in 57, at any rate, clearly assumes a Christian presence in Rome by the late 40s. Less than a decade after Paul's Epistle to the Romans, the widespread presence of Christians in the capital was attested by Tacitus's chilling description of Christianity as a "pernicious superstition" and of Christians as "a class of humanity loathed for their vices."[83]

Mary Beard expresses the unique relationship between nascent Christianity and the Roman Empire in these words:

> The success of Christianity was rooted in the Roman Empire, in its territorial extent, in the mobility that it promoted, in its towns and cultural mix. From Pliny's Bithynia to Perpetua's Carthage, Christianity spread from its small-scale origins in Judaea largely because of the channels of communication across the Mediterranean world that the Roman Empire had opened up and because of the movement through those channels of people, goods, books, and ideas. The irony is that the only religion that the Romans ever attempted to eradicate was the one whose success their empire made possible and which grew up entirely within the Roman world.[84]

81. In Paul's second mission journey, in particular, synagogues and Sabbath gatherings provide the initial context for proclaiming the gospel in Philippi (Acts 16:13), Thessalonica (17:1), Berea (17:10), Athens (17:17), and Corinth (18:4), whereas cities presumably without synagogues, such as Amphipolis and Apolloni, are bypassed (17:1).

82. See Nock, *Conversion*, 66–76.

83. Tacitus, *Ann.* 15.44.

84. Beard, *SPQR*, 520. We should emend Beard's judgment by clarifying that the success of Christianity *in the West* was rooted in the Roman Empire; as we shall see, Christianity's remarkable expansions eastward were largely or wholly unrelated to the empire.

The Roman sense of *adventus*—the pageantry of victorious generals arriving in *urbs Roma*—was a powerful image of the imperial age. It was no stretch for Christians like Eusebius to see in the coronation of Constantine as emperor in the fourth century the ultimate *adventus*—the victory of the gospel in the empire.[85] Eusebius believed that divine providence had ordained that the "brilliant lamp" of the gospel should first shine in the Roman Empire.[86] "Heavenly providence," he declares, ordered "that the word of the Gospel might have an unimpeded beginning, and traverse the earth in all directions. Thus by the power and assistance of heaven the saving word began to flood the whole world with light like the rays of the sun."[87] Eusebius was not alone in this belief, for when the first of the great ecumenical councils was convoked at Nicaea in 325, the invitation list was restricted to bishops inside the Roman Empire.[88] The defeat of the Roman army by the Persians some forty years later, in 363, drove both the Roman army and Christians living under their protection west into the fold of the empire and made Nicaea's guest list look divinely prescient.

The triumph of Christianity in the fourth century was so remarkable that it is tempting to take Eusebius's jubilation as a *vaticinium ex eventu*—a projection of his present onto earlier eras. However reasonable that might seem, it would be mistaken. A particular—one might even say stubborn—identification of the gospel with the Roman Empire is traceable long before Constantine. Nor was its realization dependent on the future accession of a Christian emperor; rather, it came from something inherent in the "brilliant lamp" of the gospel itself. A century before Eusebius, Origen, who was himself martyred by the Romans in 254, hailed the role of the Roman Empire as *praeparatio evangelium*, the divinely ordained "righteousness and fullness of peace" that flowered in the Pax Romana and prepared the way for the gospel. "God prepared the nations for his teaching," Origen writes, "by causing the Roman emperor to rule over all the world."[89] In the century before Origen, which was punctuated by martyrdoms under Pliny the Younger and Bar Kokhba, and especially by the celebrated martyrdoms of Polycarp, Blandina, and Perpetua, Irenaeus anticipated the victory of the faith in the empire. Writing in about the year 150, he testified to the "dispersion of the church throughout the whole world, even to the ends of the earth"—to Germania, Spain, Gaul (present-day France), and points east in Egypt and Libya. Many

85. See Luke, *Ushering in a New Republic*.
86. Eusebius, *Hist. eccl.* 4.7.1.
87. Eusebius, *Hist. eccl.* 2.2.6; 2.3.1 (LCL). See also 2.14.3; 4.26.7.
88. Frankopan, *Silk Roads*, 51.
89. Origen, *Cels.* 2.30 (ANF 4:443–44).

nations and languages and far-flung locations embraced the faith, but the faith they embraced was "one and the same throughout the whole world."[90] Irenaeus's contemporary Clement of Alexandria, writing to the emperor Marcus Aurelius (r. 161–80), explicitly linked the church's missionary success to Rome: "Our philosophy first grew up among the barbarians, but its full flower came among your nation in the great reign of your ancestor Augustus, and became an omen of good to your empire, for from that time the power of the Romans became great and splendid. You are now his happy successor, and shall be so along with your son, if you protect the philosophy which grew up with the empire and began with Augustus."[91]

Also in the mid-second century, a Roman baptismal liturgy, the *Symbolum Romanum* (known today as the Apostles' Creed), was formulated; it would become the standard baptismal confession for all Western churches.[92] Earlier still, at the close of the first century, Clement thanked God for harmony and peace on earth, vowing to "render obedience . . . to our rulers and governors on earth," because God had "given them the power of sovereignty" through God's majestic and inexpressible might, so that "they may blamelessly administer the government."[93] This conviction regarding the divine election of the Roman Empire was not predicated on the particular virtues of the empire. Far from it. When Justin and Clement addressed their works to second-century Roman emperors, Christians were being martyred in the empire. The book of Revelation, written near the close of the first century, portrays Rome contemptibly as the Great Harlot of Babylon, "mother of whores and abominations on earth" (Rev. 17:5). To repeat what we said at the outset of this section, Rome was not the obvious destination for the Christian mission. According to the above witnesses, its significance for early Christianity was determined not by human choice but by divine election. The book of Acts voices this election in three divine assurances to the apostle Paul that he must bear witness before Caesar in Rome,[94] and it closes with Luke's acknowledgment of its fruition: "And so we came to Rome" (Acts 28:14).

Let our final word in this chapter recall the remarkable chronicle of Christianity in the Roman Empire. The ministry of Jesus was consciously restricted to the provincial confines of rural Galilee and its primarily Jewish inhabitants.

90. Irenaeus, *Haer.* 1.10.1–2. See also Hengel, *Studien zum Urchristentum*, 332.

91. Eusebius, *Hist. eccl.* 4.26.7 (LCL). For a similarly irenic letter of the same era, see Justin, *1 Apol.* 12.

92. Rabenau, *Latinitas christiana*, 17.

93. 1 Clem. 60.4–61.3.

94. Acts 19:21; 23:11; 27:24. One notes a similar sense in Josephus, who, during the First Revolt, argued that divine fortune was bringing all nations, Jews included, into the empire (*J.W.* 5.362–74).

Jesus avoided the major cities of Galilee, Sepphoris and Tiberias, and his journeys to Jerusalem were dictated by liturgical rhythms rather than by mission strategy. The named individuals who participated in Jesus's ministry amounted to some twenty-five persons, and all his itinerations fell between Jerusalem and Sidon, a distance of some 140 miles. Within a mere thirty years of his death, the movement and mission founded by Jesus exploded from the confines of his ministry all the way to the capital of the Roman Empire. The Christian mission became robustly cosmopolitan, flourishing no longer in the villages of Galilee—Capernaum, Bethsaida, and Nazareth—but in the influential urban centers of the Roman world—Antioch, Ephesus, and Rome. We have record of more than one hundred named individuals who ministered along the Jerusalem–Rome corridor with the apostles Paul, Peter, and John; with the missionaries Priscilla and Aquila, Lydia, and Apollos; and with the bishop Ignatius. The missionary journeys of the apostle Paul alone covered no fewer than ten thousand miles. The seed of Jesus's ministry that was planted in Galilee flowered in the Roman Empire.

3

From Jerusalem
to the East and South

The Jerusalem–Rome corridor was not the only mission corridor of early Christianity.[1] The commission of Jesus to bear witness "to the end of the earth" (Acts 1:8) and the analogous description in 1 Clement of Paul's missionary expansion "to the limit of the west" (5.7) included Rome but also superseded it. The Greek word *oikoumenē*, meaning the whole inhabited world or "world-at-large,"[2] referred to the known world, and the known world exceeded the limits of the Roman Empire. In the last chapter, we noted Luke's reference to "certain men from Cyrene and Cyprus" (Acts 11:20) who proclaimed the gospel to gentiles in Antioch. Although Antioch lay within the Roman Empire, it served as a hub for the defense of Rome's eastern frontier, and as such it became an early staging point for Christian expansion east of the Greek-speaking Roman Empire. These unnamed individuals of Acts 11:20, regardless of where and when they became Christians, remind us that persons both came to Christian faith and extended the Christian faith in the *oikoumenē* of whom the New Testament preserves little or even no record. Luke was not unaware of the mission activity of Christians in these additional regions. He mentions several regions that composed the eastern and

1. Even today, Western historians too easily identify Christianity as a primarily or exclusively Western religion. See, for example, Beard, *SPQR*, 520: "The only religion that the Romans ever attempted to eradicate was the one whose success their empire made possible and which grew up entirely within the Roman world."
2. Isa. 24:1 LXX; Luke 4:5; Rev. 12:9.

southern missions of the church in recounting the equipping of believers at Pentecost.[3] As we noted earlier, however, Luke omits from the book of Acts all endeavors that do not contribute to its narrative, which is focused on the advancement of the gospel along the Jerusalem–Rome corridor. It is these additional missions that we turn to in this chapter, and they confront us with a painful conundrum, for the thick record of the advance of Christianity along the Jerusalem–Rome corridor is matched by a thin and fragmentary record of its advance in all other directions.

In virtually every respect, our sources for the expansion of the gospel east and south of Jerusalem pale in comparison with those for the Jerusalem–Rome corridor. With regard to persons in the record, the New Testament and Apostolic Fathers produce more than a hundred *named* individuals, all datable to the first century, associated with the Pauline, Petrine, Johannine, and Ignatian missions on the Jerusalem–Rome corridor. In addition to these names, we know of freelance missionaries such as Priscilla and Aquila, Lydia, Apollos, and Philip. Nothing remotely similar exists with regard to early Christian missions east and south of Jerusalem. Only a handful of names—Addai/Thaddaeus, Aggai, Thomas, Pantaenus, and Mari—appear in the record of the eastward expansion of the gospel, and in the record of the southward expansion, only a dozen names (those of the Scillitan martyrs) appear. Some of the foregoing names may even be apocryphal, and none of them can be positively situated in the first century.

In addition to lacking first-century sources, we are faced with a second and even greater adversity—namely, the scarcity, lateness, and often apocryphal nature of the sources we do have for considering missions east and south of Jerusalem. Of the few extant written sources, none is earlier than the late second century. The most reputable of these is the account of the Scillitan martyrs in North Africa in the year 180. Only two sources allege to report on the spread of Christianity in the first century, both of which—the Abgar-Jesus correspondence and the Acts of Thomas—are more apocryphal than historical. It is possible, of course, that sources related to the spread of Christianity east and south of Jerusalem have been lost; after all, a great number of ancient sources, perhaps even most, have perished. Nevertheless, no early Christian writer whose works have survived—including none of the historians of the era such as Irenaeus, Eusebius, or Jerome—makes mention of such sources. This unanimimous silence makes it doubtful that such sources ever existed.[4]

---

3. These included the eastern regions of Parthia, Media, Elam, and Mesopotamia (Acts 2:9) and the southern regions of "Egypt and the parts of Libya belonging to Cyrene" (Acts 2:10).

4. Moffett, *Christianity in Asia*, 1:80, contends that the earliest reliable record of Syrian Christians carrying the gospel to Persia and beyond to the Asiatic nomads and the edges of the

Our journey in this chapter must be undertaken with a few old maps and crude navigational instruments, as it were. Accordingly, both the nature and genre of this chapter are affected. The intermittent sunlight of our modest and often tentative conclusions is, as a rule, overshadowed by the heavy cloud cover of what we do not know. A chapter such as this is often relegated to an epilogue or appendix. Although that may be wise in some instances, I do not think it so in this instance, and for two reasons.

First and most importantly, to relegate mission expansion apart from that to Rome to an epilogue can imply that the evangelization of the East and South was of lesser importance than the evangelization of the West. That would be a mistake, especially today. The East and South appear to have been evangelized as early, and as completely, as was the West. As I have noted above, the expansion in these directions is less documented, but it is not less important. One could argue, in fact, that it was more important. The eastern mission was far more extensive than the mission to the Jerusalem–Rome corridor, and the obstacles that needed to be overcome in both the eastward and southward expansions were equal to if not greater than those encountered along the Jerusalem–Rome corridor. And given the vitality of Christianity in many parts of the Global East and South today (sometimes in contrast to its inertness in the West), it is important to acknowledge and document, to the best of our ability, the early and fruitful outreach of Christianity to these regions—regions that have often been dominated by faiths and ideologies other than and sometimes antagonistic to Christianity.

The second reason for retaining this chapter within the story of earliest Christianity is that the scarcity and lateness of historical sources we have to contend with here is the norm in Christian history rather than the exception. Western Christians too easily take the existence of the book of Acts for granted. In reality, a thematically coherent and complete narrative such as Acts is rare and inestimable in Christian history. The survival of such a document, especially one written by a non-apostle, is an anomaly in the history of ancient Christian texts. If epilogues are reserved for anomalies in research

---

Hindu Kush dates to two hundred years after the death of Jesus. Similarly, Koch, *Geschichte des Urchristentums*, 421–26, argues that there is reputable historical evidence for Christian presence as of the year 150 throughout Palestine and Syria, the several regions that now compose modern Turkey and modern Greece, and southern Italy as far north as Rome. Koch's survey thus confirms our own regarding first-century Christian mission along the Jerusalem–Rome corridor. With regard to Egypt and North Africa, Koch finds no certain evidence of Christianity until the year 180, roughly the same time that evidence of Christianity begins to appear in Spain and Gaul (France). His survey concludes without any reputable historical second-century evidence of Christianity in Mesopotamia, Armenia, Georgia, Persia, India, and China. These areas, in fact, are not even mentioned in his book.

and data fields, then—to speak facetiously—it would be the chapters in this book dependent on the book of Acts rather than this chapter that would be relegated to an epilogue.

Special Characteristics of Christianity in the East and South

Let us begin by noting several characteristics that differentiated the eastward and southward expansion of Christianity from its expansion along the Jerusalem–Rome corridor. The first and most unique was its indebtedness to the Silk Roads linking the Roman Empire to Mesopotamia, and stretching from there farther east to Persia and India, and ultimately to the Far East in China.[5] From Syrian Antioch the primary Silk Road ran east to Aleppo and northeast to Edessa, and then east to Nisibis, whence it followed the flow of the Tigris River past Arbela, Baghdad, and Seleucia-Ctesiphon. From Seleucia-Ctesiphon this Silk Road proceeded due east through Persia to Nishapur, Bokhara, Samarkand, and Kashgar, from which it continued eastward via either northern or southern routes around the Taklamakan Desert. At the eastern end of the desert, the routes rejoined in western China, at Dunhuang, where they continued east to Yumen and into the Chinese interior. Nearly all the above cities, like nodes on a vine, became centers of Christian communities and mission. Early Christian missions thus followed the primary merchant arteries eastward, and early Christian missionaries were themselves often merchants. Indeed, our earliest account of a named missionary to the East is the Acts of Thomas, in which the apostle Thomas is sold as a slave to a merchant named Abban, who is bound for India.[6]

A second defining characteristic of the spread of Christianity to the east and south was its dependence on Jewish communities and synagogues. This dependence was also typical of the spread of Christianity along the Jerusalem–Rome corridor; but it was probably even more characteristic of early Christian mission in the East, for eastern churches did not form secondary alliances with the indigenous cultures as strongly as western churches did with Roman culture. Already in Genesis 10:21–32, the territories associated with modern Syria, Iraq, and Iran are identified with the tribe of Shem (i.e.,

---

5. See Frankopan, *Silk Roads*, ch. 3, "The Road to a Christian East." The term "Silk Road," first coined by Baron Ferdinand von Richthofen in his 1877 geographical atlas, is a modern designation for an ancient network of overland roads between China and the Mediterranean. In the vicinity of major urban hubs, the roads were vigorous arteries, but in the expansive hinterlands they were often no more than capillary paths. See Valerie Hansen, *The Silk Road: A New History* (Oxford: University Press, 2012), 6–8.

6. Acts Thom. 1–2.

with the Semitic peoples). The book of Esther reports the dispersion of Jews throughout the East—from India to Ethiopia (Esther 8:9). A large Jewish community remained in Mesopotamia after the Babylonian exile in the sixth century BC, where the Babylonian Talmud was produced nearly a millennium later, in the fifth century AD. Jewish scholars translated the Hebrew Old Testament into the Greek Septuagint in Alexandria (i.e., North Africa) in the third century BC. In both Babylonia and Alexandria, Jews lived in perhaps greater numbers and prosperity than anywhere else in the Roman Empire. Jewish communities were the incubation grounds from which Christian missions spread. Many accounts of Christian missions to the east and south of Palestine contain references to preexisting Jewish communities, some of which are more favorable toward Jesus followers than those in the book of Acts and in the Apostolic Fathers.

A third characteristic of Christianity east of the Roman Empire was its shaping on the anvil of opposition and persecution. This same anvil, of course, shaped Christianity in the West until the fourth century, when Constantine legalized Christianity and adopted it as the licit religion of the empire. At that point, at least in the West, the anvil became something of a hammer, with Christianity assuming shaping influence in the empire. This reversal did not occur east of the Roman Empire, however. There Christianity remained a minority movement subject to dominant and sometimes hostile powers. In only one place—Armenia, where Rome retained an active role—did Christianity attain the status of a state religion (around the year 300). Otherwise, the rising star of the church's fortune in the West was accompanied by its decline in the East. Throughout the fourth century, the Sassanids, a dynasty of Persian kings, persecuted the church. And the precipitous rise of Islam in the seventh century effectively halted Christian missions in the Middle East. Thereafter, Christian communities were weakened, isolated, and sometimes eliminated. Among the few Christian communities that sustained their existence and identity in Islamic regions were those of Iberia and what is now Georgia, between the Black and Caspian seas; the church in Armenia to the south; and still farther south, the Assyrian Aramaic Church in Mesopotamia (modern Iraq).

A fourth characteristic of Christianity in the East was its frequent heterodoxy (at least with reference to the Chalcedonian Formula of 451).[7] With the exception of the Melkites (from the Syriac *malkaya*, "imperial"), who affirmed the definition of Chalcedon and remained in communion with

---

7. Chalcedon affirmed the union, without confusion or separation, of the divine and the human in the incarnate Jesus.

Constantinople and spread to various points eastward, the churches east of the empire customarily rejected the definition of Chalcedon. In Egypt, the dominant Christian confession became Miaphysite.[8] And in Mesopotamia and eastward, Christian communions tended to be Nestorian, or, as they preferred to be called, the Church of the East.[9] The liturgical language of the Church of the East was Syriac, and followers of Nestorius predominated in Mesopotamia, Arabia, and Persia. Churches of Nestorian persuasion almost certainly extended farther east, for in the late thirteenth century Marco Polo identifies them as such all along the Silk Roads, including in Kanbalu (modern Beijing), China. The Christianity most frequently encountered by the conquering Islamic invaders of the seventh and eighth centuries was Nestorian, and its emphasis on Christ's humanity likely played a role in Islam's rejection of the divine sonship of Jesus.

Fifth and finally, long before the Council of Chalcedon, Christianity east of the Roman Empire began to diverge from elements that characterized both Greek-speaking (what would become Orthodox) and Latin-speaking (what would become Catholic) Christians of the empire in the West. The character of Eastern Christianity in the latter half of the second century was both typified and influenced by Tatian. Tatian was initially tutored in the Christian faith by Justin Martyr, whose theology was orthodox, but he parted ways with Justin by rejecting Greco-Roman civilization as wholly incompatible with Christianity. Tatian accentuated the power and pervasiveness of evil in the world, in response to which he promulgated a form of rigorous asceticism, including proscription of human sexuality and an emphasis on demonology. Tatian believed that the fall of Adam had resulted in the latter's damnation, and he adopted a form of Gnosticism, also advocated by Marcion, that ascribed the creation of the world and the religion of Judaism to a lower and inferior God who was not the Father of Jesus Christ.

The combined effect of the foregoing factors produced a character in Christianity east of the Roman Empire distinct from Christianity within the empire. The gospel's eastward expansion followed an economic trade network on the Silk Roads through many diverse cultures, whereas its westward expansion proceeded along a corridor with a more homogeneous Roman culture. The Roman culture was a formative and cohesive influence in the West, whereas the varied eastern cultures made the character and complexion of Eastern Christianity more diverse. In contrast to the power and privilege that the church

8. Miaphysites held that the incarnate Christ possessed only one nature (Gk. *physis*), a combination of both divine and human.

9. Nestorianism held that two separate natures, one human and one divine, existed in the incarnate Christ.

in the West enjoyed under the Byzantines, the churches in the East remained disenfranchised minorities, and with the conquest of Islam, circumscribed minorities. Repudiation of the Formula of Chalcedon furthered the theological, political, and cultural separation of Eastern churches from Western churches. Tatian's radical juxtaposition of gospel and world, in particular, impelled Eastern churches toward insularity, whereas churches within the empire pioneered syntheses of gospel and culture.

The Progression of Christianity Eastward

We have noted the cardinal role that Syrian Antioch played for the Jerusalem–Rome corridor.[10] This city played an equally important role in the spread of early Christianity eastward. Luke mentions that, in addition to Paul and Barnabas, "many others were also proclaiming the word of the Lord" in Antioch (Acts 15:35). The "many others" would have included Semitic-speaking Christians (those speaking Aramaic, Syriac, and perhaps Hebrew) who moved eastward to Mesopotamia, Persia, India, and ultimately China.

The Syriac language that predominated in Mesopotamia was a dialect of the Aramaic spoken by Jesus and the early Palestinian church.[11] In Antioch, Syriac Christianity developed in conjunction with Greek-speaking Christianity. But east of Antioch, Syriac Christianity developed into a largely unhellenized form of Christianity. Syriac Jewish converts to Christianity who still retained a knowledge of Hebrew translated the Old Testament into Syriac directly from the Hebrew rather than from the Greek Septuagint.[12] Syriac Christianity combined elements rare in Greek-speaking Christianity—including biblicism, apophaticism, extreme asceticism (Encratism), mysticism, Gnosticism, and a distinctively Jewish character (though anti-Judaism was sometimes part of the mix as well).[13] Some of these elements were in tension with one another, and they failed to form an integrated whole. "Syrian

10. See ch. 1, pp. 7–11.

11. The Syriac literature of Aphrahat (d. 345) and Ephrem the Syrian (d. 373) in the fourth century represents the sole surviving linguistic form of the indigenous Semitic Christianity of the early Jesus movement. It is my belief, however, that the Hebrew Gospel attested by many church fathers also preserved the early gospel tradition in Hebrew. This Gospel may have been produced and disseminated in Mesopotamia by the mid-first century. See Edwards, *Hebrew Gospel*.

12. See Horn, Lieu, and Phenix, "Beyond the Eastern Frontier," 93: "The existence of an independent Syriac translation of the Hebrew Bible . . . seems to reflect that Syriac Christianity adapted the Hebrew text that was used by Jews in Palestine and Syria in the first century CE, which in turn may point to the close connections between Judaism and the earliest Syriac Christians."

13. On the character of Syriac Christianity, see Burkitt, *Early Eastern Christianity*, 40–43; Brock, *Introduction to Syriac Studies*, 1–10.

Christianity is perhaps the nearest to a form of Christianity which embraces both Jewish-Christian character and Gnostic or mystical traits congenial to Gnostics," writes James Dunn.[14] A number of these elements characterize the apocryphal Acts of Paul and Thecla, which resulted in the cult of Thecla "becoming one of the most popular in the Christian East."[15] The Spanish pilgrim Egeria attests to the tenacity and influence of the Syriac tradition in Jerusalem as late as 384/85, when Syriac was second only to Greek as the dominant liturgical language in the Holy City.[16] Syriac was the most important language of the Christian East, influencing the theological character not only of the orthodox Christian communities (i.e., those who affirmed Chalcedon), such as the Melkites, but also the various Nestorian Churches of the East, the Miaphysite communions, the Maronite churches, and the church in Persia.

We have suggested that Christianity spread east of the Roman Empire, as it did at many points around the Mediterranean, first via Jewish communities. As far back as the seventh century BC, Jews had settled in and around Palmyra, which lay in the region of Osrhoene, east of Antioch, and also farther east in Mesopotamia, in the region of Adiabene.[17] Josephus reports that the royal family of Adiabene was converted to Judaism by Jewish merchants during the reign of the Roman emperor Claudius (r. 41–54).[18] The quarter-century reign of the Adiabenian dowager queen Helena and her son Izates, during the reign of King Artabanus of Parthia, established a Jewish presence both in Mesopotamia and in Parthia to the east.[19] Helena and Izates died immediately prior to the Jewish Revolt in 66 and were buried in a majestic tomb dedicated to Queen Helena in the Kidron Valley outside Jerusalem.[20] Christian missions in Mesopotamia likely commenced from the Jewish community that arose from the royal house of Adiabene, for a number of early Syrian bishops have Jewish names. The sixth-century *Chronicle of Arbela* dates the introduction of Christianity into Mesopotamia to the mission activity of Addai during the reign of the emperor Trajan (r. 98–117).[21]

14. Dunn, "Beyond the Jewish People," 200.

15. The quotation is from Harvey, "Antioch and Christianity," 43. For the Acts of Paul and Thecla, see *NTApoc* 2:239–65.

16. Gingras, *Egeria*, ch. 47.

17. On Jewish communities in Palmyra in the seventh century BC, see van der Toorn, "Egyptian Papyrus Sheds New Light," 66.

18. *J.W.* 20.17–53.

19. *J.W.* 20.54–91.

20. *J.W.* 20.95. On the tomb complex, see Pausanias, *Descr.* 8.16.5. Further, Murphy-O'Connor, *Holy Land*, 138–40.

21. According to Syriac tradition, Addai was one of the seventy-two disciples sent out by Jesus in Luke 10:1. On the introduction of Christianity to Arbela, see Metzger, *Early Versions*, 7.

The churches that developed east of the Euphrates River lay in former Seleucia. At the death of Alexander the Great in 323 BC, his general Seleucus was allotted the region that later bore his name: Seleucia. In 130 BC the Parthians drove the Greeks out of Seleucia and west of the Euphrates, resulting in Parthian and Persian hegemony in Seleucia until the early third century AD, when Rome conquered and annexed the region. By the time of its Roman annexation, Mesopotamia had been the home of Jesus followers for nearly a century, resulting in a Christianity that was more Semitic in character than Roman. Churches in the cities of Edessa (modern Urfa in southeastern Turkey), Nisibis, Arbela, and Ctesiphon (which lay farther east, along the Tigris River) became mission hubs to their surrounding countrysides.[22] As noted earlier, these churches did not adopt Greek; they retained both the Syriac language and its Semitic influences, which tethered them to their Jewish and Palestinian roots.[23]

Edessa was a particularly important site for early Eastern Christianity. It lay at the strategic juncture of two major trade routes: a north–south route running from Armenia to Egypt and the east–west Silk Roads that extended to China. Only twenty-five miles distant from Edessa was ancient Haran, the site where Terah, Abraham's father, died and where Isaac's wife, Rebecca, was born and raised. Edessa is associated with one of the two Christian traditions related to the spread of Christianity east of Palestine that presume to be set in the first century. In *Ecclesiastical History*, Eusebius quotes a letter "from the archives at Edessa" that was supposedly written to Jesus by Abgar Uchama ("the Black"), who ruled eastern Syria from Edessa in the years 9–46. According to the letter, reports of Jesus's miraculous cures had reached Edessa, and, concluding that he must be either God or a son of God, Abgar begs Jesus to come and heal him of an unspecified disease. Abgar also laments Jesus's ill treatment by the Jews and invites him to relocate to the city of Edessa. According to Eusebius, the resurrected Jesus wrote a return letter to Abgar, which was delivered by a courier named Ananias. In the letter, Jesus blesses the monarch for believing without seeing and reports that he cannot visit Abgar because he has work to do before his ascension. Jesus promises, however, to send a disciple to heal Abgar at a later time. Eusebius sets the Abgar correspondence in the context of the broader evangelization of Mesopotamia by Thaddaeus, who was reputed to be one of the seventy-two disciples commissioned in Luke 10:1. According to Eusebius, Thaddaeus was sent by the apostle Thomas to Edessa, where he performed numerous miracles, including the healing of King Abgar, who professed faith in Jesus as the Son of God and summoned the citizens

22. Metzger, *Early Versions*, 7.
23. Burkitt, *Early Eastern Christianity*, 4–9.

of his kingdom to hear the gospel proclaimed by Thaddaeus. Eusebius dates these events to the 340th year in Edessa, which equates to AD 30.[24]

The existence of the Abgar-Jesus correspondence in the archives of Edessa is independently corroborated by the Spanish pilgrim Egeria, who visited Edessa in 384–85, nearly fifty years after Eusebius died. The city of Edessa was the custodian of so many Christian sites, artifacts, and textual archives—including the Abgar-Jesus correspondence—that Egeria needed three days to see them all.[25] Ironically, she was already familiar with the famous correspondence back in Spain. By the fourth century, in other words, the letters of Abgar and Jesus had circulated as far as the western rim of the Roman Empire. The existence of the Abgar-Jesus correspondence is thus assured; but that, of course, does not guarantee its authenticity. The putative correspondence between Abgar and Jesus is characterized by elements typical of other early Christian apocrypha, including enchantment with wonders and miracles, maligning of the Jews, conversions of members of royal households, and magical qualities of the letters to protect readers—all packed into two brief documents. As for a letter from Jesus, Revelation 2–3 ascribes the letters to the seven churches to the *exalted* Jesus. But apart from the supposed letter to Abgar, no correspondence is ascribed to the earthly Jesus. Few readers can doubt, nor should they, the apocryphal status of the correspondence.[26] Eusebius himself seems to betray skepticism of the correspondence by attesting to its *existence* rather than its authenticity.[27]

The Abgar correspondence is related to a larger work called the *Doctrine of Addai*, which recounts the peaceful death of Thaddaeus (or Addai, as he was also called) and his burial with great honors by King Abgar. Addai was succeeded by a disciple named Aggai, a seller of royal garments who was martyred in Edessa by Abgar's royal successors (who had defected from

24. Eusebius, *Hist. eccl.* 1.13. For an introduction to and English translation of the Abgar-Jesus correspondence, see H. J. W. Drijvers, "The Abgar Legend," *NTApoc* 1:492–99.

25. See Gingras, *Egeria*, ch. 9. On the publication of the Abgar correspondence throughout early Christendom, see Moffett, *Christianity in Asia*, 1:80n9. The letter of Jesus was translated into all the major languages of Christendom, engraved on church archways and city gates (including the gate of Philippi in the fifth century), and preserved in church service books dating back to Saxon times. A medieval letter preserved in the British Museum accords it a position of honor immediately following the Lord's Prayer and Apostles' Creed.

26. Already in the sixth century, the so-called *Decretum Gelasianum* judged both letters in the Abgar-Jesus correspondence (along with sixty other supposedly Christian documents) to be "apocryphal." See *NTApoc* 1:38–40.

27. Eusebius, *Hist. eccl.* 1.13.5. I find no other instance in *Ecclesiastical History* where Eusebius relies on a source as obviously questionable as the Abgar legend. His recourse to the Abgar legend as a source supports our earlier conclusion (pp. 48–50) that he had no sources for his history of the church in the East comparable to the sources at his disposal for the history of the church in the West.

Christianity).[28] The *Doctrine of Addai* dates to the end of the fourth century, but like the earlier version preserved in Eusebius, it may preserve genuinely historical kernels with regard to the spread of Christianity eastward. For instance, we know from other sources that Christian missionaries made their way to Antioch, where they preached to Jews, in or around the year 40 (Acts 11:19). Antioch, after all, was more than halfway from Jerusalem to Edessa, and Edessa was within the sphere of influence of Babylon, where there existed perhaps the largest Jewish community outside Judea. It also seems plausible that early missionaries—one of whom may have been Addai/Thaddaeus, commissioned by the apostle Thomas—advanced eastward along the major trade route from Antioch to Edessa, where they preached the gospel in Jewish communities.

Corroboration of these historical kernels may be found in a collection of early hymns known as the Odes of Solomon, which derives from Edessa or its environs in approximately the year 100. Probably originally written in Syriac, the Odes consists of forty-two psalms that combine both Jewish and Christian elements.[29] The name "Jesus" does not appear in the Odes, but "Messiah/Christ" occurs throughout with reference to Jesus. There are also references to the virgin birth (19.6–7), Jesus's baptism (24.1), the incarnation (7.6), the resurrection (8.5), and the deity of Christ (29.6). As in the New Testament, the advent of the promised Messiah—through whom believers are offered eternal life and love—is depicted in terms of love, light, flowing water, and God's Word (15.10; 33.11). References to Christ in the Odes are reminiscent of references to the servant of the Lord in Isaiah 40–66.[30] The destiny of the Messiah is portrayed in character with Old Testament imagery and prophecy, especially as a fulfillment of the servant's vocation. And the Odes preserves a "high Christology," with two trinitarian ascriptions of unusual androgynous character[31] and with Christ depicted as the preexistent Son of God, reminiscent

28. See Tixeront, *L'église d'Édesse*, esp. 120–35.
29. See James H. Charlesworth, "Odes of Solomon," *OTP* 2:725–71.
30. Odes Sol. 17.6–16; 25.5; 28.9–20; 31.6–13.
31. "The Son is the cup,
    And the Father is he who was milked;
    And the Holy Spirit is she who milked him;
    Because his breasts were full,
    And it was undesirable that his milk should be released without purpose.
    The Holy Spirit opened her bosom,
    And mixed the milk of the two breasts of the Father.
    Then she gave the mixture to the generation without their knowing."
    (Odes Sol. 19.1–5)
The Holy Spirit was commonly portrayed as feminine in the early East, as in this instance, with both the Father and the Spirit offering milk from their breasts to the world. See the other trinitarian ascription in Odes Sol. 23.22.

of Philippians 2:5–11.[32] The provenance of this Jewish-Christian text in Edessa suggests that early Christian missionaries had reached Mesopotamia by the late first or early second century with a gospel more integrated with Judaism than polarized from it.[33] We cannot verify that one of these missionaries was Addai/Thaddaeus, however, for his name does not appear in the Odes.

Early Christianity North of Mesopotamia

The Georgian kingdoms of Colchis and Iberia, south of the Caucasus Mountains between the Black and Caspian Seas, trace their Christian traditions to two of Jesus's original twelve disciples: St. Andrew and St. Simon the Zealot. However, this tradition is not attested by early sources, apocryphal or otherwise. The earliest certain evidence of the existence of Christianity in Georgia and Armenia dates to the third century. Christianity flowered in these two regions from the third to the seventh century, at the time when both the Roman Empire and Sassanid Persia were facing mortal decline. Eusebius attests to the establishment of Christianity in Armenia with an account of the conversion of Trdat (Tiridates) III (r. ca. 287–330) around the year 300 through the efforts of St. Gregory the Illuminator (ca. 257–ca. 331).[34]

We know nothing of the introduction of Christianity in Colchis, on the eastern shore of the Black Sea. But farther east, in Iberia, its introduction is attributed to a Christian slave woman named Nino. During the reign of the emperor Constantine, Nino was captured and taken to Georgia, where she evangelized the Georgians and the Iberian king, Mirian III, in about the year 330.[35] The region

---

32. "The Savior who gives life and does not reject (us)
    The Man who humbled himself
    But was raised because of his own righteousness.
    The Son of the Most High appeared
    In the perfection of his Father.
    And light dawned from the Word
    That was before time in him.
    The Messiah in truth is one.
    And he was known before the foundation of the world,
    That he might give life to persons forever by the truth of his name." (Odes Sol.
        41.11–16)
See also Odes Sol. 32.2.

33. On the beginnings of the eastward expansion of Christianity, see Metzger, *Early Versions*, 3–10; Moffett, *Christianity in Asia*, 1:45–90; Horn, Lieu, and Phenix, "Beyond the Eastern Frontier," 63–93.

34. Eusebius, *Hist. eccl.* 6.46.3. On the founding of Christianity in Armenia, see Metzger, *Early Versions*, 153–57.

35. The earliest testimony to Nino comes from Rufinus in the fourth century (*Hist.* 1.10). On the introduction of Christianity in Iberia through Nino and the literature pertaining thereto, see Metzger, *Early Versions*, 182–84; Haas, "Caucasus," 122–28.

of Georgia—including both the kingdom of Iberia, in the east, and the kingdom of Colchis, in the west—initially rejected the Chalcedonian Formula of 451, but subsequently embraced it. By the late fifth century, renowned Christian ascetics from Georgia had visited the monasteries of Mar Saba near Jerusalem and St. Catherine's Monastery on the Sinai peninsula and had assisted in founding the oldest monastic community in Greece, the Monastery of Iviron (i.e., the Monastery of the Iberians) at Mt. Athos.[36] The roots of Christianity, whenever and however they were first planted, went deep into northern Mesopotamia. As a result, Armenia and Georgia, both of which were subjected to Islamic invasions in the seventh and eighth centuries, remained predominantly Christian.[37]

Persia

Christianity likely reached Persia (modern Iran) via the catechetical and missionary fonts of Edessa and Nisibis.[38] The home of Zoroastrianism (6th c. BC) and the Church of the East (Nestorianism, 5th c. AD), Persia was considered by nearly all church fathers the home of the Magi (Matt. 2:1–12). The fathers tell us nothing further about the introduction of Christianity in Persia, although there, as elsewhere in the East, its most plausible means of introduction were via long-established Jewish communities.[39] Few early Christian texts have survived in Persia, although one of the earliest records the martyrdom of Candida, a favored concubine of a late third-century Persian ruler, Bahram II. The church was well established in Persia by the sixth century, winning converts from Zoroastrianism and launching missions of its own.[40]

India

The sole exception to the general dearth of information regarding the provenance and expansion of Christianity east of Palestine is India, which retains a longer Christian memory than anywhere in central Asia. The beginnings of Christianity in India are elaborately apocryphal, as they are in Edessa in

36. For special treatments of Christianity in Georgia (especially Iberia) and its influence on Mt. Athos, see Speake, *Athonite Commonwealth*, 54–63; Trumler, *Athos*, 68–77.

37. Haas, "Caucasus," 111–41.

38. Frankopan speaks of the school in Edessa as "the focal point of the Christian east, pumping out texts, saints' lives and advice not only in Syriac, the Aramaic dialect used in Edessa, but in a range of other languages too such as Persian and Sogdian." *Silk Roads*, 53.

39. Moffett writes, "Surviving records of the earliest Christian groups in Asia outside the Roman Empire almost always have a strong Jewish-Christian tinge." *Christianity in Asia*, 1:10.

40. Horn, Lieu, and Phenix, "Beyond the Eastern Frontier," 94–109. On the influential role of Christianity in Persia, see again Frankopan, *Silk Roads*, ch. 3.

the Abgar tradition. Indeed, Syriac-speaking missionaries made their way from Edessa to India. The tradition of the arrival of Christianity in India derives from the Acts of Thomas, which (in contrast to the two-paragraph Abgar-Jesus correspondence of Mesopotamia) is a book-length document of seventy-five pages. The Acts of Thomas is attributed to Judas Thomas, who is the same as the apostle Thomas, and begins thus: "[Following the ascension of Jesus], we apostles were all in Jerusalem, . . . and we divided the regions of the world, that each one of us might go to the region which fell to his lot, and to the nation to which the Lord sent him."[41] This introduction attests to a consciousness of world mission rather than simply Roman mission. The Judas Thomas in question apparently derives from the apostolic lists in Luke 6:16 and Acts 1:13, where "Judas (the son [or brother] of) James" is mentioned in place of "Thaddaeus" (who was associated with Thomas) in the corresponding apostolic lists of Matthew 10:3 and Mark 3:18. According to the Acts of Thomas, evangelization of India fell by lot to Judas Thomas, who twice refused the Savior's command to go there. Thereupon Jesus made Judas Thomas a slave and sold him to a merchant named Abban, who ferried him by ship to India.[42] There Thomas first converted a little Jewish flute girl[43] and, later, the king of India, named Gundaphorus.[44] Thomas traveled thereafter throughout India, preaching and performing charming miracles, including converting the wives of cruel kings, resurrecting a virtuous maiden killed in a lover's quarrel, and even converting a herd of wild asses, which then proclaimed the gospel to disbelievers and skeptics.[45] Thomas met his end in martyrdom under King Misdaeus.[46]

Composed probably in the third century, the Acts of Thomas is a long hagiographic patchwork of endearing stories, tedious digressions, wild improbabilities, and occasionally plausible history. Among its historical plausibilities is the skeletal tradition that, in the first century, (Judas) Thomas went to India, where he converted its king and died a martyr's death. This tradition is repeated and affirmed by fourth-century witnesses, including Ephrem the Syrian, Gregory Nazianzus, Rufinus, Jerome, and Paulinus of Nola. Other factors commend this skeletal tradition. First-century travel from the Levant to India was more common than might be supposed. It would have been unremarkable for a Christian missionary to proceed there either by sea or

41. Acts Thom. 1, in *NTApoc* 2:399.
42. Acts Thom. 1–4.
43. Acts Thom. 5–8.
44. Acts Thom. 17–29.
45. Acts Thom. 30–158.
46. Acts Thom. 159–170.

overland by the Silk Road through Persia.[47] King Gundaphorus, moreover, was a dominant historical monarch in mid-first-century India.

The *Didascalia apostolorum*, written in Syriac (perhaps in Edessa) around the year 250, corroborates the evangelization of India by Thomas. The *Didascalia* chronicles the spread of the gospel by various witnesses to various destinations—James to Jerusalem, Mark to Egypt, Peter to Syria and Rome, and Thomas to India. With regard to the last, which is not attested in the New Testament, the *Didascalia* maintains, "India, and all its countries, and those bordering on it even to the farthest sea, received the Apostle's Hand of Priesthood from Judas Thomas, who was guide and ruler in the Church which he built there."[48] These data do not prove the veracity of the narrative line of the Acts of Thomas, but they do enhance its plausibility. The church in South India fervently embraces the foregoing skeletal narrative and commemorates its first-century founding by the apostle Thomas in story and song.[49]

Farther East

Whether Christianity pushed east from India in the first century, we cannot say. We do know that a flourishing Christian community developed along the Silk Roads in late antiquity in East Turkestan of Central Asia, where primarily Nestorian texts were committed to writing. The Sogdian language of East Turkestan assumed the role of lingua franca in Central Asia—similar, although on a smaller scale, to the role that Greek played in the ancient Mediterranian. The earliest cache of Sogdian texts is dated to the seventh century, but its richness, including New Testament Gospels and Epistles, the Shepherd of Hermas, and liturgical and ecclesiastical texts, assumes the introduction of Christianity into East Turkestan much earlier than the seventh century.[50] From Sogdiana, the Silk Road continued east to China, where the earliest *recorded* Christian was a Syrian teacher, fittingly named Aluoben (Syriac for "teacher"), whose arrival in China in 635 is hailed by the Syriac Church as the official entry of Christianity into China.[51]

47. Lieu and Parry, "Deep into Asia," 173–77. In the thirteenth century Marco Polo computed the sea route between Baghdad and India to be a distance "of seventeen days' navigation." Komroff, *Travels of Marco Polo*, bk. 1, ch. 6.

48. Quoted in Moffett, *Christianity in Asia*, 1:33.

49. For a full and informative discussion of the Acts of Thomas and its relevance for the founding of the church in India, see Moffett, *Christianity in Asia*, 1:24–44.

50. See Metzger, *Early Versions*, 279–81.

51. Lieu and Parry, "Deep into Asia," 159–71.

The Progression of Christianity Southward to Egypt

The early history of Christianity in Egypt and North Africa is obscured by the same cloud of uncertainty that hangs over the church's eastward expansion.[52] For the first two centuries of the Christian era, we know little for certain about the spread of the gospel to Alexandria, and from there either southward up the Nile or westward across North Africa. The dearth of documentation here is more perplexing than that for the eastward expansion of Christianity, however; for Egypt was closely allied with Palestine geographically, histori-cally, and culturally. Adolf Harnack writes in agony: "Our near-complete ignorance of the history of Christianity in Alexandria and Egypt is the most painful deficiency in our knowledge of early church history."[53]

The year after Octavian defeated Mark Antony and Cleopatra at the Battle of Actium in 31 BC, he annexed Egypt to the Roman Empire. Thus, for nearly a century before the introduction of Christianity there, Egypt had been part of the empire. Palestine's religious ties with Egypt were, of course, far older than that. Historically speaking, Egypt had been a predictable place of refuge for Israelites—from Abraham (Gen. 12:10) and the sons of Jacob (Gen. 42), in search of famine relief, to the flight of the holy family from Herod's wrath (Matt. 2:13–23). Archaeologists have recently discovered evidence of Jewish colonies located six hundred miles up the Nile, on the island of Elephantine (where the Aswan Dam is located today), that date to the fifth century BC.[54] The Letter of Aristeas reports the resettlement of one hundred thousand Jews in Egypt in the third century BC, a third of whom were dispersed throughout the land.[55] It also recounts the translation of the Hebrew Old Testament into the Greek Septuagint in Alexandria, following the resettlement, in order to accommodate the Greek-speaking Jewish minority in Egypt. Philo (ca. 20 BC–ca. AD 50), the most prolific pre-Christian Jewish author and a contem-porary of Jesus, hailed from Alexandria. In the New Testament, Luke records the presence of Egyptians, Lybians, and Cyrenians in Jerusalem at Pentecost (Acts 2:10). Apollos, the early Christian missionary tutored by Priscilla and Aquila, hailed from Alexandria (Acts 18:24–28). The conversion of a finance minister of the queen of Ethiopia by Philip (Acts 8:24–40) links Christianity to Egypt's contiguous neighbor to the south. Frequent references to Egypt in

52. On its sparse, late, and often apocryphal sources, see Choat et al., "World of the Nile."
53. Harnack, *Mission und Ausbreitung*, 2:706–7 (my trans.). Harnack's despair is echoed by Hengel, *Studien zum Urchristentum*, 332: "The absence of a single report from the first century with regard to Christian mission in Alexandria and Egypt is a complete mystery" (my trans.).
54. Van der Toorn, "Egyptian Papyrus Sheds New Light," 34–35.
55. Let. Aris. 13.

the Epistle to the Hebrews,[56] coupled with its high-caliber Greek and thoroughgoing thesis of the superiority of Christianity to Judaism, make the Jewish elite of Alexandria a plausible intended audience of Hebrews. The Epistle of Barnabas may also be linked to Alexandria, since Barnabas is filled with allegory (which was characteristic of Alexandrian literature). Clement of Alexandria, in fact, is the earliest witness to Barnabas.[57] And the port of Caesarea Maritima, on the coast of Palestine, was the first stop on the sea route from Alexandria to Rome; it was from this port that Paul embarked as a prisoner on a grain ship sailing from Alexandria to Rome (Acts 27:1–2).

All the above knit Egypt, and Alexandria in particular, to the same geographical, historical, religious, and imperial fabric as Israel. This close association renders the dearth of documentation on the beginnings of Christianity in Egypt all the more bewildering. Scholars have sought to account for this dearth in various ways. In the 1930s, Walter Bauer argued that early Alexandrian Christianity was overwhelmingly Gnostic and that later orthodox theologians, in an attempt to expunge the heresy, expunged the early history of Christianity in Alexandria as well.[58] This rather conspiratorial theory is largely argued from silence. Material remains do not support it, for the various papyri and fragments of codices found in situ in Egypt that can be safely dated to the second century, although often heterodox, do not exhibit the pronounced Gnostic character argued by Bauer.[59] There is historical evidence for a more practical explanation: the massive destruction wreaked on Alexandria by Rome in 117 in retaliation for the Jewish revolt in Egypt during the reign of the emperor Trajan in 115.[60] The retaliation virtually annihilated the Jewish community in Egypt. If Christians constituted a minority group among the larger Jewish community, they too would have perished with the destruction of the Jewish community.[61]

The first specific reference to the evangelization of North Africa dates from the fourth century. Both Eusebius[62] and Jerome[63] report that the evangelist Mark took the Gospel, which he had written in Rome at the request of Peter, to Alexandria, where he formed large Christian communities of ascetic

---

56. Heb. 3:16; 8:9; 11:22–29.
57. Holmes, *Apostolic Fathers*, 372–73.
58. Bauer, *Rechtgläubigkeit und Ketzerei*, 49–64. For an English edition, see Bauer, *Orthodoxy and Heresy*. For a critique of Bauer's thesis, see Hartog, *Orthodoxy and Heresy*, esp. 6–33, 60–88.
59. Choat et al., "World of the Nile," 190.
60. Eusebius, *Hist. eccl.* 4.2.
61. Choat et al., "World of the Nile," 207; Birger A. Pearson, "Alexandria," *ABD* 1:153.
62. *Hist. eccl.* 2.16.1–2.
63. *Vir. ill.* 8.3.

character. This tradition is older than the fourth century, for both Eusebius[64] and Jerome[65] attribute it to Clement of Alexandria in the second century and, earlier still in the second century, to Papias. Clement locates the most primitive base of Christianity outside Judea in Antioch on the Orontes—from which the faith quickly spread south to the Nile Delta, where the Alexandria of Apollos and Saint Mark the Evangelist became an early seat of Christian learning.[66] Christianity, as we have seen, was established in Antioch already in the 40s, so its extension "shortly" thereafter to Alexandria would place it in Egypt perhaps in mid-first century. There is no archeological or epigraphical evidence for Christianity in Egypt in the second century—indeed none of either before the fourth century. Nevertheless, the thriving catechetical school of Clement (ca. 150–ca. 220) and Origen (185–254) in Alexandria, the Christian and quasi-Christian texts recovered from the sands of Nag Hammadi and Oxyrhynchus, and the bishopric of Demetrius, already mature by the late second century, all attest to a vital Christian presence in Egypt in the second century. Such a presence does not develop overnight. All this reinforces the claim of Clement noted above, that Christianity made its way to Egypt in the first century, shortly after its introduction to Antioch.

North Africa

Rome ruled North Africa for nearly six centuries, from 146 BC until AD 439, during which the Pax Romana afforded the southern rim of the Mediterranean remarkable prosperity. After Octavian defeated Mark Antony and Cleopatra at the Battle of Actium in 31 BC, he employed the plenary power of his imperial office as Caesar Augustus in forging a new world order—introducing massive public works projects and developing key cities. Carthage, the old Punic capital of North Africa, benefited extravagantly from Augustus's largesse. Already before the birth of Jesus, Carthage was a leading Hellenistic city; it had a theater, odeon (for musical performances), baths, a Roman forum, amphitheater, and a seventy-five-mile aqueduct sluicing water from mountain headwaters in the south to the coastal capital. A half century later, the emperor

---

64. *Hist. eccl.* 2.15.2.

65. *Vir. ill.* 8.1.

66. See the florid description by A. Cleveland Coxe, "Introductory Note to Clement of Alexandria," *ANF* 2:165: "Alexandria becomes the brain of Christendom: its heart was yet beating at Antioch, but the West was still receptive only, its hands and arms stretched forth towards the sunrise for further enlightenment. From the East it had obtained the Scriptures and their authentication, and from the same source was deriving the canons, the liturgies, and the creed of Christendom."

Nero (r. 54–68) widened Augustus's largesse from Carthage in particular to North Africa as a whole, designating it the breadbasket of the empire.[67]

The earliest material evidence of a Christian presence in North Africa dates to the late second century. Given the peace, economic prosperity, and established trade routes in the Mediterranean, however, Christianity must have established itself in North Africa much earlier. Indeed, Luke's reference to Christian evangelists from Cyrene (Acts 11:20) on the north coast of Africa (modern Libya) implies a Christian presence in North Africa already in the first century. The oldest written document of the North African church, and oldest Latin document from Christian North Africa, is an account of heroic Christian martyrdom known as the Acts of the Scillitan Martyrs. The village from which the martyrs hailed, Scilli, lay most probably in Numidia, west of Carthage. On July 17, 180, the Roman proconsul of North Africa, Vigellius Saturninus, arraigned twelve Christians—seven men and five women—in his courtroom in Carthage. The proconsul ordered them to abandon what he considered a pernicious superstition and "return to a sound mind," swearing by the "genius of our lord the Emperor" and ceasing to neglect the customs and sacred rites of Rome. The spokesman for the accused, Speratus, professed that he and the others had committed no crimes, neither done nor spoken ill, and paid all required taxes. He insisted, in fact, that even when ill-treated, "[we] pay heed to our Emperor." Unimpressed, the proconsul ordered them to forsake their "folly," to which one man responded, "We fear no one but God." A woman declared, "We honor Caesar as Caesar, but we fear God"; another woman, "What I am, that I wish to be"; and yet another woman, "I am a Christian." All twelve professed likewise. "What was Speratus clutching to his chest?" demanded the proconsul. "Books and epistles of Paul, a just man," came the reply. The proconsul offered the believers a stay of thirty days to reconsider their decision. They declined. There was nothing to reconsider. Saturninus put them all to the sword the same day. "Thanks be to God," they declared, "today we are martyrs in heaven." "And so," the account concludes, "they all together were crowned with martyrdom."[68]

This dramatic account offers several insights into early North African Christianity. Christianity had presumably spread to the home of the martyrs

67. On North Africa and the origins of Christianity there, see Merdinger, "Roman North Africa," 223–60.

68. For an introduction and English translation, see Andrew Rutherfurd, "The Passion of the Scillitan Martyrs," *ANF* 10:281–85. The original Latin with English translation can be found in Gwatkin, *Selections from Early Writers*, 79–83. For further discussion of the Scillitan martyrs, see Merdinger, "Roman North Africa," 233–34; Bauer, *Anfänge der Christenheit*, 161–62; Quasten, *Patrology*, 1:178–79.

in rural Scilli from Carthage, which presumes a Christian presence in Carthage several decades before 180. Five of the accused were women, whose testimony is represented in the account as equal to the men's, suggesting a level of gender equality among them. The nine Latin and three Berber names of the martyrs similarly suggest that the faith was embraced by both Roman and indigenous populations.[69] The "books and epistles of Paul" in the possession of Speratus are also noteworthy. They appear to distinguish the proto-canonical status of the Pauline corpus among Christian writings, and also to identify the Scillitan martyrs with normative Christianity.[70] Furthermore, reference to the documents in Speratus's possession as *libri* and not *volumen* (scrolls) implies a codex or book form, a subject to which we devote chapter 14. The refusal of Speratus to part with his Christian texts may have been a resolve not to deny the faith by surrendering the Scriptures to imperial authorities. Failure to surrender such documents inevitably resulted in martyrdom. The clarity with which Speratus differentiates between political claims that Christians may and may not obey indicates that the Scillitan martyrs were well tutored regarding legitimate and illegitimate claims of the Roman imperium vis-à-vis Christian faith.

Summary

This chapter completes a two-part examination of the earliest expansion of the gospel from Jerusalem to the nations. In several respects, the expansion of the gospel from Jerusalem to the east and south mirrors its expansion from Jerusalem to Rome, which we considered in the last chapter. Most importantly, the gospel apparently moved east and south from Antioch concurrently with its more documented westward expansion to Rome. Expansions of the gospel in all directions benefited from the political and social stability afforded by the Pax Romana. Early Christian evangelists all capitalized, at least initially, on their affiliation with Jews as the earliest recipients of the gospel, and with synagogues as starting points of Christian mission. And all Christian missions, whatever their destinations, identified keenly with urban culture.

Beyond these commonalities, however, the picture of Christianity outside the Jerusalem–Rome corridor exhibits several distinctive characteristics. In contrast to the one-hundred-plus first-century Christians named in relation to the Jerusalem–Rome corridor, fewer than two dozen names are associated

---

69. The nine martyrs with Latin names are the leader Speratus (m.), Donata (f.), Vestia (f.), Secunda (f.), Felix (m.), Aquilinus (m.), Laetantius (m.), Januaria (f.), and Generosa (f.). The three with Berber names are Nartzalus (m.), Cittinus (m.), and Veturius (m.).

70. The proto-canonical status of the Pauline Epistles is also suggested in 2 Pet. 3:15–16.

with Christian missions in all other directions, half of which comprise the Scillitan martyrs. Not all these latter names are historically identifiable, however, and those of the Scillitan martyrs date to the late second century. In contrast to the plethora of information for the spread of Christianity to the west, its spread in all other directions is characterized by fewer, later, and frequently apocryphal sources. The result is a mottled record rife with gaps and incompletenesses.

In the East, the expansion of the gospel was determined more definitively by the Silk Roads than by any other network. The Silk Roads, in turn, allied the expansion of the gospel with merchant classes and commerce; indeed, several of the names in this chapter are identified as merchants. The eastward expansion of the gospel also mandated the adoption of Syriac, rather than Greek, and thereafter the adoption of a plethora of languages related to the diverse cultures, religions, ethnicities, and geographies of the East. The church in the West, by contrast, and this also includes the church in North Africa, was able to forge a synthesis of the gospel with the more homogeneous Greco-Roman culture. The greater distances and diversities that the church encountered in its eastward expansion required it initially—and still require it today—to live and spread its faith in pluralistic environments.

4

From Hebrew to Greek

The most striking irony about the language of first-century Christianity is that Jesus and his Galilean disciples were nurtured exclusively on sacred Semitic texts, both Hebrew and Aramaic, yet not a single first-century text of the Jesus movement survives in either Hebrew or Aramaic. All first-century Christian texts are in Greek, and only Greek. The global transition from a Semitic-mediated to a Greek-mediated faith is the subject of this chapter.

The Status of Hebrew and Aramaic in First-Century Judaism

Hebrew and Aramaic are close linguistic siblings, both sharing the same alphabet. Syriac, a third sibling, is a dialect of Aramaic that is written in a variant cursive script. All three languages are written right to left. Syriac is the first language into which the New Testament was translated, but its translation, made in the second century, falls beyond our present purview.[1] Although Hebrew and Aramaic belong to the same linguistic family, Aramaic was not particularly distinctive of Judaism; for a millennium it was spoken in many dialects throughout the ancient Near East. Hebrew, on the other hand, was specifically and almost exclusively unique to Jews.[2] Second Kings

1. According to Burkitt, *Early Eastern Christianity*, 1–43, the churches of Mesopotamia that produced the Syriac translation composed the single branch of early Christianity that had "roots in a realm outside the Roman Empire" (vii). On the relation of Syriac to Aramaic, see J. F. Healey, "Script, Syriac," *GEDSH* 363–64.

2. The expanse of spoken Aramaic in the ancient Near East is signified by the decision of the third century BC Buddhist emperor of India, Asoka, to publish his edicts not only in Sanskrit but also in Aramaic and Greek.

preserves an illuminating reference to both Hebrew and Aramaic from the Assyrian siege of Jerusalem (ca. 701 BC). Hebrew was then the common tongue of Jerusalem, and the city leaders implored Sennacherib's besieging general to speak in Aramaic rather than in Hebrew so the people would not understand him. It was a vain ploy. "Has my master sent me to speak these words to your master and to you," scoffed the general, "and not to the men sitting on the wall, who are doomed with you to eat their own dung and to drink their own urine?" (18:27 RSV). By the Christian era, however, the tables had turned in Palestine, and Aramaic was more widely spoken than Hebrew. The occurrence of occasional Aramaic words and phrases in the Greek New Testament attests to its common use in Jesus's day.[3] In an attempt to be historically accurate (at least regarding language), the 2004 movie *The Passion of the Christ* cast all dialogue (with the exception of Latin, spoken by Roman officials) in Aramaic.

Aramaic was not the only spoken language of first-century Palestine, however. Following the conquests of Alexander the Great three centuries earlier, Greek had steadily eclipsed other vernaculars in the Middle East, and by the first century it was the standard language throughout the Roman Empire. The Greek vernacular and its larger Hellenistic culture influenced Jews greatly, both those living in the diaspora and those in Palestine. Indeed, much of the influence on Christianity that might be ascribed to "Judaism" was, to some degree, Hellenistic. We have noted, for example, how the large and influential Jewish population in Alexandria produced the Septuagint, the translation of the Hebrew Scriptures into Greek. This was because, by the third century BC, their facility in Greek had surpassed their facility in Hebrew.[4] Greek had extended its roots into other Jewish literature as well. Many texts in the Apocrypha[5]

3. New Testament Aramaisms include *talitha koum*, "Arise, little girl" (Mark 5:41); *ephphatha*, "Be opened" (Mark 7:34); *Abba*, "Abba" (Mark 14:36); *Golgotha*, "Golgotha" (Mark 15:22); *Elōi elōi lema sabachthani*, "My God, my God, why have you forsaken me" (Mark 15:34; Matt. 27:46); *Kēphas*, "Peter" (John 1:42; plus eight references to this Aramaic name of Peter in 1 Corinthians and Galatians); *Marana tha*, "Our Lord, come" (1 Cor. 16:22).

4. According to Jewish tradition, some seventy translators produced for the library at Alexandria a translation of the Hebrew Scriptures into Greek. The work was begun in the third century BC and concluded in the second century BC. The seventy translators account for the Latin name of the translation, "Septuagint" (abbreviated as LXX). The Septuagint includes several books that are not in the Hebrew Old Testament (see "Apocrypha" in the following footnote). The Septuagint became the primary version of the Bible used by Greek-speaking Jews and early Christians. For the traditional account of the production of the Septuagint, see the Letter of Aristeas (*OTP* 2:7–34).

5. The word "Apocrypha" (meaning "hidden") refers to the books of the Greek Old Testament, the Septuagint, that are not included in the thirty-nine books of the Hebrew Old Testament. The Apocrypha traditionally includes First and Second Esdras, Tobit, Judith, Additions to Esther, Wisdom of Solomon, Ecclesiasticus (Wisdom of Jesus the Son of Sirach), Baruch, Letter of Jeremiah, Susanna, Bel and the Dragon, Prayer of Manasseh, and First and Second Maccabees.

and Pseudepigrapha[6] of the Old Testament are extant only in Greek. Ironically, First and Second Maccabees, which recount the successful defense of Jewish Palestine from the onslaught of Seleucid Hellenism, is no longer extant in Hebrew but only in Greek.[7] Both Philo and Josephus, the two major Jewish writers of the first century, wrote in Greek. Greek made significant inroads into Galilee as gentiles settled there in large concentrations. Hence the expression "Galilee of the Gentiles."[8] Jerusalem itself was multilingual, as evidenced by the sign that Pilate affixed to the cross of Jesus, which was written "in Hebrew, Latin, and Greek" (John 19:19–20). "Hebrew" in the inscription probably means Aramaic, and Hebrew, Aramaic, and Greek were all what we today would call "street languages."[9] Latin, on the other hand, was probably limited to the Roman enclaves in Caesarea Maritima and Jerusalem, and thus not widely spoken in Palestine.

Aramaic was the tongue of home and marketplace in first-century Palestine, but it was not the sole linguistic medium of Jews, as is sometimes supposed, for Hebrew retained its status as the language of Jewish religious culture, especially *written* religious culture.[10] Very few first-century Aramaic documents survive. Even Greek surpassed Aramaic with regard to written Jewish religious texts.[11] The most common Aramaic texts to survive are translations of the Hebrew Scriptures known as targums, which were not considered as authoritative as the Hebrew text they translated or paraphrased. In order to be regarded as inspired, the Jewish Scriptures needed to be "written in the Assyrian character (= Hebrew), on leather, and in ink."[12] The dictate of the

6. The word "Pseudepigrapha," meaning "falsely named," refers to a body of writings that were ascribed to persons other than their real authors for the purpose of enhancing their authority. Included in the Pseudepigrapha are a large miscellany of Jewish works that were written in the centuries immediately before and during the Christian era and are not included in either the Old Testament or the Apocrypha.

7. First Maccabees may have been originally composed in Hebrew, but it was most widely circulated and read in Greek.

8. Isa. 9:1; 1 Macc. 5:15; Matt. 4:15.

9. The word *Hebraisti* in John 19:20 probably denotes Hebrew rather than Aramaic. For the distinction between Hebrew (Gk. *Hebraisti*) and Aramaic (Gk. *Syristi*) in the LXX, see 2 Kings 18:26; Isa. 36:11; Dan. 2:4; Ezra 4:7. For the same distinction, see Josephus, *Ant.* 10.8.

10. Edward Cook, "Aramaic," *EDEJ* 360–62, refers to Aramaic as the "'default' language for most communication between Jews" and to Hebrew as the language of poetry, legal documents, theology, and biblical commentary.

11. Rabbis generally regarded Aramaic as "low diction" for religious texts. Both *m.* Meg. 1:8 and *m.* Git. 9:6, 8, for example, validate Hebrew marriage and divorce certificates that were translated into Greek but not those translated into Aramaic (Rabin, "Hebrew and Aramaic," 2:1033–37). Treu, "Die Bedeutung des Griechischen," 133, notes that Jewish sages preferred Greek translations over Aramaic translations, which were generally considered inferior and vulgar.

12. See *m.* Yad. 4:5.

Mishnah that the Sacred Scriptures must be read in "the Holy Tongue" (Hebrew) destined Hebrew as the language of worship and liturgy in both temple and synagogue.[13] Religious objects such as tefillin (small Jewish phylacteries) also required Hebrew texts, and Hebrew inscriptions appear on Jewish ossuaries and synagogues far into the Christian era.[14] Virtually all extant sacred Jewish literature from the Babylonian exile in the sixth century BC until the production of Babylonian Talmud in the fifth century AD—a full millennium later—exists in Hebrew. This includes the Old Testament (with the exception of its minor Aramaic sections),[15] the vast majority of the Dead Sea Scrolls, the majority of the Bar Kokhba letters of the second century, the entire Mishnah of the second century and the longer Tosefta that parallels it, and the majority of the Palestinian (Jerusalem) and Babylonian Talmuds of the fourth and fifth centuries, respectively.[16] These foundational texts of Judaism are all written in Hebrew.

The victory of the Maccabees over the numerically and tactically superior forces of the Seleucids in the second century BC seems to have revitalized the use of Hebrew in Roman-dominated Palestine.[17] Two vignettes may attest to its revitalization. When Paul was arrested in the temple in approximately the year 60, he petitioned the Roman tribune to be allowed to address the riotous crowd, and when permitted to do so, he spoke "in the Hebrew language."[18] Paul needed to assert his Jewishness in the crisis, and he did so by speaking in Hebrew. Josephus acted likewise during the First Jewish Revolt, in one instance addressing contrary Jewish crowds in "*tē patriō glossē*" (the language of their fathers),[19] and another time in "*Hebraizōn*" (Hebrew).[20]

Hebrew was thus not a dead language in first-century Palestine. It retained its currency as the primary language of sacred Jewish texts and religious culture, especially as those texts and culture were commemorated in temple and

13. See *m.* Sotah 7:2.

14. For ossuaries, see Meyers and Chancey, *Alexander to Constantine*, 50. Hebrew inscriptions have been discovered in synagogue floor mosaics in Israel from as late as the fifth century AD at Sepphoris, Khirbet Wadi Hamam, Huqoq, Beth Alpha, Hammath Tiberias, Yaphiʻa, and ʻEin-Gedi.

15. The Aramaic sections of the Old Testament are Ezra 4:8–6:18; 7:11–26; Jer. 10:11; Dan. 2:4b–7:28—a total of 269 verses.

16. For the Hebrew of the Babylonian Talmud, which consisted of an Aramaic dialect, see Eliezer Berkovits, "Talmud, Babylonian," *Enc. Jud.* 15:763.

17. On the wider prevalence of Hebrew in first-century Palestine, see Milik, *Ten Years of Discovery*, 130.

18. Acts 21:40; 22:2.

19. *J.W.* 5.361.

20. *J.W.* 6.97. For fuller discussion and defense of these references to *Hebrew* rather than Aramaic, see Edwards, *Hebrew Gospel*, 166–78.

synagogue. We may summarize the three major tongues in Palestine in the first century by saying that Aramaic was the most widespread language in daily use; Hebrew was almost certainly understood—and perhaps also spoken, especially on religious occasions—by a majority of the Jewish population; and Greek, the least common of the three, was nevertheless the linguistic medium of a significant minority.[21]

The Supremacy of Greek in Early Christianity

The Jesus movement would have seemed destined to follow first-century Jewish religious culture in its adherence to Hebrew and Aramaic. The complete absence of extant Christian literature in either language, therefore, is nothing short of astounding. The word *extant* is important here, for we know that the early church produced at least one Hebrew Christian document. Two dozen ancient sources have left some seventy-five attestations, extending from the second to the ninth century, to the existence of an early Gospel written in Hebrew. No known copy of the Hebrew Gospel is extant today, but I have argued elsewhere that portions of it are credibly preserved in those sections of the Gospel of Luke that find no parallel in the Gospels of Mark and Matthew.[22] We noted in the last chapter that early Semitic Christianity in Mesopotamia provides a logical *Sitz im Leben* for such a Hebrew Gospel. The relevance of the Hebrew Gospel for our present purposes is that all attestations of it are in *Greek*. The ancients are unanimous that it was written in Hebrew, but that all extant quotations of it exist in Greek translation indicates that by the mid-first century, or shortly thereafter, Greek superseded Hebrew and Aramaic as the language of Christianity. The Hebrew Gospel itself therefore conforms to our above conclusion, that all *extant* Christian literature of the first century, even when originally written in Hebrew, survives only in Greek.

Historical absolutes such as this are rarely accidental. That Hebrew did not become the dominant linguistic medium of the Christian church was due to several factors, some obvious and others less so. The single most important factor was ethnic and linguistic rather than religious. In the eastern provinces of the Roman Empire, the common language was Greek, and the proclamation of the gospel to gentiles in such areas required Greek, and only Greek.

21. See the statistical linguistic analysis of first-century Palestine by Michael Wise, *Language and Literacy*, 288–345, who acknowledges the predominance of Aramaic in the spoken culture, with facility in Greek among perhaps 30 percent of the population. With reference to Hebrew, Wise concludes: "our data show that 65–80 percent of Judea spoke a form of Hebrew. . . . [Hebrew] was essentially as widely used among Judeans as it had ever been" (296).

22. See Edwards, *Hebrew Gospel*.

As we have noted, the opening moves of the Hellenist Jewish Christian mission that are introduced in Acts 8 included Roman cities rather than Galilean towns and villages. Already in the 40s, at the latest, Hellenist Christians made their way to cosmopolitan Antioch (Acts 11:19–26), and by the late 40s, the Council of Jerusalem formally validated the Roman and urban character of their gentile mission. The westward advance of the gospel, from Roman city to Roman city along the Jerusalem–Rome corridor, and its southward advance, from Jerusalem to Alexandria and then west along the north coast of Africa, were both undertaken in Greek. A dedicated gentile mission, as affirmed at the Council of Jerusalem, was by nature primarily urban; and a gentile urban mission, at least in the Roman Empire, mandated Greek. Greek was not, however, the only language in which the gospel spread in urban gentile cultures. As we noted in the last chapter, the eastward advance of the gospel was probably conducted primarily or exclusively in Syriac, although we have no first-century written attestation of it in Syriac.[23] Even putative first-century attestations of the eastward expansion of Christianity—namely, the Abgar-Jesus correspondence and the Acts of Thomas—are in Greek. It is particularly important to highlight two of the above points: first, although the early gentile mission was conducted in both Greek and Syriac, its only remaining first-century evidence is in Greek (hence the Greek mission branch necessarily determines the discussion in this chapter); second, and equally important, both Greek and Syriac mission branches abandoned Hebrew in favor of gentile vernaculars.

The Christian adoption of Greek was motivated by sociological factors as well. The culture that Rome inherited from Greece and disseminated throughout the Mediterranean retained much of its Greek ethos. Education at a foremost academy in the Roman era—at Alexandria or Antioch or Athens, for instance—presupposed a mastery of Greek language and literature. Greek manners and dress prevailed over village rusticity, native deities were identified with Greek gods and goddesses, and native names were frequently augmented or replaced by Greek names.[24] Nor was the Hellenizing influence limited to the urban scene. Native customs such as ritual prostitution and various taboos often survived with Greek veneers. The language of first-century mystery

---

23. The earliest written evidence of Syriac occurs in non-Christian tomb inscriptions dating from the first century. Precise datings of the translation of Old and New Testaments into Syriac are not ascertainable. The earliest known Syriac Christian writings are the translation of the Hebrew Old Testament into Syriac and Tatian's Gospel harmony (the Diatessaron), both dating to the latter half of the second century. The New Testament was probably first translated into Syriac ca. 400. On the question of Syriac translations of the Bible, see Metzger, *Early Versions*, 8–10; 36–39; and R. B. ter Haar Romeny and C. E. Morrison, "Peshitta," *GEDSH* 326–31.

24. See Ramsay, *Church in the Roman Empire*, 41–42.

cults, whose "mother" sites proliferated in bucolic settings, was almost always Greek (and thus theoretically accessible to any inhabitant of the empire). The cults of Cybele and Attis, and others too, enlarged their footprints to include Rome, where Greek was primarily spoken.[25] The apostle Paul penned his famous Epistle to the Romans in Greek, and Greek continued to be spoken in Rome long after Paul, for fully three-quarters of Rome's catacomb inscriptions are in Greek.[26]

The powerful tide of Hellenism, as we have seen, raised the boats of Jewish populations no less than those of other populations. Historical sociologists estimate that as many as five or six million Jews lived in the diaspora, compared to the perhaps one million Jews living in Palestine.[27] Five or six million people constituted roughly ten percent of the total population of the empire.[28] Jews were thus a very significant minority, and their significance was enhanced by the fact that they often played influential roles in the empire. The Roman exemption of Jews from military service and emperor worship and the not-infrequent intermarriage of Jewish women with Roman officials, including emperors, reflect the range of their influence. And diaspora Jews—like Alexandrian Jews, mentioned earlier—had so acculturated to the Roman Empire that Greek had replaced Hebrew and Aramaic as their primary language.

Religion is typically resistant to the winds of cultural change. By the first century, however, Judaism had long since unfurled its sails to the Greco-Roman winds. Greek literary styles and practices noticeably influenced Hebrew and Aramaic literary forms in the three centuries after Alexander's conquest of the Levant, inspiring new bodies of literature as well as new literary styles.[29] The foremost Greek literary event in Judaism was the production of the Septuagint, the significance of which is hard to overstate. Elias Bickerman declares it "the most important translation ever made." He says, "It opened the Bible to the world and the world to the Word of God. Without this translation London and Rome would still be heathen and the Scriptures would be no better known than the Egyptian Book of the Dead."[30] The Septuagint replaced the Hebrew Old Testament as *the* Bible of first-century Christians. The influence of Greek on Jewish literary tradition did not end with the Septuagint, however. As noted

25. See Nock, *Conversion*, 36–41.

26. Stark, *Rise of Christianity*, 58, notes a near-total absence of Hebrew and Aramaic catacomb inscriptions. They make up only 2 percent of inscriptions, while Latin inscriptions make up 20 percent.

27. Again, Stark, *Rise of Christianity*, 57.

28. Harnack, *Mission and Expansion*, 8–9, offers one of the lowest estimates of Jews in the empire at about 7 percent.

29. See Doering, *Ancient Jewish Letters*, 15.

30. Bickerman, *Jews in the Greek Age*, 101.

earlier, the two major Jewish writers of the first century, Philo and Josephus, composed their immense bodies of work—eleven volumes in the Loeb series for Philo and nine volumes for Josephus—exclusively in Greek.

In chapter 2 we noted factors that favored the survival and spread of Christianity. We close this section with another factor that, though seldom noted, deserves mention. Greek literature of all sorts—including poetry, philosophy, history, mathematics, astronomy, and physics—proliferated in the centuries before and after the advent of Christianity. Twenty major Greek authors can be counted in the third century BC,[31] ten in the second,[32] and seven in the first.[33] Then nineteen flourished in the second century AD,[34] followed by twelve in the third.[35] In the first century AD, by contrast, there were only four major Greek writers: Philo, Josephus, Plutarch, and Dio Chrysostom.[36] Latin authors abounded in these same centuries, with more than thirty flourishing in the first century AD. The dearth of first-century Greek writers is made more severe by the fact that Philo's and Josephus's works are limited to Jewish history and culture. That leaves only two Greek-language exponents of the Greco-Roman tradition: Plutarch, a historian, and Dio(n) Chrysostomus, a philosopher of self-sufficiency. This paucity created an enviable reading market for first-century Greek *Christian* writers. The New Testament Epistles and Gospels, the book of Acts and the Revelation of John, and the additional documents comprising the Apostolic Fathers, all written in Greek, appeared in a century when their lights shone bright in a starless season of Greek literature. In combination with other factors we have considered—including the Pax Romana, pirate-free sea lanes, well-traveled Roman roads, political stability, and a Greek vernacular—the hiatus of first-century Greek literature afforded the church a propitious

31. Their names are Philitas, Lycophron, Aratus, Theocritus, Timon of Phlius, Callimachus, Apollonius Rhodius, Herodas, Euphorion, Crates, Arcesilas, Cleanthes, Zenodotus, Eratosthenes, Philochorus, Berosus, Manetho, Euclid, Aristarchus, and Archimedes.

32. Their names are Moschus, Nicander, Aristophanes of Byzantium, Aristarchus, Dionysius Thrax, Polybius, Apollodorus, Carneades, Panaetius, and Hipparchus.

33. Their names are Bion, Antipater of Sidon, Meleager, Diodorus Siculus, Strabo, Dionysius of Halicarnassus, and Posidonius.

34. Their names are Epictetus, Marcus Aurelius, Babrius, Arrian, Appian, Aelian, Ptolemy, Pausanias, Apollonius Dyscolus, Herodian, Julius Pollux, Alexander of Aphrodisias, Herodes Atticus, Lucian, Galen, Sextus Empiricus, Alciphron, Athenaeus, and Clement of Alexandria.

35. Their names are Oppian, Dio Cassius, Herodian, Origen, Plotinus, Cassius Longinus, Porphyry, Xenophon of Ephesus, Heliodorus, Longus, Philostratus III, and Diogenes Laërtius.

36. Dio Chrysostom was also known as Dio Cocceianus. The dating of two other Greek authors, Dioscurides (botanist) and Longinus (critic) is too uncertain to place them confidently in the first century. For a complete list of Greek and Latin writers of antiquity, see Harvey, *Companion to Classical Literature*, 455–62.

opportunity to disseminate gospels, epistles, and sermons.[37] That could only have been done in Greek.

Greek and the Beginnings of the Concept of Biblical Inspiration

The table of references at the end of the twenty-eighth edition of the Nestle-Aland Greek New Testament lists some twenty-eight hundred references to various Jewish scriptural traditions that are either quoted or alluded to in the New Testament. The same table lists only eleven allusions to Greco-Roman sources. Jewish tradition, especially as transmitted via the Septuagint, was the overwhelming source and authority for the Christian scriptural tradition. The Old Testament was regarded as the progenitor of the Christian tradition. Indeed, early Christians coined a new word, *theopneustos*—meaning "God breathed" or "God inspired" (2 Tim. 3:16)—to characterize the Old Testament, including its Greek translation in the Septuagint.[38] *Theopneustos* derives from the imagery of Genesis 2:7, where God fashions the first human being from the dust of the earth and, through divine inbreathing, inspires a "living being." The early church regarded the Septuagint as a literary analogy of Genesis 2:7: God's breath vivified written words into living words. The Apostolic Fathers retained the veneration of 2 Timothy 3:16 for the Old Testament. First Clement directs its readers to "the Sacred Scriptures, which are true, which were given through the Holy Spirit."[39] Clement refers to such Scriptures as *hieras graphas*, "Sacred Scriptures," rather than *theopneustos*; but both terms are highly reverent descriptions of the Septuagint. The church expressly identified itself as the heir of the history and promises of Israel.

The Septuagint became a wedge that separated mainstream Christianity both from Judaism and from marginal, heterodox Christian movements. The Christians' widespread embrace of the Septuagint caused Jews to reject it and produce *three* new Greek translations of the Hebrew Scriptures in the second century to replace it.[40] Heterodox Christian movements also rejected

37. For a discussion of factors favoring the spread of Christianity in the early centuries, see ch. 2.

38. Eusebius, *Hist. eccl.* 5.8.10, for example, refers expressly to "the Scriptures of the Seventy [the Septuagint]" as "inspired" (Gk. *theopneustos*).

39. 1 Clem. 45.2.

40. The new translations that Jews deemed more compatible with their interests were those of Aquila (a disciple of Rabbi Akiba), Theodotion, and Symmachus. According to Rahlfs, "History of the Septuagint Text," xxiv, the translation of Aquila was so wooden that "it perpetrated the most appalling outrages to the whole of the Greek language." Hengel quotes Heinz Schreckenberg, who, in *Die christliche Adversus-Judaeos-Texte und ihr literarisches und historisches Umfeld* (Peter Lang: Frankfurt/Berlin, 1982), 399, writes, "The Christian reception

the Septuagint—indeed, the Old Testament itself. In the mid-second century, Marcion, a bishop of Rome, caricatured the God of the Old Testament as an inferior, vengeful God who was not the God and Father of Jesus Christ. The majority church did not follow Marcion; indeed, had it followed him, Christianity would have severed itself from the story of Israel and reduced the faith to an ahistorical idea. Marcion's radical challenge almost certainly stimulated the second-century church to begin defining its canon of Scriptures to include both Old and New Testaments.[41]

The concept of a list of writings considered sacred—a "canon" (Gk. *kanōn*, "rule" or "standard")—was common to Judaism as well as to numerous Greco-Roman cults.[42] It was wholly anticipated that the church would transfer the concept of *theopneustos*, "inspiration," to its own writings that celebrated Jesus Christ as the divine fulfillment of Old Testament prophecy. Papias's use of *theopneustos* with reference to the book of Revelation may be the first instance of its use for a document destined to be included in the New Testament.[43] The concept of inspiration and the term *theopneustos*

---

of the Septuagint and its use as an anti-Jewish apologetic weapon alienated it from the Jews themselves. . . . Judaism [withdrew] . . . both theologically and religiously into its own Hebrew linguistic sphere, and Christianity took possession of both the tradition and intellectual property of the Greek Bible" (Hengel, "Septuagint as a Collection," 68).

41. Unfortunately, the rejection of Marcionism in the second and following centuries did not eradicate malignancy toward Judaism from the bloodstream of the church. The second-century resistance to Marcion must be reclaimed in each age of the church. A troubling quotation of Adolf Harnack indicates a jaundiced prejudice against Judaism from one of the church's great scholars: "To have rejected the Old Testament in the second century was a mistake that the main body of the church was correct in avoiding; to retain it in the sixteenth century was a historical fact that the Reformation was not yet in a position to escape; but to go on conserving it within Protestantism as a canonical authority after the nineteenth century is the consequence of a paralysis of religion and church" (quoted in Pelikan, *Melody of Theology*, 113). The German Christian movement of the Third Reich and many so-called alt-right political movements in the West today are reminders of the ongoing challenge of Marcionism to the church.

42. Josephus, *Ag. Ap.* 1.42–43, testifies to the Jewish veneration of Scripture: "We have given practical proof of our reverence for our own Scriptures. For, although such long ages have now passed, no one has ventured either to add or to remove, or to alter a syllable; and it is an instinct with every Jew, from the day of his birth, to regard them as the decrees of God, to abide by them, and, if need be, cheerfully to die for them. Time and again before now the sight has been witnessed of prisoners enduring tortures and death in every form in the theatres, rather than utter a single word against the laws and the allied documents" (LCL). On the concept of inspiration throughout antiquity, Grant, *Roman Hellenism*, 130–31, writes, "The Christian conception of the inspiration of the New Testament writings resulted not only from a transfer or extension of Jewish veneration for the Hebrew Scriptures (and also for additional books belonging to various sects, e.g., those of the group at Qumran or the Essenes described by Josephus or the Therapeutae described by Philo); but it also resulted in some measure from the influence of contemporary pagan veneration for canons of religious or philosophical works."

43. Pap. *Frag.* 10.

proliferated widely in the church.[44] The first-century church did not develop a formal doctrine of inspiration, however. For at least a century after the death of Jesus, the church was content to assert *that* the Scriptures were inspired without attempting to explain *how* they were inspired. Most historians of doctrine agree that the beginnings of an actual doctrine of Scripture began with Justin Martyr in the mid-second century.[45]

Lack of a formal doctrine of inspiration, however, did not mean that first-century Christians failed to regard the Gospels and the Epistles of Paul, for example, as unique and authoritative witnesses to the faith. Already in the earliest New Testament documents, we see hints that the kerygma, as the summary outline of divine revelation in Jesus Christ, was imputed with divine authority. Paul's statement that "the righteousness by faith speaks thus" (Rom. 10:6) implies that *God* speaks through righteousness by faith. More plainly, in declaring that "Scripture foresaw that God would justify gentiles by faith" (Gal. 3:8) or that "Scripture imprisoned all things under sin" (Gal. 3:22), Paul uses "Scripture" as a circumlocution for God. Indeed, in Romans 11:32, Paul repeats the last passage nearly verbatim with "God" substituted for "Scripture." The clearest example of the interchangeability of God and Scripture in the New Testament is Romans 9:17: "For the Scripture says to Pharaoh, 'I raised you up for the express purpose of demonstrating my power in you, so that my name might be declared in all the earth.'" The quotation comes from Exodus 9:16 (LXX); but in Exodus, "God" rather than "Scripture" speaks to Pharaoh through Moses. In such passages, the apostle interchanges God and Scripture, imputing divine provenance and authority to Scripture.

The early church saw Jesus Christ as the fulfillment of the promises, types, prophecies, and purposes of God's first covenant with Israel. Early Christianity witnesses to this conviction in many and various ways. Quoting Paul, Luke diagnoses the old covenant with an inability that can be overcome only in the gospel of Jesus Christ: "Let it be known to you, my kinsmen, that through [Jesus] pardon from sins is proclaimed to you, and from everything from which you could not be justified by the law of Moses" (Acts 13:38). The Fourth Gospel testifies that Jesus fulfilled the purposes of the temple—indeed, that he replaced the temple (John 2:19–22). The apostle Paul addresses the same dynamic in terms of law rather than temple. The gospel proclaims salvation apart from law (Rom. 8:2), a salvation that fulfills the law (Rom. 8:4). Defining the relation of old and new covenants in typological terms,

44. See the full column of patristic references to the term in *PGL* 630.
45. So von Campenhausen, *Entstehung der christlichen Bibel*, 106; Hengel, "Septuagint as a Collection," 50.

Paul describes the law of Moses as a "ministry of death" and the gospel as a "ministry of the Spirit" and "of righteousness," and hence of God's glory (2 Cor. 3:7–9). Above all, Jesus Christ is the actualization of the new covenant anticipated in Jeremiah 31:31–34; indeed, adds Paul, the old covenant was a veil obscuring the understanding of those who knew it alone, a veil that could be removed only by the new covenant in Christ. But Paul is equally capable of abandoning types and images and declaring with simple finality, "All the promises of God are fulfilled in Jesus" (2 Cor. 1:20).

The Apostolic Fathers also advance the belief of the christological fulfillment of the Old Testament. First Clement 16 interprets each strophe of Isaiah 53 with reference to its fulfillment in Jesus Christ. Ignatius understands the Old Testament prophets to be guided not by Judaism but by the light of Christ that had not yet appeared: "The most-godly prophets lived in accordance with Christ Jesus. This is why they were persecuted, being inspired as they were by his grace in order that those who are disobedient might be fully convinced that there is one God who revealed himself through Jesus Christ his Son, who is his Word."[46]

Some of Ignatius's parishoners argued that the revelation of God in the Old Testament—"the archives" of God, as they referred to it—was superior to the new Christian writings; indeed, they refused to believe anything in the new apostolic writings that was not attested in the "archives." Ignatius reverses and corrects these opinions, asserting that the ultimate "archives" are the gospel rather than the Old Testament. "For me," he declares, "the 'archives' are Jesus Christ, the unalterable archives are his cross and death and his resurrection and the faith that comes through him."[47] Ignatius thus tectonically shifts the center of inspiration and authority from the Septuagint to its fulfillment in the kerygma of Jesus Christ. Diognetus, the most lyrical of the Apostolic Fathers, extends the Christ event to cosmic proportions: "For God loved humanity, on whose account he made the world, to whom he subjected all things on earth, to whom he gave reason, to whom he gave intelligence, to whom alone he permitted a vision of heaven, whom he created in his own image, to whom he sent his Only-Begotten Son, to whom he promised the kingdom in heaven, which he will give to those who have loved him."[48]

For Jews, the Torah is the font of divine revelation, and thus the font of subsequent Jewish tradition. So fundamental is the Torah that the term frequently denotes the entirety of the Jewish Scriptures. A tally of the citations

---

46. Ign. *Magn.* 8.2.
47. Ign. *Phld.* 8.2. See the discussion in Lightfoot, *Apostolic Fathers*, 2:269–73.
48. Diogn. 10.2.

of the Septuagint in the New Testament reveals, interestingly, that Christian writers did not locate the God-breathed epicenter of Scripture in the Torah (i.e., in the five books traditionally ascribed to Moses). The Psalms are cited more frequently in the New Testament than are any other Old Testament book, and citations of the prophets exceed those of the Pentateuch. For the church, the defining core of the Old Testament was no longer law but prophecy, particularly as fulfilled in Jesus Christ.[49] We saw Ignatius's testimony to prophetic inspiration above. When Paul declares that "the promise to Abraham and his offspring that he would be the heir of the world did not come through the law but through righteousness by faith" (Rom. 4:13), he shifts the saving significance of divine revelation in the Old Testament from law to God's promises and their fulfillment in Jesus Christ.

Conclusion

Let us conclude by briefly reviewing the seminal factors that cut the scion of the first-century Jesus movement from its Semitic stock and grafted it onto a Greek stock. The overriding factor was the gentile mission, which ipso facto required Syriac in the East and Greek in the West. As the common tongue of the first-century Roman Empire and the primary medium of Hellenistic culture itself, Greek became the receptor language of the Hebrew Old Testament in the third and second centuries BC and, in the West, the *sole* language of Christian mission, liturgy, and literature in the first century and the majority of the second century. This, along with the unusual paucity of Greek literature in the first century, opened an opportune door for Greek Christian literature.

Greek irrevocably shaped and defined Christianity. It provided a new word and concept of inspiration, *theopneustos*, "God-breathed." The Septuagint assumed a singular and formative role in the early church; and the church's embrace of the Septuagint provoked the synagogue to shun it. The Septuagint may also have enabled the early church to retain the Old Testament in its canon rather than reject it, as did the radical Marcionites.[50] Finally, so constitutive was the gentile mission of early Christianity that it mandated both a Greek

49. See Hengel, *Septuagint as Christian Scripture*, 110–11.
50. Some Septuagintal renderings—such as the offering of "bread and wine" to Abraham by Melchizedek (Gen. 14:18), which seemed to foreshadow the Eucharist, and the reference to the young woman of Isa. 7:14 as a "virgin" whose offspring would be called "Immanuel"— enhanced the proleptic value of the Septuagint for Christians. See Hengel, *Septuagint as Christian Scripture*, 41, who suggests that the Septuagint permitted the early church to retain the Old Testament rather than jettison it, as Marcion did in the second century.

medium and a new hermeneutic of the Old Testament. The nucleus of the Old Testament was no longer law, as in Judaism, but prophecy, the fulfillment of the promises and purposes of God in Jesus Christ, who was the Savior not only of Israel but of the *world*. The commission of the church to take the gospel into all the world could be fulfilled only by embracing Greek.

5

From Jesus Movement
to Gentile Mission

Siblings Who Viewed Their Parents Differently

Jesus was a Jew. His family line could be traced back to Abraham (Matt. 1:1–16) or even Adam (Luke 3:23–38). He was circumcised on the eighth day (Luke 2:21), and he regularly attended synagogues in Galilee (Luke 4:16) and festivals in the temple in Jerusalem (Luke 2:41–42; John 5:1).[1] Fellow Jews considered him an authorized rabbi (John 3:2); he recited the Shema (Mark 12:28–30); and, in general, he was Torah-observant (Matt. 5:17–18). Rarely did he travel outside the bounds of Jewish Palestine.[2]

---

1. The ministry of Jesus should be dated to the late 20s. This time period accords with two fixed dates in the New Testament. One is the setting of Jesus's early ministry in the forty-sixth year of the construction of Herod's temple (John 2:20). According to Josephus (*Ant.* 15.380), Herod began building the temple in the eighteenth year of his reign. Herod's reign began in 38 BC, which would date the start of temple construction to 20/19 BC (see the discussion in Schürer, *History of the Jewish People*, 1:292n12), and thus the commencement of Jesus's ministry would have been forty-six years later, in AD 27/28. A second fixed date is found in the reference to the fifteenth year of the reign of Tiberius (Luke 3:1). Tiberius became emperor at the death of Augustus, in the year 14, and fifteen years later (any part of a year was usually counted as a full year) sets the commencement of Jesus's ministry again to the year 28. On the dating in Luke 3:1, see Edwards, *Gospel according to Luke*, 103.

2. Challenges to Jesus's Jewishness are rare and unsuccessful. The most desperate (and infamous) attempt to deny the Jewishness of Jesus was made by the Nazi Institute for Research and Removal of Jewish Influence in German Ecclesiastical Life during the Third Reich, in which Professor Walter Grundmann argued that Jesus was not a Jew because his father was not Joseph but, rather, a Roman soldier named Pandera (or Panthera), a paramour of his mother, Mary. This malicious

His apostles were equally Jewish (Matt. 10:1–4). They participated with him in the above endeavors and made the temple in Jerusalem the epicenter of their ministry as they awaited the fulfillment of the kingdom of God after his death (Acts 1:6). They also carefully observed ritual cleanliness, refraining from unclean foods (Acts 10:14) and from unclean persons, such as a Samaritan woman (John 4:27) or a Syrophoenician woman (Mark 7:24–30).

In these respects, Jesus and his followers stood in accord with other rabbis and their followers in Jewish Palestine. But this is not the sum of the matter. Jesus focused on Jews, but gentiles were present in his peripheral vision. In the same chapter that Jesus identifies his mission with "the lost . . . house of Israel" (Matt. 10:5–6), he declares that his disciples will bear witness to the gentiles (10:17–18). Jesus taught that salvation was *from* the Jews (John 4:22), but his ministry extended beyond them. He occasionally ventured to gentile regions east of the Sea of Galilee—and not simply because such regions were unavoidable. On one occasion, Jesus and his disciples crossed the lake to the Decapolis, where he exorcized a formidable demoniac and then sent him to proclaim in the Decapolis "all that the Lord has done for you and been merciful to you" (Mark 5:19). He later undertook a longer journey to gentile Tyre, where he healed the daughter of a Greek Syrophoenician woman. From Tyre, he traveled farther north, to gentile Sidon, after which he returned to the Decapolis, where he healed a deaf man of a speech impediment and fed four thousand gentiles in an open-air feast that resembled his earlier feeding of five thousand Jews. In Luke 4:25–27, a Syrophoenician woman and a Syrian leper—both of whom stood outside a traditional understanding of Israel's mission—are declared to be within the *missio Dei* as represented by Jesus. When Jesus speaks of people coming from east and west, and north and south, to recline in the kingdom of God, he is referring to *gentiles* (Luke 13:29). Such endeavors and teachings were atypical of Jewish rabbis; indeed, there is no precedent of other rabbis undertaking similar missions in gentile regions.

What accounts for this anomaly in the ministry of a Jewish rabbi? These gentile initiatives may have been anomalous, but they were not baseless. The Gospels hint that they were motivated by the same factor that motivated Jesus's ministry as a whole: the fulfillment of the divine plan as announced in the Jewish Scriptures. The Gospel of Mark tells of Jesus healing a man in the Decapolis of a speech impediment, which it describes as a "*mogilalon*" (Mark 7:32). The only other occurrence of this word in Scripture is in Isaiah

---

rumor circulated as early as the third century (Str-B 1:39; Origen, *Cels.* 1.32, 69) and was later promoted in a medieval pseudo-history of Jesus called the *Toledot Yeshu* (see Schlichting, *Leben Jesu*, esp. 53–83). For Grundmann's role in propagating this scurrilous fiction in Nazi Germany, see Hertel and Martin-Luther-Gymnasium, *Gratwanderungen—Das "Entjudungsinstitut" in Eisenach*.

35:5–6, where the "eyes of the blind will be opened and the ears of the deaf unstopped, . . . and the tongue of the dumb [*mogilalōn*] will shout for joy," thus revealing God's glory to the *nations* (i.e., gentiles). This prophecy of Isaiah 35 is addressed to Lebanon, the same region to which Jesus journeys in Mark 7–8. The Gospel of Mark understands Jesus's mission to Tyre, Sidon, and the Decapolis as fulfilling the promise that Lebanon would "see the glory of the LORD, the splendor of our God" (Isa. 35:2).

The ministry of Jesus was consistent with several threads from the Old Testament that understood Israel's vocation as being not that of a dam, collecting and retaining the divine abundance for itself, but that of a conduit—conveying God's saving initiatives to all nations. The book of Isaiah culminates with the prophecy that "all flesh" will worship Israel's God (66:17–23). Second Chronicles records Solomon praying that God would hear the supplication of gentiles in the temple (6:32–33). Isaiah's enigmatic servant of the Lord would fulfill his divine commission by becoming "a light for the nations, that [God's] salvation may reach the end of the earth."[3] All three Synoptics cite the servant of the Lord as a prototype of Jesus's ministry.[4] The servant is not an *exception* to God's purpose in Israel but a *culmination* of it. A gentile mission is further assumed in God's commission of Jonah to preach in Nineveh, a commission that Jesus cites with reference to his own ministry.[5] Above all, the foundational declaration of the gentile mission occurs in God's promise to Abraham: "All peoples on earth will be blessed by you" (Gen. 12:3).[6] In his sermon in the Jerusalem temple, the apostle Peter proclaims that the resurrection of Jesus fulfills God's covenant, that "in [Abraham's] seed, all peoples of the earth shall be blessed" (Acts 3:25–26). The declaration of the apostle Paul that in Christ there is "neither Jew nor Greek, neither slave nor free, neither male and female" is likewise predicated

3. Isa. 49:6; see also 42:6; 51:4; 60:3.

4. Matthew interprets Jesus's open-air ministry among the crowds with reference to the servant (Matt. 12:18–20 // Isa. 42:1–4). In Mark 3:27, the emancipating servant (Isa. 49:24–26) is the model of Jesus's powerful parable of liberation. Throughout the Second Gospel, in fact, the premier title for Jesus, Son of God, seems to be interpreted in terms of Isaiah's humble servant of the Lord. See Edwards, "Servant of the Lord," 49–63. According to the Third Gospel, righteous Simeon waits in the temple for the Messiah, "the light of revelation to the gentiles" (Luke 2:32). And Luke identifies the programmatic characteristics of Jesus's ministry with those of Isaiah's servant of the Lord—the proclamation of good news to the poor, captives, and prisoners (Luke 4:18–19; Isa. 61:1).

5. Matt. 12:41 // Luke 11:32. For more on Jesus and the gentile mission, see Evans, *From Jesus to the Church*, 49–57.

6. On the concept and possibility of a gentile mission in Judaism, see Dunn, "From the Crucifixion," 34–36. Dunn acknowledges a precedent for Paul's gentile mission in the Old Testament, although he admits that the promise to Abraham was "much more neglected" in Judaism.

on "the seed of Abraham" (Gal. 3:28–29). Eusebius cites Genesis 12:3 as the divine precedent for Jesus's ministry. Christianity is not a departure from the Old Testament witness to God, he maintains, but its fulfillment, for "only among Christians throughout the whole world is the manner of religion taught to Abraham found in practice."[7] The promise of God to Abraham in Genesis 12 runs like an artery through the Old Testament Prophets and into early Christianity.

Jesus's commission of the Twelve to be his witnesses "to the end of the earth" (Acts 1:8) transmitted the promise of Abraham to the early church. Jesus did not tell the Twelve, however, how the commission would be fulfilled. That would require the unfolding of subsequent events. An all-important first step in its fulfillment was taken by the Hellenists of Acts 6.[8] All seven deacons appointed from the Hellenist community in Jerusalem have Greek names (Acts 6:5). The early Jerusalem leaders prudently decided that problems arising from the Greek-speaking community could best be resolved by members of the same community. Hellenists already incorporated elements of Greek culture into their synagogues, thus preparing their members, Stephen and Philip in particular, to spread the gospel among "the dispersed" Jews in Samaria (Acts 8:4–25), Phoenicia, and Cyprus—and then, finally, to gentiles in Antioch (Acts 11:19–21). The gentile mission of the church drew on the same Old Testament precedents that informed Jesus's ministry. In chapter 3 we traced the early spread of the gospel to Mesopotamia, for which there was precedent in God's compassion for Nineveh (Jon. 3–4). The vast eastward expansion of the gospel echoed the witness of Esther in the kingdom of Xerxes, which included not only Media and Persia but also India, farther east, and Nubia, farther south (Esther 1:1).

The gentile mission is properly understood not as an alien or contrary innovation of early Christianity but as a development in character with the Old Testament itself, one that was exhibited by Jesus and fulfilled by his followers. The apostle Paul, the apostle to the gentiles (Gal. 2:9), was not a gentile but a zealous Jew who considered his call an affirmation (rather than a denial) of Israel's call. "All the promises of God are fulfilled in Jesus," he declares.[9] In the book of Acts, according to Seán Freyne, Luke intends "to show the beginnings of the mission to the Gentiles as being the work of Greek-speaking Jews who were Jesus-followers from Jerusalem."[10] The proclamation of the gospel to both Jews and gentiles—without obliging the latter to adopt the

---

7. Eusebius, *Hist. eccl.* 1.4.12–15 (LCL).
8. On Hellenists, see ch. 2, pp. 21–23.
9. 2 Cor. 1:20; also Rom. 15:8.
10. Freyne, *Jesus Movement and Its Expansion*, 205–6.

norms of the former, such as circumcision and Sabbath and food regulations, in order to be considered bona fide Christians—was not the invention of the apostle Paul, as many suppose, but rather the extension of the gospel via Greek-speaking *Jewish* believers to Greek-speaking *gentiles*. And it is this that enabled the Christian faith to become a world faith.[11]

When early Christians such as the Hellenists or the apostles Paul and Peter embraced gentiles without qualification, they did something that no other Jews did; but in so doing, they did not cease to think of themselves as Jews. How did this happen? The answer lies chiefly in a different understanding of the same Scriptures that both Christian Jews and non-Christian Jews considered foundational. To think of this matter rightly, we need to jettison a common misunderstanding of Christianity as a child of Judaism. As I understand the texts and history related to this question, the parent-child analogy needs to be replaced by a sibling analogy. Christianity is not the child of Judaism but rather its sibling. Jesus followers stood in relation to other Jews like siblings in the same family who understood their common parentage differently.[12] Both siblings claimed their common parental tradition as it was transmitted to them via the history of Israel and the Old Testament Scriptures, yet they found within that one tradition precedents for the development of daughter traditions that differed fundamentally from one another.

Cohesion

Being so accustomed to the separation—and sometimes antagonism—of Christians and Jews, we tend to forget that they did not begin separately, nor did they intend to separate. The reasons and forces for Jews who believed in Jesus and Jews who did not believe in Jesus to cohere were, in fact, many and strong—including ethnic, linguistic, cultural, and religious bonds. Jesus operated self-consciously within the institutions of synagogue, Sabbath, Torah, and temple. And he never instructed his followers to operate otherwise. He did not instruct them to form a church. After his ascension, Jesus's followers in Jerusalem immediately identified—at least for a time—with the same structures that he did. The earliest Jesus followers would not have identified themselves as anything other than Jewish, for wherever one was born or raised, "loyalty

11. More fully on this final point, see Hengel, *Paulus und Jakobus*, 1–58; or, for an English translation, see Hengel, *Between Jesus and Paul*, 1–29.
12. The sibling metaphor is not original with me. One of its early exponents was Alan F. Segal, with his 1986 book *Rebecca's Children*. Later exponents include Michael Holmes (*Apostolic Fathers*, 9) and Joan Taylor, who speaks of the parting of Judaism and Christianity in terms of a "family feud" ("Parting in Palestine," 99).

to the temple and acceptance of the customs, rituals, and practices associated with this worship were the primary criteria for being named a *Ioudaios*."[13] Even as this elemental and cohesive force waned, a united tradition remained between Jews who followed Jesus and Jews who did not. The bond that united the various sects within Judaism should not be underestimated. First-century Jews—whether Pharisees, Sadducees, Essenes, Herodians, Zealots, simple *am ha-aretz* (people of the land), or Jesus followers—all identified themselves, despite their differences, as Jews. Indeed, Jesus followers were in closer theological agreement with Pharisees, for example, who played the dominant role in defining Judaism following the First Revolt, than were perhaps any of the other Jewish sects.

The individual who was probably most responsible for keeping early Jesus followers within the Jewish fold was James the brother of the Lord. Paul calls this James a "pillar" of the church in Jerusalem (Gal. 2:9). The tabernacle, like the temple after it, was supported by load-bearing pillars (Exod. 40:18). And the reference to James as a "pillar" indicates Paul's judgment of his importance, even if Paul did not always agree with him. Unlike for Hellenist Jews and even Peter (whose influence in early Jewish Christianity was second only to James), we have no indication that James ever left Jerusalem. He remained in the Holy City and sought to expand the new faith within Judaism as others extended it beyond Judaism. The ancient world was, with few exceptions, a world of autocratic rule. In all the various spheres of life—whether political, military, social, or religious—people looked to strong individuals for leadership. James emerged at the Council of Jerusalem as such a leader for Jewish Jesus followers. His qualifications were unique among all the early Christians: he was the blood brother of Jesus, who appeared to him after his resurrection (1 Cor. 15:7), and his uncompromising piety, diet, clothing, and manner of life granted to him alone of all Jesus followers the privilege "to enter into the [Jewish] sanctuary."[14] James was apparently held in esteem even by *non-Christian* Jewish sects and "obeyed by them all."[15] No other Jewish leader, not even Peter, was so endowed to lead the early church within the context of Judaism.[16] After his death, James was esteemed by various Jewish-Christian

---

13. Freyne, *Jesus Movement and Its Expansion*, 16.
14. Eusebius, *Hist. eccl.* 2.23.6.
15. Eusebius, *Hist. eccl.* 2.23.8–11.
16. Von Campenhausen, in *Aus der Frühzeit*, 135–36, strongly opposes both Harnack's judgment, that James's Jewish-Christian synthesis resembled a "caliphate," and Eduard Meyer's judgment, that James's vision for the church was analogous to Islam and Mormonism. "In reality," writes von Campenhausen, "we have no right to apply such ideological stereotypes either to early Christianity or to later Jewish-Christianity" (my trans.).

sects—including Ebionites, Nazarenes, Syrian Christians, some Gnostic groups, and especially the community associated with the Hebrew Gospel. The issue for James was not whether the church should expand to include gentiles. His decision at the Council of Jerusalem, which he based on Amos 9:11–12 (LXX), clearly endorsed the inclusion of gentiles (Acts 15:13–29). The citation of Amos 9:11–12 is important, for it again shows that early Jesus followers justified their mission on the precedent of the Old Testament. The issue for James, rather, was whether the church needed to leave the fold of Judaism—or worse, turn against it—in order to achieve the goal of gentile inclusion. James lived in the conviction that the church could be true to God's promises to Israel while remaining within the structures of Israel. He also died for that conviction. According to Eusebius, his confession of "Jesus Christ as the Son of God" before all the people led to his martyrdom at the temple of Jerusalem.[17] Peter Stuhlmacher summarizes the influence of James on early Christianity thus: "During his entire life, James tried to keep Jewish and gentile Christians together, and in this sense he functioned as the head of the original Jerusalem community as the mother community of all Christians."[18]

The book of Acts intimates that even when Hellenist (Greek-speaking) Jesus followers were driven from Jerusalem following Saul's persecution (8:1), Hebrew Jesus followers continued to be tolerated there by traditional Jews, "for the church throughout all Judea and Galilee and Samaria enjoyed peace" (9:31). Assuming that Saul was converted to Christianity in the early 30s, this text implies that Jesus followers in Palestine coexisted in and with Jewish synagogues for a few years following Jesus's crucifixion.[19] This should not surprise us, for Judaism accommodated not only the various sects that we noted above but also another class of adherents, known as "Godfearers," who were altogether less Jewish than Jesus followers were. The book of Acts refers to this class of individuals variously as "Godfearers,"[20] "proselytes,"[21] and "God worshipers,"[22] all of which designate gentiles who were attracted to the monotheism, moral character, and perhaps ethnic cohesiveness of Judaism but who chose not to observe the Mosaic law with respect to food laws and

17. *Hist. eccl.* 2.23.2. Eusebius cites Josephus (*Ant.* 20.200–203), Clement, and Hegesippus as earlier witnesses to the martyrdom of the apostle James.

18. Stuhlmacher, "Christ in the Pauline School," 162. Important discussions of James can be found in von Campenhausen, *Aus der Frühzeit*, 25–33; Evans, *From Jesus to the Church*, 59–77; Dunn, *Neither Jew nor Greek*, 509–97; Dunn, "Beyond the Jewish People."

19. See the discussion in Harnack, *Mission and Expansion*, 45–46.

20. Acts 10:2, 22, 35; 13:16, 26.

21. Acts 2:11; 13:43.

22. Acts 13:43, 50; 16:14; 17:4, 12 (perhaps), 17; 18:7.

the requirement of male circumcision.[23] These caveats relegated Godfearers to "associate" status in Judaism—second-class status, in reality—as evidenced by their invariable placement second to ethnic Jews in ancient written sources.

Subordinate though they were, Godfearers were often present in great numbers in ancient synagogues.[24] The earliest archaeological evidence for Godfearers comes from a nine-foot marble doorjamb of the synagogue in Aphrodisias (modern western Turkey). Two faces of the pillar are inscribed in Greek with the names of 120 donors to the synagogue. Sixty-nine of the names are Jewish, three belong to proselytes (i.e., gentiles who cut ties with their families, were circumcised, and called themselves "sons of Abraham"), and fifty-four belong to Godfearers. That nearly half the names on the pillar are those of Godfearers and proselytes attests to the attraction of the Jewish synagogue for gentiles. The attraction may have been particularly strong at Aphrodisias, where Greco-Roman religion and myth were promoted extravagantly. Inscriptions related to the emperor cult abound in Aphrodisias, as do marble statues of gods and goddesses, especially Aphrodite, for whom the city was named. As the goddess of fertility, fornication, and fun, Aphrodite was a popular deity for such a city. The monotheism and morality of Judaism must have been especially appealing for gentiles who were affronted by the display of eros and bloodlust in Aphrodisias. The placement of the names on the pillar is telling, however, for the names of Godfearers and proselytes, who are designated as "*theosebeis*," are inscribed on the lower half of the pillar, *below* Jewish names, as a visual reminder of their secondary status.[25] Lacking the distinctions of Jewish birth, circumcision, and perhaps various elements of Torah observance (such as keeping kosher), the *theosebeis* were shadow members of the synagogue.

The ubiquity of Godfearers and their second-class status in synagogues are crucial to understanding the appeal of Christianity for them: Christianity offered the monotheism and moral standards attractive to Godfearers, but it did not relegate gentiles to second-class status or require them to observe circumcision and food laws.[26] The conversion of the Roman centurion Cornelius

23. Danker, BDAG 918, defines "Godfearers" as "former polytheists who accepted the ethical monotheism of Israel and attended the synagogue, but who did not obligate themselves to keep the whole Mosaic law; in particular, the males did not submit to circumcision."

24. Josephus, *Ant.* 14.110, informs readers that both Jews and Godfearers were spread throughout the Roman world. For studies on Godfearers, see Wander, *Gottesfürchtige und Sympathisanten*; Edwards, "*Nomen Sacrum* in the Sardis Synagogue," 816; Chilton, "Godfearers."

25. On Aphrodisias, see Charlotte Rouche, "Aphrodisias," *EEECAA* 1:85–86; Reynolds and Tannenbaum, *Jews and Godfearers at Aphrodisias*; Chilton, "Godfearers."

26. See here Stark, *Rise of Christianity*, 59.

(Acts 10:1–11:18) is a classic example of a gentile whose status as a Godfearer became the first step in his acceptance of Christian faith (Acts 15:6–11).

What was particularly remarkable in the Pauline mission was that ethnicity—being Jewish or Greek—was no longer primary, as it was in both Judaism and the Roman Empire, but subordinated to an ultimate and abiding unity in Christ.[27] In Paul's famous dictum, "there is neither Jew nor Greek, neither slave nor free, neither male and female, *for you all are one in Christ Jesus*" (Gal. 3:28). The new order in Christ elicits new terminology from Paul. Standard categories such as nation (*ethnos*), race (*genos*), and people (*laos*)—which were central to the social and political thought of the ancient world—are relativized and supplanted by "brothers and sisters," "assemblies," "holy ones," "believers," "the spiritual," and corresponding metaphors of family (Eph. 3:14–19), body (1 Cor. 12:12–27; Rom. 12:4–5), spatial metaphors (Eph. 2:11–18), and citizenship (Phil. 3:20).[28]

This renaming upended the prevailing social and religious categories. When Jews within Christian communities eschewed idolatry, for example, they were not persecuted by non-Christian Jews; they were affirmed for adhering to Torah. When gentiles became Christians and eschewed idolatry, however, they were considered by non-Christian gentiles as "atheists" (i.e., deniers of Greco-Roman deities). Paul's counsel in this instance addresses both groups with a new reality, for Jewish Christians (who passed the test of idolatry with regard to Torah) needed to know that the ultimate test of idolatry concerns the lordship of Jesus Christ. "For us there is one God," he decrees, "who is the Father from whom all things come, and for whom we ourselves exist; and one Lord Jesus Christ, through whom all things come, and through whom we exist" (1 Cor. 8:6). Paul addresses other divisive issues such as sexual morality, Sabbath observance, circumcision, marriage, and food rules similarly. His theological compass in such matters is oriented to what might be called christological pragmatism—that is, judging behaviors according to their conformity with Christ and their effect in the community of Christ. The "early Christian movement was . . . constitutionally disinclined to define itself in culturally specific ways," writes John Barclay; rather, it judged ideas, worship styles, and behaviors by christological norms (Col. 3:17).[29] In stating that "Christians dwell in the world, but are not of the world,"[30] the Epistle to Diognetus alludes to the paradox of Christianity: unlike the Roman Empire

27. Among the many relevant texts here, see 1 Cor. 1:22–24; 9:20–21; 10:32; Gal. 2:11–21; 3:28.

28. See Barclay, *Pauline Churches*, 13–14.

29. See Barclay, *Pauline Churches*, 15–25 (quotation from p. 19).

30. Diogn. 6.3.

(which annexed and absorbed the cultures around it) and unlike Judaism (which segregated itself from the cultures around it), Christians, whether Jews or gentiles, sought to be conformed to the image of Jesus Christ (Gal. 4:19).

Pushback from Judaism

Following the First Revolt,[31] rabbinic leaders migrated north to form academies in Galilee for the purpose of reconstituting Judaism. The rabbinic program employed a new rhetoric to label and ostracize groups that were deemed nonconformist or heretical. One class of individuals was called the *"minim"* (heretics). The *minim* are described as "wicked," "slanderers," and "enemies"—as are similar classes of individuals in the Dead Sea Scrolls. The *minim* are never specifically identified as "Christians," however, and it is unclear to what extent Christians were the intended objects of this imprecation.[32]

An unambiguous denunciation of Christians, however, appears in the word *aposynagōgos* (expelled from the synagogue), which occurs with reference to Jesus followers only in the Gospel of John.[33] These are the only occurrences of *aposynagōgos* in all Greek literature, and its use in the Gospel of John in the late first century, with specific reference to confessing Jesus as Messiah (John 9:22; 12:42), heightens the probability of its reference to Christians.[34]

---

31. On the First Jewish Revolt, see ch. 6, pp. 103–6.

32. The *Birkat ha-Minim* (benediction concerning heretics) was the twelfth of the Eighteen Benedictions of the Amidah (a Jewish prayer recited while standing). These benedictions were customarily recited at the conclusion of Jewish worship services in Second Temple Judaism. The twelfth benediction, the *Birkat ha-Minim*, invokes God's wrath on "slanderers," "wickedness," "Thine enemies," and "the kingdom of arrogance." These imprecations are often assumed to refer to Christians, but the evildoers are nowhere specifically identified as Jesus followers or Christians. The specific relevance of the *Birkat ha-Minim* for Jewish attitudes toward early Christians is debatable, because the Eighteen Benedictions, as they are incorporated into the Talmud (5th c.), represent a much later period than the one we are concerned with in this book. More relevant for our purposes are the nine brief passages in the Mishnah (late 2nd c.) that refer to *minim* (Ber. 9:5; Rosh Hash. 2:1; Meg. 4:8; 4:9; Sotah 9:15; Sanh. 4:5; Hul. 2:9; Parah 3:3; Yad. 4:8). Only one passage in the Tosefta, which contains supplemental material of approximately the same dates as the Mishnah, refers to the *minim* (Ber. 3:25). The texts in the Mishnah and Tosefta do not refer to Christians either. The only two groups that can be identified as proscribed in them are the Sadducees and those who collaborated with the enemy (i.e., Rome). With regard to a specific imprecation of Christians in the Mishnah, Shaye Cohen gives this clarification: "[Christians] are invisible in the Mishnah. The Mishnah's *minim* are not Christians. . . . The editors of the Mishnah have little interest in *minim*, no interest in heresy, and no interest in Christians" ("In Between," 207–36).

33. *Aposynagōgos* occurs in John 9:22; 12:42; 16:2. Additionally, the Fourth Gospel portrays Jesus followers in ambiguous relationships with Jewish synagogues. In some instances, their faith in Jesus is impaired because of their allegiance to synagogues (8:31–59). In other instances, they find themselves at odds with synagogues (7:25–31; 10:31–42; 11:19, 45; 12:9–11, 37–43).

34. Wolfgang Schrage, *"aposynagōgos,"* *TWNT* 7:845–50.

In the mid-second century, Justin Martyr writes that Christians were regularly cursed in the synagogue and that Jesus was mocked and reviled as Son of God and King of Israel.[35] Whether such imprecations were employed in the first century, we cannot say for sure, but we know that Christian writings were cursed in the late first century. Christian writings, including the Gospels, were not difficult to identify because they were written in Greek rather than Hebrew and written in codices rather than on scrolls. Rabbis called them *gilyōnim* and targeted them for burning.[36] From a Jewish perspective, a Gospel written in Hebrew posed a particular danger because it purveyed content considered illicit by Jews in an otherwise trusted medium. The Hebrew Gospel, widely known and cited in the first Christian millennium but no longer extant, likely fell casualty to the ban on *gilyōnim*.[37] A text from the Babylonian Talmud, ostensibly dated to the late first century, condemns the "Gospel" (of Matthew?) as "sin pages."[38]

Not surprisingly, Jesus was an occasional target of anti-Christian polemic by Jewish rabbis. The two most common charges leveled against him were that he practiced magic and that he led Israel astray as a deceiver. Further references report that he called five disciples,[39] was an idolater,[40] and was misled by Balaam.[41] Precisely when these indictments arose is unclear, for the bodies of literature in which they are contained (the Mishnah, Tosefta, and Talmuds) were compiled over several centuries.[42] Whether any of the above testimonies circulated in the first century is not known.

The Jewish historian Shaye Cohen states that "Christian literature from c. 100 to 150 CE is uniformly hostile to Jews and Judaism."[43] Cohen further notes,

35. *Dial.* 16.4; 35.8; 46.4; 96.2; 97.4; 137.2.

36. The singular *gilyōn* (Hb. "parchment") may also have connoted "tablet" or "codex." See *HALOT* 1:193.

37. See *b.* Shabb. 116a–b.

38. Edwards, *Hebrew Gospel*, 228–33.

39. See *b.* Sanh. 43a.

40. See *b.* Sanh. 103a; Ber. 18a.

41. See *b.* Sanh. 90a. For a complete review of Jewish texts and testimonies that refer to Jesus, see Dalman, *Jesus Christ in the Talmud*. Philip Alexander also surveys the relevant Jewish material in "Parting of the Ways."

42. The Mishnah (Hb. "second [law]"), completed in about 200 by Rabbi Judah the Prince, is a written compilation of Jewish rabbinic teaching, arranged in sixty-three tractates that comprise six major divisions. The Mishnah is second in importance in Jewish life only to the Hebrew Scriptures. The Tosefta (Hb. "supplement") consists of longer supplements that parallel the Mishnah. The Talmud (Hb. "learning," "instruction") constitutes the summation of the Jewish rabbinic tradition, comprising the Mishnah and its supplements in the Tosefta and Gemara (Aramaic commentary on the Mishnah). The Palestinian (or Jerusalem) Talmud was completed in Tiberias in the fourth century, and the longer and more authoritative Babylonian Talmud was completed in Babylon in the fifth century. With the exception of the Gemara, the above bodies of literature are all written in Hebrew.

43. See Cohen, "In Between," 212.

however, that Jewish literature of the same era is much less antagonistic to Christianity; indeed, Christianity is by and large excluded from consideration and ignored in such literature. The Mishnah, produced around the year 200, when Christiantiy was developing independently of the synagogue, exemplifies this indifference.[44] By the early second century, Cohen concludes, synagogue and church had developed into fully distinct and separate bodies. "There were no mixed communities of Jews and Christians."[45] Other Jewish sources appear to echo this judgment. Josephus, the Jewish historian who wrote both his *Jewish War* and his *Antiquities of the Jews* at the end of the first century, devotes single paragraphs to Jesus, John the Baptist, and James (the leader of the church in Jerusalem), but nothing further with reference to "Christianity."[46] The fifth-century Babylonian Talmud, which was compiled after Christianity had become *religio licita* (legal religion) in the Roman Empire, contains only sparing references to Christianity and only six brief and dismissive references to Jesus.[47]

Roman writers were no better informed about Christianity than were Jewish writers. The three earliest Roman writers to mention Christianity label it a *superstitio*—something strange, foreign, and undeserving of serious consideration. Tacitus and Suetonius mention the new faith with reference to Nero's savage persecution of Christians in 64. Both writers condemn Nero's brutality, but Christianity itself remains a "mischievous superstition" to them.[48] Pliny the Younger, governor of Bithynia, likewise sums up Christianity as a "depraved and excessive superstition."[49] Tacitus, in particular, was responsibly informed about Judaism,[50] but neither he, nor Suetonius, nor Pliny were

44. On the Mishnah, see the quotation of Shaye Cohen at the end of note 32 above.

45. See Cohen, "In Between," 232–33: "The evidence surveyed here supports the view, once regnant among scholars but now unaccountably out of fashion, that by the early second century C.E. Jews (that is, ethnic Jews who did not believe in Christ) and Christians (that is, ethnic gentiles who did believe in Christ) constituted separated communities, each with its own identity, rituals, institutions, authority figures and literature. . . . The simplest explanation for this phenomenon is that after around 100 C.E. Christian communities were distinct from Jewish communities, not only the Hebrew-writing sages of Roman Palestina but also the Greek-writing Jewish communities of the Diaspora."

46. Josephus on Jesus (*Ant.* 18.63–64), John the Baptist (*Ant.* 18.116–19), and James (*Ant.* 20.200).

47. It claims that Jesus was born out of wedlock, his mother having been seduced by a paramour (*b.* Sanh. 107); that he learned magic in Egypt (*b.* Shabb. 12); that he called himself God (*b.* Ta'an. 65b); that he was tried by the Sanhedrin as a deceiver and teacher of apostasy (*b.* Sanh. 103a; Ber. 18); that he was executed on the eve of Passover (*b.* Sanh. 43a); and that he had five disciples (*b.* Sanh. 43a). See Dalman's *Jesus Christ in the Talmud*, and especially the introductory essay by Heinrich Laible.

48. Tacitus, *Ann.* 15:44; Suetonius, *Nero* 16.

49. Pliny, *Ep. Tra.* 10.96.

50. Tacitus, *Hist.* 5.1–13.

comparably informed about Christianity; indeed, they were content to dismiss it as a *superstitio*. For the first century of the existence of Christianity, and perhaps longer, both Jewish and Roman literatures were generally indifferent to Christianity.[51]

Enduring Influences of Judaism on Christianity

Even after Jesus followers separated from synagogues, the Jewish roots of the Christian faith continued to be positively perceived in Christian communities far removed from Palestine. To the gentile Corinthians, Paul argues for the authenticity of his apostleship on the basis of its "Hebrew" and "Israelite" character (2 Cor. 11:22). To believers in Philippi, he argues that his heritage and status as a Jew is grounds for "confidence in the flesh" (Phil. 3:4–6). Similarly, he repeatedly refers to Peter as a model for the church—in each instance using Peter's Hebrew name, "Cephas."[52] Texts later than Paul continue to attest to the same alliance between Christianity and Judaism. In chapter 3 we saw that the Odes of Solomon, written around the year 100, holds "high" Christian theology in harmony with traditional Jewish doctrines.[53] A second and later document, the Pseudo-Clementines, composed around the year 200, reflects a distinctly accommodating view of Jews and Christians to one another: "Thus, the Hebrews are not condemned because they did not know Jesus . . . provided only they act according to the instruction of Moses and do not injure him whom they did not know. And again, the offspring of the Gentiles are not judged, who . . . have not known Moses, provided only they act according to the words of Jesus and thus do not injure him whom they did not know."[54]

Even the Jerusalem temple seems to have played a more positive role in the early church than it did in the ministry of Jesus. As we noted earlier in this chapter, the early church initially identified with the temple, and James maintained his leadership of the church from the temple. Luke's omission of the word "church" from the first seven chapters and the last seven chapters of Acts, where the narratives are located in the temple, suggests his deference to the temple. Even after church and synagogue had effectively parted, the temple remained a positive metaphor for some aspects of Christianity. Paul identifies believers as living temples: "Do you not know that your body is a

---

51. On the ignorance of and indifference to Christianity in first-century Roman writers, see Wilken, *Christians as the Romans Saw Them*, 48–50.

52. See 1 Cor. 1:12; 3:22; 9:5; 15:5.

53. See ch. 3, pp. 57–58.

54. Ps.-Clem. *Hom.* 8.7.1–2, in *NTApoc* 2:525.

temple of the Holy Spirit living in you?" (1 Cor. 6:19). More comprehensively and surprisingly, in both Romans and 1 Peter, language that expressly reflects the temple and its liturgy is employed to describe the holiness and divine acceptability of the *gentile* mission of the church.[55] Both texts adopt temple imagery to signify that the salvation of gentiles is the rightful fulfillment of the salvation of Israel.

The Apostolic Fathers also employ the temple metaphor in their letters. First Clement admonishes readers to be as devout in their moral lives as is a priest in the temple.[56] They tell Jesus followers, "Guard your bodies as the temple of God,"[57] for "our heart . . . is a holy temple dedicated to the Lord."[58] "Let us therefore become a perfect temple for God."[59] The temple can symbolize the church as well as the individual believer. Ignatius exhorts the Ephesians, "that we may be God's temple and God may be in us."[60] The temple is an allegory of the church: "for you are stones of a temple, . . . hoisted up to the heights by the crane of Jesus Christ, which is the cross, using as a rope the Holy Spirit."[61] Therefore, Ignatius concludes, "Let all of you run together as to one temple of God, as to one altar, to one Jesus Christ."[62] Jesus Christ is the ultimate consummation of temple imagery—for as the temple was the place where humanity met God, in Jesus Christ God meets humanity.[63] Even the Epistle of Barnabas, among the most antagonistic of the Apostolic Fathers to Judaism, appeals to the spiritual significance of the temple for the church.[64]

After the separation of church and synagogue, the influence of Judaism on the church continued to be extolled by Eusebius, who attests that the first fifteen bishops of Jerusalem were "all Hebrews by origin," for "their whole church at that time consisted of Hebrews who had continued Christian from the Apostles down to the siege [of Hadrian]."[65] For Eusebius, the

---

55. Rom. 15:15–16; 1 Pet. 2:4–6.

56. 1 Clem. 40–41.

57. Ign. *Phld*. 7.2; 2 Clem. 9.3.

58. Barn. 6.15.

59. Barn. 4.11.

60. Ign. *Eph*. 15.3.

61. Ign. *Eph*. 9.1.

62. Ign. *Magn*. 7.2.

63. For a detailed account of temple terminology in early Christianity, see Wardle, "Pillars, Foundations, and Stones."

64. Barn. 16.

65. Eusebius, *Hist. eccl.* 4.5.1–2 (LCL). The siege to which Eusebius refers was Hadrian's destruction of Jerusalem during the Second Jewish Revolt (132–35), a critical turning point in Christianity's transition from being a predominantly Jewish movement to being one that was predominantly gentile. After Hadrian's destruction of Jerusalem, "the church, too, was composed of gentiles" (*Hist. eccl.* 4.6.4 [LCL]). On the Second Revolt, see ch. 6, pp. 111–13.

Second Jewish Revolt of 132–35 finally severed the bond between Judaism and Christianity, which until then remained at least theoretically intact.[66] Long after synagogue and church had said farewell, the late second-century Christian prophet Montanus named two villages in Phrygia "Jerusalem," by which he hoped to recover the charismatic immediacy of the Holy Spirit that he believed characterized the early church.[67] We thus witness a decided retention of Jewish imagery in early Christianity even after church and synagogue parted ways.

The "Parting of Ways" between Jews and Christians

Our post-Holocaust era has made Christians painfully aware that although Christian theology did not cause the Holocaust, a long history of negative and sometimes hateful profiling of Jews in Christianity abetted its acceptance.[68] The Holocaust delivered a moral ultimatum to both Jews and Christians—but especially to the latter—to rethink, reconsider, and reframe their relationship. In response to that ultimatum, Christians and Jews have begun revisiting the history leading up to the "parting of the ways" between them. Scholars have drawn attention to the fact that no one event or moment in history can be

66. For a review of the vitality of Judaism and its coexistence alongside Christians in Palestine until the Second Jewish Revolt of 132–35, see Taylor, "Parting in Palestine."

67. Eusebius, *Hist. eccl.* 5.18.1–2.

68. Pejorative references to Judaism in Christian scholarship cannot be limited to Adolf Harnack, but the influence of his *Mission and Expansion* has made his anti-Semitic views particularly deleterious. Harnack's opening line refers to Jewish synagogues as *fontes persecutionum*, "fonts of persecution," for Christian communities (1). Thenceforth the invective against Jews is relentless. The apostle Paul is portrayed as teaching that "the day of Israel . . . had now expired" and that "Jewish Christian churches that did not unite with the Gentile Christian churches . . . forfeited . . . their very right to existence" (56). Harnack portrays Jews in the book of Acts without exception as malicious opponents of Christians (57). Only when Christians left the Hebrew world and embraced "the greater freedom of the Greek spirit," he declares, did Christianity come of age, leaving Judaism behind as a "husk" (64). His final judgment abdicates rational scholarship for a racial tirade: "The Jewish people . . . were always in error, an error which shows that *they never were the chosen people*. The chosen people throughout was the Christian people" (66). The Old Testament was a Christian book, he maintained, with which Jews have nothing to do. "Every Christian must therefore deny them the possession of the Old Testament. It would be a sin for Christians to say, 'This book [the Old Testament] belongs to us and to the Jews.' No: *the book belonged from the outset as it belongs now and evermore, to none but Christians*, whilst Jews are the worst, the most godless and God-forsaken, of all nations upon earth, the devil's own people, Satan's synagogue, a fellowship of hypocrites" (66). Because of "their obstinacy and hostility to Christ," declares Harnack, in conclusion, "they [Jews] relieve Christians" from the responsibility of converting them (67). The above italics are Harnack's. Such anti-Jewish fulminations, not surprisingly, fueled the malignant "German Christian" movement that arose in Nazi Germany.

determined in which a categorical break between Jews and Christian actually occurred.[69] The absence of a definite point of cataclysm has caused some scholars to characterize the struggle between Jews who followed Jesus and Jews who did not as an intramural struggle from beginning to end. This has led some to conclude that Christianity has never ceased being an organic expression of Judaism and thus remains within its walls.

Eric Meyers seems to invoke this perspective for the early church in Galilee. On the basis of archaeology, he argues that in lower Galilee, Christians and Jews lived in close proximity without any perceptible borders between them, "apparently peacefully alongside one another" well into the Byzantine era.[70] Freyne considers the power struggles in embryonic Christianity as similarly intramural, and each faction in the various struggles as equally legitimate. "Deeply suspicious of . . . claims by the champions of orthodoxy,"[71] Freyne rejects a single Christian metanarrative. He rejects attempts by the early church to argue for a particular understanding of the gospel over against false understandings; indeed, he regards second-century attempts to promulgate "the rule of faith," or apostolic succession, or orthodoxy versus heresy, as theological and ecclesiastical bullying. The ultimate apologist for the intra-mural view is Daniel Boyarin, a Jewish scholar who regards Christianity the same way he regards the Enoch traditions, for example. Both Judaism and Christianity, he maintains, remained within "the province of Israel." "Once we fully take in that 'Christianity' is simply part and parcel of ancient Juda-ism, this very way of posing the issue [that Christianity parted ways with Judaism] becomes immaterial."[72] According to Boyarin, Jews and Christians never parted ways. Few scholars follow Boyarin to this final conclusion, but many, cognizant of the fact that neither Jews nor Christians can point to a specific time and place when they became "Jews" and "Christians," leave the question open.

The above options will strike most readers as inadequate, and the final one as seriously so. The fact that Christians and Jews coexisted peacefully in lower Galilee, as Meyers maintains, entails no assertion of their common identity. Freyne's judgment reveals his own theological pluralism, but it seems irrelevant with respect to how Jews and Christians regarded their ultimate

69. Many scholars assign the separation of synagogue and church to the fourth century (e.g., Alexander, "Parting of the Ways," 2). On the other hand, Annette Yoshiko Reed argues that "it may not be possible to pinpoint the historical moment that shaped 'Christianity' and 'Judaism' in all their diverse forms and regional expressions—either before the fourth century or after" ("Parting of the Ways," *EDEJ* 1031).

70. Meyers, "Side by Side in Galilee," 145–50.

71. Freyne, *Jesus Movement and Its Expansion*, 348–50.

72. Boyarin, "Parables of Enoch," 63–64.

relation to one another. Boyarin's dictum, above all, blurs the identities of Judaism and Christianity in order to maintain a hypothetical unified camp, and in so doing it dishonors the integrity of both. Peter Schäfer reproaches Boyarin for demeaning a profound problem: "We have learned by now that the old model of the 'parting of the ways' of Judaism and Christianity needs to be abandoned in favor of a much more differentiated and sophisticated model, taking into consideration a long process of mutual demarcation *and* absorption; but to maintain that '"Christianity" is simply (!) part and parcel of ancient Judaism' means to replace one evil with another."[73] The histories of Jews and Christians, Schäfer rightly reminds readers, demand something more than a denial of the identities unique to each.

Conclusion

The chief purpose of this chapter has been to demonstrate the inherent cohesiveness of early Christianity with Judaism. Both Jewish Jesus followers and Jews who did not follow Jesus understood themselves to be rightful heirs of the promises of God to Israel. When Jewish Jesus followers parted from Jews who did not follow Jesus over the issue of the role of gentiles in God's saving purposes for Israel, they did not think of themselves as less Jewish or less faithful to the divine script of Israel's story. They thought the opposite of themselves, in fact—that they were those destined to fulfill the mission of God in Israel. The crux of the difference was the conviction of the early church that the ultimate purpose of salvation history was not centripetal, having to do with the salvation of Israel, but centrifugal, having to do with the salvation of the gentile world through Israel. Early Christians believed that Israel was chosen to be a light to the nations. The tension between these two convictions frayed and ultimately rent the inherent cohesion between Jewish Jesus followers and Jews who did not follow Jesus. Despite the lack of a given event or time when the two parted ways, the fact remains that Christians and Jews have identified and defined themselves independently of one another for nearly two millennia.

In the next chapters, we will consider other issues, both internal and external, that divided Jews who followed Jesus from Jews who did not. Chief among the internal issues was the scandal of Christology—for Jews, an irreconcilable offense, but for Christians, Israel's providential consummation. Before we consider the essential role that Christology played in the parting of the ways, however, we need to consider the most crucial external force that divided Jesus followers and Jews who did not follow Jesus: the Roman Empire.

73. Schäfer, *Jewish Jesus*, 84.

6

From Jesus Movement to Roman Persecution

In the last chapter, we spoke of Jewish Jesus followers and Jews who were not Jesus followers as two siblings, like Jacob and Esau in Rebecca's womb, contending for the name and identity of their common parentage in Israel. Ultimately, the contention ended in division. Here I introduce a new image to convey how Jesus followers eventually parted fellowship from Jews who were not Jesus followers. The image is that of a drop of water elongating into an oval and then continuing to stretch until it divides, forming two separate droplets. Something similar happened with Judaism and Christianity. Despite the forces of cohesion between them, and despite the fact that we cannot pinpoint either an exact time or a particular precipitating event when believers in Jesus separated from nonbelievers in Jesus, an ever-widening differentiation within the synagogue ended in two independent communions.

When early Jesus followers reflected on the Jewish roots of their faith, they reflected on the familiar. They considered their calling as Jews to be perfected according to the gospel of Jesus Christ, but they did not understand the gospel to separate them from Judaism. When they found themselves confronted with the gentile mission, on the other hand, they stood before something new and unprecedented. Indeed, from a conventional Jewish perspective, the gentile mission was alien. For early Jesus followers, the Jewish roots of their faith were "scripted," so to speak, but not so their accommodation to the gentile world. Nevertheless, the gentile mission grew quickly and in great numbers. In baptizing the gentile Roman centurion Cornelius, the apostle Peter attests to the inexorable momentum of the gentile mission that confronted the church: "If God gave the same gift to them [gentiles] that he gave to those of us who believed in the Lord Jesus Christ, who was I to hinder God?" (Acts 11:17).

In this chapter, we will consider the forces that acted both on and in the early church—particularly as those forces presented themselves in the Roman Empire—forces that, within a mere seventy-five years, would result in both Judaism and Christianity defining themselves independently of each other.

Tensions in Rome

The earliest identifiable breach between Jewish and gentile Jesus followers occurred with the edict of the emperor Claudius (r. 41–54), who, in the words of the Roman historian Suetonius, "expelled Jews from Rome for constantly making disturbances at the instigation of Chrestus."[1] Luke alludes to this expulsion in reporting that, in Corinth, Paul joined forces with Aquila and Priscilla, "who had recently come from Italy because Claudius had ordered all the Jews to leave Rome" (Acts 18:2). Claudius had earlier expelled both Greek and Jewish rioters from Alexandria in 41, and he acted with similar dispatch in 49 by expelling Jews from Rome for causing "disturbances." Writing in the early second century, Suetonius associates the "disturbances" with the name "Chrestus." "Chrestus" is a variant spelling of the more common "Christus," as used by Tacitus with reference to Jesus Christ in Nero's persecution in 64.[2] Claudius appears to have expelled Jews from Rome because of disturbances caused by the introduction of the gospel into Roman synagogues. With Jews absent from Roman synagogues for five years, gentile Godfearers and Jesus followers adapted synagogue programs and practices away from issues of disagreement with Jews—such as circumcision, food laws, Torah cultic laws, and perhaps even Sabbath, all of which were nonobligatory for gentiles. When Claudius died in 54 and his edict lapsed, Jewish Christians returned to reestablish themselves in Roman synagogues that had become much more gentile in character in their absence. Paul wrote his Epistle to the Romans probably in the year 57, three years into the process of Jewish and gentile Christians reacclimating to one another in Rome. The readjustment was not seamless. On the basis of his experience with "all the churches of the gentiles" (Rom. 16:4, 26), Paul attempted to ameliorate tensions between Jewish and gentile Jesus followers in Rome (14:1–12). However

---

1. *Claud.* 25.4.
2. For another instance of the variant spelling "Chrestus," see Tertullian, *Apol.* 3. For Tacitus's description of Nero's persecution, see *Ann.* 15.44.

successful the Epistle to the Romans may have been in repairing the breach between the two groups initially, unity would not last for long.

Fifteen years after the Edict of Claudius, the divergence that Suetonius noted had become a distinct separation between Jesus followers and Jews who did not follow Jesus. The two communities had become like two separate drops of water. Tacitus recounts that in the year 64, the emperor Nero attributed a conflagration that destroyed the greater part of Rome to "a class of persons, hated for their vices, whom the crowd called 'Christians.'"[3] Tacitus's use of the word "Christians" is especially significant, for it indicates that, by Nero's day, Jesus followers in Rome were no longer considered a sect of Judaism, as they were in Claudius's day, but a "class" of persons separated from Jews.[4] Jews are not mentioned as a guilty party in the fire, nor were they persecuted as a result of it. On the contrary, Jews were held in high regard by many Romans and were spared blame for the conflagration.[5] Christians, however, were "hated" (*invisos*) in Rome, according to Tacitus, and they alone were blamed and subjected to hideous tortures and deaths. The hatred was mitigated by a grain of pity, however, for the population believed "that [Christians] were being sacrificed not for the welfare of the state but to the ferocity of a single man."[6] The fate of the gospel in Rome is thus apparent. During the reign of Claudius, Jesus Christ was the cause of discord within synagogues; but in the reign of Nero, fifteen years later, he had become the cause of division between Christians and Jews. Thirty years after the death of Jesus, Romans regarded Jews and Christians as two distinct entities.[7]

First Jewish Revolt

The two Jewish revolts, the first in 66–70 and the second in 132–35, were the only major disruptions of the Pax Romana in the first two centuries of the

3. *Ann.* 15.44.

4. Dunn's statements in "From the Crucifixion," 42, that Nero's agents ferreted out Christian scapegoats from "marketplace gossip"—indeed, that "there is no hint that they were regarded as 'Christians' as distinct from Jews"—seems to me a defective reading of Tacitus, *Ann.* 15.44. Williams, "Jews and Christians at Rome," offers a more defensible reading: in Rome, Christian Jews became divided and distinguished from non-Christian Jews over the messiahship of Jesus within twenty years of Jesus's death.

5. Nero's wife was, in fact, Jewish.

6. Tacitus, *Ann.* 15.44 (LCL).

7. See Williams, "Jews and Christians at Rome," 152: "Separation of Christians from Jews, then, must have started extremely early in the imperial capital, if within a generation of the death of Jesus of Nazareth neither the common people nor the authorities had any difficulty in distinguishing between the adherents of those two closely related 'superstitions,' as elite Romans disparagingly referred to them."

Christian era. Whereas Nero's fire separated Christians from Jews in Rome, the two Jewish revolts, and especially the second, effectively separated Christians from Jews in the broader empire.

In the year 66, militant Jewish factions rebelled against the Roman occupation of Palestine, massacring the Roman garrison in Caesarea Maritima. Rome retaliated by slaughtering twenty thousand Jews in Caesarea—in one hour! Despite the deployment of Rome's combined military forces in Palestine and Syria against the Jewish rebels, by the end of the year the rebels had succeeded in routing the Roman forces and establishing Jewish rule in Palestine under the authority of military commanders in Galilee, Judea, and Jerusalem. Rome responded with unmitigated force. Throughout 67 and 68, the Roman general Vespasian pressed systematically south through Galilee with six legions,[8] including the crack Tenth Legion (Fretensis), subduing cities that surrendered and destroying those that resisted. In early 69, with only Jerusalem remaining unconquered, Vespasian was summoned to Rome to succeed Nero as emperor, who had died the year before. The final siege of Jerusalem was bequeathed to Vespasian's son Titus, who, in late summer 70, completely destroyed Jerusalem, razed the temple, massacred its defenders, and deported captive Jews as slaves to Rome. Three years later, Titus's adjutant general Flavius Silva concluded the First Revolt with his siege and destruction of the remnant Jewish rebels at Masada.[9]

The Jewish War was more than a Roman victory over Jewish rebels. It came close to annihilating Judaism itself. Four of the major Jewish parties—the Sadducees, Essenes, Herodians, and Zealots—were exterminated. The destruction of the Sadducees resulted, concomitantly, in the destruction of the Sanhedrin as well, thus eliminating the centralized authority of first-century Judaism.[10] Only two Jewish parties survived the Götterdämmerung of AD 70. One was the Pharisees, who had abstained en masse from the revolt and survived to restore, and in some respects reinvent, Judaism according to rabbinic beliefs and practices. The other party, which also abstained from the

8. A Roman legion consisted of five to six thousand soldiers.

9. The Jewish writer Josephus initially fought against Vespasian as commander of Jewish forces in Galilee. Later, having surrendered, he advocated for the Romans in their cataclysmic destruction of Jerusalem. Josephus's *History of the Jewish War against the Romans* recounts the entire epic in seven books, much of it narrated from his personal involvment.

10. Alexander, "Parting of the Ways," 3. Freyne summarizes the disastrous consequences of the First Revolt thus: "The destruction of the Jerusalem temple and the dissolution of the Sanhedrin and the priesthood, followed by Titus's triumphant return to Rome with some of the spoils of war, including precious treasures from the temple and many captives to be sold at the slave markets, were measures meant to demoralize Judean resistance." In addition, "a [Roman] legion was located permanently at its center in Jerusalem." *Jesus Movement and Its Expansion*, 326.

revolt, was Jesus followers. At the end of the Jewish War, Jerusalem looked like Berlin at the end of World War II. The fact that the Synoptic Gospels, which were written in the immediate aftermath of the revolt, contain no explicit mention of it indicates the extent to which the early church had separated from Judaism by the year 70.

Christianity and Pharisaism embarked on their respective and divergent courses following the revolt. Christianity rapidly redefined itself along gentile lines, while rabbinic Judaism was absorbed in reconstituting itself as the sole defining heir of Judaism. The forces propelling Christianity toward gentile expansion were bolstered by the outcome of the First Revolt, for the victorious Roman Tenth Legion, which remained as an occupation force in Judea, brought a massive gentile contingent into the heart of Palestine.

A poll tax imposed on surviving Jews in the aftermath of the destruction of Jerusalem further divided the disciples of the Pharisees and the disciples of Jesus. In 70, the emperor Vespasian levied a "Jewish tax," *fiscus Judaicus*, in place of the half-shekel tax that Jews had paid to support the temple prior to its fall (Exod. 30:11–16). The half-shekel tax, the equivalent of two days' wages, is the tax referred to in Matthew 17:24–27. The *fiscus Judaicus* differed from the half-shekel tax in two onerous respects, however. First, it was imposed not only on Jewish males, as the half-shekel tax had been, but on *every* Jew—male and female, young and old, both inside and outside Palestine. Second, the *fiscus Judaicus* was used to fund a *pagan* temple—the temple of Jupiter Capitolinus in Rome. In the words of Josephus, "[Vespasian] imposed a poll-tax of two drachmas on all Jews, wherever they lived, to be paid annually into the Capitol as they had formerly contributed to the temple in Jerusalem."[11] The *fiscus Judaicus* was levied for thirty years, until the reign of the emperor Nerva at the end of the first century.[12] Its imposition on Jews alone split the church along its most sensitive ethnic vein, pulling Jewish Christians away from fellowship with gentile Christians by requiring them to identify with the synagogue. At the same time, it induced gentile Christians to disassociate from Jewish Christians to avoid both the financial burden of the tax and the problem of being required to fund a pagan temple. The overall result of the First Revolt was thus disastrous for the unity of Jewish and gentile Jesus followers. The onset of the revolt had driven Jesus followers out of Jerusalem to seek refuge in the caves of Pella, on the east side of the Jordan. In the aftermath of the revolt, the *fiscus Judaicus* penalized Jewish Jesus followers

---

11. *J.W.* 7.216–18 (LCL).

12. Suetonius, *Dom.* 12.1–2. For more on the *fiscus Judaicus*, see Moussaieff, "New Cleopatra"; Williams, "Jews and Christians at Rome," 159–66.

financially while at the same time rewarding gentile Jesus followers financially for separating from them.

Many in the early church regarded the fall of Jerusalem as God's judgment on Judaism. The Epistle of Barnabas claims that the Jerusalem temple "had been torn down because [the Jews] had gone to war." This dates Barnabas after the fall of Jerusalem. But it continues, "Now [the Jews] were hoping to rebuild it"—which dates the epistle more precisely, close to the end of the first century. Such hopes were utterly futile, according to Barnabas, for Jews "went astray in setting their hope on the building rather than upon their God who had made them as God's house." The temple was destroyed, according to Barnabas, so that believers, and not a building, could become God's true and lasting temple. "When we have received the remission of our sins and when we hope in his name, we ourselves become new. . . . God's true dwelling place is God dwelling in us."[13] For Barnabas, God's covenant is no longer shared by Jews and Christians but belongs to Christians alone. *Their* temple, *their* circumcision, and *their* sacrifices have been superseded by *our* repentant heart.[14] As William Horbury notes, for Barnabas, "the Christian claim to the Jewish heritage is total and exclusive."[15]

The *fiscus Judaicus* and anti-Christian invective of Jewish rabbis were thus two forces that polarized Jesus followers within and from the synagogue in the late first century. These two forces were joined by a third, which, like the *fiscus Judaicus*, was instituted by the Roman Empire but, unlike the *fiscus*, was exerted against gentile Christians rather than against Jews. This third force was the emperor cult.

Divine Honors for Caesar

A brief history of ruler worship in the Mediterranean world provides a helpful background for understanding the Roman emperor cult. In principle, early Greeks and Romans were opposed to the deification of rulers as practiced in Persia and Egypt, for example. The concept of a deified king was first introduced to the Greeks by Alexander the Great (d. 323 BC), who was addressed by the priest of the cult of Amon in Egypt as "the son of Amon/Zeus." Thereafter, Alexander promoted himself as a divine ruler, particularly in the East, where the attribution of deity to rulers was more commonly accepted and widely practiced than it was in the West. The first Roman emperor to

13. The above quotations are from Barn. 16.
14. See Barn. 16; 9.6; 2.4–10.
15. Horbury, "Jewish-Christian Relations," 335. Also on Barnabas, see Chester, "Parting of the Ways," 273–78; Freyne, *Jesus Movement and Its Expansion*, 331–34.

promote himself and his reign as deified was Augustus (r. 31 BC–AD 14). Like Alexander, Augustus considered himself to have been miraculously conceived by a serpent.[16] A few years before Jesus was born, Augustus hailed himself as a god whose "birthday signaled the beginning of good news for the world."[17] Thereafter, Augustus styled himself as God, son of God, and savior and his reign as a utopian age of peace and prosperity.[18] First-century Romans resisted a deified-emperor cult, however. Writing in about 115, Tacitus dismissed the cult of Augustus as a vanity, mocking Augustus as a very "mortal deity."[19] Following Augustus, the emperor cult remained largely dormant in the western half of the Roman Empire until the latter part of the first century. Tiberius, Claudius, Vespasian, and Titus made no attempt to invoke the status of deity.[20] The two major chroniclers of the first-century Roman principate, Tacitus and Suetonius, devote frequent attention to the superstitions of these emperors— their compulsions with portents, omens, auguries, and dice playing—but references to divine honors are rare and insipid. Both Caligula (r. 37–41) and Nero (r. 54–68) vaunted their deity, but their aspirations, like those of Augustus, were more persuasive in their imaginations than in the minds of their Roman subjects. Nero killed Christians in 64 by throwing them to wild beasts, crucifying them, and burning them alive, but the ancient accounts nowhere attribute his persecution to the failure of Christians to render him divine honor. Nero's savagery was a diversion, rather, to deflect charges from

16. "Such an omen," states Suetonius, "had befallen no one save Alexander the Great" (*Aug.* 94 [LCL]). Additionally, Augustus exhumed Alexander's body from its sarcophagus and placed a crown on its head (*Aug.* 18.1).

17. This quotation is from an inscription discovered at Priene (south of Ephesus) and is dated to 9 BC. See Deissmann, *Light from the Ancient East*, 366–67. According to Tacitus, *Ann.* 4.37, Roman emperor worship commenced when Augustus built a temple to himself at Pergamon in 29 BC. Pergamon, however, was in the East and not the West, where veneration of rulers was less popular. See Suetonius, *Aug.* 52.

18. See Augustus's inscription at Halicarnassus (modern Bodrum), cited in Kleinknecht, *Pantheion*, 40; and the long and ostentatious description of his accomplishments in the *Res Gestae divi Augusti*, discovered at Antioch of Pisidia and Ancyra, cited in Barrett, *New Testament Background*, 1–5.

19. See Tacitus, *Ann.* 1.10, 59.

20. According to Tacitus, Tiberius (r. 14–37) reigned with "grinding despotism" (*Ann.* 5.3) and repeatedly disavowed cultic honors (*Ann.* 1.72; 2.87). Claudius (r. 41–54) limited ascriptions of divinity to a minimum, allowing only the pro forma honor of deification at his death (*Ann.* 12.69). The imperial cult is not mentioned in relation to the three brief rulers of the year 69: Galba, Otho, and Vitellius. The Flavian emperors stabilized the tottering empire after the decadence of the Julio-Claudian emperors. Vespasian (r. 69–79) strengthened and reformed the empire, especially the law courts (Suetonius, *Vesp.* 8 and 10), but he refused the title "Father of his Country" (*Vesp.* 12). The brief reign of his son and successor, Titus (r. 79–81), was munificent and virtuous by Roman standards and free of infatuation with divine honors.

being directed at himself for having set fire to Rome.[21] Until the 80s of the first century, divine honors were applied to Roman emperors either sparingly or only at their deaths.[22] The apostle Paul's assertion, generally favorable to Roman rulers, that Caesar "is God's servant for your good" (Rom. 13:4) and his commendation of the empire as a restraining force against evil (2 Thess. 2:3–12) are scarcely conceivable if there was an emperor cult inimical to Christians.[23] The similarly favorable attitude toward the Roman army in the New Testament, and especially toward centurions, also belies an inimical emperor cult at the time.[24]

This changed in the latter part of the first century, however, when Domitian (r. 81–96) imposed the imperial cult at the edge of the Roman sword, expecting Roman governors to render him obedience as "Lord" (*dominus*) and "God" (*deus*).[25] Political observance was thereafter synonymous with sacred observance. Soldiers and public officials in the empire were required to swear by the emperor's genius, celebrate the days of his birth and accession to the throne, and burn incense or offer sacrifices to his image. These observances were not generally required of private citizens, however. Domitian's

21. Tacitus, *Ann.* 15.44. The above review contrasts with that of Bruce Winter, *Divine Honours for the Caesars*, 296–306, who argues, on the basis of occasional evidence of deified rulers in the eastern regions of the empire in the first century, for the prevalence of emperor worship also in western regions of the empire. Rulers were associated with deities earlier and regularly in the East, as exemplified in Alexander's promotion of his putative divine status and eastward expansion of his empire. The deification of Roman rulers gained little traction in western regions of the empire, however, until the reign of Domitian. Winter's assumption that Nero brutalized Christians in 64 because of their failure to offer him divine honors would likely surprise Tacitus (*Ann.* 15.44), who attributes Nero's persecution of Christians to an attempt to scapegoat them for the fire in Rome, making no mention of the imperial cult. Koch, *Geschichte des Urchristentums*, 456, sees no evidence of failure to observe the emperor cult being the cause of Nero's lightning pogrom against Christians, which lasted less than a week. The reasons for Nero's persecution of Christians, according to Koch, generally echo the report of Tacitus— namely, Christians, unlike Jews, were not protected; they were profiled as instigators of crimes and social problems in Rome; and this was because Roman ignorance and misunderstanding evolved into prejudice, with many Romans deriding the faith as a "superstition."

22. Note Tacitus's closing dictum regarding Nero: "The honor of divinity is not paid to the emperor until he has ceased to live and move among men" (*Ann.* 15.74 [LCL]).

23. It is important to recall that Nero (r. 54–68) was emperor when Paul wrote Romans. Nero's first ten years as emperor, and thus the time during which Paul wrote his Epistle to the Romans, were characterized by satisfactory and sometimes commendable policies. In the last five years of his reign, however, Nero's infamy reached extremes.

24. See Edwards, "Public Theology," esp. 236–45.

25. Suetonius, *Dom.* 13. The erection of a temple to Domitian at Ephesus in the 80s attests to the intensification of the emperor cult at that time, and it elevated Ephesus to the distinction of *neōkoros* (temple guardian) of the emperor cult. Ephesus achieved the distinction of four temple guardianships in its Roman history, more than any other city in the empire, including Pergamon, which attainted three temple guardianships.

successors, especially Trajan (r. 98–117), Hadrian (r. 117–38), and Marcus Aurelius (r. 161–80), attributed divine titles so avidly and often to themselves— savior (Gk. *sōtēr*), benefactor (Gk. *euergetēs*), divine (Lat. *divus*), son of god (Gk. *huios theou*), master (Gk. *autokratōr*), great one / venerable (Gk. *sebastos*; Lat. *augustus*)—that the titles became inseparable from their names. Such titles were rare in public inscriptions until the late first century, but they abounded thereafter—on statues, monuments, arches, pillars and columns, stelae, and coinage; and they became common in imperial processions and holidays throughout the empire. These later emperors vastly expanded the authority of the emperorship by consolidating political (Lat. *princeps*), military (Lat. *imperator*), and religious (Lat. *pontifex*) authority under the laurel wreath and scepter of the Roman emperor.

Descriptions of the imperial cult typically strike moderns, for whom God is "wholly other," as offensive and absurd. The divide between human and divine was not as wide in the polytheistic worlds of Greece and Rome, however, as it is in the modern mind. To be sure, some ancients were also annoyed with the cult. Tacitus sports with it when he says that even "princes . . . were equivalent to deities."[26] When the mother of Tiberius was proposed for divine honors at her death, and when the same was proposed for the four-month-old child of Nero at its death, Tacitus was dismissive.[27] When Nero dismissed and banished his first wife, Octavia, so that he could marry Poppaea, and when he further satisfied Poppaea's bloodlust by suffocating Octavia, cutting off her head, and presenting it to Poppaea to gloat over—after which he made a temple offering as a sham expiation!—Tacitus hurled an acid reproach: "As often as the emperor ordered an exile or murder, so often was a thanksgiving addressed to heaven."[28]

The only ethnic group in the Roman Empire exempt from rendering divine honor to emperors was the Jews. Aware of Jewish aversion to polytheism, Rome absolved Jews of emperor worship. A daily sacrifice in the temple of Jerusalem on behalf of the reigning emperor was accepted by Rome as a proxy offering on behalf of the Jewish people. Jews—including Jewish Christians—were thus exempted from observance of the emperor cult. Gentile Christians, however, were not exempted. Like all other non-Jewish citizens and inhabitants of the empire, they were fully accountable to the potential obligations of the emperor cult. The word *potential* is important here. Since only official representatives of the empire—soldiers, administrative officials, and priests—were required to observe the cult publicly, other inhabitants were exempted from rendering such observance. Roman officials could demand the

26. *Ann.* 3.36.
27. *Ann.* 5.2; 15.23.
28. *Ann.* 14.64 (LCL).

offering of prayers and incense to an emperor from ordinary Romans, however, if they doubted their fidelity to the empire. Pliny did so with Christians in Bithynia in the early second century, and Roman officials did so with Polycarp in the mid-second century. This perilous policy was imposed unevenly and arbitrarily: seasons of dormancy could be interrupted by sporadic bursts of persecution, both corporal and capital.[29] The emperor cult thus held gentile Christians in a potential state of mortal jeopardy.

Christian martyrdoms at the hands of Romans were sporadic until the mid-second century.[30] This has led some scholars to argue that the emperor cult was not an actual peril to Christians until the mid-second century.[31] As is evident from the foregoing discussion, scholars disagree in their judgment of the pervasiveness of the imperial cult. Some see it as a deadly reality from the first century onward; others, such as myself, see it as a latent concern for gentile Christians until the reign of Domitian, after which it became a periodic danger.[32] There can be no doubt, however, about its effect on the relationship

29. The uneven enforcement of the imperial cult is one reason, among others, why Maier, *New Testament Christianity in the Roman World*, argues that there was not a single imperial cult that ruled the empire but, rather, an array of forms of emperor worship that were more local in character.

30. Jesus (Mark 15) and James the brother of John (Acts 12:2) were killed by the Romans. The martyrdoms of Stephen (Acts 7) and James the brother of Jesus (Eusebius, *Hist. eccl.* 2.23) were the result of Jewish persecutions. Outside the New Testament record, Christians were martyred in Rome under Nero in AD 64 (Tacitus, *Ann.* 15.44), Christian tradition attests to the deaths of Peter and Paul in Rome (1 Clem. 5; Eusebius, *Hist. eccl.* 2.25.8), the family of David died at the hands of Vespasian (Eusebius, *Hist. eccl.* 3.12, 17), Ignatius was martyred in Rome (Ign., *Rom.* 5), and other possible martyrdoms are alluded to by Pliny the Younger (*Ep. Tra.* 10.96).

31. Koch, *Geschichte des Urchristentums*, 475–83, argues for an intensification of the emperor cult after Hadrian, but with fewer martyrdoms than is often supposed. Freyne, *Jesus Movement and Its Expansion*, 318–34, similarly, argues that although imperial power and policies became more punitive in Trajan's reign, the general religious tolerance of the empire extended throughout the second century.

32. The Roman emperor cult is not infrequently misrepresented. Lohmeyer's early monograph *Christuskult und Kaiserkult*, 17, mistakenly assumes that "the emperor cult encompassed the entirety of the Roman imperium" (my trans.) and that the characteristics for which the emperor cult was justly infamous in the second century prevailed in the first century as well. Winter argues similarly in *Divine Honours for the Caesars*. Even though the emperor cult was more widely promoted in the East than it was in the West, we have no evidence in either the East or West of the emperor cult being invoked in order to punish or execute Christians, at least not until the time of Domitian. Much of Wright's claim in *Paul and the Faithfulness of God*, 311–47, that the emperor cult was as active and inimical in the West as it was in the East, is based on data from the East. In the opposite vein, Harnack, *Mission and Expansion*, 297, is too idealistic when he asserts that "Christians repudiated the imperial cultus in every shape and form. . . . Unhesitatingly they reckoned it a phase of idolatry." The imperial cult was a hydra of many heads, some heads of which did not compromise Christian faithfulness and hence did not need to be rejected. In 1 Cor. 8 and 10, for example, Paul argues that Christians can eat meat offered to idols (including idols of the emperors) without denying their faith. The conclusion

between Jewish and gentile Christians. It created a safe harbor for Jewish Christians that was forbidden to gentile Christians, exposing the latter to the harrowing waters of divine honors for the emperor. The *fiscus Judaicus*, as we have seen, drove a wedge between Jewish and gentile Christians by penalizing Jews but sparing gentiles; the emperor cult drove a further wedge by penalizing gentiles but sparing Jews. As a result, by the end of the first century, Christians were regarded throughout the empire much as they were in Rome in Nero's day—as a religious sect distinct from Judaism. Pliny's questions to the emperor Trajan in the early second century, it will be recalled, related solely to "Christians," with no reference to Jews. Martin Goodman's judgment in this respect is well formed: "It seems to me no accident that a clear distinction between Jews and Christians begins regularly to appear in pagan Roman texts after A.D. 96."[33] The Roman Empire had again been influential in shaping separate identities for Judaism and Christianity.[34]

Second Jewish Revolt

If there was a straw that broke the camel's back regarding the separation of Jews and Christians, it was the Second Jewish Revolt, in 132–35. Following the revolt, Jews and Christians appear not only divided but also often antagonistic. In a defense of Christianity addressed to the emperor Antoninus Pius (r. 138–61), Justin Martyr writes that Jews "count us foes and enemies; and, like yourselves, they kill and punish us whenever they have the power, as you can well believe. For in the Jewish war which lately raged [= Second Jewish Revolt], Bar Kokhba, the leader of the revolt of the Jews, gave orders

---

of Goguel, *Birth of Christianity*, 445–46, that "Paul was ready to comply with all [Rome's] demands provided they did not conflict with what belonged to God" accords fairly with evidence in the Pauline epistles. It also finds support from Paul's contemporaries and successors. Philo lavished praise on the emperor as "Master" (*Embassy* 271, 276, 291), "Lord" (*Embassy* 286, 356), and even "savior" (*Embassy* 22). Even the polemical Tertullian refers to the emperor as "Lord" without jeopardizing the true lordship of God (*Apol.* 34.1). Finally, it should be recalled that Luke, especially, frequently portrays the Roman Empire in positive terms, including the offices of the centurion and tribune, which without fail in Luke-Acts advocate for Christians rather than against them (see Edwards, "'Public Theology,'" esp. 239–40). For a nuanced and insightful discussion of the relationship between early Christianity and the Roman Empire, including the emperor cult, see Barclay's "Response to N. T. Wright" in *Pauline Churches*, 373–87.

33. Goodman, "Diaspora Reactions," 33–34.

34. The emperor cult, in particular, may help us understand the appeal in the Epistle to the Hebrews for believers not to renounce Christianity for Judaism. If Christians under the reigns of Domitian or Trajan, at the end of the first century, found their property and lives imperiled by the imperial cult, we can well imagine the appeal of returning to—or even converting to— the safe haven of Judaism to escape the peril.

that Christians alone should be led away to cruel punishments, unless they should deny that Jesus is the Christ and utter blasphemy."[35] Eusebius later elaborates that Bar Kokhba "killed the Christians with all kind of persecutions when they refused to help him against the Roman troops."[36] Later still, Jerome describes Bar Kokhba as "the leader of the Jewish faction, [who] slaughtered the Christians with various punishments."[37]

We have no eyewitness historian for the Second Revolt like we have in Josephus for the First Revolt. We do have a cache of letters relating to the revolt, however, some of them written by Bar Kokhba himself, which have been retrieved from caves at Nahal Hever, south of Qumran on the west side of the Dead Sea.[38] No particular incident is known to have triggered the revolt, but it assumed quasi-eschatological proportions, for Jewish rebels introduced a new calendar and new legal documents at its outbreak. Its leader, a certain Simon, was hailed by the famous Rabbi Akiba as "Bar Kokhba" (Son of the Star). "Son of the Star" was a messianic reference to Numbers 24:17, "the star coming out of Jacob." Coinage struck in Judea bearing an image of a star above the temple promoted Bar Kokhba as the Messiah. Unlike the centripetal combat of the First Revolt, contracting from the hinterlands of Galilee into the epicenter of Jerusalem, the combat of the Second Revolt was centrifugal, expanding outward from Jerusalem, like lava from a volcano, to the caves and wadis of the rugged Judean wilderness. The devastation of the Second Revolt surpassed even that of the First Revolt sixty years earlier, with nearly six hundred thousand Jewish men perishing, according to Dio Cassius.[39] Following the defeat of Bar Kokhba and the Jewish rebels, Jerusalem was transformed into a pagan mecca. Hadrian renamed the city Aelia Capitolina,[40] the Jewish temple was replaced with a temple to Zeus/Jupiter and Aphrodite/Venus, and Jews were banned on pain of death from entering the city. In the words of Eusebius, "[Hadrian] commanded that by a legal decree and ordinances the whole nation should be absolutely prevented from entering thenceforth even the district round Jerusalem, so that not even from a distance could it see its ancestral home."[41] Gentiles, however, including gentile Christians, were allowed to live in Jerusalem. Once again, Rome divided Jews and Christians.

35. Justin, 1 Apol. 31.5–6 (ANF 1:173).
36. Eusebius, Hist. eccl. 4.8.4 (LCL).
37. Jerome, Vir. ill. 21.3 (Halton trans.).
38. See Lewis, Yadin, and Greenfield, Greek Papyri.
39. Dio Cassius, Hist. rom. 69.14.3.
40. After Hadrian (Aelius Hadrianus) and Zeus (Jupiter Capitolinus).
41. Eusebius, Hist. eccl. 4.6.1–4 (LCL). For treatments of the Bar Kokhba Revolt, see Schürer, History of the Jewish People, 1:543–57; Meyers and Chancey, Alexander to Constantine, 165–73.

Christians were unable to render allegiance in any form to a messianic pretender like Bar Kokhba (Matt. 24:4–5), who then exacted severe reprisals, including martyrdom. Justin's report to the emperor attests to the fratricidal breach between synagogue and church. Bar Kokhba repeated the pre-Christian Paul's persecution of Jesus followers on a grand scale, in "furious rage forcing believers to blaspheme" (Acts 26:11). Christians had been persecuted in many ways within the Jerusalem–Rome corridor.[42] These persecutions reached a peak in Bar Kokhba's attack on Christians, but not an end. Twenty years later in Smyrna (modern western Turkey), Jews "shouted out in unison that Polycarp should be burned alive." Indeed, they participated in his martyrdom, assisting in preparing the pyre; and once he was immolated, they appealed to Roman officials not to surrender his body to the Christians.[43] Martin Hengel sums up the antagonism to nascent Christianity thus: "By the end of the first century the synagogue had driven Jewish Christians out. Christian communities themselves did not initiate the breach with Judaism but were, as the example of the Pauline mission shows, . . . forced out step by step. There was no more room in the synagogue for their messianic disturbance of the peace."[44]

Apart from the Bar Kokhba era, open persecution of Christians by Jews may not have been as common as is sometimes supposed. Nor did the violence remain a one-way street from Jews to Christians. Close on the heels of the Second Revolt, Marcion vilified Judaism as the product of an inferior and malevolent god.[45] As the new faith gained ground in the empire, especially with the accession of the emperor Constantine in the fourth century, Christians not infrequently persecuted and oppressed Jews.

Conclusion

The separation of church and synagogue naturally brings a *religious* conflict to mind. The separation was certainly a religious conflict; indeed, primarily

42. Harassments (Acts 8:1–4), calumnies (Acts 13:45; 16:20–21; 17:1–15; 18:6, 12–17; 19:9), plots (Acts 14:5–6; 20:3, 19), physical attacks and beatings (Acts 16:22–23; 21:35–36; 23:10), trials (23:1–10; 26), arrests (Acts 9:1–2; 21:37; 28:16), imprisonments (12:5; 16:24; 24:27), expulsions and deportations (Acts 17:13–14; 23:20–35; 27:1), riots (Acts 19:23–40; 21:30–36), stoning (Acts 7:58–59; 14:19), martyrdoms (Acts 7; 12:1–5), or combinations of these (2 Cor. 11:23–33).

43. Mart. Pol. 12.2; 13.1; 17.2; 18.1.

44. Hengel, *Studien zum Urchristentum*, 330 (my trans.). The foregoing evidence argues against Stark's judgment that, in the mid-second century, "the church still was dominated by people with Jewish roots and strong current ties to the Jewish world." *Rise of Christianity*, 63–65.

45. On Marcion, see ch. 4, p. 78. Grant first attributed Marcion's anti-Judaism to Bar Kokhba's persecution of Christians (*Gnosticism and Early Christianity*, 121–28).

so. But it was not exclusively religious. This chapter has examined the instrumental role that Rome played in the parting of ways between Christians and Jews. The emperor Claudius's expulsion of Jews from Rome in 49 and Nero's persecution of Christians for the Roman fire fifteen years later, in 64, set precedents that were soon followed throughout the empire. The combined catastrophes of the First Jewish Revolt of 66–70 and the Second Jewish Revolt of 132–35, the intervening *fiscus Judaicus*, and the pressures of the Roman emperor cult—all contributed to the eventual separation of Jews and Christians. That is not to say that the separation would not have occurred apart from these influences. Christology alone, as we will see, was sufficient to ensure such a separation. What we can say with near certainty is that without Rome's instrumental role, the separation would have been a more gradual and less inimical divorce.

7

From Torah to Kerygma

External events and forces were not the sole factors that drove Jews and Christians apart. Had there been no internal fissures between the two, the events surveyed in the last chapter would have affected Jesus followers no differently than they affected Pharisaic rabbis, for instance, who were driven out of Jerusalem after the First and Second Revolts but not out of Judaism. However, the external events and forces seeped like permeating water and prying roots into existing fissures between Jews and Christians, cracking and splitting into pieces what had once been whole. Some of the fissures were slight, and, left unstressed, would have divided Christians from Jews at only a superficial level (as they divided Pharisees from Sadducees, for example). Other fissures were deeper, capable of cleaving the rock in two. One such fissure was the matter of gentile inclusion, which we have considered. But the deepest fissure, the Christian claim "Kyrios Iēsous" (Jesus is Lord), fundamentally and irrevocably determined the genus of Christianity in distinction from Judaism.[1]

Kerygma

Nearly one-fifth of the book of Acts consists of speeches, primarily of Peter in the first half and of Paul in the second half, but also of Stephen, James,

1. The title "Lord Jesus" or the claim "Jesus is Lord" (both are translations of the Gk. *Kyrios Iēsous*) occurs more than 130 times in all literary layers of the New Testament, including the Gospels, Acts, the Pauline and General Epistles, and Revelation. Grant, *Roman Hellenism*, 155–58, rightly emphasizes that the understanding of Jesus as Lord, based on his resurrection from the dead, was the first and foundational conviction of early Christianity: "Christianity began with Christ's *Resurrection*, not his death, and not the Sermon on the Mount. It is the Risen and Glorified Lord of the Christian cult who is described as 'Lord'" (156).

Apollos, and, in the last ten chapters, of trial testimonies. When the various speeches are compared with one another, a three-point core emerges that is common to nearly all. The first and third points can be summarized in single sentences, but the second entails several subpoints:

1. The promises of God in the Old Testament are now fulfilled.
2. Jesus of Nazareth is the long-awaited Messiah, born of David's line, who
   a. did good and mighty works by the power of God,
   b. was crucified according to the purpose of God,
   c. was raised from the dead by God and exalted to his right hand,
   d. now reigns in heaven as Lord, and
   e. will come again to judge and restore all things for the purpose of God.
3. Let all who hear repent and be baptized.

This outline of the history of salvation provided the framework for the proclamation of early Christian missionaries, preachers, and teachers. It was not a straitjacket but, rather, a skeleton that could be fleshed out as specific situations and audiences required. A single verse suffices in some contexts (e.g., Acts 17:3), and others call for fully developed narratives.[2] The New Testament refers to the gospel summary as *kerygma* (Gk. "proclamation"), which early Christians deemed essential for the presentation of the gospel. Paul describes the kerygma as "the revelation of the eternal mystery" of the gospel (Rom. 16:25) and "the proclamation that saves those who believe" (1 Cor. 1:21). The author of Colossians accentuates its universal and cosmic significance: "proclaimed to every creature under heaven" (Col. 1:23). Its content is solely and wholly determined by Jesus Christ—especially by his cross (1 Cor. 2:2–4) and resurrection (1 Cor. 15:14). The kerygma constituted the commission and mission of the church.[3]

At the turn of the second century, Ignatius refers to the kerygma as the "dogma of the Lord and apostles," the authoritative and life-giving proclamation of faith and love, in the name of the Holy Trinity, that is the "beginning and end" of the gospel.[4] Similar to Colossians 1:23, cited above, the Shepherd of Hermas speaks of "the Son of God who has been proclaimed to the

---

2. E.g., Acts 2:14–41; 13:16–41.
3. See esp. 2 Tim. 4:5, 7, 17; Titus 3. On the kerygma as a whole, see Gerhard Friedrich, "*kerygma*," *TWNT* 3:714–17; Otto Merk, "*kerygma*," *EDNT* 2:288–92.
4. Ign. *Magn.* 13.1.

ends of the earth," the refuge of all who believe in him.[5] In the second and following centuries, kerygma defined not only the content of the gospel and the task of the church but also the distinction of both from heresy. Kerygma thus constituted *orthodox* proclamation, the way properly to glorify God. For Eusebius, kerygma is the "uncorrupted virgin" that protects the "healthy rule of the Savior's proclamation."[6] The Greek word for "rule," *kanōn*, attests to the consolidation of the gospel within a recognized corpus of witnesses, which Eusebius refers to as "the unerring tradition of the apostolic preaching."[7]

The early church understood itself to be the repository, manifestation, and transmitter of the kerygma. In contrast to many philosophies and schools of thought that proliferated in the Greco-Roman world, kerygma was a truth that could be *lived*, and its lived expression, both individually and corporately, was the greatest witness to its truth. Reminiscent of Jesus's saying that "a tree is known by its fruit" (Matt. 12:33), Ignatius reminds readers that "those who profess to be Christ's will be recognized by their actions."[8] The first century did not bifurcate faith and works; it adhered closely to a gospel of "knowing and doing" (John 13:17). The universal and univocal testimony of the Johannine literature is, "If you love me, you will keep my commandments."[9] The Pauline literature similarly exhorts Christians to "walk in newness of life" (Rom. 6:4), "not according to the flesh but according to the Spirit" (Rom. 8:4). Second Clement expresses the correspondence of thought, word, and deed thus: "How do we confess [God]? By doing what he says and not disobeying his commandments, and honoring him not only with our lips but with all our heart and all our mind."[10] The only gospel capable of convicting and redeeming the world is the *lived* gospel; conversely, as 2 Clement admonishes, failing to live the gospel jeopardizes the salvation of those to whom it is proclaimed, "For when pagans hear from our mouths the oracles of God and marvel at their beauty and greatness, and then discover that our works are not worthy of the words we speak, they turn from wonder to blasphemy, saying that it is a myth and delusion."[11] The bifurcation between theology and ethics, between faith and works, that typifies later ages of the church is not apparent

---

5. Herm. Sim. 8.3.2.

6. *Hist. eccl.* 3.32.7.

7. *Hist. eccl.* 4.8.2.

8. Ign. *Eph*. 14.2. For Ignatius, the social engagement of Christians distinguishes them from heretics: "They [heretics] have no concern for love, none for the widow, none for the orphan, none for the oppressed, none for the prisoner or the one released, none for the hungry or thirsty" (Ign. *Smyrn*. 6.2).

9. John 14:15; see also 1 John 2:3.

10. 2 Clem. 3.4.

11. 2 Clem. 13.3.

in the New Testament and Apostolic Fathers. Even grace and law are held in greater complementarity than they are in subsequent ages. The gospel of the first century was not merely an idea; it was a holistic commitment to divine revelation that transformed individual life and universal cosmos.

The kerygma needed to be articulated and proclaimed, learned and taught. Which means the church needed to be a training society as well as a worshiping community. Worship and education were both essential to transforming believer and community according to the image of Christ. The personal and corporate significance of kerygma is well summarized by Adolf Harnack:

> Neophytes had to get accustomed or to be trained at first to a society of this kind. It ran counter to all the requirements exacted by any other cultus or holy rite from its devotees, however much the existing guild-life may have paved the way for it along several lines. That its object should be the *common edification of the members*, that the community was therefore to resemble a single body with many members, that every member was to be subordinate to the whole body, that one member was to suffer and rejoice with another, that Jesus Christ did not call individuals apart but built them into a society in which the individual got his place—all these were lessons which had to be learned.[12]

The Preeminence of Jesus Christ

The apostle Paul speaks of "learning Christ" (Eph. 4:20). What, in particular, had to be learned? The one thing of unrivaled preeminence in Christianity, the sole content of the kerygma, the primary subject of all Christian preaching—which, even when not expressly the subject, is nevertheless the reference point for all other points under consideration—is the sole sufficiency of Jesus Christ for salvation. When the gospel was either embraced or rejected, whether by Jews or by gentiles, it was inevitably the person and work of Jesus Christ that was embraced or rejected. When embraced, Jesus was "the author of life" (Acts 3:15); when not, he was a "stone of rejection" (Acts 4:11). His singularity derived from his presumption to speak and act not only *for* God but *as* God—a presumption that both his followers and his opponents recognized.[13]

Jesus as God

A great many of the early church's beliefs were inherited from Judaism. Even Christian dogmas that differed from Judaism were frequently different

12. Harnack, *Mission and Expansion*, 433.
13. John 5:18; 10:30–31. See Dunn, "From the Crucifixion," 49.

interpretations of essential elements of Judaism. The theological cornerstone of Judaism is monotheism, the belief in only one God. The Mosaic mandate sanctioned only one God, and it abided no contenders alongside the one God: "Hear, O Israel: The LORD our God, the LORD is one" (Deut. 6:4). Israel guarded this mandate zealously. In the Old Testament, the name YHWH is applied to no one besides Israel's God; and in subsequent Judaism, to call any being "God" other than YHWH was deemed a capital offense.[14] It is precisely this offense of which early Christianity was guilty—although in ascribing deity to Jesus, the church, then as now, did not intend to affirm that Jesus was a second God but, rather, that he was a person ontologically one with and equal to the only God. Already in the New Testament and in the Apostolic Fathers, Jesus is referred to as "God." In some instances, this is stated directly.[15] More often, it is implied. Jesus is defined as "equal to God" or "one with the Father."[16] Early believers are instructed to "think of Jesus as God."[17] The earliest known remains of a church in Israel, a third-century structure located at the foot of Tel Megiddo, has a beautiful floor mosaic that reads, "To God Jesus Christ."[18] Attributes that belong solely to God—creation, for example—are expressly ascribed in the New Testament to Jesus Christ.[19] The presence of Jesus's name in baptismal formulations equates him with both God the Father and God the Holy Spirit.[20] Unlike the teachings of some mystery cults, the deity of Jesus was not treated as privileged knowledge that was to be concealed from outsiders because it belonged only to initiates. The Gospel of Matthew records the chief priests and the scribes taunting Jesus at the crucifixion, telling him to come down from the cross, "for he said 'I am the Son of God'" (27:43). Non-Jews were aware of the same divine claim, for Pliny the Younger reported to the emperor Trajan early in the second century that Christians in Bithynia gathered weekly and

14. On the derivation and understanding of YHWH (the tetragrammaton), see ch. 14, p. 245.

15. John 1:1, 18; Rom. 9:5; 1 John 5:20; 1 Cor. 10:1–4; Col. 2:9; Phil. 2:5–6; Ign. *Eph.* 18.2; Ign. *Rom.* 3.3; Ign. *Smyrn.* 1.1.

16. John 5:18; 10:30; Ign. *Magn.* 7.2.

17. 2 Clem. 1.1.

18. See Tzaferis, "'To God Jesus Christ.'" All three words in the inscription (God, Jesus, Christ) are *nomina sacra* (abbreviated forms—first and last letters beneath a horizontal line—used for roughly two dozen common names and theological terms in early Christianity). Such abbreviations attest to the antiquity of reverence associated with the terms—which, in the present instance, implies that Jesus was considered God well before the third century. For more on *nomina sacra*, see ch. 14, pp. 245–46.

19. John 1:3; Col. 1:16; Heb. 1:2.

20. Matt. 28:19; Acts 2:38, 41; 8:12, 16; 10:48; 19:5; Rom. 6:3; 1 Cor. 12:13; Gal. 3:27; Did. 7.1; Herm. Vis. 7.3.

"sang a hymn to Christ as to God."[21] The preeminence of Jesus Christ was not a theological extravagance but an essential tenet of Christian belief. It was God's revelation, "in the fullness of time" (Gal. 4:4), to the family of Israel and, through them, to the world. "I make known to you, fellow family members," writes Paul to the Galatians, "that the gospel that was preached by me is not a human invention; I did not receive it from a human source nor was I taught it, but it came to me through a revelation of Jesus Christ."[22]

Jesus as Lord

For every reference to Jesus as "God" in the New Testament, there are a hundred references to him as "Lord."[23] "Lord" may connote to modern readers something less than "God," but this was not its connotation to ancient Jews, for whom *kyrios* (Lord) was the standard Greek translation in the Septuagint for the exalted divine name: YHWH.[24] So exalted was the name YHWH in Judaism that it was (and still is) regarded too holy to pronounce.[25] Among the wealth of references to Jesus as Lord, perhaps the single most important is the Christ hymn of Philippians 2:5–11, where the apostle Paul's three-stage Christology of divine preexistence ("[Jesus] existed in the form of God"), incarnation ("[Jesus] emptied himself . . . and became human"), and heavenly exaltation ("God exalted [Jesus], . . . in order that at the name of Jesus every knee should bow in heaven and on earth and under the earth") is represented

21. "Essent soliti stato die ante lucem convenire carmenque Christo quasi deo dicere." *Ep. Tra.* 10.96.

22. Gal. 1:11–12; see also vv. 15–16.

23. There are more than seven hundred references to Jesus as Lord in the New Testament, and there are fully five hundred references to him as Lord in the Apostolic Fathers. The New Testament word count is that of Joseph Fitzmyer, "*kyrios*," *EDNT* 2:329; the Apostolic Fathers count is my own.

24. "Lord" (Gk. *kyrios*) was also commonly used for Greco-Roman heroes and rulers, but as an honorary distinction rather than as an ontological equivalent for "God." The claims attributed to Jesus as Lord are attributed to no Greco-Roman "Lord" (e.g., Phil. 2:5–11; Col. 1:15–20; Heb. 1:1–3).

25. Joseph Fitzmyer, "*kyrios*," *EDNT* 2:330, reminds us that the translation of the Hebrew "YHWH" by the Greek "*kyrios*" is based on the evidence of the great fourth- and fifth-century Greek codices, whereas in pre-Christian Greek manuscripts of the Hebrew Scriptures, such as those known by Origen and Jerome, "YHWH" was typically inserted into the Greek text in Hebrew or paleo-Hebrew characters. Nevertheless, notes Fitzmyer, the widespread use of the Aramaic "*mareh*" (Lord) in pre-Christian Jewish texts indicates that "there was clearly a custom beginning among Palestinian Jews of the last two centuries BC of referring to God as '(the) Lord.'" Despite the lack of absolute certainty, noted by Fitzmyer, that Greek-speaking Jews of Jesus's day referred to YHWH as "Lord," we may be assured that the use of "*kyrios*" for "YHWH" in the fourth- and fifth-century Greek codices fully conformed to Jewish understanding and custom, for an aberrant Greek translation of the all-important divine name would scarcely have been tolerated by Greek-speaking Jews in the Christian era.

in the single term *kyrios* (Lord): "Every tongue shall confess that Jesus Christ is Lord, to the glory of God the Father." The placement of *kyrios* (Lord) before *Iēsous Christos* (Jesus Christ) in the Greek syntax of verse 11 makes it emphatic. It should be recalled that Philippians is a datable epistle, written no later than the mid-50s. Within twenty years of his crucifixion, in other words, Jesus was being called Lord. Indeed, the title was almost certainly in use even earlier, for the mastery of the hymn's vocabulary, meter, and stylistic symmetry attest to a period of formation before it was quoted by Paul. The Christ hymn must have been circulating no later than the 40s, and it might have circulated even earlier.[26] The widespread attribution of "Lord" to Jesus is thus evidence of an elevated Christology among Jesus followers quite early. Indeed, Paul's conclusion of 1 Corinthians with the Aramaic vocative *marana tha*, "Lord, come!" (16:22) indicates that Jesus was called "Lord" already in early Aramaic-speaking Christianity. The early Aramaic confession of Jesus as Lord lived on in a lovely benediction quoted in the Didache:

> May grace come, and may this world pass away.
> Hosanna to the God of David.
> If anyone is holy, let him come;
> If anyone is not, let him repent.
> Maranatha! Amen. (10.6, Holmes trans.)

Jesus as Christ

Another title for Jesus, nearly as popular as "Lord," was *Christos* (Christ), which is the Greek translation of the Hebrew "Messiah." "Christ" occurs in every book of the New Testament except for 3 John, a total of 530 times; and it appears in the Apostolic Fathers 150 times. Like "Lord," "Christ/Messiah" is wholly determined by its usage in the Old Testament and in the expectations of Second Temple Judaism. Both the Greek word "Christ" and the Hebrew word "Messiah" derive from the root meaning "to anoint (with oil)." In the Hebrew tradition, three classes of people—kings, priests, and prophets—were anointed with oil as a means of legitimating their divine installation to office.[27] None of these uses, however, refers specifically to the Messiah. With the demise of the monarchy, and especially with the fall of Jerusalem to Nebuchadnezzar in 586 BC, the concept of a new and greater king like David emerged in Israel

---

26. See the important and enduring conclusion of Ernst Lohmeyer, in *Die Briefe*, 90–99, that the Christ hymn was pre-Pauline, perhaps originally functioning as a eucharistic text.

27. The tradition relates many anointings of kings (e.g., 1 Sam. 9:27–10:1; 1 Kings 1:32–40), fewer of high priests (throughout Leviticus; 1 Chron. 29:22; Sirach 45:15), and fewer yet of prophets (1 Kings 19:16; Isa. 61:1).

as a pattern for a God-ordained deliverer. "'The days are coming,' declares the LORD, 'when I will raise up to David a righteous branch, a King, who will reign wisely and do what is just and right in the land'" (Jer. 23:5).[28] The Old Testament does not develop a formal doctrine of the Messiah, however. And even in postexilic Judaism, the concept of the Messiah remained fluid. Only once in the Old Testament is "Messiah" used as an absolute title (Dan. 9:26); and at Qumran, where it is also used absolutely (1QSa 2.12), it refers to *two* Messiahs.[29] The most specific form of the otherwise general messianic conception in pre-Christian texts is that of an eschatological king. Even this majestic Messiah, however, would be a *mortal* earthly ruler rather than an eternal being.[30] As we saw earlier, Rabbi Akiba believed Bar Kokhba, the leader of the Second Jewish Revolt, to be the Messiah—and Bar Kokhba perished in the revolt.[31] The Messiah would be a king chosen by God to deliver Israel from its enemies and to cause Israel to live in peace and tranquility thereafter.[32] He would deliver Jerusalem from the gentiles, gather the faithful from dispersion, and rule in justice and glory.[33] Jesus, however, rejected the association of the Messiah with sword and scepter, with military might and political dominance (associations that had become central for Jews in Roman-occupied Palestine); hence, Jesus was reluctant to use the title, and he frequently commanded those who would use it of him to remain silent.[34] Neither Jesus nor early Christians rejected the concept of God's divinely anointed Messiah, of course; but in the Gospels (unlike in Paul), the title is used with restraint in order to preserve its theological integrity from political and military triumphalism.[35]

The title "Christ" is commonly (mis)understood today as a reference to Jesus's deity. In the early church, the deity of Jesus would be conveyed by

---

28. Old Testament messianic texts include Isa. 9:1–6; 11:1–10; Jer. 30:8–11; 33:14–18; Ezek. 17:22–24; 34:23–31; 37:15–28; Mic. 5:1–5; Zech. 9:9–13.

29. In accordance with Num. 24:15–17 and Deut. 33:8–11, see 4QTest 5–10; 4QFlor 1.13a. One of the expected messianic figures at Qumran was a son of David as military deliverer; the other was a son of Aaron as high priest (1QS 9.11). The expectation of a messianic high priest seems to have been limited to Qumran, however, and to have exerted little if any influence on subsequent Judaism. See García Martínez, "Messianische Erwartungen."

30. The Jew Trypho declares that the Messiah will be *"anthrōpos ex anthrōpōn genomenos"* (a human born of humans). Justin, *Dial*. 67.2 (cf. 48.1; 49.1).

31. On Bar Kokhba and the Second Jewish Revolt, see ch. 6, pp. 111–13.

32. Sib. Or. 3.286–294.

33. Pss. Sol. 17.23–30.

34. See Irenaeus, *Haer*. 3.18.4: "[Jesus] rebuked Peter because he supposed Jesus to be the Christ according to the common conception of the people."

35. For discussions of the messianic expectation, see Str-B 4/2:799–1015; Moore, *Judaism in the First Centuries*, 2:323–76; Schürer, *History of the Jewish People*, 2:488–554; Hofius, "Ist Jesus der Messias?"; Ferdinand Hahn, "*Christos*," EDNT 3:478–86.

"Lord" and "Son of God," but less so by "Christ," which refers to a divine commission rather than a divine nature. This title designates Jesus as the divinely *anointed one*, who was foreshadowed in the Old Testament and was to fulfill Israel's destiny. The Messiah occupied a singular office in Israel, one for which no parallels have been found elsewhere in the ancient Near East and one that, within Israel, was not blended or equated with any other office. Other Old Testament deliverers—the Servant of Yahweh and the Son of Man, for example—are not assigned or co-opted by messianic expectations. In Israel, the word "Messiah" is principally anchored as a royal title to the Davidic tradition.[36] Among all the peoples of the earth, Israel was God's chosen people, and the Messiah was God's chosen person among that people. The Messiah was God's specific savior of God's specific people. Jesus laid claim to that tradition when he interpreted his messianic status to two bewildered travelers on the road to Emmaus: "Beginning with Moses and all the prophets, he explained to them in all the Scriptures the things concerning himself" (Luke 24:27). Jesus followers early and absolutely identified their master as the divinely ordained and empowered Savior of Israel.

Jesus as Son of God

Whereas "Christ"—and, to an extent, "Lord"—practically became second names for Jesus in the early church, "Son of God" appears with less frequency in the literature but with greater theological precision. There are some eighty occurrences of "Son of God" in the New Testament, and roughly the same number in the Apostolic Fathers. It is the most robust christological title applied to Jesus. Like "Lord" (Gk. *kyrios*), "Son of God" (Gk. *huios theou*; Lat. *filius Dei*) occurs regularly in Greco-Roman inscriptions with reference to rulers and heroes; but as with the Greco-Roman use of "Lord," its connotations are more honorific than ontological, and the attributes of those to whom it is ascribed are less exalted and cosmic than are those ascribed to Jesus. The roots of the divine sonship ascribed to Jesus are not in the Greco-Roman world but in the Old Testament. If "Messiah" conveys divine commission more than divine nature, "Son of God" conveys both in equal measure. As Isaac was the "beloved son" of Abraham (Gen. 22:2, 12), so Israel was the beloved son of God. Moses identifies Israel as such when, speaking on behalf of God, he declares to Pharaoh, "Israel is my firstborn son" (Exod. 4:22–23). The term "son of God" was later reserved for the king, who, at his coronation, became

---

36. Apart from the Davidic tradition, "Messiah" became an honorific title for the high priest in postexilic Judaism. In a highly unusual occurrence, the title is given to Cyrus, king of Persia, in Isa. 45:1. A full survey of the term is offered by K. Seybold, *"masiah," TDOT* 9:43–54.

both the ruler and representative of Israel before God (Ps. 2:7). Later still, the plenary imagery and terminology of divine sonship are bestowed upon Jesus when, at his baptism, God declares, "You are my beloved Son, in whom I am well pleased" (Mark 1:11). Early Christians saw in Jesus's baptism—and in his subsequent life, death, and resurrection—the consummation of divine sonship: Jesus was Israel reduced to one, who fulfilled Israel's initial vocation from Abraham onward and who restored wayward and disobedient Israel to its original divine sonship.

In the New Testament, and particularly in the Pauline Epistles, Son of God Christology encompasses the plenary narrative of redemption: the preexistence of the Son, who is sent by the Father; the Son's self-sacrifice on the cross, effecting God's salvific purpose and plan; the Son's enthronement as Messiah, united in filial love with the Father; and the Son's presiding as final judge of all. Philippians 2:5–11 is a quintessential exposition of Son of God Christology, and Galatians 2:20 is a quintessential account of Son of God Christology experienced in the believer's life: "It is no longer I who live, but Christ who lives within me; the life I now live in the flesh, I live by faith in the Son of God, who loved me and handed himself over on my behalf." This redemptive, self-giving love was not an episodic anomaly but the climax of a long-orchestrated salvation, including its divine realization "in the fullness of time" (Gal. 4:4), when the Father sent his Son to redeem humanity from sin in order to fulfill the divine eschatological plan: "that God might be all in all" (1 Cor. 15:28).[37]

Son of God Christology flows as strongly through the arteries of the Apostolic Fathers as it does through those of the New Testament writers. The Son of God is present and active in the creation of the world,[38] and his self-sacrifice in history "sums up" all that is required to atone for human sin: "Therefore, the Son of God came in the flesh for this purpose: to offer full restitution for the sins of those who persecuted his prophets to death."[39] As the Son of God, Jesus is the supreme Savior,[40] the full revelation of God,[41] son of David in the flesh but Son of God in the Spirit,[42] who is both Lord and Messiah.[43] As the Son of God, Jesus will judge the world in truth and righteousness.[44] And he will rule in cosmic authority (as we see, for instance, in Col. 1:15–20) for all eternity.[45]

---

37. See Rom. 5:10; 8:3, 32; Gal. 4:4–6. On Son of God Christology, see Edwards, "Son of God."
38. Barn. 6.12; Herm. Sim. 9.12 (repeatedly emphasized).
39. Barn. 5.11.
40. Barn. 5.9; 7.2, 9; Diogn. 10.2; 11.5; Herm. Sim. 8.11.1; 9.12.5.
41. Ign. *Magn.* 8.2.
42. Ign. *Smyrn.* 1.1.
43. Barn. 12.8, 10, 11; Herm. Sim. 5.5–6 (repeated in various forms ten times).
44. Did. 16.4; Barn. 15.5; Herm. Vis. 2.2.8.
45. Herm. Sim. 8.3.1; 9.12.2; 9.13–14 (several references).

The eternal sonship of Jesus, especially apparent in the Pauline epistles, plays a pronounced role in the fathers, who use "Son of God" more frequently with reference to Jesus's eternal sonship than to his incarnate sonship.[46] We witness the early church's wholesale abandonment of the title "Son of Man," which was Jesus's preferred self-designation in the Gospels but came to be regarded as a reference to his human nature alone.[47] The fathers' emphasis on the exalted nature of the Son of God resulted in a heightened sense of the union of the Son of God with believers, and of discipleship as union with Christ. The fathers refer to believers as "sons of God" more frequently than New Testament writers do.[48] Ignatius tells believers to sing "in union with one voice through Jesus Christ to the Father, in order that he may . . . acknowledge that [they] are members of his Son."[49] Believers are likewise baptized in the name of the Father, Son, and Holy Spirit;[50] and the one in whose name they are baptized is the only one whom they worship. The Martyrdom of Polycarp declares martyrs worthy of honor, but it declares the Son of God alone as worthy of worship.[51] The fathers acknowledge the totality of the Son of God narrative, which, like Philippians 2:5–11, encompasses everything from the preexistence of the Son to his role as the final judge of all. The Shepherd of Hermas foresees the end of time: "When all the nations under heaven have heard and believed on the name of the Son of God, they will have received the seal, having one thought, one mind, one faith, and one love."[52] The divine sonship of Jesus is the proclamation and content of all God's preachers, whether prophets or servants, apostles or teachers.[53] Preaching in the name of the Son of God is the sum and "seal of the church's proclamation."[54]

Jesus as Savior

The major titles above are complemented by numerous other titles for Jesus in the first century. One of the more important, "Savior" (Gk. *sōtēr*), occurs twenty times in the New Testament (half of them in the Pastoral Letters) and nine times in the Apostolic Fathers. The noun "salvation" occurs

---

46. Ign. *Eph*. 20.2; Barn. 12.10; Diogn. 7.4.

47. In its three occurrences in the New Testament outside the Gospels, "Son of Man" appears with reference to the exalted Jesus (Acts 7:56; Rev. 1:13; 14:14), and its two occurrences in the Apostolic Fathers refer to Jesus's human rather than divine nature (Ign. *Eph*. 20; Barn. 12.9).

48. See the references cited in *PGL* 1426.

49. Ign. *Eph*. 4.2; further, Ign. *Rom*. 1.1 (twice); Herm. Sim. 2.6; 2.11.

50. Matt. 28:19; Did. 7.1, 3.

51. Mart. Pol. 17.3.

52. Herm. Sim. 9.17.4.

53. Herm. Sim. 9.15.4.

54. Herm. Sim. 9.16.5.

frequently both in the New Testament and in the fathers,[55] but the title "Savior" appears very infrequently. The sparing use of "Savior" in early Christianity may be a reaction against its wide and indiscriminate use in the Roman imperial cult.[56] The use of "Savior" in conjunction with God the Father in salutations and benedictions in both the New Testament and the Apostolic Fathers guards it from association with the emperor cult.[57] However, "Savior" appears with reference to Jesus in decisive New Testament texts. In the angelic announcement to the shepherds regarding Jesus's birth (Luke 2:11), the title is used to counteract the claims and cult of Augustus Caesar (who appears in 2:1). Jesus is the Savior of more than the Roman Empire. He is the Savior of the *kosmos*, the world (John 4:42), "whom God exalted at his right hand as Founder and Savior."[58] As Savior, Jesus is endowed with power to save the powerless.[59]

Jesus as Creator

The New Testament makes the astonishing assertion that the Son, in concert with the Father, was the agent of the world's creation.[60] The New Testament and the fathers identify the primary reference of the "image of God" (Lat. *imago Dei*) not with humanity in general but with Jesus in particular.[61] Only because Jesus is the *imago Dei*—or, to use Paul's framing, the *second Adam*—is he alone capable of redeeming fallen humanity. As the second Adam, "he renewed us by the forgiveness of sins, made us people of another type, . . . as if he were creating us all over again."[62] In the words of Paul, the result of the Son's redemption is, literally, a "new creation."[63]

55. See, for example, the lengthy review of salvation history in Barn. 5.

56. The New Testament generally avoids using titles associated with the imperial cult. In addition to "savior" (Gk. *sōtēr*), the following Greek titles proliferated in the Roman imperial world but are rare in the New Testament: *euergetēs* ("benefactor," only in Luke 22:25), *autokratōr* ("absolute ruler," absent in the New Testament), *huios tou theou* ("Son of God," used in the New Testament only of Jesus in defined contexts), *megas/megistos* ("great," "supreme," rare in the New Testament), *kratistos* ("most excellent," only Luke 1:3; Acts 23:26; 24:3; 26:25), and *sebastos* ("revered," "august," only in Acts 27:1). Josephus also frequently couples "savior" and "benefactor" in political and nationalistic associations (*J.W.* 1.530; 3.459; 4.146; 7.71; *Ant.* 11.278; 12.261; *Vita* 244; 259).

57. See 2 Clem. 20.5; Ign. *Eph.* 1.1; Ign. *Magn.* 1.1; Pol. *Phil.* 1.1; Mart. Pol. 19.2.

58. Acts 5:31; see also 2 Clem. 20.5.

59. "Having now revealed the Savior's power to save even the powerless, [God] willed that . . . we should believe in his goodness and regard him as nurse, father, teacher, counselor, healer, mind, light, honor, glory, strength, and life" (Diogn. 9.6, Holmes trans.).

60. John 1:1, 10; Col. 1:16; Heb. 1:2–3.

61. See 2 Cor. 4:4; Col. 1:15; Barn. 6.12–13.

62. Barn. 6.11; see also Rom. 5:12–21.

63. Gal. 6:15; 2 Cor. 5:17.

Jesus as Revealer of God

Jesus is also said to be the unique revealer and saving representative of God. To know Jesus is to know God. Ignatius exhorts the Ephesians to "become wise by receiving God's knowledge, which is Jesus Christ."[64] The author of Second Clement begins his "epistle," which may be "the oldest surviving complete Christian sermon outside the New Testament,"[65] with a climactic opening line: "Brothers and sisters, we ought to think of Jesus Christ as we think of God."[66] Both the Gospel of John and the fathers refer to Jesus as *monogenēs*, "the only-begotten Son."[67] According to the Epistle to Diognetus, the only-begotten Son alone is capable of restoring humanity to its created image of God.[68] Nearly as sublime as *monogenēs* is the reference to Jesus as the "Word of God," which is also featured in the prologue of the Fourth Gospel. As the "Word of God," Jesus was with God—indeed was God—becoming incarnate in human flesh both to reveal God and to save the world.[69] The Epistle to Diognetus emphasizes Jesus as the "Word": "This is the one who was from the beginning, who appeared as new yet proved to be old, and is always young as he is born in the hearts of saints."[70] The title "Word of God" embodies the essential paradox of the incarnation—that Jesus is both *with* God and *is* God. In Oscar Cullmann's words, "The word of God *proclaimed* by Jesus is at the same time the word *lived* by him; he is himself the Word of God."[71] As God in the flesh, Jesus is both God and revealer of God.

Two further images of Jesus as divine revealer are worthy of mention. Ignatius speaks of Jesus as "the archives of God," the sum of all that can be known of God: "The unalterable archives of Jesus Christ are his cross and death and his resurrection and the faith that comes through him."[72] Ignatius also refers to Jesus as the Great Physician, and in so doing he reintroduces the above paradox of the Word of God. The Great Physician, according to Ignatius, is one being in two natures: "There is only one physician, who is both flesh and spirit, born and unborn, God in man, true life in death, both of Mary and of God, now suffering but then beyond suffering, Jesus Christ our Lord."[73]

---

64. Ign. *Eph.* 17.2.
65. Holmes, *Apostolic Fathers*, 132.
66. 2 Clem. 1.1.
67. John 1:14, 18; 3:18; Mart. Pol. 20.2.
68. Diogn. 10.2. See also John 3:16; Heb. 11:17; 1 John 4:9.
69. John 1:1, 14, 16–18.
70. Diogn. 11.3–5 (Holmes trans.).
71. Cullmann, *Christology*, 267.
72. Ign. *Phld.* 8.2.
73. Ign. *Eph.* 7.2.

Jesus as Eschatological Judge

Finally, early Christians also referred to Jesus as the eschatological judge of the world. Here too, and without qualification, the church identified both God and Jesus with a single role, for Paul speaks of God as judge and equally of Jesus as judge.[74] In some New Testament passages—Acts 7:56, for example— God and Jesus adjudicate simultaneously. Jesus appears as the final judge in several parables.[75] The Christ hymn of Philippians 2:5–11 again highlights Jesus Christ as the perfect executor of the divine plan, for God has given to the Son full dominion over creation, including its final judgment. Curiously, the office of Jesus as judge of the living and the dead plays only a minor role in the Apostolic Fathers,[76] which could imply that the first Christian generations were less preoccupied with the early return of Christ than scholars often assume.

The Scandal of the Incarnation

The above titles, images, metaphors, and allusions are subsumed in the central proposition of the kerygma—that Jesus, the anointed one of God who was sent to the world as its redeemer, was crucified and raised from the dead.[77] The central point of the kerygma is that, in Jesus, *God became a human being* in order to be and do for humanity what humanity could not be and do for itself. God's ability to assume the human condition, which includes taking upon Godself the abject level of human suffering and death, is the scandal of the incarnation. It is important to remember that becoming human does *not* belong to non-Christian definitions of God. No other religion besides Christianity has considered becoming human essential to its confession of God.[78] From the earliest days of the church, this "descent on the part of God" perplexed and offended critics of Christianity. Was it not possible, Celsus asked in derision, that God could achieve the betterment of the human race by his *divine power* rather than by a disgraceful humiliation into human weakness in the supposed incarnation of Jesus Christ?[79] The apostle Paul was aware

74. God as Judge: 1 Thess. 3:13; Rom. 3:5; 14:10. Jesus as Judge: 1 Cor. 4:5; 2 Cor. 5:10; 2 Tim. 4:1, 8.

75. Matt. 25:1–33.

76. See 2 Clem. 1.1; Pol. *Phil.* 2.1; Barn. 7.2.

77. The foregoing review of titles—especially "God," "Son of God," and "Lord"—reveals the patent error in Bart Ehrman's popular but erroneous claim: "The idea that Jesus was divine was a later Christian invention, one found, among our Gospels, only in John" (*Jesus, Interrupted*, 249).

78. See Edwards, *Jesus the Only Savior?*, 113–15.

79. Origen, *Cels.* 4.2–3.

of the scandal of the incarnation, perhaps even tempted to be ashamed of it (Rom. 1:16). God's identification with human weakness resulted in Jesus's appalling death on a cross. The speeches in Acts, likewise, rarely mention the cross, emphasizing rather the divine favor on Jesus, his Servant, in resurrecting him from the dead. Ignatius captures the essence of Paul's declaration that Jesus "became a lowly human, obedient to death" (Phil. 2:8) in powerful and poetic redundancy:

> Be deaf, therefore, whenever anyone speaks to you apart from Jesus Christ, who was of the family of David, who was the son of Mary; who really was born, who both ate and drank; who really was persecuted under Pontius Pilate, who really was crucified and died while those in heaven and on earth and under the earth looked on; who, moreover, really was raised from the dead when his Father raised him up. In the same way, his Father will likewise also raise up in Christ Jesus us who believe in him, who apart from him have no true life.[80]

This dogma—that God's Son was sent to take upon himself human weakness, sin, and death—profoundly offended Celsus, mentioned above, and the elite detractors of Christianity in the second and following centuries. Celsus feared that the conversion of the patrician classes to Christianity would destabilize and irrevocably threaten the social and religious order on which Roman society depended.[81] It was clear to all, whether lovers of Christ or haters of Christ, that proclaiming the scandal of the incarnation exposed Christians to the greatest of dangers. If the scandal of the gospel was simple folly, why were early Christians so vehemently denounced and persecuted? Paul asks the Galatians, rhetorically, why he is being persecuted by Judaizers if he is not proclaiming "the scandal of the cross" (Gal. 5:11). If Christ did not truly descend into the human state and suffer humiliation and death, then, writes Ignatius, "I am not truly in chains. And why do I submit myself to death, to fire, to sword, and to beasts?"[82] Did not Jews in the mid-second century curse Justin Martyr and other Christians for worshiping a crucified man, whose crucifixion attested that he was justly accursed by God?[83] The particularity of Christology especially offended the monotheism of Jews and the dignity of the Greek pantheon. This scandalous dogma, so indefatigably promoted by Christians, accounted for the martyrdoms of Stephen[84] and James,[85] the

---

80. Ign. *Trall.* 9.
81. Freyne, *Jesus Movement and Its Expansion*, 324–25.
82. Ign. *Smyrn.* 4.2; Ign. *Trall.* 10.
83. Justin, *Dial.* 96.
84. Acts 7:52; see also 9:1–2.
85. Eusebius, *Hist. eccl.* 2.23.2, 10, 13–14.

descendants of David following the First Revolt,[86] Jewish believers in Christ at the hand of Bar Kokhba,[87] and Polycarp.[88] Justin decreed that this dogma alone—that one so abased was divine and worthy of worship—resulted in the wholesale rejection of Christianity by Judaism.[89]

The titles, images, and assertions made of Jesus are appropriate for no other figure in the history of Israel—not for Adam or Moses, not for Samuel or David, not for Elijah or any of the other prophets. Jesus is the unique agent of God in both revelation and redemption because he shares the divine nature itself. Christian claims regarding Jesus Christ found no counterparts in either Judaism or polytheism. The hope of Jews for a future Messiah was, for Christians, already fulfilled in the crucifixion and resurrection of Christ. The Christian doctrine of incarnation upended the Greco-Roman goal of deification and apotheosis of humanity. The titles "Lord" and "Son of God," attributed to Jesus, vastly exceeded the Jewish messianic expectation. Likewise, the titles ascribed to Jesus (e.g., Acts 2:36) and the description of his person and mission (e.g., Phil. 2:5–11) divided Christianity categorically from both Jewish monotheism and Hellenistic polytheism.[90] For Jews, the Christian claim of a crucified Messiah was a shameful and fatal contradiction—for the Messiah they expected was, by definition, a victorious king who would restore Israel and preside over Israel in a long and prosperous reign.[91] For polytheists, the Christian claim of the *incarnation*—not merely occasional and transitory appearances of gods in human form but the complete union of the divine with human suffering and death—was equally fatal, for the unique New Testament claim that in Jesus of Nazareth God had become a true human being seemed to render the Christian witness absurd. "What is the meaning of such a descent upon the part of God?" mocks Celsus. If God cannot make humanity good by way of almighty heavenly knowledge and power, he argues, how could God

86. Eusebius, *Hist. eccl.* 3.12; 3.17.
87. Justin, *1 Apol.* 31.5–6.
88. Mart. Pol. 17.2.
89. Justin, *Dial.* 16.4; 96.2.
90. "The falling out between Jews and Christians already discernible in Jerusalem had its roots in the confession of the πιστεύοντες [*pisteuontes*, "believers"]. The insight and conviction that God made Jesus of Nazareth into the Κύριος καὶ Χριστός [*Kyrios kai Christos*, "Lord and Christ"] (Acts 2:36)—the same Jesus whom the Romans had crucified at the behest of the Sanhedrin—and on Golgotha presented a once-for-all atonement for the people of God (Rom. 3:25–26) brought about a separation between those who followed this confession and those who considered it erroneous or even blasphemous." Stuhlmacher, "Christ in the Pauline School," 170.
91. See the conclusion of Evans, *From Jesus to the Church*, 145–49; esp. 148: "We may conclude that the primary objection to Christian claims that the crucified Jesus of Nazareth is in fact Israel's Messiah was the fact of his death, and a shameful one at that. From a Jewish perspective, this objection was fatal."

conceivably make humanity good, as Christians claim, by becoming a weak and fallible human?[92] Martin Hengel rightly identifies "the load-bearing core of Christology" that differentiated Christianity from its Jewish and Greco-Roman contexts. To summarize Hengel: the radical grace of the incarnation of the Son of God is the single most important and formative factor in the proclamation of the early church, the impulse of its gentile mission, and the formation of the Christian church.[93]

The turn of the second century was an important line of demarcation for early Christianity. Ignatius of Antioch straddled the line. With one foot in the first century, he was the last churchman for whom "Jesus Christ alone," without further elaboration, sufficed as the defining content of Christianity.[94] With the other foot in the second century, although not the first to deal with the issue of docetism,[95] Ignatius was the first to realize its peril to an unqualified confession of Jesus Christ alone and thus the need further to define and defend the Christian confession. He emphatically repeats that Christ "was truly born," "truly ate and drank," "truly died,"[96] that his resurrection body was truly human and not an unsubstantial ghost,[97] and above all, that the cross of Christ was not a stumbling block to a faithful Christology.[98] Ignatius was thus the first of the fathers to set the stage for a robust theological engagement with the heterodoxies and heresies of the second and following centuries.[99]

Behind and beneath the Christology of Ignatius and his first-century predecessors is the conviction that the essential claims made of Jesus are the same claims that belong to the properties of God. First-century Christians framed the person and work of Jesus Christ in cosmic and supernatural categories.

92. Origen, *Cels.* 4.3 (*ANF* 4:498). Freyne, *Jesus Movement and Its Expansion*, 324–25, argues that Christology was the single point that made Christianity uncompromisingly odious to the Greco-Roman world. This included, in addition to its dogma of the incarnation (*Cels.* 4.3), an offense to the oneness of God in the claim of Jesus's deity (*Cels.* 7.3); the claim of virgin birth, which Celsus regarded as a Christian fabrication to disguise Mary's infidelity with a Roman soldier named Pandera/Panthera (*Cels.* 1.32); and the claim of resurrection—which, Celsus argued, was a hallucination of "a half-frantic woman," since "no one really dead ever rose with a true body" (*Cels.* 2.55).

93. Hengel, *Studien zum Urchristentum*, 317–25.

94. Ign. *Eph.* 14.2; Ign. *Magn.* 4.1; 10.3; Ign. *Rom.* 3.3; Ign. *Trall.* 6.1.

95. Docetism (from Gk. *dokeō*, "to appear or seem") was a tendency in early Christianity to regard the humanity and sufferings of Jesus as apparent rather than real. In teaching that Jesus *seemed* human but was not truly human, docetism denied the incarnation. Docetist tendencies are alluded to in 1 John 4:1–3; 2 John 7; and perhaps Col. 2:8–9.

96. Ign. *Trall.* 9; Ign. *Smyrn.* 1, 2, 3; Ign. *Magn.* 11.

97. Ign. *Smyrn.* 3.

98. Ign. *Eph.* 18; Ign. *Magn.* 9, 11; Ign. *Trall.* 2, 8; Ign. *Phld.* 3; Ign. *Smyrn.* 1, 5, 6. For more on Ignatius and docetism, see Lightfoot, *Apostolic Fathers*, 1:375–76.

99. See von Campenhausen, *Urchristliches und Altkirchliches*, 270–71.

The promises and prophecies of God are fulfilled in Jesus Christ (2 Cor. 1:20).[100] In leading believers to Christ, the divine purpose of Torah is fulfilled (Gal. 3:24); and in the teaching of Christ to love one's neighbor (Gal. 5:14) and bear the burdens of the other (Gal. 6:2), all the commandments of Torah are both summarized and fulfilled. Jesus is, and has always been, "the first and the last" (Rev. 1:17). For first-century Christians, Jewish monotheism in the Old Testament cannot be rightly understood apart from Jesus's claim: "I and the Father are one" (John 10:30). The cosmic significance of Jesus is proclaimed in Ephesians 1:10: all things have been summed up in Christ. And the cosmic scope of the Christ event is affirmed in 1 Corinthians 15:28: "When all things are subjected to [Jesus], then the Son himself will be subjected to the one who subjects all things to him, so that God may be all things in all."

---

100. See 2 Cor. 3:14–18; Heb. 8:7–13.

8

From Synagogue to Church

In the previous chapter, we referred to an inner core of the Jesus movement that remained constant through the external changes that transpired from the death of Jesus to the day of Ignatius. That unchanging core shaped and conformed the movement and its adherents, both individual and communal, to its character.[1] The shaping reality was the adamantine conviction of Jesus followers that the master who had called them into fellowship with himself had died on the cross for their sins and had been resurrected from the dead for their justification (Rom. 4:25).[2] But the significance of Jesus was not limited to his sacrificial death and resurrection, matchless though they were. Believers understood themselves, in a very real sense, to have died and been resurrected with and through him. And they further believed that the Lord who had been present in their earthly fellowship was, in his celestial reign,

1. Although Karl Barth did not write *Church Dogmatics* with specific reference to the development of the early church, his understanding of the shaping nature of revelation, as attested in Scripture, is descriptive of our present task. Barth understands Jesus Christ, as he is attested in Holy Scripture, as the lifeblood and living Lord of the church. In its connection with divine revelation, "Scripture is in the hands but not in the power of the Church. It speaks as it is translated, interpreted and applied. But always in and even in spite of all these human efforts, it is Scripture itself which speaks" (*CD* I/2, 682–83).

2. In contrast to a view popular among liberal twentieth-century New Testament scholars, that the apostle Paul was an innovator in doctrine and the essential founder of Christianity, I adhere to the view that Paul was a faithful interpreter of the "tradition" and "remembrance" of Jesus (1 Cor. 11:23–26) and neither the founder of Christianity nor an essential rival to other exponents of the Christian tradition, such as Peter and James. This position is ably articulated and argued by Stuhlmacher, "Christ in the Pauline School."

equally present and efficacious in the church through the Holy Spirit. As we saw in the last chapter, soon after Jesus's death and resurrection, his followers formulated the essentials of salvation in skeletal form: the kerygma. Even before they articulated their faith, however, they joined in a community that bore witness as the firstfruits of the kingdom Jesus introduced. Their "called-out community" (Gk. *ekklēsia*) is the subject of this chapter.

The Peculiarity of the *Ekklēsia*

Arthur Darby Nock insightfully observes that the success of Christianity was first and foremost "the success of an institution" that embodied and promoted the gospel. According to Nock, the ancient world first became aware of Christianity not through the gospel but through two expressions of it that differed from the expressions of all other cults and religions. The first expression was the structured community of the church, the *ekklēsia*; the second was its martyrs, who bore witness to the faith. Christians died for their beliefs when necessary, and they formed themselves into communities that exemplified their beliefs before the world. The world saw the face of Christianity in church and martyrdom before it heard its voice in the gospel.[3]

We easily forget the uniqueness of a philosophy that instantiated itself in organizational form. Judaism, of course, did so in the synagogue, which was as important for Judaism as the church was for Christianity. Apart from Judaism and Christianity, however, no other philosophy (neither Stoicism, nor Cynicism, nor Pythagoreanism) and no other cult (neither that of Isis, nor of Mithra, nor of Cybele, nor even of the Roman emperor) formed identifiable communities that, like the Christian church, were organized in microcosm, affiliated in macrocosm, and convoked weekly to commemorate their founding and transmit themselves. The Christian "philosophy" was only one of many philosophies that pulsated through the first-century world. Most of these philosophies and movements surely appeared to their contemporaries more likely than Christianity to succeed. But the Christian philosophy was characterized by one distinctive that gave it an edge over all the others: its community, the church, which equipped Christianity to survive and ultimately to transform ancient culture itself.

Acts reports that already at Pentecost, fifty days after Jesus's resurrection, a distinctive community of Jesus followers existed in Jerusalem, observing "the teaching of the apostles" (the kerygma), fellowship, common meals, and prayer (Acts 2:42–47). The last three of these distinctives would also have been

---

3. Nock, *Conversion*, 192–93, 210–11, 241.

shared, if in somewhat different forms, by Jews who did not believe in Jesus. The major distinctive in the list is the first element: the apostolic confession of Jesus as Messiah, even as *kyrios* (Lord). The saving uniqueness of Jesus remained at the forefront of the Christian proclamation. We see it again in Acts 4, when members of the Jesus community are arrested in the temple for "proclaiming, in Jesus, the resurrection from the dead" (v. 2) and when believers appear as custodians of "the apostolic testimony to the resurrection of the Lord Jesus" (v. 33). As a consequence of this testimony, the apostles Peter and John were tried and reprimanded by the high priestly Sadducean family and then "sent away to their own people" (v. 23).

Who were "their own people"? This unassuming phrase must refer to the community, described in Acts 2:42, that participated in the temple community of Jerusalem but maintained its separate fellowship was well. That fellowship was the church in its embryonic form. Thereafter in Acts, Jesus followers are identified no longer with the temple but with churches in Jerusalem and all Judea, Galilee, and Samaria (9:31); in Antioch (13:1); and in Phrygia and Galatia (14:21–27). At the gathering of the Council of Jerusalem in the late 40s, all participating units are called "*ekklēsiai*," churches (15:22).

There are elements in the Epistle of James that seem appropriate to a worship setting that included both Jewish and gentile Jesus followers. James is the only New Testament epistle to refer to believers worshiping in both synagogues (2:2) and churches (5:14). In its opening line, "to the twelve tribes in the dispersion," James refers to Jesus followers as the consummation of salvation history in Israel (1:1). If, as has been traditionally maintained, the epistle was authored by James—the Lord's brother, who maintained ties with the temple leadership in Jerusalem—then its references to religion and its understated Christology would have played well in a Christian worshiping community closely affiliated with Judaism.[4]

The size and diversity of the church in Jerusalem was soon increased by members from Hellenistic synagogues of the diaspora, some of whom were probably Godfearers and most of whom spoke Greek.[5] These hybrid communities beat an early and wide path from Judaism to Christianity. Luke testifies to such persons and their influence on early Christian missions in the Jewish diaspora in Acts 6–7. The newly converted Paul first proclaimed the gospel in a Hellenistic synagogue in Damascus (Acts 9:20), and thenceforth synagogues became starting points for his preaching and mission on the

---

4. For "religion," see James 1:26–27. "Jesus Christ" appears only in 1:1 and 2:1. For a similar reconstruction of the Epistle of James and of early Acts, see Evans, *From Jesus to the Church*, 35–37.

5. On Godfearers, see ch. 5, pp. 89–91.

Jerusalem–Rome corridor.[6] The critical point to grasp here is that Hellenistic synagogues were the initial points of contact for Christian missions within the Jewish diaspora, and perhaps even within Greco-Roman culture at large. Christian missionaries did not found synagogues, however. They founded *churches*.[7] From its inception in Acts, the apostolic community in Jerusalem is called only a church, never a synagogue. This is more noteworthy than it may appear to gentile Christian readers of Acts, for the earliest Jesus followers in Jerusalem were all Jews who had regularly participated with Jesus in Galilean synagogues. But in Jerusalem, they are not expressly identified with synagogues.[8] The New Testament and the Apostolic Fathers never refer to a community founded by Paul or other Christian missionaries as a synagogue. No Christian epistles, whether from Paul or any other church leader, are written to synagogues. Especially in the diaspora, Christian missionaries witnessed to the gospel in synagogues, but they founded churches. Paul's experience in Ephesus was typical: he preached in the synagogue of Ephesus (Acts 19:8), but it was from the *church* in Ephesus that he summoned elders to meet him in Miletus (Acts 20:17). Jesus followers were identified by the word "church" (Acts 5:11) even before they were identified as "Christians" (Acts 11:26).[9] The church was essential to the identity of believers, who received it as the community instituted by God, as the body of Christ.[10]

The Greek word for "church," *ekklēsia*, occurs 115 times in the Greek New Testament. Half the occurrences are plural, referring to individual churches; the other half are singular, referring to the *one* church, the collective unity of which each individual congregation is a microcosm. The plural and singular are not fundamentally different, however, for churches are individual lights powered by a single source, the one gospel in the universal

6. Acts 13:5, 14, 43; 14:1; 17:1, 10, 17; 18:4, 7, 19; 19:8. For more on Hellenistic synagogues in Christian mission along the Jerusalem–Rome corridor, see ch. 2, pp. 21–22.

7. The only New Testament epistles in which the word *ekklēsia* does not appear are 2 Timothy, Titus, 1–2 Peter, 1–2 John, and Jude.

8. Even in Acts 6, the conflict between Greek-speaking and Hebrew-speaking Jewish Jesus followers is not identified with a synagogue. A diaspora synagogue in Jerusalem, in fact, leads the opposition against Stephen (v. 9).

9. A prayer in the Didache calls on God to oversee the church like a shepherd: "Lord, remember your church, to deliver it from all evil and to perfect it in your love, and from the four winds gather the church that you have sanctified into your kingdom, which you have prepared for it; for the power and glory are yours forever" (Did. 10.5).

10. On the use of "*ekklēsia*" in the New Testament, see Karl L. Schmidt, "*ekklēsia*," *TWNT* 3:502–39; Jürgen Roloff, "*ekklēsia*," *EDNT* 1:410–15. Reference to the church is sometimes made even without the word *ekklēsia*, as when believers are called the house of Christ (Heb. 3:6) or "partners of Christ" (Heb. 3:14).

body of Christ.[11] In Acts 15, Luke names different individuals attending the Council of Jerusalem from different places and churches as belonging to "the whole church" (15:22). The root meaning of *ekklēsia* in classical Greek is "assembly," with specific reference to political assemblies in the Greek *polis*. Luke, in fact, uses *ekklēsia* in this political sense in his description of the riot in Ephesus.[12] The Jewish synagogue rather than Greek *polis*, however, determined the conceptual framework of *ekklēsia* in the New Testament. "Remember your congregation," prays the psalmist to God, "which you acquired long ago and redeemed to be the tribe of your heritage" (Ps. 74:2). The Hebrew word for "congregation" here is *'edah*, and in the Septuagint is the Greek *synagōgē*. The apostle Paul alludes to this verse in his parting speech to the elders of the church of Ephesus (Acts 20:28), but he substitutes the word *ekklēsia* for *'edah/synagōgē*. In so doing he links the Christian *ekklēsia* to the communities of Israel's faith in the Old Testament. *Ekklēsia* became the commonly accepted designation for Christian assemblies, whether they were composed of Jewish Christians or gentile Christians, or both. It was not one term among others; it was the only term used, whether of a local congregation or of the broader institution. The constituency of the church was, of course, human. But its founder was the Lord, and its mission was a divine mandate. *Ekklēsia* is never used with reference to one of the "pillars" of the early church; we never hear, for example, of the church of Paul (or Peter or John or James). *Ekklēsia* is used always and only with reference to its Lord—"the church of God" or, occasionally, "the church of Christ."

The Church: Old, New, and Whole

In the earliest formal definition of the Christian faith, the Roman symbol of the mid-second century, the church is called "holy" and "catholic." The Nicene Creed of 325 adds two more defining articles: "one" and "apostolic." The orthodox confession of "one, holy, catholic, and apostolic church" accentuates the church's unity, sanctity, universality, and apostolicity. In the following conceptual categories of old, new, and whole, I attempt to demonstrate the foundation of the orthodox confession of the church already in the New Testament and Apostolic Fathers.[13]

---

11. This is illustrated in the book of Revelation, where the word *ekklēsia* occurs twenty times, and almost always in the plural—*ekklēsiai* (churches)—meaning communities of the one church.

12. Acts 19:32, 39. The few occurrences of *ekklēsia* in the Gospel of Matthew (16:18; 18:17) might refer to a Jesus assembly.

13. My three categories, though not taken from a particular source, are closest to the summation of the early church as *a people* that was both *primitive* (old) and *new* in Harnack, *Mission and Expansion*, 251–65.

Old

Unlike moderns, for whom "old" is usually pejorative, connoting something outdated, the ancients typically looked on "old" positively, as indicating something that had withstood the test of time and was thus valuable. Early Christians thought of the antiquity of the church as something positive. If the church per se was not ancient, it was nevertheless the repository of the ancient and venerable revelation of God.[14] The church was heir of all that had gone before in God's dealings with Israel, bringing together the random notes and isolated melodies of Israel's history into a symphonic finale. We see this in Luke's use of the word "church," which, in contrast to his use of the word "Christian," for example, is not introduced as the result of a process of historical development. We do not see a point where the Jesus fellowship within the Jewish synagogue *becomes* the Christian church. The liturgical calendar commonly refers to Pentecost as the beginning or "birthday" of the church. Pentecost, however, is mentioned only three times in the New Testament (never in the Apostolic Fathers), none of which designates the church's beginning.[15] In Acts, the descent of the Holy Spirit on the church signifies not the formation of the church but the equipping of the church for witness to the mighty works of God in various languages and mission to gentiles (Acts 1:8). Throughout the New Testament, the church, the *ekklēsia*, exists wherever and whenever individuals hear and respond to the kerygma in faith.[16] This understanding began with Jesus himself, who, in calling twelve apostles, reconstituted the twelve tribes of Israel. The prophets before him had appealed to the precedents of Torah or Moses in Israel's formative years, without which Israel would have ceased being Israel. Following the exile, Zerubbabel, Ezra, and Nehemiah appealed to the same basis for a restoration of Israel's mission. It was to this saving strain in Israel that Jesus coupled the apostolic community. Early in Acts (5:11), Luke refers to this community as the "church," and in doing so he reappropriates the strain that had been sustained by God's grace throughout Israel's history.

We see something similar in Paul. The argument of Romans 4, that Abraham was justified by faith, attests to the eternal and enduring core of the gospel throughout the history of Israel. Romans 9–11 develops the point

14. Lake, "Introduction," 1:xv, summarizes Eusebius's understanding of the teaching of Christianity and the race of Christians in *Hist. eccl.* 1.4.1–15 as follows: "The teaching of Christianity was neither new nor strange. What was new was the Church, the race of Christians. Their corporate existence, their general piety, and their increasing influence were indeed new, but their teaching was not."

15. Acts 2:1–13; 20:16; 1 Cor. 16:8.

16. Acts 8:3; Col. 4:15.

similarly, where Paul refers to the history of Israel as a story of two Israels; he speaks of an "Israel within Israel," a *remnant Israel* as an enduring kernel of God's salvific line, the children of promise within the external husk of *ethnic Israel*, the children of disobedience (9:6–13). Paul's subsequent reference to the "root" of the olive tree, onto which both Jews and gentiles must be engrafted for salvation, presupposes a redeemed community in the history of Israel (11:13–24). At two points in the New Testament this saving strain is consummated in a new covenant that was promised in Jeremiah (31:31–34). The first is the baptism of Jesus, where the Spirit descends on Jesus and God declares "You are my Son,"[17] thereby ratifying and completing the divine intention for Israel to be the firstborn son of God (Exod. 4:22–23). At the baptism, Jesus is Israel reduced to one; and in Jesus, Israel's destiny is fulfilled. The second point is Pentecost, where God bestows the Spirit on the community of Jesus, the church, thereby empowering it to carry forth the mission of Jesus to gentiles (Acts 2:1–4).

The church carried forth its legacy with Judaism and the Old Testament in several obvious respects. One of the most important was in following the synagogue rather than the temple as the prototype of the gathered community of believers. Temples, whether the Jewish temple in Jerusalem or pagan temples throughout the Greco-Roman world, were anchored to sacred places, as were mystery cults.[18] To access the efficacy of such a cult, one had to go to the place where it was located. Church and synagogue, by contrast, were mobile communities that accompanied believers wherever they were located. In this respect, believers did not go to churches and synagogues, but rather, churches and synagogues went with Christian and Jewish believers, from which they bore witness in their respective communities. The New Testament and the Apostolic Fathers refer to the church in this mobile sense, as the "sojourning" people of God, guiding believers through the pilgrimage of life.[19] The ever-present metaphor of the church as a "tower" in the Shepherd of Hermas, by contrast, captures its fastness but fails to convey its mobility.

The Jewish synagogue also provided the template for Christian worship, including Scripture readings, prayers, song, oral interpretation, and common meals. The church followed the synagogue in omitting animal sacrifices, which were practiced in the Jerusalem temple and in virtually all polytheistic cults. And the vocabulary of the new faith was indebted to the Jewish tradition, including key concepts such as righteousness, grace, works of the law, (new)

17. Matt. 3:17; Mark 1:11; Luke 3:22.
18. For more on mystery cults, see ch. 1, p. 13.
19. James 1:1; 1 Pet. 1:1; 1 Clem. 1.1; 2 Clem. 5.1

covenant, servant of God, divine Sonship, (Holy) Spirit, and many others.[20] These terms contributed to the skeletal theological structure that Christians inherited from Judaism. If the musculature of the new faith moved the old bones in new ways, the bones themselves belonged to the story of salvation contained in *both* Testaments.

Along with vocabulary, the church inherited a theological worldview from Judaism. Apart from Zoroastrianism in Persia and perhaps exceptional pharaohs in Egypt, the concept of monotheism, foundational to both Judaism and Christianity (and later to Islam), was anomalous in the ancient world outside Israel. Similarly, creation myths of the ancient Near East presupposed preexisting (and usually warring) material forms from which the cosmos was fashioned, whereas the God of Israel, and thus the God of Christians, is portrayed as creator *ex nihilo*. Another unique characteristic is this God's self-revelation in history. In contrast to the deities of the ancient Near East, which reflected and were accessed by the cycles of nature and the rotations of heavenly bodies, the God of the Judeo-Christian tradition directs *history* to a purposeful end. The concept of absolute morality was also inherent in both Judaism and Christianity. More than custom and ceremonial observance, true religion was the subordination of life—public and private, individual and corporate—to the regulations of a supreme ethical code that was valid in all walks of life. Like the cardinal points of the compass, the above theological convictions oriented Christian life as they did Jewish life.

Finally, the church's heritage intersected with eternity itself. This is already assumed in the New Testament. The prologue of the Fourth Gospel describes the "Word" being with God before time and becoming "the Word made flesh" in time (John 1:1–14). Paul speaks of Jesus Christ existing eternally in form and equality with God (Phil. 2:6), the visible image of the invisible God, in whom all things were created (Col. 1:15–16), who in the fullness of time became human to redeem fallen humans (Gal. 4:4–6). Hebrews speaks of Christ as "the radiance of God's glory, the very imprint of his nature, who upholds the cosmos by the word of his power" (Heb. 1:3). These are, first and foremost, christological declarations rather than ecclesiastical affirmations, but they include the church, for the church is the "body of Christ," which "God chose . . . before the foundation of the world to be holy and blameless before him in love" (Eph. 1:4).[21] If Christ ordained believers before creation, and if believers *are* the church, then the church itself participates in Christ's

20. See here the brief but careful documentation of essential Christian vocabulary in Evans, *From Jesus to the Church*, 22–23.

21. No verse is more essential to Karl Barth's imposing discussion of eternal election in Jesus Christ than Eph. 1:4 (*CD* II/2, §§32–35).

eternal nature. Second Clement affirms this coeternality: "Therefore, brothers and sisters, when we do the will of God our Father, we are one with the first church, which was spiritual and indeed created before the sun and moon."[22] The witness of other Apostolic Fathers concurs. The Shepherd of Hermas portrays the church in an allegory as an elderly woman who hands Hermas a book (the Scriptures). "Who is she?" asks Hermas. "She is the church," replies an attending angel, "and she is elderly because she was created before all things; therefore, she is elderly, and for her sake the world was formed."[23] The image of the church that redounds throughout the Shepherd is that of "a great tower built upon the waters out of shining stones."[24] The tower, as noted earlier, signifies the impregnability of the church, ever unmoved. In his dissertation on the church early in *Ecclesiastical History*, Eusebius avers that Jesus Christ was active as the Logos throughout the history of Israel and that it was he in whom those who then believed were saved, even if they knew him not by name.[25] The church preserves and perfects its ancient heritage, indeed its testimony to the Ancient of Days (Dan. 7:9; Rev. 1:14). "In all the world," declares Eusebius, "it is only among Christians that Abraham's manner of religion is put into practice."[26]

New

The church was the spiritual heir of God's promises to Israel. But it was also, and above all, the community of Jesus Christ, who had fulfilled the promises of God that Israel failed to fulfill. In this latter respect, the church is unique from, and completes, its inheritance from Israel. In the words of Arthur Darby Nock, "The Church of the second century thought of itself as the new people of God, the spiritual Israel, which had entered into the enjoyment of those promises which Israel after the flesh had lost by blindness of heart. Both to themselves and to outsiders they appeared as a people . . . [who] were unique."[27]

---

22. 2 Clem. 14.1. Further, "Now the church, being spiritual, was made manifest in the flesh of Christ" (2 Clem. 14.3).

23. Herm. Vis. 2.4.1.

24. Herm. Vis. 3.2.4.

25. Eusebius, *Hist. eccl.* 1.4.1–15.

26. Eusebius, *Hist. eccl.* 1.4.14. Harnack, *Mission and Expansion*, 253–56, address the same point: "Christians embody the fundamental principles of that divine revelation and worship which are the source of human history, and which constitute the primitive possession of Christianity, although that possession has of course lain undiscovered till the present moment" (256).

27. Nock, *Conversion*, 241.

New elements appear in church worship, including prophecy, admonition, glossolalia, and readings of apostolic letters and gospels. New times for worship are introduced in shifting worship from Saturday to Sunday (a subject discussed in ch. 12, below). New worshipers appear, as we have seen, in the full inclusion of gentiles in Christian churches. This last phenomenon was of such magnitude that it virtually mandated new worship communities, for gentile Godfearers and proselytes did not stand on equal footing with Jews in synagogues.[28]

The changing face of Christian congregations included more than gentiles, however, for women were present in greater number and in more diverse functions than they were in Jewish synagogues. The prominence of women had begun in Jesus's ministry. Luke 8:1–3 names Mary Magdalene, Joanna, Susanna, and "many other women" who financially supported Jesus's ministry. The *kai . . . kai* (both . . . and) Greek grammatical structure in Luke 8:1–2 sets the women in parity with the Twelve. This is a remarkable testimony to the seminal role of women in Jesus's ministry, for which there is no parallel among Jewish rabbis. Women appear as protagonists in Jesus's parables,[29] and they sit "at his feet"—the posture of an approved disciple in Judaism—when he teaches (Luke 10:39).[30] Mary Magdalene appears in all four Gospels as the first herald of the resurrected Lord.[31]

Women appear in equally prominent roles in Acts and the Epistles. Women and children are mentioned as bona fide members of Christian churches, "worthy of all the saints," as Paul says of Phoebe (Rom. 16:1–2).[32] Women bear persecution for the sake of the gospel.[33] They serve in the Pauline mission as "fellow athletes" (Phil. 4:2–3). And Paul attests to the load-bearing role of women in the church of Rome by naming ten women at the conclusion of Romans as "fellow workers," "chosen," "tested and approved," and "dear friends" (Rom. 16:1–16). Indeed, he commends both Andronicus and

28. On Godfearers and proselytes, see ch. 8, pp. 89–91.

29. Luke 13:20–21; 15:8–10; 18:1–8.

30. On the many and various roles of women in the ministry of Jesus, see Duff, *Jesus Followers*, 147–50.

31. Mary Magdalene appears in Matt. 28:1 (with "the other Mary"); Mark 16:1, 9 (with "the mother [or wife] of James, and Salome"); Luke 24:10 (with "Joanna, and Mary, the mother [or wife] of James, and the other women with them"); and John 20:1–18. Mary's name heads each list, and she is the first to proclaim the resurrected Christ.

32. Acts 5:14; 8:12; 9:2; 16:14; 18:2; 21:5; Did. 4.9–10; 1 Clem. 1.3; 2 Clem. 19.1; 20.2; Ign. *Smyrn.* 13.1; Pol. *Phil.* 4.2. Paul signals the presence of women in Christian gatherings by adding "daughters" to a quotation from Isaiah 43:6: "And I shall be your father and you shall be sons *and daughters* to me" (2 Cor. 6:18).

33. Acts 8:3; 22:4. In his letter to the emperor Trajan, Pliny (*Ep. Tra.* 10.96) reports torturing two young Christian women who were "deaconesses."

Junia (a feminine name!) as "prominent among the *apostles*" (Rom. 16:7). First Timothy 3:8–13 includes women in the discussion of deacons, assigning them virtually the same qualifications as men, which implies that women too served as deacons. By the turn of the century, the Greek word for "deacon" appears in both masculine (*diakonos*) and feminine (*diakonissa*) forms, indicating both male and female diaconal officers.[34] Women assumed other leadership roles in early Christianity as well. Priscilla (usually mentioned before her husband, Aquila)[35] tutors Christian leaders (Acts 18:24–28), and Christian fellowships meet in women's homes.[36] The "Elder" addresses his Second Epistle to a woman (whose Greek title, *kyria*, is the feminine form of "lord"), and the public reading of the letter would have upheld *kyria* as a feminine model of leadership (2 John 1).[37]

Luke likewise acknowledges the special roles of three women in Acts: Mary, mother of John Mark, who hosts the church in her home in Jerusalem (Acts 12:1–16); Lydia, who is instrumental in forming a church in Philippi (Acts 16:16–40); and Priscilla (just mentioned), who tutors missionaries in Asia (Acts 18). Along with Phoebe, who heads the long honor role at the end of Paul's Epistle to the Romans and personally delivers the epistle from Corinth to Rome (Rom. 16:1–2),[38] these women are distinguished leaders in first-century Christianity.

We have noted the names of women in the eastern and southern missions of early Christianity, the important role of Nino in the conversion of the region

34. Pliny's letter (*Ep. Tra.* 96) referring to the "two deaconesses" (Lat. *ministrae*) is the earliest known occurrence of the word "deacon" in feminine form. The Greek form, *diakonissa*, appears from the second century onward with reference to an office of women who ministered to women and assisted in women's baptisms. See *PGL* 352.

35. Acts 18:18, 26; Rom. 16:3; 2 Tim. 4:19.

36. Acts 12:12; 16:14; 2 John 1–5.

37. In *Ephesian Women*, Karaman argues from evidence in Ephesus that Greco-Roman cultural norms played a determinative role in the formation of Christian social practices, and especially in the inequality of husbands and wives in marriage (see esp. ch. 4). Whether Greco-Roman cultural norms were as homogenous, and whether they influenced Christian social practices as much as Karaman suggests, is debatable. In Rome, for example, there was divergence and debate on women's roles. Tacitus records vociferous debate on the subject of wives and concubines accompanying Roman troops on their frequent expeditions to Germania, with strong opinions voiced against and for—and with no decision taken (*Ann.* 3.33–34). Tacitus further notes the unprecedented nature of the leadership role of Agrippina, the eldest daughter of Germanicus: "It was an innovation, certainly, and one without precedent in ancient custom, that a woman should sit in state before Roman standards" (*Ann.* 12.37 [LCL]). Some women's roles in Rome, and presumably elsewhere in the empire, were thus subject to debate. Moreover, several roles ascribed to women in the New Testament—e.g., Junia as apostle, Phoebe as courier of Paul's Epistle to the Romans, and Priscilla as tutor of Apollos—seem unconventional by known Greco-Roman standards.

38. The sister of Crescens would play a similar role in delivering Polycarp's epistle to the Philippians (Pol. *Phil.* 14).

of Iberia, the martyrdom of Candida in Persia, and the Scillitan women who were martyred. The names of these seven women equal in number those of men in the same missions—although women's names are more historically verifiable.[39] The prominence of women in the first century along the Jerusalem–Rome corridor and in the early church is also evident in problems and controversies. In some instances they join with leading men in opposing the Christian mission (Acts 13:50). In others their disagreements disrupt the church (Phil. 4:2). And in Corinth (1 Cor. 11:1–16) and the Pastorals (1 Tim. 5:3–16), we see that their gifts and needs require special consideration from the church. In the Christian apocryphal tradition of the early second century, heroines appear in the personalities of Thecla, Maximilla and Iphidama, and Eucleia.[40] The number of women and the various roles they played in the church were exceptional in the ancient world, in relation to both Jewish synagogues and Greco-Roman society at large.[41]

The prominence of women in the church was indirectly related to an increase in three subgroups: widows, orphans, and the poor. The widespread practice of female infanticide in the non-Jewish ancient world resulted in a preponderance of males in Greco-Roman society. The refusal of the Christian church to expose or abort babies, or to sell female babies into slavery, resulted in a higher percentage of women in Christian communities than in Greco-Roman society in general. Girls throughout the ancient world tended to marry soon after puberty, sometimes as early as age thirteen, and often to older men, who usually preceded them in death. These factors combined to produce a disproportionately high number of widows in Christian communities.

Similarly, the refusal of the early church to sell orphans into slavery, as was common in the Greco-Roman world, resulted in more orphans in Christian communities. As for slavery itself, first-century Christianity frequently upheld the practice of extreme social degradation as a model of discipleship. Jesus expressed his saving mission in terms of servitude—giving his life as a ransom

---

39. On Nino, see ch. 3, pp. 58–59. On Candida, see ch. 3, p. 59. On the Scillitan women, see ch. 3, pp. 65–66.

40. On Thecla, see the Acts of Paul and Thecla, *NTApoc* 2:239–70. On Maximilla and Iphidama, see the Acts of Andrew, *NTApoc* 2:136–51. On Eucleia, see the Acts of Andrew, *NTApoc* 2:139–40.

41. See Meeks, *First Urban Christians*, 70–71: "The role of women in the Pauline churches is much greater and much more nearly equal to that of men than in contemporary Judaism." This statement is true of more than only Pauline churches, however. For further discussion of women in early Christianity, see Duff, *Jesus Followers*, 161–69. For sociological analyses of women's roles in early Christianity, see Stark, *Rise of Christianity*, 95–128; Stegemann and Stegemann, *Jesus Movement*, 361–407.

for many (Mark 10:45). Slaves appear in a positive light in the Gospels.[42] Paul claims "slave" (Gk. *doulos*) as a primary metaphor for apostleship in four epistles attributed to him,[43] and his ethical admonitions include the humane treatment of slaves as well as principles that would fundamentally undermine slavery itself.[44] In his Letter to Philemon, Paul calls a slave a "brother"; and brother Onesimus may have become the bishop of Ephesus.[45] The early church's commitment to human dignity resulted in a higher proportion of persons whose needs required the benevolence of the church for survival. The benevolence was not primarily utilitarian—a way of gaining converts, for example. "We know of no cases," writes Adolf Harnack, "in which Christians desired to win, or actually did win, adherents by means of the charities which they dispensed."[46] Standing admonitions in early Christian literature not to neglect widows or forget orphans, and to remember the poor and treat slaves humanely, attest to the moral importance of these persons for the early church.[47]

Virtually every chapter of this book has mentioned the groundbreaking gentile mission of early Christianity. This revolutionary characteristic was the result of a unique consciousness of mission in early Christianity that far surpassed the same sense in either Judaism or Roman religion. Mission was not absent in Judaism, but neither was it vital. Jesus refers to scribes and Pharisees traveling "around the sea and land" to make converts (Matt. 23:15), but this lone reference in the New Testament to Jewish mission—and mission seemingly limited to Israel—indicates its general lack of importance.[48] Mission assumed priority in Christianity because it reflected the theological reality at the heart of the gospel, *the sending of God's Son*. The Fourth Gospel, in particular, repeatedly emphasizes the sending of the Son in the drama of salvation. God is a sending God, and hence the *missio Dei* defines the nature

---

42. Matt. 8:5–13; Luke 16:1–8; 22:26.

43. Rom 1:1; Gal 1:10; Phil 1:1; Titus 1:1.

44. Acts 16:16–18; Rom. 1:1; Gal. 3:28; Col. 3:11; 4:1.

45. That Onesimus is named in a sister epistle to Philemon, Colossians (4:9), and that Ignatius refers to Onesimus, bishop of Ephesus, without further qualification (Ign. *Eph.* 1.3; 6.2), seems to imply the Onesimus familiar to the church from Paul's Letter to Philemon. For more on this, see Peter Lampe, "Onesimus," *ABD* 5:21–22.

46. Harnack, *Mission and Expansion*, 386.

47. Mark 12:40–42; Luke 2:37; 7:12; 18:1–8; Acts 6:1–7; 1 Tim. 5:1–16; 1 Clem. 8.4; Barn. 20.2; Ign. *Smyrn.* 6.2; 13.1; Ign. *Pol.* 4.1; Pol. *Phil.* 4.3; 6.1; Herm. Vis. 2.4.3; Herm. Mand. 1.10; Herm. Sim. 1.8; 3.7; 26.2; 27.2. Fox, *Pagans and Christians*, 308–11, notes that in Augustan Rome widows were penalized if they did not remarry within two years. The early church discouraged forced second marriages and elevated widowhood to an honorable status, worthy of the church's beneficence. The church's policy of not discarding orphans resulted in a corresponding status of honor and beneficence for orphans and the needy.

48. Paget argues that outside Palestine there seems to have been generally no missionary consciousness among Jews. "Jewish Missionary Efforts."

and character of the church. Jesus sent his disciples in mission before they had a proper understanding of him; indeed, one might argue that mission was essential to their gaining a proper understanding of him. Throughout the New Testament, mission is not something the church *does* but something it *is*, its very nature.[49]

We noted in the introduction that a missionary champion like the apostle Paul does not reappear in the history of the church. This has led some scholars to imagine the post–New Testament church as a conglomeration of smaller reclusive communities.[50] Such judgments need to be reconsidered. The non-appearance of another missionary like Paul is irrelevant, for the missionary nature of the church was neither indebted to Paul nor limited to him, prodigious though he was. All leaders of the first-century church of whom we are informed were involved in mission—including Paul, of course, but also the early unnamed missionaries from Cyprus and Cyrene who evangelized Antioch, and who were followed in other missions by Barnabas, Timothy, Titus, Sosthenes, Peter, Apollos, Priscilla, and Aquila. Paul's references to the Thessalonians (1 Thess. 1:9–10) and Corinthians (1 Cor. 12:2) turning from idol worship are not wholly self-referential; they also imply broader mission networks. The "troublers" in Galatia were missionary agents (Gal. 1:6–9), as were the "schismatics" in Corinth (1 Cor. 1:10–17). The Didache, written in the late first century, dedicates three chapters to itinerant apostles and prophets who traveled in the name of the Lord, strengthening and expanding the church.[51] At the close of the first century, the community associated with the apostle John established new Christian communities or strengthened preexisting ones in Roman Asia. Bishop Ignatius did the same only a few years later. The fact that we do not know the names of the missionaries who carried the faith south to North Africa and east to Mesopotamia, Persia, India, and eventually China does not change the fact that mission achieved the expansion. The church was the child of kerygma; kerygma was not a force of nature but a story, a history, that had to be proclaimed. And proclamation

---

49. On the missional nature and mandate of the church, see Guder's *Be My Witnesses* and *Incarnation and the Church's Witness*.

50. For example, MacMullen, *Christianizing the Roman Empire*, 111: "After New Testament times and before Constantine, very little open advertising of Christianity is attested. Celsus mentions some exorcising and healing in public, but he reminds his readers, too, of the dangers entailed in open preaching. Likelihood and chance descriptions from other sources direct us, rather, to private houses as the chief locus of conversion. Even there we should probably not expect to find any very active or official mission. Missionaries are just not mentioned." Harnack, *Mission and Expansion*, 86, adds that, with the rise of the catechumenate, "missionary preaching" had effectively become extinct in the church by about 200.

51. Did. 11–13.

required sending believers to encounter, proclaim, teach, catechize, and model the gospel (Rom. 10:14–17). "The early church mission was grounded in the messianic sending of Jesus," writes Martin Hengel. "Jesus's ministry as an itinerant preacher, the call and sending of his disciples, and Jesus's helping openness to all the lost and despised—non-Jews included—form the final point of departure for the later mission of the church."[52]

The characterization of Christian communities as diffident and inconspicuous, which I have argued against, seems to have been truer of heterodox sects than of mainstream churches. Gnostic and Marcionite Christians tended to propagate their versions of the gospel in "pacified" areas already evangelized by Christians. Their presence and influence were strongest among elites in metropolitan areas—such as Rome, Alexandria, Ephesus, and Antioch. Their teachings tended to accommodate the gospel to prevailing currents of thought, especially to variants of Platonism, Neoplatonism, and Encratism.[53] We know of no exponent of a heterodox form of Christianity being martyred. The church of the New Testament and Apostolic Fathers, on the other hand, was a church on the front lines of the Roman world, where—unlike the heterodox—persecution and martyrdom were both potential and actual.

Whole

A final characteristic of the church in early Christian literature is contained in the Greek word *teleios*, which denotes something sound, mature, complete, or perfect. *Teleios* includes the idea of being directed to or shaped by an inherent purpose, hence the English derivative "teleology." In considering this third and final characteristic of the early church, I intend the word "wholeness" to sum up the sense of the *teleios*. When the apostle Paul refers to God's purpose as a mystery that has been partially and imperfectly revealed in Israel but is now fully and finally revealed in the gospel of Jesus Christ,[54] he refers to the wholeness of the divine plan, of which the church is both firstfruit and witness. Early Christians believed that the end and purpose of salvation history had been fulfilled in the gospel, of which they were custodians (1 Cor. 10:11).

52. Hengel, *Studien zum Urchristentum*, 134–35.

53. Platonism and Neoplatonism were widely influential in the ancient world, ascribing supreme, unchangeable, and eternal status to ideas and ideals, but corruption and transience to material realities. Platonic and Neoplatonic versions of Christianity typically devalued or denied the doctrine of the incarnation. Encratites, on the other hand, stressed extreme forms of asceticism, such as the rejection of wine, meat, and often marriage. Interactions with these heterodoxies appear as early as 1 John and the Apostolic Fathers, and they become even more common in the late second-century apologists.

54. E.g., 1 Cor. 2; 13:10; Eph. 3.

Three convictions of the early church express its understanding of whole-ness. Two can be given in concrete images—a body and a family—and the third in a concept: "catholicity." The first conviction is that believers are united with Christ as the "bride of Christ";[55] the "house of Christ" (Heb. 3:6); "part-ners of Christ" (Heb. 3:14); or, most commonly, the "body of Christ."[56] These images are more than similes. The church is not simply *like* a bride or house or body; in a real sense, it *is* the bride, house, partner, and body of Christ. The Greek word for "body" is not *sarx* (flesh), which signifies physicality and materiality, but *sōma* (body), a body of material form that is animated by a nonmaterial spirit. "Body of Christ" is a load-bearing metaphor for the church that extends throughout early Christianity. The apostle Paul uses the image in Romans and 1 Corinthians to signify diverse parts that function together as a single whole.[57] The church is not a community of sameness but of differ-ent peoples and cultures, of multi-giftedness, and of different forms of call and service. These differences result in unity rather than fragmentation, just as different musical instruments combine to form a symphony rather than a cacophony. "The one body has many parts," says Paul, "but all parts belong to the body" (1 Cor. 12:12), and their entelechy—another English derivative of *teleios*, meaning "the purpose for which a thing exists"—is not disparateness but congruence with the larger body to which they belong.

Body-of-Christ terminology does not occur in the Gospels, but the High Priestly Prayer of Jesus in John 17 speaks of a unity of believers with Christ that stands in correlation with the unity of the Son and the Father. Similarly, 1 Clement encourages Christians to think of social disparities in terms of mutuality: "The strong must not neglect the weak, and the weak must respect the strong. Let the rich support the poor; and let the poor give thanks to God for those who serve their needs."[58] The body metaphor also serves Ignatius, for whom the church is the custodian and guarantor of the treasures of the gospel; the treasures include the "precepts of the Lord and apostles," the virtues of the faith, and the triunity of the Godhead. As such, the church is in spiritual communion with God as well as in physical communion with the world.[59] Later in the second century, 2 Clement refers to the church as both the "body" and "bride" of Christ. "The living church is the body of Christ," which, like Jesus himself, is "spiritual" in nature, having existed from all eternity but revealed in the last days for our salvation.[60]

---

55. See 2 Cor. 11:2; Eph. 5:29–32; Rev. 19:7; 21:2, 9.
56. Rom. 7:4; 1 Cor. 10:16; 11:3; 12:27; Eph. 4:12; Col. 2:17.
57. Rom. 12:4–8; 1 Cor. 12.
58. 1 Clem. 38.2.
59. Ign. *Magn.* 13.
60. 2 Clem. 14.2.

A second image of the wholeness of the church is the family. Family is a place of belonging and identity, and the epistles of Paul, in particular, abound with these characteristics. Believers are set apart as "holy ones,"[61] "elect,"[62] "called,"[63] "(be)loved,"[64] and "known."[65] The family metaphor especially conveys the bond of Christian community. Believers are often called brothers and sisters in early Christianity, and more so by Paul than by any other early writer. They are also called children, both God's children and Paul's children.[66] God is typically called the Father of believers. With emotional intensity, Paul transposes the same metaphor to himself, reminding the Corinthians: "You may have thousands of instructors in Christ, but not many fathers, for in Christ Jesus I personally fathered you through the gospel" (1 Cor. 4:15). Paul appeals to Philemon to receive the runaway slave Onesimus, whom Paul calls "my own child, begotten in my (prison) chains" (Philem. 10). To the Thessalonians, Paul describes himself as "gentle among you, as a nurse would care for her own children" (1 Thess. 2:7). He speaks of separated congregations as "orphaned" (1 Thess. 2:17). The powerful and intimate bond of the family becomes the model of *philadelphia*, familial love extended to the larger social world.[67]

Third and finally, the universal compass of the church is conveyed in "catholicity." The church consists of different ethnicities, races, nationalities, genders, and classes of people. Its totality is captured in the Greek word *katholikos*, meaning "general" or "universal." The second-century bishop Polycarp was especially fond of acknowledging the one united "universal church throughout the world."[68] The book of Revelation does not employ the world *katholikos*, but it repeatedly emphasizes the Christian congregation as one of "every nation, tribe, people, and tongue," swelled with "myriads of myriads and thousands of thousands" who sing a new song to the Lamb, the Christ of God.[69] Ignatius was the first to christen this all-encompassing nature of the church as "catholic." "Wherever Christ Jesus is, there is the catholic church," he declares.[70] Catholicity did not mean harmony and agreement on all matters;

61. Rom. 1:7; 1 Cor. 1:2; 2 Cor. 1:1; Eph. 1:1; Phil. 1:1; Col. 1:2.
62. Rom. 8:33; Eph. 1:4; Col. 3:12; 1 Thess. 1:4.
63. 1 Cor. 1:9; 7:15, 17–24; Gal. 1:6, 15; 5:8; 1 Thess. 2:12.
64. Rom. 1:7; Col. 3:12; 1 Thess. 1:4; 2 Thess. 2:13.
65. 1 Cor. 8:3; Gal. 4:9.
66. 1 Cor. 4:14, 17; 2 Cor. 6:13; 12:14; Gal. 4:19; Phil. 2:22; Philem. 10.
67. Rom. 12:10; 1 Thess. 4:9; Heb. 13:1; 1 Pet. 1:22; 2 Pet. 1:7. On the use of familial terminology in Paul, see Meeks, *First Urban Christians*, 85–94.
68. Mart. Pol. Salutation, 8.1; 16.2; 19.2.
69. Rev. 5:8–13; 7:9–17; 10:11; 11:9; 13:7; 14:6; 15:3–4.
70. Ign. *Smyrn.* 8.2.

rifts are recorded in the New Testament—for example, between Paul and Barnabas (Acts 15:36–41); Paul and Peter (Gal. 2:11–14); and, within the wider church communion, the Council of Jerusalem (Acts 15:1–35). In themselves, such rifts do not jeopardize the inherent unity of the church any more than disagreements or misfortunes jeopardize a healthy marriage. The catholicity of the church, Harnack notes, was an *experience* of believers before it was a doctrine or tenet of the church.[71] The distinctiveness of individual Christian communities is attested in the New Testament Epistles, in Revelation, and in the Apostolic Fathers, all of which regularly refer to churches in the plural. The individuality of a given church is nevertheless superseded by its belonging to and identity with a larger whole, *the* church. It was precisely this catholicity that second-century voices of heterodoxy—Cerinthus, Cerdo, Valentinus, Basilides, and Marcion—denied, elevating particular church communities over the one *catholic* community. The New Testament and Apostolic Fathers, by contrast, assert *catholicity* as characteristic of the true church over schismatic churches: "the saints with all those who call upon the name of our Lord Jesus Christ in every place" (1 Cor. 1:2).[72] In the fifth century, Vincent of Lérins would summarize the universality, antiquity, and consensual unity of the church in brilliant simplicity, as that which has been believed "Ubique, semper, ab omnibus" (everywhere, always, and by all).[73]

The Third Race

Harnack offers an insightful description of the subject of this chapter, the church:

> Every [church] community was at once a unit, complete in itself; but it was also a reproduction of the collective church of God, and it had to recognize and manifest itself as such. Such a religious and social organization, destitute of any political or national basis and yet embracing the entire private life, was a novel and unheard-of thing upon the soil of Greek and Roman life, where

71. See Harnack, *Mission and Expansion*, 483–84:
   The [catholic] federation had no written constitution. It did not possess one iota of common statutes. Nevertheless, it was a fact. Its common denominator consisted of the apostles' creed, the apostolic canon, and belief in the apostolical succession of the episcopate. . . . Externally, this unity manifested itself in inter-communion, the brotherly welcome extended to travelers and wanderers. . . . The Christian was at home everywhere, and he could feel himself at home, thanks to the inter-communion. He was protected and controlled wherever he went. The church introduced, as it were, a new franchise among her members.
72. On the church as a "worldwide people," see Meeks, *First Urban Christians*, 107–10.
73. See Pelikan, *Christian Tradition*, 1:332–39.

religious and social organizations only existed as a rule in quite a rudimentary form, and where they lacked any religious control of life as a whole. . . . What a sense of stability a creation of this kind must have given the individual! What powers of attraction it must have exercised, as soon as its objects came to be understood! It was this, and not any evangelist, which proved to be the most effective missionary. In fact, we may take it for granted that the mere existence and persistent activity of the individual Christian communities did more than anything else to bring about the extension of the Christian religion.[74]

Harnack describes the church as "embracing the entire private life, . . . a novel and unheard-of thing upon the soil of Greek and Roman life." Indeed, it was equally novel with respect to Jewish life. In the last two chapters, we have described Christianity in terms of the particularity of Jesus Christ and the peculiarity of the church. The result of its christological particularity and ecclesiastical peculiarity produced an understanding of life, both individually and corporately, that differed from the two major alternatives of the first-century world: Judaism and Greco-Roman culture.

The new faith was buffeted by the winds of both Judaism and Rome, of course, but it set sail to a different point on the compass from either. Toward the end of the first century, a new Greek term, *genos* (meaning "race" or "people"), was used to characterize this new faith. The Epistle to Diognetus describes Jesus followers as "this new race."[75] Polycarp describes them as "the race of Christians."[76] And thereafter, Tertullian differentiates Christians as a "third race."[77] "Christianity was making good its claim to be a 'third race,'" writes W. H. C. Frend, "independent of both Judaism and paganism."[78] As a third race, Christianity did not bring another cult that could be added to the portfolio of polytheistic Greco-Roman cults; it brought a single security that replaced the portfolio. As a third race, Christianity did not augment

74. Harnack, *Mission and Expansion*, 432, 434.

75. Diogn. 1.1.

76. Mart. Pol. 3.2. Similarly, in Mart. Pol. 12.2, Polycarp is derided by his persecutors as "the father of Christians."

77. *Nat.* 1.8. Aristides differentiates Christians from barbarians, Greeks, and Jews as "a new people with something divine in their midst" (*Apol.* 15; *ANF* 10:278). Clement of Alexandria describes Christians, in distinction from Greeks and Jews, as worshiping God "in a new way, in the third form" (*Strom.* 6.5.39). Eusebius refers to Christians similarly as "a confessedly new race" (*Hist. eccl.* 1.4.1). The most inimitable descriptions of the third race (although they do not use the exact term) are in Diogn. 5 and Aristides, *Apol.* 16 (see Conclusion, pp. 254–55).

78. Frend, *Rise of Christianity*, 257. Barclay, *Pauline Churches*, 24–25, notes that by the second century "Christians" were being considered a distinct category, whereas earlier Jews, in particular, participated in "Jewish" and "Christian" gatherings without being called anything other than "Jews."

Judaism with another sect; it was, rather, a new community that saw itself as the fulfillment of God's promises to Israel. Unlike Judaism, the third race of Christianity was not ethnically isolated. It was consciously independent of the prevailing religious currents in the ancient world. And unlike Greco-Roman religions, Christianity was not theologically pluralistic and endlessly absorbent. Its social uniqueness extended to all levels of life—including family, local community, *polis*, and empire—and to its relation to the history of Israel. Its distinctiveness made Christianity an easy target of suspicion and hostility, of course. As a vulnerable community, it prayed for the protection of rulers and leaders.[79] The particularity of Jesus Christ and the peculiarity of the church as the third race generated a viable means of living out the theological identity of early Christians as the body of Christ.[80]

---

79. See 1 Clem. 59.3–61.3.

80. For more on the third race, see Harnack, *Mission and Expansion*, 240–78; Fox, *Pagans and Christians*, 325–37; Koch, *Geschichte des Urchristentums*, 450–52; and, most recently, Sittser, *Resilient Faith*, 1–4, 101–2, 173–78.

9

From Jewish
to Christian Ethos

In chapters 5–8 we charted factors that resulted in the transformation of a predominantly Jewish Jesus movement into a predominantly gentile Jesus movement. The factors were many and varied—including historical events that helped push Jesus followers out of synagogues; the taproot conviction of Christians that Jesus was the Messiah and Son of God; the mission consciousness of early Christianity, which included gentiles without compromise in the church; and various other ways in which both the theology and ecclesiology of the church, though clearly indebted to Judaism, parted ways from it. Now I focus on Jesus followers themselves, who adhered to the kerygma and affiliated with churches. What did the gospel preachers, Christian writers, and teachers of the faith expect of Jesus followers? What did they want them to become in distinction from the Jews and Romans among whom they lived? When Hebrews 6:1 exhorts believers to leave behind the elementary doctrines common to Jews and Christians and advance to "maturity" (Gk. *teleiotēs*), what kind of maturity is envisioned? What were the contours and character of life to which the kerygma called believers and in which the church nurtured them?

Several publicly identifiable practices characterized the Jewish world in which Christianity arose. Adherence to these practices rendered one an observant Jew. A review of these practices sets the stage for our consideration of the practices and goals that subsequently characterized Christian life. Four primary features of Judaism—in order of least to most important—were fasting, purity regulations, circumcision, and Sabbath observance. We will deal with the first three here and reserve consideration of Sabbath for chapter 12.

Fasting

Jewish piety was generally expressed through prayer, almsgiving, and fasting. Christians shared prayer and almsgiving with Jews, but they were more reserved with regard to fasting. Judaism mandated fasting only on the Day of Atonement (Yom Kippur),[1] but Jews sometimes fasted in times of tragedy and crisis, and for other personal reasons. In the first century, Pharisees normally fasted on Mondays and Thursdays.[2] The Gospels record Jesus fasting occasionally (e.g., Matt. 4:2), but not regularly. More frequently, the Gospels record his warnings against fasting (Matt. 6:16–18). This troubled the Pharisees—as did Jesus's justification of his warning on tacitly messianic grounds: "the sons of the bridegroom do not fast when the bridegroom is with them" (Mark 2:18–20). Jesus followers shared Jesus's reserve regarding fasting—for, with the exception of two places in 2 Corinthians, references to fasting in the New Testament vanish after Acts 14.

Only three texts in the Apostolic Fathers mention fasting. The Didache commends fasting on the behalf of persecutors of Christians,[3] and also for a day or two prior to baptism.[4] It identifies no further role for fasting, however, other than to differentiate Christians from Jews.[5] The Shepherd of Hermas discounts fasting more completely, calling it "worthless." The chief value of the practice is as a metaphor. True "fasting," according to Hermas, is committing no evil, keeping a pure heart, and performing works of moral righteousness that please God, including works of justice for the oppressed and of mercy for the hungry, naked, and needy.[6] The Epistle of Barnabas sees no value in fasting for the battle against evil, twice noting that even the fasting of Moses was unable to prevent the Israelites from committing apostasy in the wilderness.[7] True "fasting" is "humiliation of the soul,"[8] for whatever is required and achieved by Old Testament fasts, declares Barnabas, has been

1. Lev. 16:29–30; *m.* Yoma 8:1–2.
2. Did. 8; *b.* Taʿan. 12a.
3. Did. 1.3.
4. Did. 7.4.
5. Did. 8.1: "Do not let your fasts coincide with those of the hypocrites. They fast on Monday and Thursday, so you must fast on Wednesday and Friday" (Homes trans.).
6. Herm. Sim. 5.1. The only other value of fasting, according to Hermas, is as an aid to understanding divine revelation (Herm. Vis. 2.2.1; 3.1.2; 3.10.6).
7. Barn. 4.7; 14.2.
8. Barn. 3.1.

fulfilled in the suffering of Jesus Christ on the cross.[9] Indeed, Christ's self-sacrifice on the cross is the once-for-all effectual offering for the sins of his people. The role of fasting is, of course, revived in the Christian asceticism of late antiquity and in subsequent spiritual traditions, especially in Orthodoxy and Catholicism. But by the close of the postapostolic era, fasting had been de-emphasized in Christianity as Christianity broke from its association with Judaism.[10]

Purity

Purity regulations, especially the distinction between clean and unclean, played a strong role in Judaism. Sacrificial offerings were an element in all ancient religions, and ritual cleanness was required of both the offerings and those who offered them. Jewish purity regulations were incomparably complex, a "thick forest of rules for distinguishing between holy and common, between *tahor* (Heb. 'clean') and *tameh* (Heb. 'unclean')," in the words of Paula Fredriksen.[11] The two-hundred-page sixth-and-final division of the Jewish Mishnah is devoted solely to purity regulations, including clean vessels, meal offerings, animal sacrifices, grain offerings, and libations. For observant Jews, "clean" and "unclean" designated *ritual* rather than hygienic purity; thus a worshiper spattered with the blood of a ritually slain animal was regarded clean (Exod. 24:8), whereas a person fresh from a bath who saw a corpse in a tent was rendered unclean (Num. 19:14). Consumption of, and contact with, certain animals rendered one unclean.[12] Bodily discharges from the genital area rendered one unclean: in the case of males, discharges of semen and fluxes; and in the case of females, menstruation, childbirth, miscarriages, and abortions.[13] Various skin diseases, and especially leprosy, rendered one unclean, as did proximity to corpses or tombs.[14] Ritual uncleanness required washing of hands before prayer and entire bodies in *miqva'ot*—full immersion bathing pools—before weekly synagogue services.[15] The material from

9. Barn. 7.3–5.

10. On fasting in the Old Testament and Jewish tradition, see Str-B 4/1:77–114. On fasting in the early church in comparison to Jewish and gentile customs, see Fox, *Pagans and Christians*, 395–96.

11. Fredriksen, "Purity Laws?," 22.

12. Lev. 7:19–27.

13. Lev. 12:1–8; 15:1–30. *m.* Tehar. offers a comprehensive treatment of ritual cleanness and defilement.

14. Lev. 13–14; 21:1–3.

15. *m.* Miqv. offers a comprehensive treatment of necessary properties, especially living (flowing) water rather than standing water, for immersion pools.

which an eating utensil was made rendered it clean or unclean; thus a bowl carved from natural stone was considered clean, but a bowl made of porous ceramic transmitted impurities that rendered it unclean. The intrusive addition in Mark 7:3–4—for the benefit of Mark's gentile readers—indicates the extent and complexity of ritual cleanness.

Ritual uncleanness included unclean persons as well as unclean objects and behaviors. Proper observance of purity regulations required knowledge of Torah—and, by contrast, those ignorant of Torah were unclean.[16] Disregard of food laws and the worship of idols obviously rendered gentiles unclean. But Jews could also be unclean. A large segment of the Jewish population, the *am ha-aretz* (people of the land), was considered ritually unclean.[17] Purity regulations were not limited to *temple* purity; they pertained to Jewish life as a whole, including for Jews far removed from the temple, such as the Essenes or diaspora Jews. Ritual purity was proximate to holiness.[18]

Jesus complied with many purity regulations. He dined with Pharisees without being accused of violating ritual cleanness (Luke 14:1). He went regularly to Jerusalem for festivals—for Passover (Mark 11), Sukkot (John 7:10), and an unspecified feast (John 5:1). Entry into the temple at Passover required special purification, and purification required immersion in *miqva'ot*. Neither Jesus nor his disciples are slighted in the Gospels for failing to observe such regulations.

Jesus did not follow purity regulations with regard to persons, however. He ate with unclean sinners and tax collectors (Luke 15:1–2). He touched ritually defiled bodies: women with (gynecological) blood flows (Mark 5:25–34), lepers (Mark 1:41), and corpses (Luke 7:14). The early church understood him to dispense with food laws (Mark 7:19). Not least telling in this respect was that Jesus called all twelve of his disciples from the *am ha-aretz*, the class of Jews who failed to satisfy the criteria of ritual cleanness. Some *am ha-aretz*, of course, complied with many requirements of ritual cleanliness. Peter complied with food observances, for instance (Acts 10:14). Nevertheless, the early church exhibited a wholesale disregard for ritual cleanliness. We know of two instances, in fact, when attempts by Jesus followers to observe ritual cleanness were judged to be *violations* of the gospel.[19]

16. See *m.* Avot 2:6: "An ignorant man cannot be saintly" (Rabbi Hillel).

17. "Am-Haaretz ('People of the land') [is] the name given to those Jews who were ignorant of the Law and who failed to observe the rules of cleanness and uncleanness and were not scrupulous in setting apart tithes from the produce." Danby, *Mishnah*, 794.

18. See Moore, *Judaism in the First Centuries*, 2:76; Sanders, *Judaism*, 213–40; Poirier, "Purity beyond the Temple."

19. Acts 10:14–15; Gal. 2:11–14.

The topic and vocabulary of purity fall off precipitously in the New Testament[20] and Apostolic Fathers.[21] Only in meat offered to idols are food regulations again raised in early Christianity.[22] The Didache strictly forbids believers from eating food offered to idols because "they have to do with the worship of dead gods."[23] Paul, on the other hand, renders a verdict on the effect that eating such foods might have on fellow believers, whether Jews or gentiles. In so doing, he bases his judgment on *ethics* rather than on uncleanness per se. The law of Christian love is the final arbiter on food matters.

More than any other New Testament narrative, Acts 15 reveals the indifference of the early church to Jewish purity regulations and the influence of its indifference in separating Christians from Jews. The stage is set for the narrative already in Acts 9:43, with the apostle Peter staying in the house of Simon the tanner beside the sea. Persons who skinned and processed unclean animals were considered unclean in Judaism. The Mishnah restricts tanneries to city outskirts, and rabbis allowed a woman married to a tanner to divorce him if she could not endure the stench.[24] It is in such a house that Peter lodges. While there he receives a thrice-repeated vision of unclean animals (reptiles and birds) and a divine command to "kill and eat." Peter refuses, swearing, "I have never eaten anything common and unclean" (Acts 10:9–16). Immediately following the vision, Peter is summoned by Cornelius, a Roman centurion, who asks to hear "all things commanded to you by the Lord" (10:33). Finally, in chapter 15, which falls at the midpoint of Acts, gentiles are granted full acceptance in the church. The narrative sequence of Acts abolishes the concept of ritual uncleanness, whether unclean work (tanning), unclean places (tanneries), unclean food (the animals in Peter's vision), or unclean persons (gentile centurions). Peter's summary judgment speaks for early Christianity as a whole: "God showed me not to regard any human common or unclean"

20. The word for "ritual uncleanness" (Hb. *tame*; Gk. *akathartos*), which occurs three hundred times in the Old Testament, occurs seldom in the New Testament, and then primarily with reference to "unclean spirits" rather than to ritual purity. "Uncleanness" (Gk. *akatharsia*) occurs nine times in the Pauline letters with reference to moral uncleanness; "unwashed" (Gk. *aniptos*) occurs only in Matt. 15:20 and Mark 7:2; "common" (Gk. *koinos*) occurs in Mark 7:2, 5; Acts 2:44; 4:32; 10:14, 28; 11:8; Rom. 14:14; "polluted" (Gk. *miainō*) occurs only four times and, with the exception of John 18:28, only with reference to moral rather than cultic uncleanness.

21. "Common" (Gk. *koinos*) and "unwashed" (Gk. *aniptos*) do not occur in the fathers; "unclean" (Gk. *akathartos*) and "uncleanness" (Gk. *akatharsia*) occur two times each, with reference to moral uncleanness (Barn. 19.4; Herm. Vis. 1.7) and oral sex (Barn. 10.8); and "polluted" (Gk. *miainō*) occurs only twice—in Herm. Mand. 5.1.3 and 5.1.6, with reference to anger polluting a godly spirit.

22. See 1 Cor. 8–10; Did. 6.3.

23. Did. 6.3.

24. See *m.* B. Bat. 2:9; *m.* Ketub. 7:10.

(10:28). The gospel of Jesus Christ, "who is the Lord of all" (10:36), opens the door to the gentile mission and closes the door to ritual purity judgments in all forms.

Circumcision and the Law

More defining for Jews than either fasting or purity was the practice of circumcision as a sign of Torah obedience. The single most influential catalyst in the breach between Judaism and Christianity was, as we have seen, the destruction of the Jewish temple in the year 70. But gentile Christianity's rejection of circumcision was a second deal breaker. According to Genesis, circumcision was instituted by God with Abraham and his descendants as a sign of promise, that "my covenant shall be in your flesh for an everlasting covenant" (Gen. 17:13).[25] So central was circumcision to Jewish identity that "uncircumcised" became a term of opprobrium for non-Jews. Circumcision and Sabbath were the right and left arms of Judaism. Circumcision, in fact, may have been the stronger arm, for circumcision of a male child on the eighth day took precedence over the law of the Sabbath.[26] Circumcision and the prohibition of idolatry were nonnegotiables for Israelites: both required of Jews the ultimate sacrifice, martyrdom, rather than the violation of either. Jews who uncircumcised themselves—as some did in the Maccabean era to accommodate the Seleucid oppressors (1 Macc. 1:15)—were considered heathens who had renounced their religion.[27]

Such were the associations that Jews brought to the table when they converted to Christianity. Among the surprises in the first seventy-five years of the Jesus movement, few are greater than the swiftness and completeness with which the early church dispensed with circumcision. In the words of J. D. G. Dunn: "That circumcision was not required of these first non-Jewish members of the [Christian] sect is the really astonishing feature—astonishing also that the Acts of the Apostles passes over the development in a single sentence (Acts 11:20) without comment."[28] The watershed event that decided the role of circumcision in the fledgling church was, once again, the Council in Jerusalem in the late 40s, where Jesus followers gathered to consider the

25. "Circumcision is central to the identity of the Jew and of Judaism, the *sine qua non* for all males who are heirs of the covenant promises given to Abraham and the patriarchs (Genesis 17:9–14)," writes Dunn. "From the Crucifixion," 37.

26. See *m.* Shabb. 18:3–19:3; John 7:22–23.

27. On circumcision, see Str-B 4/1:23–40; Moore, *Judaism in the First Centuries*, 1:333–35; 2:16–39; Sanders, *Judaism*, 213–40.

28. Dunn, "Beyond the Jewish People," 191.

claim of certain believers of the sect of the Pharisees that it was necessary to be circumcised and keep the law of Moses in order to be saved (Acts 15:1, 5). Why would the council, asks Peter rhetorically, "place a yoke upon the neck of the disciples that neither our fathers nor we ourselves were strong enough to bear" (15:10)? By "yoke" Peter refers to the "yoke of the Law" (the sign of which was circumcision) that rabbis declared essential for salvation.[29] After hearing testimony from Peter, Paul, Barnabas, and others, James (the leader of the church in Jerusalem, who was certainly sympathetic to the claim of the circumcision party) issued a letter in the name of the council that left the practice of circumcision *unmentioned* in a list of observances expected of diaspora Christians. In releasing the church from imposing "the yoke of the Law" upon gentile converts, the council set in motion a chain reaction that determined the essential nature of the church. In declaring the distinction between gentiles and Jews irrelevant for salvation and church membership, the council opened the door for gentiles to enter the church, not as Godfearers or proselytes of lower status, but as full and unconditional members. The church was free to pursue its mission with gentiles as it had with Jews, and to receive gentile converts as fully as it had received Jewish converts. The inclusion of gentiles furthered the chain reaction begun by the council's decision, for the church (in the West) proclaimed and transmitted the gospel in Greek and claimed the Septuagint as its Scripture.

It is relatively certain that the decision of the Council of Jerusalem caused a dissenting minority of Jewish Christians to break fellowship with the Jesus followers gathered in Jerusalem. But the greater church was willing to go to the mat to defend the oneness of the church and the uncompromised equality of its members. Paul, in particular, promoted the ecclesial unity of Jews and gentiles indefatigably and without exception in his epistles. "Circumcision is nothing and uncircumcision is nothing," he declares, "but keeping God's commandments" is what counts (1 Cor. 7:19).[30] The synagogue, of course, was adamant in requiring circumcision of Jewish members. For late first-century rabbis in Tiberias and Sepphoris, relaxing circumcision laws was anathema—indeed, grounds for excommunication from the synagogue.[31] The

29. On "the yoke of the Law," see *m.* Avot 3:5. On its usage, see Moore, *Judaism in the First Centuries*, 1:465–66.

30. Following the Council of Jerusalem and early in the second mission journey, Paul's decision to circumcise Timothy (Acts 16:3), son of a Jewish mother and gentile father, should be understood in the same light as his teaching on meat offered to idols (1 Cor. 8:1–12; 10:23–33). Circumcision and foods were decided on the basis of their practical effect on those to whom the gospel was proclaimed rather than on any inherent efficacy in either circumcision or foods.

31. The Palestinian recension of the *Birkat ha-Minim* declares: "May the Christians (*noṣerim*) and the heretics (*minim*) perish in an instant." Quoted in Alexander, "Parting of the Ways," 7.

issue of circumcision thus divided Christians and Jews irrevocably from one another. Shaye Cohen writes, "A non-Christian Jewish community that admitted Jews and non-Jews alike, without prejudice and (in the case of males) without circumcision, is nowhere attested in antiquity."[32] In this sentence, Cohen succeeds in identifying the fundamental difference between the Jewish synagogue and the Christian church—namely, that what was intolerable in the synagogue was mandatory in the church: the full inclusion of uncircumcised gentile believers.

The early church's position on circumcision extended unchallenged into the postapostolic era. With the exception of one passage, circumcision vanishes from the written corpus of the church between the close of the New Testament and the writings of the apologists in the mid-second century. The exception appears in the Epistle of Barnabas, where the sole remaining function of circumcision is metaphorical. Readers are enjoined to have "circumcised hearts" (obedient faith) and "circumcised ears" (receptive hearing of the word of faith). The epistle not only rejects physical circumcision, but it also regards it a subterfuge of an evil angel: "The circumcision in which [Jews] have trusted is abolished, for [the Lord] declared circumcision not to be a matter of the flesh. [Jews] disobeyed, however, for an evil angel beguiled them."[33] First Clement follows the Council of Jerusalem in joyfully identifying grace rather than law as the "yoke" of salvation. "You see, beloved friends, the pattern that has been given to us, that as the Lord so humbled himself, should we not do the same who came to him through the yoke of grace"?[34]

The Christian Way

If fasting, ritual purity, circumcision, and Sabbath were not normative for the early church, what was? What were the forms and character of the redeemed life proclaimed in the kerygma and embodied in the church? Our focus here is the influence of the gospel on ordinary believers, the "normal" Christian life. Five elements appear in the New Testament and Apostolic Fathers as constitutive of the new life in Christ. These five are not dogmatic and final, for others of equal merit could be cited, but they provide the contours of "mere" early Christianity and offer important insights into the values and priorities of the early church. The first is early Christianity's tendency to form lists of virtues and vices considered axiomatic of lived Christian faith. The second

32. Cohen, "In Between," 209.
33. Barn. 9.4.
34. 1 Clem. 16.17.

is a "two-ways" perspective that differentiates the Christian way from other ways in the ancient world. The third, a warning against "double-mindedness," instructs readers in the undivided allegiance required of Christians. "Imitation" is the fourth, cited as a means of Christian transformation. And the fifth and final element is the endgame: the completed believer, "the perfect athlete" of the redeemed life.

Virtues and Vices

The epistles in the New Testament and Apostolic Fathers were usually written in response to specific needs in specific churches. Moral exhortation appears in many epistles in the form of virtue and vice lists. These lists are especially typical of the Pauline literature, including the Pastoral Epistles, but they also appear in the Epistles of Peter, in Revelation, and in several documents of the fathers—including Barnabas, Polycarp, and the Shepherd of Hermas. About 250 vices appear in the sin lists,[35] and 70-plus virtues appear in the virtue lists.[36] A number of the more important virtues and vices are repeated in the various lists.

In the vice lists, sexual immorality appears more frequently than any other vice, and usually at the head of the list. Other common vices include slander, idolatry, drunkenness, murder, sorcery, orgies, and theft. Both vice lists and virtue lists emphasize *characteristics* over *deeds*. In sin lists, characteristics outnumber acts ten to one. Of foremost concern to early Christians are characteristics such as impurity, covetousness, malice, enmity, evil, greed, envy, strife, insolence, pride, heartlessness, reviling, jealousy, quarrelsomeness, conceit, crudeness, ungodliness, hostility, and partiality. Any one of these characteristics can manifest itself in scores of different acts and behaviors.

Virtues, likewise, are almost entirely qualities of character rather than simply good deeds. In the famous list of virtues in Galatians 5—love, joy, peace, patience, goodness, kindness, faith, humility, and self-control—not one is a specific act. Each is a quality of character that is capable of countless good acts. Of course, some virtuous *acts* are referred to (usually in the Apostolic Fathers), including chastity, instructing children in the love of God, not aborting or exposing children, not oppressing the afflicted, and not advocating for

35. Mark 7:21–22; Rom. 1:29–32; 1 Cor. 5:10; 6:9–10; 2 Cor. 12:20; Gal. 5:19–21; Eph. 4:31; 5:3–5; Col. 3:5; 1 Tim. 1:9–10; 6:4; 2 Tim. 3:2–4; Titus 3:3; 1 Pet. 4:3; Rev. 9:21; 21:8; 22:15; Barn. 19; 20:1–2; Pol. *Phil.* 2.2; Herm. Man. 8.1–6.
36. See 2 Cor. 6:6; Gal. 5:22–23; Eph. 4:32; Phil. 1:11; 1 Tim. 4:12; 2 Tim. 2:22; 2 Pet. 1:5; Pol. *Phil.* 2.3; Herm. Vis. 3.8; Herm. Mand. 8.9.

the wealthy against the poor.[37] But here too, good deeds are far outnumbered by virtuous characteristics: innocence, sincerity, tenderheartedness, forgivingness, purity, truthfulness, righteousness, mercy, steadfastness, godliness, knowledge, and sound conduct. Rather than simply approving good deeds and proscribing evil ones, the early church addressed both virtue and vice at their source in human character. The vice and virtue lists thus take seriously Jesus's teachings that "the good person brings forth good from the treasure of his heart" (Luke 6:45) and that "evil deeds come from within and defile a person" (Mark 7:21–23).

Ironically, none of the lists treats the Ten Commandants or the Old Testament laws as definitive accounts of the life pleasing to God. The observance of Sabbath—from the fourth commandment (the longest and arguably the most important of the Decalogue)—does not appear in any of the lists; love of parents, from the fifth commandment, appears in only one list (Rom. 1:30). Fasting, ritual purity, and circumcision are also summarily omitted. Judging by the lists, the Christian understandings of virtue and vice do not generally replicate those in the Torah or in Stoicism. Rather, the virtue lists accent the transformation of character according to the image of Jesus—who embodies the true character of God, to which, by the power of the gospel, Jesus followers are being conformed.

The virtue-and-vice lists focus primarily on personal responsibilities rather than on what we today call "social ethics." Early Christians were, of course, neither unaware of nor unconcerned with such things. Many were slaves. Many were refugees, driven from homes and loved ones. And many had experienced manifold injustices and forms of violence. The autocracies of the ancient world, and of the Roman Empire in particular, afforded early Christians far fewer avenues to redress systemic evils—slavery, war, cruelties of the arena, blood sports, and corporal and capital punishments—than are available to modern Christians in Western democracies. First-century Christians attended to social issues—especially with respect to widows, orphans, the needy, and slaves—within their individual and ecclesial powers.[38] The primary objective of the virtue and vice lists, however, was *the transformation of individual life*—and this included by extension *the transformation of the communal life of believers* in the church—so that the world would see Christians' good works and glorify their Father in heaven. The powerful

37. See Pol. *Phil.* 2.3; Barn. 19.2; 20.1–2.
38. On widows, orphans, and the needy, see ch. 8, pp. 144–45. Regarding slavery, Paul's appeal to Philemon to receive his runaway slave Onesimus "no longer as a slave, but more than as a slave, as a brother" (Philem. 16) clearly reveals Paul's attitude toward slavery, if not his ability to alter it.

transformation of personal character, especially when replicated within a community of transformed individuals, played an incomparable role in the ultimate transformation of the ancient world.

Two Ways

Early Christians frequently spoke of the Christian way as an all-important choice between two ways. The book of James sets before readers the earthly wisdom from below and the heavenly wisdom from above (3:13–18). The Didache commences with an ultimate choice: "There are two ways, one of life and one of death, and there is a great difference between these two ways." It then summarizes the way of life: "First, you shall love God your maker; second, your neighbor as yourself."[39] "Way" is a metaphor of walking, and walking is a behavior, participatory in nature. For the Didache, believers follow the way by observing the Ten Commandments, shunning evil in all forms, practicing humility, avoiding hypocrisy, and honoring God.[40] "The way" is not one among other equal or lesser ways; it is the singular way that comprises "the whole yoke of the Lord," the way of perfection.[41]

The two ways are rooted in Hebraic soil. The category of Jewish teaching known as halakah (from the Hb. *halak*, "to walk") encompasses regulations related to personal, social, and political relationships. Psalms and Proverbs, in particular, depict the divine command in terms of the way of wisdom versus the way of folly, the way of life versus the way of death. The Testaments of the Twelve Patriarchs, similarly, develop various themes according to the ways of truth and the ways of error.[42] The Testaments present a world divided between good and evil, requiring of the faithful a choice between the way guided by angels of the Lord and the way of the sinful angel Beliar. Jesus himself cast his mission in terms of two ways—the narrow way that leads to life and the broad way that leads to death (Matt. 7:13–14)—and the impossibility of serving two masters, God and mammon (Luke 16:13).

The two ways also play a role in the Apostolic Fathers. We noted above the two ways in the Didache. Ignatius, likewise, refers to the two ways of life and death.[43] The Shepherd of Hermas depicts Christian life as a choice between the straight way of righteousness and the crooked way of unrighteousness,

39. Did. 1.1–2.
40. Did. 1–4.
41. Did. 6.2.
42. The Testament of the Twelve Patriarchs is a pseudepigraphical Jewish text written perhaps in the third century BC that offers readers moral encouragement and spiritual consolation.
43. Ign. *Magn.* 5.

or between an angel of righteousness and an angel of wickedness.[44] The climactic exhortation of the Epistle of Barnabas appears in the choice between the way of divine light and virtues versus the way of satanic darkness and evil.[45] For 2 Clement, the way encompasses the eternal destinies of individuals and the world; one must choose between two masters (God and Satan), two lives (one of virtue and one of vice), and two worlds (heaven and hell).[46]

Double-Mindedness

As the poet Robert Frost recognized, the trouble with having two ways is that one cannot travel both. A choice of one over the other is required. The importance of choosing steadfast and undivided faith is a prominent refrain in the Apostolic Fathers, especially in the Shepherd of Hermas. The exhortation to steadfastness often comes in the warning not to be wavering, hesitant, or divided in faith. The Greek word associated with this warning is *dipsychos*, meaning "double minded." The Epistle of James warns that such a person is driven to and fro like waves of the sea, "unstable in all his ways" (1:8), double-minded rather than pure in heart (4:8).

The warning of James becomes a virtual mantra in the Apostolic Fathers. For 1 Clement, Lot's inconstant wife, who looked back and became a pillar of salt, symbolizes the error of double-mindedness.[47] The Shepherd labels such inconstancy the "daughter of the devil."[48] A doubled-minded person inevitably becomes "double-tongued."[49] The ultimate danger of double-mindedness is not simply mental deadlock but actual sin. The sins of double-mindedness are legion—including grief,[50] dissensions,[51] slander,[52] fascination with the occult (especially fortune tellers),[53] and vulnerability to false prophecy and spirits of error.[54] For the double-minded, the gospel ultimately becomes alien and offensive,[55] leaving them open to wickedness, hypocrisy, blasphemy,[56] and

44. Herm. Mand. 6.1–2.
45. Barn. 18–20.
46. 2 Clem. 6.
47. 1 Clem. 11.2.
48. Herm. Mand. 9.9.
49. Did. 2.3; Barn. 19.7.
50. Herm. Mand. 10.1.1.
51. Herm. Sim. 8.8.5; 8.9.4; 8.10.2.
52. Herm. Sim. 8.7.2.
53. Herm. Mand. 11.2; 11.4.
54. Herm. Mand. 11.1; 11.13.
55. Herm. Sim. 1.3.
56. Herm. Sim. 9.18.3.

"dead works."[57] Wavering in faith breeds profanity, abortion, infanticide, and covetousness.[58] The double-minded do not persist in hope;[59] they do not believe God's promises;[60] and as such, they are faithless.[61]

Double-mindedness is the antithesis of true and whole-hearted faith, to which James 4:8 summons readers.[62] The essence of saving faith is sincerity, conviction, and steadfastness. These foundational pillars undermine and overcome double-mindedness.[63] God reveals the divine will so that humanity can know and believe in God.[64] But the double-minded do not trust in God, and not to trust God is to be separated from God and without forgiveness of sin.[65] God wills undivided faith, not double-mindedness.[66]

The opposite of being double-minded (*dipsychos*) is being *adiakritos*, which means "constant," "steadfast," or "unwavering." Like *dipsychos*, *adiakritos* occurs in the New Testament only in the Epistle of James; in combination with "unhypocritical," it refers to the unwavering wisdom of God (3:17). Ignatius repeatedly appeals to being *adiakritos* as the virtuous antidote to being *dipsychos*. The way of the world is double-mindedness, but the way of God is resoluteness and steadfastness. Steadfast faith is virtuous because it reflects the nature of God, whereas double-mindedness reflects the sinfulness of humanity. Ignatius describes Jesus Christ as "our unwavering life."[67] Similarly, he praises the Magnesians for possessing "an unwavering spirit, who is Jesus Christ."[68] When this divine attribute is reproduced in Christian behavior, it becomes the virtue of steadfastness. Filled with God's grace, believers become "unwavering,"[69] even "of unwavering endurance";[70] they rejoice "without wavering in the suffering of our Lord."[71] The apostle Paul concludes his magisterial chapter on the resurrection of Jesus Christ with an appeal to the virtue of steadfastness among believers: "Therefore, beloved brothers and sisters, become steadfast, immovable, always abounding

57. Herm. Sim. 9.21.2.
58. Did. 4.4; Barn. 19.5.
59. 2 Clem. 11.5.
60. 2 Clem. 11.2.
61. 2 Clem. 19.2.
62. Herm. Vis. 3.3.4; 3.10.9; 4.1.4; 4.1.7; 4.2.4; 4.2.6.
63. 1 Clem. 23.2–3; Herm. Vis. 2.2.7.
64. Herm. Vis. 3.4.3; 3.11.2; Herm. Mand. 12.4.2; Herm. Sim. 6.1.2.
65. James 1:8; Herm. Vis. 2.2.4; 3.2.2; 3.7.1; Herm. Mand. 5.2.1; Herm. Sim. 8.8.3; 8.9.4; 8.10.2; 8.11.3.
66. Herm. Mand. 9.
67. Ign. *Eph.* 3.2.
68. Ign. *Magn.* 15.
69. Ign. *Rom.* (Salutation).
70. Ign. *Trall.* 1.1.
71. Ign. *Phld.* (Salutation).

in the work of the Lord, knowing that your labor in the Lord is not in vain" (1 Cor. 15:58).

Imitation

The early church adopted norms and vocabulary appropriate to the gospel as "good news." There are, of course, prohibitions in early Christian teaching (such as those in the sin lists noted above), but negatives are not the essence of Christianity. Eliminating evil does not result in a state of virtue; indeed, it may invite the return of greater evil (Matt. 12:43–45). The good news of the gospel is that life can be more than the state of nature, and especially of fallen nature. The promise of the gospel is a new and abundant life that grows by imitating Jesus Christ.

On more than one occasion, the apostle Paul speaks of "undressing" the old sinful self and "dressing" oneself anew in the person of Christ.[72] This mundane image of "putting on Christ" illustrates the concept of imitation, the process of reproducing in oneself what is honorable in another. Imitation is frequently upheld as the means by which believers embrace the good (3 John 11), the Christian faith (Heb. 13:7), or even God (Eph. 5:1). Believers are exhorted to imitate the characteristics of Christ wherever they appear—in other believers, for example, as "the heirs of the promise" (Heb. 6:12), or in fellow churches (1 Thess. 2:14). Paul also encourages his converts to imitate his own example, which exhibits God's promise for human life.[73]

The principle of maturing by following examples of strength and health maintained vital signs in the postapostolic era. Ignatius enjoins the congregations in Ephesus and Tralles, as Paul earlier enjoined the Ephesians, to "imitate God."[74] The Epistle to Diognetus describes charitable behaviors as imitations of God: "Whoever bears the burden of a neighbor, or wishes to help someone worse off than oneself, or provide for those in need, such a person becomes God to those who receive them, indeed this one is an imitator of God."[75]

Believers are to imitate Christ as Christ imitates the Father.[76] The supreme example of imitating Jesus Christ is bearing witness to one's faith with one's life, martyrdom.[77] True martyrdom is not a single act at the end of life, however, but bearing witness to the gospel in daily life through "patient

---

72. Rom. 12:2; 2 Cor. 4:16; Gal. 3:27; Eph. 4:24; Col. 3:9–10.
73. See 1 Cor. 4:16; 11:1; Phil. 3:17; 1 Thess. 1:6; 2:14; 2 Thess. 3:7, 9.
74. Ign. *Eph*. 1.1; Ign. *Trall*. 1.1.
75. Diogn. 10.5–6.
76. Ign. *Phld*. 7.2; Ign. *Eph*. 10.3.
77. Mart. Pol. 17.3.

endurance,"[78] imitating the "goodness of the Lord,"[79] and the example of the Lord himself.[80] In so doing, believers are "God-bearers" and "Christ-bearers."[81] To imitate God or Christ is to imitate their characteristics, the sufferings of Christ, for instance,[82] or the gospel itself, which is the word of Christ.[83] The "heroes of faith"—Elijah, Elisha, Ezekiel, Abraham, Job, Moses, and, above all, David—exhort believers to exemplary obedience, according to 1 Clement.[84] Such individuals are not simply past heroes but living examples in the present. The martyrdom of Polycarp is upheld as a supreme example to imitate.[85] But Ignatius also exhorts the church in Smyrna to imitate their *living* bishop, Burrhus, "who is a model of service to God."[86] In life and death, all these became icons through whom believers could see God; and when believers imitated them, or "put them on," they too became icons of God.

The Perfect Athlete

The apostle Paul exhorts believers "to attain to perfection, to the measure of the stature of the fullness of Christ" (Eph. 4:13). The Greek word *teleios*, here translated "perfection," means "fully mature," "meeting the highest standard," "perfect." No standard could be higher. The early church did not speak of the Christian way in terms of ease and comfort, of low demands or no demands, but as a rigorous and demanding contest. The author of Hebrews commends his readers for enduring the "hard struggle" of faith (10:32). The Greek word for "hard struggle," *athlēsis*, alludes to a tough athletic contest. Believers should expect "manifold trials" (James 1:2), but they should not lament them. Rather, they should prepare for them, like a great expedition for which rigorous preparation is indispensable for success. Believers should greet the challenges of the expedition with joy, training their bodies (1 Tim. 4:7–8), competing like athletes in "the great contest of faith" (1 Tim. 6:12), fighting like soldiers in "the good campaign,"[87] "striving to enter through the narrow gate" (Luke 13:24). The contest is earnest and can entail mortal combat, "wrestling with beasts," as Paul writes in 1 Corinthians 15:32.

78. Pol. *Phil*. 8.2.
79. Diogn. 10.4.
80. Pol. *Phil*. 10.1.
81. Ign. *Eph*. 9.2.
82. Ign. *Rom*. 6.3.
83. Mart. Pol. 22.1.
84. 1 Clem. 17–19.
85. Mart. Pol. 1.2; 19.1.
86. Ign. *Smyrn*. 12.1
87. 1 Tim. 1:18; 2 Cor. 10:4.

Whether Paul intends "beasts" literally or metaphorically is not certain.[88] Ignatius used the same image literally of his impending death in the Roman Coliseum and metaphorically of his struggles "on land and sea, by night and day" as he traveled to Rome.[89] The hardships that Christians had to face required self-discipline and abstinence (2 Pet. 1:6), but such sacrifices were worth making for the sake of the prize (Phil. 3:14) of receiving the crown of righteousness and glory,[90] indeed, the eternal crown of life itself (Rev. 2:10) prepared for those who "fought the good fight, finished the race, and kept the faith" (2 Tim. 4:7).

Stadiums, hippodromes, racecourses, and theaters were ubiquitous in the Roman world, and early Christian metaphors for discipleship stemming from them were powerful and effective. The culture of physical contest and combat even made inroads into the Palestinian Jewish world—for Herod the Great constructed an amphitheater and hippodrome in the heart of Jerusalem, the one city in the ancient world perhaps most resistant to Roman influences.[91] Athletic metaphors were more than attempts at cultural relevance, however. They were appropriate to the gospel itself, for the artistry of conceiving and executing an athletic feat was analogous of the artistry of theology and ethics. In the words of Paul: "Do you not know that all competitors in the stadium run, but only one receives the prize? Run so you will win. Everyone who competes trains rigorously—but all for a fading crown. We compete for an unfading crown! I do not run pointlessly, nor am I a mere shadowboxer. I punish my body and discipline it, lest having preached to others I be found unworthy myself" (1 Cor. 9:24–27).

The most complete athletic metaphor for the Christian life in the post–New Testament era occurs in 2 Clement 7, where a description of the Roman stadium serves as an exhortation to Christian faithfulness. "Compete so that we may be crowned," it says, for "not all are crowned, but only those who have trained hard and competed well." The author was aware, as are all church leaders, that Christians fall short of moral perfection. "If we cannot all be

---

88. The phrase is usually understood metaphorically, but a literal sense is not impossible. Gladiatorial combats occurred in Ephesus already in the first century BC, and the death referred to in 1 Cor. 15:32 is physical rather than metaphorical. In 1 Cor. 16:8–9 Paul speaks of facing many dangers and much opposition in Ephesus, and in 2 Cor. 1:8–9 he testifies that the dangers in Asia were so great that he despaired of rescue from them. However he intended it, Paul employed the expression "wrestling with beasts" absolutely seriously. The Christian apocryphal tradition in the Acts of Paul (ch. 7), by contrast, undermines the seriousness of 1 Cor. 15:32 by its portrayal of Paul being thrown to a lion in the arena of Ephesus: the lion—which Paul had previously baptized!—refuses to harm him, allowing Paul to go free.

89. Ign. *Rom.* 5.1.

90. See 2 Tim. 2:5; 4:8; 1 Pet. 5:4; Rev. 3:11.

91. Josephus, *Ant.* 15.268; *J.W.* 2.44. See Richardson, *Herod*, 186–88.

crowned," he concedes, "let us at least come close to it." Some in the author's fellowship had failed because they "corrupted" the faith. He likens them to athletes who cheat in races. Such athletes are disqualified, flogged, and thrown out of the stadium. "What will be done to cheaters in the heavenly competition?" the author asks pointedly; he then quotes Isaiah 66:24 as a warning to those who attempt to gain approval of their actions by perverting the gospel. Second Clement's admonition to believers to keep trying, even if they do not fully succeed, conveys seriousness about the demands of the gospel as well as pastoral sensitivity to those who struggle with its claims upon their lives.

The exhortation of Ignatius to the young bishop Polycarp sounds like a pep talk to a cross-country team. "Press on in your race," he writes, "bearing the infirmities of all, as the perfect athlete." To be sure, he adds, "it is hard work, but there is great gain."[92] As bishop, Polycarp is "God's athlete,"[93] and the mark of a great athlete is to be bruised.[94] The ultimate bruising of the athlete results in his death—martyrdom. The word "martyrdom" derives from the Greek *martyreō*, "to bear witness." Death is not the only means to bear witness to the gospel, and not necessarily even the most important; for believers bear witness to the gospel in thousands of ways and days throughout their lives. But death is the final witness—and as such, the most distinctive.

Already in 1 Clement, written late in the first century, Peter and Paul, who "were persecuted and fought to the death," are called *athlētas* (athletic champions).[95] The use of athletic imagery with reference to martyrdom reaches a zenith in the Martyrdom of Polycarp, which narrates the bishop's martyrdom as an athletic contest. The repeated emphasis on the stadium frames the martyrdom.[96] Polycarp is made a public spectacle,[97] and the roar of the crowd, as in athletic spectacles, drowns out all other sounds.[98] Like a heavenly coach, a divine voice exhorts Polycarp as he enters the arena, "Be strong, Polycarp, and courageous."[99] In martyrdom, Polycarp becomes "the perfect athlete," worthy of commemoration because of his faithfulness, but also "for the training and preparation of those who will do so in the future." His victory of martyrdom is hailed as his eternal "birthday."[100]

92. Ign. *Pol.* 1.2–3. See here Lightfoot, *Apostolic Fathers*, 4:335–36.
93. Ign. *Pol.* 2.3.
94. Ign. *Pol.* 3.1.
95. 1 Clem. 5.1–7.
96. Mart. Pol. 6.2; 8.3; 9.1–2; 12.1.
97. Mart. Pol. 6.2.
98. Mart. Pol. 8.3.
99. Mart. Pol. 9.1.
100. Mart. Pol. 18.3 (Holmes trans.). Similarly, Perpetua is portrayed as anointed for the athletic contest in her martyrdom (*Passion of the Holy Martyrs Perpetua and Felicitas* 3.2; ANF 3:702).

As late as the fourth century, the strivings and struggles of Christians continued to be cast in athletic imagery. Those whose valor won trophies in contests with demons and unseen adversaries were "athletes of piety."[101] Like Polycarp, the martyrs of the era were celebrated as victorious athletes. Among the greatest, whose narrative is both the longest and the most traumatic in Eusebius's *Ecclesiastical History*, is that of a Christian servant named Blandina, "a noble athlete" who, throughout unspeakable tortures, "put on the great and invincible athlete, Christ," thereby gaining for herself "the crown of immortality."[102]

Treasure in an Earthen Vessel

The apostle Paul pictures the relationship of the gospel and the church to each other in terms of a treasure in an earthen vessel (2 Cor. 4:7). Lest we imagine that the early church was flawless, or especially virtuous in comparison to the church today, the metaphor of an *earthen* vessel signifies Paul's undeluded judgment of the early church. In every age, the church is an earthen vessel, a misfit of goodness and folly, both an honor and a shame to its Lord. It was the uncomprehending and flawed Twelve whom Jesus called and sent into mission (Mark 8:14–21). It was the compromised and misguided Corinthians about whom Paul wrote the following: "Not many of you were wise by human standards, not many powerful, not many of noble stock. But God chose the foolish things of the world to shame the wise, he chose the weak things of the world to shame the strong, and he chose unimportant things, indeed despised things—things in fact that don't exist—to nullify things that do exist" (1 Cor. 1:26–28)."

It is precisely such individuals, in whom there is often little to emulate, who were instructed in the Christian way. It is these same individuals, and their disciples, who crossed the major frontiers we consider in this book, who made the journey from Jesus movement to Christian church. We have considered the various facets of this unusual and remarkable development, the strangeness of the gospel—an offense to Jews and folly to Romans—that birthed the Christian church. The strangeness did not diminish once Jews and Romans became acquainted with the church. The more they learned of Christianity, in fact, the stranger it seemed. And if it was strange to outsiders, it was even more so to insiders, to Christians themselves. For they knew firsthand—as Christians today also know—that through fallible people God had wrought

101. Eusebius, *Hist. eccl.* 5.1.
102. Eusebius, *Hist. eccl.* 5.1.19, 42 (LCL).

something uncharacteristic of human fallibility. Indeed, through their fallibility God created a new people, "a third race." The inimitable words of the second-century Epistle to Diognetus capture the divine mystery of the treasure of Christ in the earthen vessel of the church.

> Christians are not distinguished from the rest of humanity by country, language, or custom. For nowhere do they live in cities of their own, nor do they speak some unusual dialect, nor do they practice an eccentric way of life. This teaching of theirs has not been discovered by the thought and reflection of ingenious people, nor do they promote any human doctrine, as some do. But while they live in both Greek and barbarian cities, as each one's lots was cast, and follow the local customs in dress and food and other aspects of life, at the same time they demonstrate the remarkable and admittedly unusual character of their own citizenship. They live in their own countries, but only as nonresidents; they participate in everything as citizens, and endure everything as foreigners. Every foreign country is their fatherland, and every fatherland is foreign. They marry like everyone else, and have children, but they do not expose their offspring. They share their food but not their wives. They are in the flesh, but they do not live according to the flesh. They live on earth, but their citizenship is in heaven. They obey the established laws; indeed in their private lives they transcend the laws. They love everyone, and by everyone they are persecuted. They are unknown, yet they are condemned; they are put to death, yet they are brought to life. They are poor, yet they make many rich; they are in need of everything, yet they abound in everything. They are dishonored, yet they are glorified in their dishonor; they are slandered, yet they are vindicated. They are cursed, yet they bless; they are insulted, yet they offer respect. When they do good, they are punished as evildoers; when they are punished, they rejoice as though brought to life. By the Jews they are assaulted as foreigners, and by the Greeks they are persecuted, yet those who hate them are unable to give a reason for their hostility. In a word, what the soul is to the body, Christians are to the world. (Diogn. 5.1–6.1, Holmes trans.)

10

From Passover to Eucharist

The Lord's Supper as the Fulfillment of Passover

The taproots of Judaism and Christianity extend to the inbreaking of God into human history. For Jews, the constitutive inbreaking was the exodus from Egypt; for Christianity, it was the crucifixion of Jesus. Both historical events are commemorated in liturgical ceremonies—the exodus in Passover and Jesus's crucifixion in the Eucharist.

We must already pause for a caveat, however, for the Eucharist is generally considered by Christians to be a "sacrament"—that is, a means by which believers participate in the mystery of Jesus Christ. Centuries of controversy over how the elements of bread and wine relate to and convey the presence of God have caused us to think of them, and the ceremonies associated with them, as modes of revelation that differ from other modes of revelation (such as Scripture and preaching). Nowhere in the New Testament, however, does the Greek word *mystērion*, often translated "sacrament," fulfill our definition of sacrament.[1] Not until late antiquity—perhaps the fifth century—did "word" and "sacrament" become viable classifications of ecclesiastical traditions. In the early church, word and sacrament were not separate modes of revelation but, rather, two parts among others in the greater economy of salvation.[2]

---

1. *Mystērion* is rendered "sacramentum" in the Latin Vulgate in Eph. 1:9; 3:9; Col 1:27; and 1 Tim. 3:16. See D. S. Schaff, *NSHERK* 10:141–44, "The term was applied to Christian rites in the time of Tertullian, but can not be traced further back by any distinct testimony" (141).

2. See Pelikan, *Melody of Theology*, 213–16; and especially Nock, *Early Gentile Christianity*, 126: "We have all grown up with the category of sacraments as things of a specific kind; we are all aware of the centuries of controversy about their meaning and number. There

Jesus followers observed a number of his practices, including baptism (Matt. 28:19), common meals (1 Cor. 11:25), washing of feet (John 13:14), laying on of hands (Matt. 9:18), anointing (including of the sick, Mark 6:13), confession of sins (Matt. 3:6; James 5:16), and casting out demons (Mark 6:13). We do not know exactly how many of these practices made their way into early Christian worship and liturgy, and of those that did, how long they prevailed. We know only that baptism and common meals established themselves in church practice from the outset of the Christian movement— and not as elite, exclusive observances (such as the taurobolium in Mithraism or the ascent of the "perfect" to the upper echelons of the *Plērōma* in Gnosticism) but as practices observed "from the least to the greatest" (Heb. 8:11). The Johannine tradition locates "word" and "sacrament" in the body of the incarnate Christ: words flow from his mouth, and water and blood flow from his pierced side.[3] The one incarnate Lord is both word and sacrament, and hence word and sacrament are means of a single revelation. In 1 Corinthians 12:13, Paul combines baptism and Lord's Supper, washing and drinking, in a single image: "For in one Spirit we all were baptized into one body, whether Jews or Greeks, whether slaves or free persons, and we all drank one Spirit." He combines them, likewise, earlier in the same letter: "I do not wish you to be ignorant, brothers, that our fathers were all under the cloud and all passed through the sea and all were baptized into Moses in both the cloud and the sea, and all ate the same spiritual food and all drank the same spiritual drink; for they drank from the spiritual Rock that followed them, and the Rock was Christ" (1 Cor. 10:1–4). Karl Barth correctly sums up the New Testament witness to sacraments in declaring that Jesus Christ, as the incarnation of God, is the "first sacrament" of God, to whom all other sacraments testify.[4]

For Paul, the hasty Passover meal and the parting of the sea at the exodus were *types* that prefigured the Christ event. Both enacted and spoken modes served the same purpose as admonitions against sin and disobedience and exhortations to the endurance of faith (1 Cor. 10:6–13).[5] Paul's reference to *types* provides a strong argument, if one is needed, for locating the *prototypes* of baptism and the Lord's Supper in Israel rather than in the Greco-Roman world. Arguments that the Lord's Supper derived from Greco-Roman meals

was no such category in the first century of our era and even in the fifth century what we call sacraments were not set sharply apart from other aspects of the Christian revelation. Then, as in the first century, baptism and the Eucharist were part of the whole economy or dispensation of salvation."

3. John 19:34; 1 John 5:6.

4. Barth, *CD* II/1, 53–54.

5. Nock, *Early Gentile Christianity*, 126–28.

are implausible,[6] as are those that would root the Lord's Supper in mystery religions.[7] The argument for pagan prototypes of the Lord's Supper founders not only on the weakness of the putative parallels but also on the more evident parallels between the Supper and the Jewish Passover.[8] Central to all accounts

6. Duff, *Jesus Followers*, 204–12, argues for "strong parallels between the meals of the cultic associations and the ritual meals of the first-century assemblies of Jesus followers." This is an untenable argument. Early Christian meals as described in Acts 2:42, for example, may conform in some respects to Greco-Roman meals (*deipna*), but the similarities are neither "parallel" nor "strong," and the latter are scarcely prototypes of the Lord's Supper. That the Lord's Supper is called a *deipnon* (Luke 22:20; John 13:2, 4; 21:20; 1 Cor. 11:20–21) is of minor significance, for virtually *all* meals were called such. The idea that the cup of the Passover meal is modeled on a Greco-Roman libation, as Duff suggests, is severely discredited by the fact that pouring out wine as a "toast" to the gods was condemned in Israel (Jer. 7:18; 19:13; and possibly Amos 6:6). Greco-Roman banquets were frequently held in temples or sacred spaces dedicated to the god honored. Paul warns the Corinthian Christians against these banquets, since eating in a temple can compromise the conscience of weaker believers (1 Cor. 8:10–11); indeed, eating at these banquets can lead believers to confuse the cup of the Lord with the cup of demons (1 Cor. 10:21). Greco-Roman banquets regularly seated guests according to their social status, a custom that Jesus opposed (Mark 2:15–17; Luke 14:7–10; 16:21). Duff's contention that 1 Cor. 11:21 and Eph. 5:18–20 indicate that the Lord's Supper was followed by a drinking banquet is incredible. Symposia were roughly the equivalent to "stag parties," where women—"flute girls" and prostitutes—were present for men's pleasure. The overlaps between Plato's *Symposium* and accounts of the Lord's Supper are meager and minor. For an objective and informative consideration of the similarities and differences between Greco-Roman meals and the Lord's Supper, see Smith, "Dinner with Jesus and Paul."

7. See Nock, *Early Gentile Christianity*, 109–45: "Any idea that what we call the Christian sacraments were in their origin indebted to pagan mysteries or even to the metaphorical concepts based upon them shatters on the rock of linguistic evidence. . . . The absence from early Christian writing of other terminology commonly applied to pagan worship, even of the less esoteric kind, tells its own story" (132–33). Metzger, *Historical and Literary Studies*, 12, lists seventeen catchwords among the mystery religions that do not appear in the New Testament. For more evidence against the mysteries as prototypes of the Lord's Supper, see Edwards, *Jesus the Only Savior?*, 132–39.

8. Evidence for the Lord's Supper as a Passover celebration includes its placement in all three Synoptic Gospels on Thursday evening, its celebration in Jerusalem rather than in the suburbs, at night rather than in the afternoon, and the singing of a hymn after the meal (Mark 14:26). The time, place, and concluding hymn argue in favor of the Lord's Supper as a Passover celebration. Arguments against this conclusion point out the absence of women at the Last Supper (in Jewish custom women are present at the Passover), that there was no blessing of the cup by a guest, and that Jesus's words were at variance with the Passover liturgy. The objection regarding women is an argument from silence and is therefore not conclusive, for women were present throughout Jesus's ministry (Mark 15:41), although only infrequently mentioned. Assuming a degree of liturgical flexibility, neither of the second two objections is decisive. The most important evidence against the Lord's Supper as a Passover celebration is the reference in John 18:28 to Caiaphas and the Jewish council not entering the Roman praetorium lest they be defiled and be unable to eat the Passover. According to John, Passover lambs had not been eaten when Jesus was crucified, which implies that the crucifixion occurred on Thursday, the day of preparation. This would place the Last Supper on the night before Passover. Jeremias, *Eucharistic Words of Jesus*, 15–88, considers these points fully. Despite John 18:28, Jeremias finds several references to the Last Supper in the Fourth Gospel that agree with the synoptic

of the Lord's Supper in the New Testament are Jesus's "words of institution."[9] The Latin *instituto*, from which "institution" is derived, means "to instruct," "to introduce," and "to establish." Jesus's commentary interprets an event and ordains its observation, again testifying that sacrament and word cannot be separated but must be understood in their combined revelatory significance. Jesus's reference to the bread closely parallels the words of Moses to Israel in the wilderness: "This is the bread that the Lord has given you to eat" (Exod. 16:15). His reference to the cup likewise echoes the words of Moses at the giving of the law on Mount Sinai: "Behold, the blood of the covenant that the Lord has made with you in accordance with all these words" (Exod. 24:8).[10] The Lord's Supper binds its participants to a temporal continuum of past, present, and future. It is a remembrance of Jesus's past vicarious death on behalf of its participants, a celebration of the present confirmation of a new covenant in Jesus's blood poured out for his disciples, and an anticipation "until he comes" of a future messianic banquet. The Lord's Supper fulfills the promises and hopes of Israel.[11]

Three additional comments are relevant regarding the words of institution. The first is the reference to blood, which repeats and heightens the reference to blood in the covenant-renewal ceremony at Sinai. After Moses recounts the words of the Lord and receives the Israelites' assent to them, he builds an altar at the foot of the mountain, on which he sacrifices oxen. He throws half the blood of the oxen on the altar and the other half on the people, binding them in covenant with God (Exod. 24:3–8). The scandal of splashing Jews with blood at Sinai is intensified at the Last Supper, where Jesus commands the disciples to *drink* his blood.[12] In Hebrew thought, blood represented the life force of a creature. Jesus's reference to "my blood" is thus a reference to his very life. Here again, sacrament is interpreted by word and word actualized in sacrament, for the ingestion of blood at the Last Supper is an enactment of Jeremiah's prophecy about the new covenant in which God would put his

---

chronology (e.g., 13:21–30), including the words of interpretation in John 6, which presume the Passover context (6:3).

9. Matt. 26:26–29; Mark 14:22–25; Luke 22:15–20; 1 Cor. 11:23–26.

10. On these parallels, see Nock, *Early Gentile Christianity*, 125.

11. "It is certainly the Jewish background," declares Schweizer, "which shaped the format of the early Christian Lord's Supper." *Lord's Supper*, 1–3.

12. The Roman critic of Christianity, Porphyry, expressed his abhorrence of the Lord's Supper thus: "Is it not, then, bestial and absurd, surpassing all absurdity and bestial coarseness for a man to eat human flesh and drink the blood of his fellow tribesman or relative, and therein win life eternal?" For the full quotation, see Harnack, *Mission and Expansion*, 229n1. In response to critics who argue that no Jew would command disciples to "drink blood," Nock writes, "It is much harder to imagine someone else inventing the words than Jesus uttering them" (*Early Gentile Christianity*, 125).

law "within Israel, writing it on their hearts."[13] The blood of the covenant is no longer *on* Israel but *in* it—nourishing and giving life.

A second comment concerns the verb "to be" in the words of institution: "This *is* my body. . . . This *is* my blood." This most common of verbs has played an epic role in discussions of the Eucharist. The language of first-century Jewish liturgical life was Hebrew, and the declaration "This is my body" in Hebrew could either include or omit "is."[14] The actual Hebrew phrase was likely "This, my body," with "is" implied. In Indo-European languages, "is" suggests a too-exact equivalent between Jesus and the bread, whereas its omission weakens the relationship to a figurative or symbolic likeness. The Hebrew, with or without the verb, means a definite though not necessarily identical relationship. The theory that Jesus's words alter the chemical substance of the bread and wine to that of his flesh and blood overinterprets the sense of the texts. In the Gospel of Mark, in fact, Jesus declares "This is my blood" *after* the disciples have drunk the cup (14:23–24).[15] Furthermore, the demonstrative pronoun *this* in "*This* is my body. . . . *This* is my blood" (14:22, 24) is neuter (Gk. *touto*). If it were meant to designate the bread and wine, it would need to be masculine (Gk. *houtos*) to agree with *bread* and *wine* (both masculine nouns in Greek). The neuter points to Jesus's body (Gk. *sōma*, neuter) rather than to either the bread or the wine.[16] Finally, the phrase "poured out for many," although it is symbolized by wine in the upper room, becomes reality only in Jesus's death on Golgotha.[17] Taken together, the rendering "The bread *means* or *stands for* my body" may best convey the sense of the words of institution.

A third and final comment can be offered in support of the Passover as the prototype of the Lord's Supper. In Genesis 14:18, Melchizedek is portrayed as offering "bread and wine" to Abraham after the latter's victory over northern kings. Given the pronounced interest in Melchizedek in Second Temple Judaism—in Philo,[18] Josephus,[19] and Qumran;[20] in the Gnostic interpretations

---

13. Jer. 31:33; Heb. 8:8–12.

14. On the use of Hebrew rather than Aramaic in first-century Jewish religious life, see Edwards, *Hebrew Gospel*, 166–74. In the Hebrew New Testaments of Delitzsch (1931) and UBS (1976), "to be" is omitted in the words of institution.

15. See Schweizer, *Mark*, 303–4.

16. Schlatter, *Matthäus*, 742.

17. See Boughton, "Shed for You/Many."

18. Philo, *Alleg. Interp.* 3.82, allegorically refers to the wine offered by Melchizedek as "reason."

19. Josephus, *J.W.* 6.438 and *Ant.* 1.180, refers to Melchizedek as the "Righteous King" who officiated as the first high priest of God and gave the name "Salem" to Jerusalem.

20. 11QMelch.

of early Christianity found in the Nag Hammadi codices;[21] and in the tradition of Christianity ably advocated in the book of Hebrews[22]—it would not be surprising if the bread and cup offered at the Last Supper by Jesus, the true high priest and Son of God, were interpreted in terms of Melchizedek, the "King of Righteousness," who offered bread and wine to Abraham. We see no reference to Melchizedek in the Lord's Supper texts of the New Testament, however, and no reference to him at all in the Apostolic Fathers. The analogy between Passover and Lord's Supper was evidently so firmly established that other plausible analogies, such the one with Melchizedek, were eclipsed.[23]

Passover is thus the prototype of the Lord's Supper in the New Testament, although the significance of the Lord's Supper exceeds the Passover. The apostle Paul employs the one cup and one bread as a symbol of the one church, the body of Christ: "Because there is one bread, we, the many, are one body, for we all partake of the one bread" (1 Cor. 10:17). The imagery of cup and bread serves ethical purposes here, reproving the Corinthians for combining pagan and Christian sacrifices. Indeed, Paul chides the Corinthians for an overly "sacramental" attitude that corrupts the Lord's Supper.[24]

In yet a different vein, the Fourth Gospel employs the Lord's Supper as a metaphor for the incarnation of Jesus Christ, "the living bread who has come down from heaven" (John 6:51).[25] "Therefore, Jesus said to them, 'Truly, truly

21. See Birger A. Pearson, "Melchizedek," *ABD* 4:688, for the role of Melchizedek in the Nag Hammadi codices. For the role of Melchizedek in the Old Testament, Second Temple Judaism, and Qumran, see the entries written by Michael Astour and George Brooke in *ABD* 4:684–88.

22. Heb. 7 is devoted entirely to arguing for Jesus as high priest and Son of God "according to the order of Melchizedek."

23. In "Supersession or Subsession?," Boulton argues for a "subsessionist" understanding of the Eucharist as a repetition, rather than a supersession, of the Passover. "By connecting the Last Supper with the Passover meal," he says, the Gospel writers "mean to typologically cast the supper as an inauguration of a new exodus—or perhaps better, not a 'new' exodus but rather 'another exodus'" (25). Boulton is correct in retaining the typology of the Lord's Supper with the Exodus Passover, but if the Lord's Supper is only a repetition of the Exodus Passover, it forfeits the distinctiveness that Jer. 31 ascribes to the new covenant and that Jesus's words of institution ascribe to the Last Supper. Jer. 31, Jesus's words of institution, and (above all) Heb. 8–10 portray the new covenant not simply as "another" covenant subsequent to the first but as a once-for-all-time covenant that fulfills the first covenant and eliminates the need for a future covenant.

24. See Schweizer, *Lord's Supper*, 5: "The Corinthians thought far too sacramentally, to the extent that they came close to the concept of a magically effective *opus operatum* (1 Cor. 10:1–22; 15:29). What Paul throws up to them is exactly this: through their sacramentalism they have actually corrupted the Lord's Supper."

25. The imagery of flesh and blood is used in Heb. 2:14 as a reference to the human nature that Jesus assumed in order to deliver humanity from sin, death, and the devil. The author of Hebrews does not mention the Lord's Supper with reference to flesh and blood, but the text comports with Lord's Supper liturgy.

I tell you, unless you eat the flesh of the Son of Man and drink his blood, you do not have life among yourselves. Whoever eats my flesh and drinks my blood has eternal life, and I shall raise him in the last day. For my flesh is true food, and my blood is true drink. Whoever eats my flesh and drinks my blood abides in me and I in him'" (6:53–56). The imagery of Jesus's body and blood complements the earlier statement in John of the necessity of being born from above (3:3–5) and the later passage in which Jesus speaks of Peter's need to be washed (13:6–8). All highlight "the offense of faith." "According to John," declares Eduard Schweizer, "the Lord's Supper witnesses to nothing other than the same offense of the full incarnation."[26]

The Lord's Supper in Early Christian Tradition

The earliest record of the Lord's Supper, written no more than twenty years after Jesus's death, is narrated already in terms of "tradition"—as something handed down. Paul received the tradition from the Lord, delivered it to the Corinthians, and the Corinthians received it in faith.

> For I received from the Lord what I also handed on to you, that on the night he was betrayed the Lord Jesus took bread, and having given thanks, he broke it and said, "This is my body that is [given] for you. Do this in my remembrance." Likewise, also the cup after the supper, saying, "This cup is the new covenant in my blood. Do this, as often as you drink it, in my remembrance." For as often as you eat this break and drink the cup, you proclaim the Lord's death until he comes. (1 Cor. 11:23–26)

Paul recites this tradition with reference to the historical and vicarious self-giving of Jesus for the disciples, which was actualized on the cross and which is symbolized in the Supper; hence the double summons to "remembrance." The remembrance is more than a repetition of a past event. The "new covenant" proclaimed by Jesus is transtemporal—foreshadowed by Moses (Exod. 24:3–8), anticipated by Jeremiah (Jer. 31:31–34), and fulfilled in Jesus's blood as a promise and pledge of the coming kingdom of God. Paul positions the Lord's Supper tradition in 1 Corinthians in the context of moral rectitude. Thus discrimination of the rich against the poor in celebrating the meal renders one "unworthy" of participation in the meal.[27]

The earliest synoptic account of the Lord's Supper, written ten years or more after 1 Corinthians, coheres closely with 1 Corinthians 11: "While they

26. Schweizer, *Lord's Supper*, 8.
27. 1 Cor. 11:17–22, 27–33.

were eating, Jesus took bread and, having blessed it, broke it and gave it to them and said, 'Take, this is my body.' And having taken the cup and given thanks, he gave it to them, and they all drank of it. And he said to them, 'This is my blood of the covenant poured out on behalf of many. I tell you truly that I will no longer drink from the produce of the vine until that day when I drink it anew in the kingdom of God'" (Mark 14:22–25).

The Gospel of Luke preserves the above narrative kernel but augments it with a prelude of nearly equal length devoted to the cup. Of all the New Testament witnesses, Luke alone emphasizes the Hebraic setting of the Lord's Supper with its prelude, in Jesus's words: "I have truly desired to eat this meal with you" (22:15); "truly desired" is a literal Greek rendering of a Hebrew infinitive absolute.[28] Luke alone retains the reference to the Lord's Supper as a "remembrance" (22:19), but all three Synoptics, as we have seen, identify the Lord's Supper as a Passover meal, and all three include the narrative chain of thanksgiving, breaking (of bread), pouring (of the cup), and giving. The emphasis on Jesus's vicarious self-sacrifice is present in all three as well, as is the eschatological anticipation of "drinking anew in the kingdom of God." Finally, the Synoptics, like Paul, set the narrative in the context of moral accountability—preceded by Judas's collusion with the Sanhedrin to betray Jesus and followed by the scandal of the disciples' adamant profession of allegiance and their shameful abandonment of Jesus at his arrest.[29]

Three further accounts of the Lord's Supper appear in the Apostolic Fathers, although none is as full as the New Testament accounts. In the Didache, the Supper has attained the formal designation of "Eucharist," the designation that thenceforth predominates in the Apostolic Fathers. The Eucharist is set not in the context of moral rectitude but in that of church order, including instructions concerning baptism, fasting, prayer, Eucharist, and teaching. The Didache prescribes the proper invocations for the cup and for the breaking of the bread.[30] It also prescribes baptism as a necessary prerequisite for partak-

---

28. Edwards, *Hebrew Gospel*, 136.

29. As noted earlier, the Fourth Gospel omits a Last Supper narrative in favor of controversy with "the Jews" in which Jesus alludes to the elements of bread and blood (wine) with reference to the incarnation (John 6:51–58).

30. For the cup: "We give you thanks, our Father, for the holy vine of David your servant, which you have made known to us through Jesus, your servant; to you be the glory forever" (Did. 9.2, Holmes trans.). For the breaking of the bread: "We give you thanks, our Father, for the life and knowledge that you have made known to us through Jesus, your servant; to you be the glory forever. Just as this broken bread was scattered upon the mountains and then was gathered together and became one, so may your church be gathered together from the ends of the earth into your kingdom; for yours is the glory and the power through Jesus Christ forever" (Did. 9.3–4, Holmes trans.).

ing in the Eucharist, and it concludes with a pastoral prayer.[31] The Didache thus preserves eucharistic prayers rather than a eucharistic liturgy and words of institution; the latter, we may assume, were firmly established by the time the Didache was composed. The prayers, notably, make no mention of the Passover, which suggests a de-emphasizing of the relationship between Eucharist and Passover. In the Didache, David (not Moses) unites the eucharistic celebration to Israel. The order of the cup appearing before the bread may be attributed to the length of the prayers associated with cup, bread, and pastoral prayer—which appear in order of increasing length. Indeed, in summarizing the elements, the Didache treats the tradition of the bread first, followed by that of the cup.[32]

Like the Didache, Ignatius refers neither to the liturgical form of the Eucharist nor to the Passover. Throughout his epistles, he appeals to the churches of Asia Minor for harmony of faith and peace among their gathered communities.[33] For Ignatius, the Eucharist is the primary symbol of the church's unity and the primary means of making that unity real for believers. "Hasten to partake of the one Eucharist," he appeals to the Philadelphians, "for there is one flesh of our Lord Jesus Christ, and one cup that unifies the church in his blood; there is one altar, just as there is one bishop."[34] The unity of the body and blood of Christ is the source of the unity of the church as the body of Christ. For Ignatius, the ecclesiastical context of the Eucharist is essential to its meaning and validity. The church is called "the place of sacrifice," because the Eucharist itself is the sacrifice.[35] The altar is thus an essential component of the celebration: "Do not be misled," he admonishes, "for unless one is at

31. For the reference to baptism, see Did. 9.5. The concluding pastoral prayer reads thus: We give you thanks, Holy Father, for your holy name, which you have caused to dwell in our hearts, and for the knowledge and faith and immortality that you have made known to us through Jesus your servant; to you be the glory forever. You, almighty Master, created all things for your name's sake, and gave food and drink to humans to enjoy, so that they might give you thanks; but to us you have graciously given spiritual food and drink, and eternal life through your servant. Above all we give thanks to you because you are mighty; to you be the glory forever. Remember your church, Lord, to deliver it from all evil and to make it perfect in your love; and from the four winds gather the church that has been sanctified into your kingdom, which you have prepared for it; for yours is the power and the glory forever. May grace come, and may this world pass away. Hosanna to the God of David. If anyone is holy, let him come; if anyone is not, let him repent. Maranatha! Amen. (Did. 10.2–6, Holmes trans.)

32. Did. 9.5: "Let no one eat or drink of your Eucharist except those baptized." It is unlikely that the Didache, which is deferential to the New Testament, would alter the sequence of a received liturgical tradition.

33. Ign. *Eph.* 13.1–2.

34. Ign. *Phld.* 4.

35. Ign. *Eph.* 5.2; Ign. *Trall.* 7.2; Ign. *Phld.* 4.

the altar, one lacks the bread of God."[36] The administration of the bishop is likewise essential: "Only that Eucharist is valid that is administered by the bishop, or his designated appointee."[37] These elements and orders are essential to the faithful and effective reception of the Eucharist by the believer. The flesh of Christ is the "bread of God" that nourishes the believer's spiritual life, and the blood of Christ is God's "incorruptible love" in and through the believer.[38] Faithful participation in the Eucharist is participation, indeed mediation, of salvation. The oneness of God's being and his salvation in Jesus Christ are reflected in the oneness of the Christian community on earth, which is expressed in the one Eucharist administered by the one servant of God, the bishop. The oneness of the church and the saving efficacy of Christ are united in Ignatius's inimitable reference to the Eucharist as "the medicine of immortality." "All of you . . . gather in one faith and in one Jesus Christ, . . . breaking one bread, which is the medicine of immortality, the antidote against death and for life in Jesus Christ forever."[39] For Ignatius, therefore, the Eucharist is soteriological and ecclesial—a celebration of the bond of unity in the church, of the saving efficacy of Jesus Christ's death, and an antidote to heresy. The Eucharist is participation in the divine life of Christ, who is its host, and also in the life of the church, which consists of the guests of its host, Jesus Christ.[40]

The final witness to the Lord's Supper that we will consider in this section is Justin Martyr, from the mid-second century. Three times in the *Dialogue with Trypho*, Justin mentions the Eucharist in connection with the atoning significance of Jesus's passion and cross.[41] All three passages refer to the Eucharist as a memorial of Christ's passion for the salvation of sinners. A more substantial witness to the Eucharist appears at the conclusion of the *First Apology*, where Justin reviews the order of the Eucharist for Antoninus Pius, to whom he addresses the apology.[42] Like the Didache and Ignatius, Justin lists baptism as a prerequisite for participation in the Eucharist, along with catechesis and moral examination. With reference to the eucharistic ceremony, Justin mentions prayer, a holy kiss, and administration of bread, followed by cup (wine mixed with water). Justin's version of the words of institution is closer to Luke 22:19 than to any other New Testament text.

---

36. Ign. *Eph.* 5.2.
37. Ign. *Smyrn.* 8.1.
38. Ign. *Rom.* 7.3.
39. Ign. *Eph.* 20.2. See also Quasten, *Patrology*, 1:66.
40. On the Eucharist in Ignatius, see Wehr, *Arznei der Unsterblichkeit*, 63–181.
41. *Dial.* 41.1 (*ANF* 1:215): "In remembrance of the suffering which [Jesus] endured on behalf of those who are purified in soul from all iniquity." See also *Dial.* 70.3–4; 111.3.
42. *1 Apol.* 65–66. Antoninus Pius was emperor of Rome (r. 138–161).

This suggests that Justin's liturgy is no longer determined by oral tradition but, at least in part, by the written Gospels. Justin follows the bread-cup sequence of the New Testament. The words of institution for the bread, "Do this in remembrance of me; this is my body," are followed by words for the cup, "This is my blood."[43] Prayer in the name of the Trinity follows the meal, concluding with a congregational "Amen." Justin's note that "Amen answers in the Hebrew language to *genoito* [so be it]" seems to suggest that "Amen" was a recent innovation in his day.[44] On the significance of the meal, Justin concludes, "As Jesus Christ our Savior, having been made flesh by the Word of God, had both flesh and blood for our salvation, so likewise have we been taught that the food which is blessed by the prayer of His word, and from our blood and flesh by transmutation are nourished, is the flesh and blood of that Jesus who was made flesh."[45] The reference to the bread and wine "transmuting" and "nourishing" our flesh and blood recalls the same idea in Ignatius. Justin's final statement that the food "is the flesh and blood of that Jesus who was made flesh" also recalls Ignatius's concept of the Eucharist as "the medicine of immortality" and could be understood as an early expression of what would become the doctrine of transubstantiation.[46]

Let us summarize the witness to the Eucharist in the New Testament, Didache, Ignatius, and Justin—which became the orthodox tradition of Christianity. Both Paul and the Gospels expressly link the Lord's Supper with the Jewish Passover, and they set its remembrance and celebration in the context of the worshiping community and in moral accountability to that community. Beginning with the Didache, the Eucharist becomes divorced from the Passover; from then on, the tradition makes no reference to Passover in relation to the Eucharist. Likewise, in the Didache and subsequent traditions, the Eucharist is no longer rehearsed in the context of moral accountability, as it is in the New Testament. Rather, it appears as a formal element of church order. The Eucharist emerges as a principal mark of the church, a defining element of its public worship and witness, and a means through which the gospel is transmitted to and made real in the lives of believers.

43. *1 Apol.* 66.3.

44. *1 Apol.* 65 (*ANF* 1:185). Original Greek text has been transliterated.

45. *1 Apol.* 66.2 (*ANF* 1:185).

46. On Justin's references to the Eucharist, see McGowan, "Liturgical Text?," 80–83. McGowan argues that 1 Cor. 11:23–25, Justin's *1 Apol.* 65–66, and Hippolytus's *Trad. ap.* 4, 9 "are the three most important liturgical 'readings' of the words of institution prior to the fourth century, and all arguably . . . [are] interpretive reflections or catecheses applied to the eucharistic meal" (85). The texts we have cited from the Didache and Ignatius also belong in the list of crucial early eucharistic texts.

The Eucharist in Heterodox Traditions

The Eucharist was not unique to the mainstream tradition of the New Testament and Apostolic Fathers. Other traditions vying for recognition and perhaps even supremacy over emerging Christianity also claimed it. The traditions of which we are aware appear to have been primarily Gnostic. The late second- or early third-century Gospel of Philip—a pseudonymous florilegium, or anthology, of 127 text units forming a rambling catechesis on the sacraments—twice refers to John 6, most likely in connection with the Eucharist. The first reference occurs in the context of Adam nourishing the animals of paradise but having no "wheat" for his own nourishment: "When Christ came, the perfect man, he brought bread from heaven in order that man might be nourished with the food of man."[47] "Bread from heaven" appears to be a reference to Exodus 16, verses 4 and 15, and Psalm 78:24 (which Jesus quotes in John 6:31). The second reference includes a loose quotation of John 6:53: "He who shall not eat my flesh and drink my blood has no life in him."[48] The Gospel of Philip here uses the singular pronoun where John 6:53 uses the plural pronoun; thus it addresses the lone believer rather than the community of believers. The idea that the believer will not be resurrected in a "contemptible body" but "naked" is predictably Gnostic, as is the idea that whoever eats the flesh of Jesus (his word) and drinks his blood (the Holy Spirit) is "clothed" for the resurrection.[49]

The Acts of Thomas, which we considered earlier in connection with the expansion of the gospel to India, also refers to the Eucharist. Like the Gospel of Philip, the Acts of Thomas is pseudonymous. It was probably written in the early third century, perhaps in Syria. Thomas, it will be recalled, is a carnival of the probable, improbable, and impossible.[50] The eucharistic reference occurs in an account of a beautiful woman whom demons tempt with sexual fantasies for five years. Thomas exorcises the demons, then converts them, and dismisses them with a benediction: "The grace of our Lord Jesus Christ be upon you forever!" The demons respond, "Amen." Then, turning to the woman, Thomas lays hands upon her in the name of the Trinity and prepares the Eucharist, inviting "Jesus, who has made us worthy to partake of the Eucharist of [his] holy body and blood," to have fellowship with them. In a concluding benediction, Thomas names the Eucharist "a love feast," at which the Holy Spirit, "the hidden mother," will perfect the "fellowship of the male."[51]

47. Gos. Phil. 15, in *NTApoc* 1:189–90.
48. Gos. Phil. 23b, in *NTApoc* 1:191.
49. Gos. Phil. 22–23b, in *NTApoc* 1:190–91.
50. On the Acts of Thomas, see ch. 3, pp. 59–61.
51. Acts Thom. 42–49, in *NTApoc* 2:357–60.

These final references reflect Gnostic interpretations of Jesus—according to which he, as a second Adam, was believed to reunite Adam and Eve as one new spiritual male fit to dwell with Christ for eternity.[52]

The Gospel of Philip and the Acts of Thomas move the Eucharist from the circle of orthodoxy to the uncircumscribed space of heterodoxy. In these texts, the Eucharist is divorced from the Jewish Passover, as well as from moral and ethical accountability within the Christian community. The divorce is even more complete, however, for in Gnosticism the addressee of the Eucharist is not the believing community but the solitary believer. Most importantly, the Eucharist is no longer a remembrance of the self-sacrifice of Jesus Christ on the cross for the salvation of believers and a means of their transformation into his likeness. Rather, the Eucharist comes to signify the abnegation of human nature—along with the abnegation of the incarnate Christ—and thus a divorce from the created world in favor of a purely spiritual union with the "All," or "*Plērōma.*"

A Concluding Note on Baptism

So far in our discussion, we have not examined baptism—which, in almost all Christian traditions, constitutes one of the two primary sacraments. Indeed, in the New Testament and other early Christian literature, baptism is mentioned more frequently than the Eucharist. And it is the more important of the two rites, for baptism belongs to the "solas" of both the scriptural confession of Ephesians 4:5–6—that there is "one Lord, one faith, one baptism, one God and Father of us all"—and the Nicene Creed, "I acknowledge one baptism for the forgiveness of sins." Baptism has been excluded in our discussion thus far not because it is unimportant but because, unlike other elements of early Christianity considered in this book, it did not undergo formal changes between the ministries of Jesus and Ignatius. The rite of baptism instituted by John the Baptizer, commanded by Jesus (Acts 1:5), and practiced from the earliest days of the Christian movement (Acts 2:38) remained essentially unaltered in the early Christian tradition.

Considering its essential significance in Christianity, however, it is fitting to conclude this chapter by discussing, briefly, the role of baptism.[53] The

52. See here Wesley W. Isenberg, "The Gospel of Philip," *NHL* 131. On the necessity of females becoming males in Gnosticism, see also Gos. Thom. 114: "Simon Peter said to them: Let Mary go away from us, for women are not worthy of life. Jesus said: Lo, I shall lead her, so that I may make her a male, that she too may become a living spirit, resembling you males. For every woman who makes herself male will enter the kingdom of heaven."

53. See Harnack, *Mission and Expansion*, 228: "From the very outset of the Christian religion, its preaching was accompanied by two outward rites, neither less nor more than two, viz., baptism and the Lord's supper."

Greco-Roman mysteries prepared candidates for admission to their cults by ceremonies, often called *hydranos*, "washing" or "sprinkling." Judaism, likewise, instituted water rites—*miqva'ot*, "immersion baths"—of purification for worship in temple and synagogue.[54] When John the Baptizer summoned Judeans to the Jordan for a washing ceremony of repentance and moral reform, he was not doing something entirely novel, but neither was his rite specifically patterned after Jewish or pagan practices.[55] All four Gospels identify John's baptism as the event at which Jesus was declared God's Son and endowed with the Holy Spirit, signaling the commencement of his salvific ministry. The Gospel of John is ambiguous on whether Jesus himself baptized, but it distinctly states that his disciples baptized during his ministry (John 3:22; 4:1–2). Following the resurrection, Jesus confirmed John's baptism as a foreshadowing of a spiritual baptism at Pentecost (Acts 1:5); and following the first major sermon in Acts, Peter summoned would-be converts to baptism "in the name of Jesus Christ for the remission of your sins and the reception of the Holy Spirit" (2:38). Baptism is rooted in the earliest conception and development of Christianity.

We find no debate over baptism in the New Testament—as we find over apostolic succession or the gentile mission, for example. Our earliest texts assume its essential role in the faith, thereby attesting to its early and wide acceptance among Jesus followers. Neither the New Testament nor the Apostolic Fathers preserves an order of service for a baptismal ceremony. Its sacred element was water. But it is unclear whether initiates were fully immersed (which the image of dying and rising with Christ in Rom. 6:3–4 suggests) or whether water was poured on standing initiates (the most common way baptism is depicted in the catacombs and early Christian wall frescoes). The Didache allows either immersion or sprinkling to satisfy the requirements of baptism.[56] The means by which the water is administered are discretionary (Gk. *adiaphora*), whereas the twice-mentioned essential element (Gk. *diapheron*) is the Trinitarian formula: "In the name of the Father and Son and Holy Spirit."[57] Christian converts were apparently baptized naked. This is

---

54. See Meeks, *First Urban Christians*, 152–53.

55. On the influence of John the Baptist on Christian baptism, see Schweizer, *Lord's Supper*, 26–27: "Baptism, which is simply presupposed in all our [New Testament] texts, was adopted by the primitive church in imitation of the baptism practiced by the disciples of John."

56. "Now concerning baptism, baptize as follows: after you have reviewed all these things, baptize in the name of the Father and of the Son and of the Holy Spirit in running [living] water. But if you have no running water, then baptize in some other water; and if you are not able to baptize in cold water, then do so in warm. But if you have neither, then pour water on the head three times in the name of Father and Son and Holy Spirit" (Did. 7.1–3, Holmes trans.).

57. Did. 7.1, 3.

explicitly instructed in the first known baptismal manual, from Hippolytus.[58] The earliest artistic depictions also show John pouring water over the head of Jesus while the latter stands naked in water.[59] In the context of baptism, the Pauline references to taking off and putting on clothes, or stripping off the old person and putting on the new, suggest nakedness as well.

Rather than the *means*, the *meaning* of baptism spawned a wealth of imagery in the New Testament. The Gospel of Matthew identifies the rite with conversion, "baptizing believers in the name of the Father and the Son and the Holy Spirit" (28:19). First Peter likens baptism to the deluge in Noah's day, signifying rescue from death and annihilation as well as preservation for new life (3:20–22). The association of baptism with receiving the Holy Spirit (Acts 1:5) is repeated in the description of Paul's baptism (Acts 9:17–18) and in connection with the gift of the Holy Spirit in 2 Corinthians 1:21–22. The most theologically consequential treatment of the subject in the New Testament is Paul's likening of baptism to dying and rising with Christ: immersion in water signifies death and burial of the old sinful person, and rising from the water symbolizes eternal regeneration in Christ.[60] The regenerated believer is united to the very body of Christ in the new community of believers. As we saw above, the new life is pictured in terms of "putting on" the new clothing of Jesus Christ himself (Col. 2:11; 3:10).[61] Similarly, the Gospel of John likens baptism to "new birth," to being born from above, born from water (John 3:3–5). The baptized believer can hear and receive genuine moral exhortation,[62] which, like the original context of the Lord's Supper, set baptism decidedly in the context of ecclesial and moral exhortation. Only believers who walk in the light on earth, admonishes the Pauline literature, will be enthroned in the heavenly places with Christ.[63]

The question whether the early church baptized infants or only adults cannot be answered with certainty. That the New Testament records only the baptisms of believing adults is not conclusive in answering the question, for the Christian movement had to begin with the baptism of adult converts, and the question of whether to baptize children may not have occurred to that first generation. However, children did figure prominently in early Christianity. The gift of salvation belongs to children as well as to adults (Acts 2:39). Two

58. *Trad. ap.* 21.
59. Meeks, *First Urban Christians*, 151.
60. Rom. 6:1–4; Eph. 2:5 (possibly); Col. 2:12.
61. See Harnack, *Mission and Expansion*, 389: "The general conviction [of the ancient church] was that baptism effectually cancelled all past sins of the baptized person . . . ; he rose from the immersion a perfectly pure and perfectly holy man."
62. Rom. 6; 8:12–17; 1 Cor. 1–4; 12; Gal. 3:26–4:6.
63. Eph. 2:4–7; Col. 2:12, 20; 3:1–4.

precedents in Judaism possibly opened the door for infant baptisms in early Christianity. The first was the presence of Jewish children in the celebration of the Passover meal, and the second was the rite of circumcision of male Jewish babies. Colossians draws a direct parallel between Jewish circumcision and Christian baptism (2:11–13). The analogy of circumcision is of particular relevance, for *all* males—young and old—were circumcised in Israelite households (Gen. 17:23–27). The New Testament preserves five accounts of baptisms of "households";[64] some of the households, presumably, included children. There thus appears to be more than one precedent in the New Testament and first-century Christianity for baptizing children and, assuming the above-mentioned households contained children, infants as well.[65]

---

64. Acts 11:14–16; 16:15, 33; 18:8; 1 Cor. 1:16.

65. For an exhaustive treatment of baptism in early Christianity, see Hellholm et al., *Ablution, Initiation, and Baptism*. More brief, but informative and balanced, is Beasley-Murray's *Baptism in the New Testament*. In *Infant Baptism in the First Four Centuries*, Jeremias argues for the probability of infant baptism in early Christianity. A case for the improbability of infant baptism until the third century, on the other hand, is presented by Aland, *Did the Early Church Baptize Infants?*

11

From Apostles to Bishops

The Twelve and the Apostles

According to the Gospels, the formal name for the inner circle of Jesus followers was "the Twelve," the individual members of which were called "apostles." "The Twelve" occurs some forty-five times in the four Gospels and is the most common designation for the Jesus cohort. "Apostles" appears ten times in the Gospels, usually in conjunction with "the Twelve."[1]

In my judgment, the earliest account of Jesus forming the Twelve occurs in the Gospel of Mark: "Jesus went up to the mountain and summoned those whom he desired, and they came to him. And he made them twelve [whom he also named apostles], in order that they might be with him, and that he might send them to proclaim and have authority to cast out demons" (Mark 3:13–15). Every aspect of this text is important for understanding Jesus's intention for the Twelve—and, by extension, for the church. First, neither here nor in earlier summons of disciples does Jesus mention any criteria for discipleship.[2] This is remarkable in itself, and all the more so when considered in light of the lengthy criteria for bishops a generation later.[3] What is emphasized, rather, is the decisiveness of Jesus in determining his inner circle of followers. The reference to "mountain," a place of prominence, and Jesus

1. For "apostle," see Matt. 10:2; Mark 3:14 (possibly); 6:30; Luke 6:13; 9:10; 11:49; 17:5; 22:14; 24:10; and John 13:16. "The Twelve" occurs in conjunction with the above passages and pericopes except in Luke 11:49; 17:5; 24:10; and John 13:16.
2. Matt. 4:18–22; Mark 1:16–20; Luke 5:1–11; John 1:35–51.
3. See 1 Tim. 3:1–7; Titus 1:5–9.

"summoning those whom he desired" signify this in Mark. Luke signifies the same by reporting that Jesus prayed through the night before "selecting" (Gk. *eklegomai*) the twelve apostles (Luke 6:12–16).

Second, although we are not told exactly why Jesus chose the Twelve, we do know something about them. None belonged to the echelons of Jewish leadership, whether as priest, or scribe, or member of the Sanhedrin; and none was a member of a Jewish sect, whether as Pharisee, Sadducee, Herodian, or Essene (with the exception of a single disciple affiliated with the Zealots). On the other hand, none was a member of the outcast and oppressed, as a slave, leper, Samaritan, or indigent. All were *am ha-aretz*, "people of the land." At least half were fishermen from Capernaum and Bethsaida, which put them in a class of competitive merchants who marketed their catch far beyond the region.[4] One of the Twelve was a venture capitalist (a tax collector) and another a political revolutionary (a Zealot). We know something, therefore, about whom Jesus called, but we are told virtually nothing about qualifications or merits that might have warranted their call.

Third, the call and inclusion of the Twelve at the outset of Jesus's ministry indicates his intention for a corporate ministry rather than a solo performance. Although we do not know why he called exactly these persons, we know the purpose for which he called them. Jesus *made* them Twelve, in Mark's words, to be with him, to proclaim (the gospel), and to cast out demons (i.e., to oppose evil). The emphasis lay not on *who* they were but on *what* Jesus would make of them. This threefold mission of being, speaking, and acting laid claim to their whole lives—relationally, verbally, and behaviorally.

Finally, the titles "apostles" and "Twelve" are important in themselves. "Apostle" was not unknown in the Greco-Roman world, and in Judaism the Hebrew *shiloach* ("an authorized member of an established community") could also be translated "apostle."[5] Neither of these uses was a prototype of a New Testament apostle, however. For in the Greco-Roman world, "apostle" usually referred to a bureaucratic official (e.g., a financial manager) or document (e.g., a cover letter, passport, or bill of lading) rather than to a person sent with a commission; and in Judaism, *shiloach* is attested only after the

---

4. No fewer than sixteen fishing ports and nearly as many towns dotted the shore of the Sea of Galilee in Jesus's day. The boats were so numerous that Josephus commandeered two hundred of them to fight the Romans in the year 68 (*J.W.* 2.635). Fish, not meat from land animals, was the primary staple derived from animals in the Greco-Roman world; fish from the Sea of Galilee were exported as far as Egypt to the south and Antioch to the north. See Murphy-O'Connor, "Fishers of Fish"; Nun, "Ports of Galilee."

5. In John 9:7 the name Siloam (Hb. *Shaluach*) is explained as "sent." *Shaluach* is the participial form of the verb *shiloach*, "to send." See Str-B 2:530.

fall of Jerusalem in the year 70.[6] The New Testament use of "apostle" differs from both of these uses. The Greek word for "apostle" (*apostolos*) derives from the root verb "to send" (*apostellō*). And with regard to New Testament apostles, apostleship is defined by the person and mission of Jesus.

In contrast to "apostles," the designation "the Twelve" is firmly rooted in and defined by the Old Testament. There were twelve pillars for the sacrifice at the foot of Mount Sinai (Exod. 24:4), twelve stones in the priestly garments (Exod. 28:21), twelve sets of tableware given for the altar (Num. 7:84), twelve sacrificial offerings at the altar's dedication (Num. 7:87), twelve oxen under the enormous laver (1 Kings 7:44), and twelve lions for the throne of Solomon (1 Kings 10:20). Joshua constructed a monument of twelve stones after crossing into the promised land (Josh. 4:8). Both the sons of Ishmael (Gen. 25:13–15) and the sons of Jacob (Gen. 49:28) formed twelve tribes. Ezekiel envisioned the restoration of Israel according to the twelve tribes of Jacob (Ezek. 47:13), which in turn became the archetype for the twelve apostles of Jesus.[7] Mark's emphasis on Jesus *making* them twelve signals his intentionality in determining their number. The four lists of the apostles in the New Testament contain minor differences in their names and sequences, but never in their number. There are always and only twelve apostles.[8] "The twelve tribes of the diaspora" in the salutation of the Epistle of James (1:1) identifies the church (5:14) not as an offshoot from, or as an opponent of, Israel, but as a direct descendant and development of Israel. As we have seen, the apostle James played a unique role in the early church by remaining in fellowship with the temple—and eventually being martyred there—testifying to his conviction that the saving history of Israel is fulfilled in the church of Jesus Christ. The salutation of his epistle attests to this conviction.[9] The Apostolic Fathers also correlate the twelve tribes and the twelve apostles.[10]

6. See Wolfgang A. Bienert, "The Picture of the Apostle in Early Christian Tradition," *NTApoc* 2:5–8. Harnack's contention, in *Mission and Expansion*, 327–33, that "apostle" was a Jewish prototype of its Christian usage lacks convincing corroborative evidence. "Apostle" does not occur in the LXX (with the exception of an uncertain text in 1 Kings 14:6), and Str-B 3:2–4 cites no use of the term prior to the fall of Jerusalem.

7. Matt. 19:28; Luke 22:30; Rev. 21:12–14.

8. Matt. 10:2–4; Mark 3:16–19; Luke 6:14–16; Acts 1:13. Two witnesses to Acts 1:26 even refer to the eleven disciples after the death of Judas as "the Twelve" (Codex Bezae; and Eusebius).

9. On the mission of James, brother of Jesus, see Evans, *From Jesus to the Church*, 25–32. First Peter is also addressed to the diaspora (1:1), although without mention of the twelve tribes. As in James 1:1, the use of the expression in 1 Peter suggests a community of Christians maintaining their roots in Hellenistic Judaism.

10. "[Jesus] gave the authority to proclaim the gospel to the Twelve as a witness to the tribes, because there are twelve tribes of Israel" (Barn. 8.3); "These twelve mountains are the twelve tribes that inhabit the whole world. The Son of God was preached to them by the

The Apostles in Early Christianity

Membership in the Twelve was nonhereditary and nontransferrable. Judas forsook his membership by betraying Jesus and was replaced as an apostle (Acts 1:15–26), but the remaining eleven who witnessed to the faith in life and death were not replaced, because faithfulness in life and death *fulfilled* their apostolic calling. The final reference to the sole authority of the twelve apostles in the early church occurs in connection with the formation of the office of deacons in Acts 6:1–6. By then the office of apostle was no longer static; it was expanding to include several individuals who were not members of the original twelve. The first was Matthias, successor to Judas (Acts 1:26). He was followed by Barnabas (Acts 4:36), James,[11] Paul (Rom. 1:1), Andronicus and Junia (Rom. 16:7), and Epaphroditus (Phil. 2:25).[12] We are not told why the title was extended to include additional apostles. Paul justified his apostleship as a commission of the resurrected Christ, and the title was probably extended likewise to others who claimed particular encounters with the resurrected Christ.[13] "The apostle of Jesus Christ," declares Wolfgang Bienert, "is first and above all a witness to the resurrection of Jesus from the dead."[14]

Following the resurrection, the apostle is no longer the only kind of Christian leader. Apostles are mentioned in conjunction with brothers (Acts 11:1), elders,[15] and prophets.[16] The office of apostle is not diminished, but it is increasingly shared with other offices. The groundbreaking decision of the early church to receive gentiles into full membership on the basis of confession of faith in Jesus Christ was the result of a decision of "apostles and elders" (Acts 15). And this is the last mention of "apostles" in the book of Acts. Paul, of course, continues to claim the term with reference to his mission, especially in the salutations of his epistles.[17] Apostolic authority remains the primary authority in the church (1 Cor. 12:28), which Paul claims for himself in order to counter the false apostles of "another gospel" in Galatia (Gal. 1:6–9). Paul

---

apostles" (Herm. Sim. 9.17.1). Just as Moses settled strife among the tribes of Israel as to which was greatest (Num. 17), so the apostles, having been tutored by the Lord Jesus Christ, settled the matter of their succession by establishing the office of bishop (1 Clem. 43–44).

11. 1 Cor. 15:7; Gal. 2:9.

12. The gender of "Junia" is almost certainly feminine, which would make Junia, who in Rom. 16:7 is called an apostle, either the wife or sister of Andronicus. See Edwards, *Romans*, 355; Moo, *Epistle to the Romans*, 921–23.

13. Paul, above all, claims apostleship on the basis of his witness of the resurrected Christ in 1 Cor. 9:1; 15:1–11; Gal. 1:15–2:10.

14. "The Picture of the Apostle in Early Christian Tradition," *NTApoc* 2:9.

15. Acts 15:2, 4, 6, 22, 23; 16:4.

16. Eph. 2:20; 3:5; Rev. 18:20.

17. Rom. 1:1; 1 Cor. 1:1; 2 Cor. 1:1; Gal. 1:1; Eph. 1:1; Col. 1:1; 1 Tim. 1:1; 2 Tim. 1:1; Titus 1:1.

places his apostleship on a par with that of Peter, John, and James the brother of the Lord.[18] "Apostle" was applied to more individuals and for a longer period of time than was the title "the Twelve," but it too was confined to the first century. The last reference to active apostles seems to be the "apostles and prophets" of the Didache who itinerated among the churches. Apostles rather than prophets, however, retained unparalleled authority: "Let every apostle who comes to you be received as the Lord."[19]

Both the apostolic authority and office continued to be held in high esteem in the early church (e.g., Rev. 2:2), and as such outlived the apostles themselves. "Remember the words spoken beforehand by the holy prophets and the commandment of the Lord and Savior through your apostles," reads 2 Peter 3:2, which also includes Paul in the venerated company of the apostles (3:15–16).[20] The Apostolic Fathers and second-century Christian writers ground their own authority as church leaders in apostolic origins. "The apostles received the good news of the gospel from the Lord Christ *on our account*," declares 1 Clement. "The Messiah, therefore, is from God, and the apostles are from the Messiah. Both, therefore, reveal the proper order of God's will."[21]

Teachers

At the end of the first century, Clement writes that as the rod of Aaron blossomed in the Old Testament (Num. 17), thus designating the tribe of Levi as God's chosen priests and ministers, so apostles were sent forth from Christ, and the firstfruits of their preaching resulted in the appointing of bishops and deacons in the church. For Clement, authority in the church is transmitted from God to Christ, from Christ to apostles, and from apostles to bishops and deacons.[22] This may have been the "official" path of ecclesial authority, but it omits two offices of unquestioned authority in early Christianity. One, which we consider here, is the office of teacher, preacher, and prophet—by which the kerygma continued to be transmitted both in the church and in the Christian mission. The other, which we consider in the following section, is the office of presbyter or elder. Unlike bishops, elders, and deacons, who were

18. 2 Cor. 11:5; 12:11–12.

19. Did. 11.3–6. Lake, *Apostolic Fathers*, 1:307n1, is correct to differentiate "apostle" from "the Twelve" in the Didache: "'Apostle' in the Didache does not mean a member of 'the Twelve,' but is merely an inspired teacher who is engaged in preaching, . . . very much [like] what is now called a Missionary." But Lake misjudges the role of apostle, because unlike prophets, apostles claim a unique commission from the Lord himself.

20. See also Jude 17.

21. 1 Clem. 42.1–2.

22. 1 Clem. 42–43.

appointed by ecclesial authority, the teaching office in the New Testament is attributed to divine call and charism.[23] The heirs to the apostolic office of proclamation of the kerygma were teachers, rather than bishops, elders, and deacons. "My child," exhorts the Didache, "remember night and day the one who speaks the word of the Lord to you, and honor him as the Lord."[24]

Of all the titles attributed to Jesus in the New Testament—including prophet, high priest, Messiah, Son of Man, Lord, Word, Son of God—none is used more frequently than "teacher," and no description of his ministry is more common than "teaching." The Gospel of John calls Jesus "the Word of God" (1:1) who teaches "the words of life" (6:68). He is the truth (14:6) who proclaims the truth (17:17). What Jesus *is*, he *does*.[25] The Synoptic Gospels, in particular, record Jesus sending the apostles into mission to teach and proclaim and to heal and cast out demons.[26] As we have seen, the primary responsibility of discipleship, according to the Gospel of Mark, is "to be with Jesus," but the secondary responsibility is to proclaim the gospel by verbal witness (Mark 3:14). The central message of the apostles is that the kingdom of God has come. The first descriptor of the gathered Christian community in Jerusalem is its "attending to the teaching of the apostles" (Acts 2:42). Teaching ranks at or near the top of summaries of ministry responsibilities in the early church.[27] Especially in the Pastoral Epistles, "sound teaching" is to be a hallmark of the church's witness.[28] In Romans 10, Paul rehearses the incarnation as a history of the "the word [Gk. *rhēma*] of faith that we proclaim" (10:8), for "faith comes from hearing, and hearing through the word of Christ" (10:17).

The association of apostleship with verbal transmission of the faith continued in the early church, and teachers and prophets emulated this verbal transmission. Unlike the offices of bishop, elder, and deacon, which were designated for and valid only within specific contexts, apostolic proclamation was *katholikos*, valid for the whole church. Adolf Harnack rightly identifies "those who spoke the word of God" (quoting Did. 4.1) as "catholic teachers (διδάσκαλοι καθολικοί [*didaskaloi katholikoi*])."[29] After the First Revolt, the Epistle of Barnabas defines apostleship as a teaching office: "[Jesus Christ]

23. On the importance of such teachers and teaching in early Christianity, see Harnack, *Mission and Expansion*, 333–46.

24. Did. 4.1.

25. On Jesus as the Word of God, see Cullmann, *Christology*, 247–69.

26. See Matt. 9:35–10:11; Mark 6:6–13; Luke 9:1–6; 10:1–12.

27. See Acts 13:1; 1 Cor. 12:28; 1 Tim. 2:7; 2 Tim. 1:11; Titus 2:7.

28. See 1 Tim. 1:10; 6:3; 2 Tim. 1:13; 4:3; Titus 1:9, 13; 2:1–2.

29. Harnack, *Mission and Expansion*, 343. On the "catholicity" of the teachers, see Heb. 13:7, 17, 24; 1 Clem. 1.3; 21.6; Did. 4.1; 11.3–5; 13; 15.1–2.

chose his own apostles who were destined to proclaim his gospel."[30] In the second century, the author of the Epistle to Diognetus repeats the same: "Since I became a disciple of apostles, I am becoming a teacher of the gentiles. To those who are becoming disciples of the truth, I seek to be a worthy servant of the teachings that have been handed down."[31] The teachers and prophets who succeeded the apostles in the early church understood themselves "to speak and act by divine commission and with divine authority."[32] Eusebius similarly understood the apostles, and the teachers and prophets who were their heirs: "The church remained a pure and uncorrupted virgin," he writes, because it preserved and disseminated the "uncorrupted" preaching and teaching of the Savior and protected its teaching and doctrines from falsehoods.[33]

Administrative Offices in the Church

Apostles, teachers, and prophets were received as witnesses appointed by divine decree. No apparent qualifications accounted for the call of the Twelve by Jesus. And although subsequent teachers certainly would have been approved according to faithfulness "to the faith once delivered to the saints" (Jude 3), the source of their call was neither human nor quantifiable. The casting of lots to replace Judas after he forfeited his apostolic office—the only instance in the New Testament of such a method of selection—seems to have been an attempt on the part of the apostles to eliminate the human element and, as in the calls of all the original apostles, allow divine charism to prevail.[34] As the churches grew in numbers and expanded across distances, however, more practical and transferrable means of succession were required. The earliest Jesus followers were Jewish Christians, and they followed the precedent of their Israelite forebears in the selection of officials. "Judges and official administrators will be given to you in all your towns that the LORD your God gives to your tribes, and they shall judge the people with righteous judgment" (Deut. 16:18). But the earliest Jesus followers lived in the Roman world as well, and Roman law and administration also influenced their organizational protocol. The church offices that emerged—bishop, elder, and deacon—were perhaps more reflective of Judaism than of Rome, but they were not exact

30. Barn. 5.9.

31. Diogn. 11.1.

32. Wolfgang A. Bienert, "The Picture of the Apostle in Early Christian Tradition," *NTApoc* 2:9.

33. *Hist. eccl.* 3.32.7–8 (LCL).

34. On casting lots in the history of Israel, including in the selection of Israel's first king (1 Sam. 10:20–21), see F. D. Gealy, "Lots," *IDB* 3:163–64.

replicas of previously existing offices in either. The early church adapted the organizational models it was familiar with according to the values and needs of its corporate life.

Elders

The office of elder (Gk. *presbyteros*) is one of the influential offices omitted from the chain of succession in 1 Clement 42–43 that we noted above. The council of elders, or "presbyters," seems to have been the first administrative body in the early church. The book of Acts identifies the first officers of the church in Jerusalem, to whom Paul and Barnabas delivered the famine collection during the reign of the emperor Claudius, as elders (Acts 11:30). Josephus reports a famine that "seized" (Gk. *katalambanein*) Palestine during the reign of Claudius, between the years 44 and 48.[35] The office of elder existed in the church of Jerusalem at that time, and possibly earlier. The office of presbyter was not new to early Christians, of course, for the members of the Sanhedrin—which consisted of scribes, Pharisees, and Sadducees—were called presbyters, and the combined body of the Sanhedrin was known as the *presbyterion* (Council of Elders).[36] Acts 11:30 suggests that Jewish Christians in Jerusalem formed a ruling body for their congregation(s) that was comparable to the Sanhedrin. The description of twenty-four elders surrounding the throne of God in Revelation 4 bears some resemblance to a celestial Sanhedrin. Paul and Barnabas, likewise, established elders in the churches they founded in the first mission journey (Acts 14:23). By the time of the Council of Jerusalem, in the late 40s, elders appear as the default leaders in the church.[37] There are no references at this time to bishops (Gk. *episkopoi*). Around the year 50, in other words, the authority of the apostles appears to have been augmented by the administrative services of councils of elders in local churches.

Bishops and Deacons

The council of elders appears to have been the college or collective from which individual members were chosen to superintend particular responsibilities in the church. Elders who proclaimed the kerygma "in word and

---

35. *Ant.* 3.320–22.

36. The New Testament normally refers to the ruling body of Jewish elders as the *synedrion* (Sanhedrin, 22 times), but occasionally as the *presbyterion* (Council of Elders, Luke 22:66; Acts 22:5) and the *gerousia* (Council of Elders, Acts 5:21). These names refer to the same institution that functioned as the judicial (including supreme court), administrative, and governmental council of seventy-one elders in Jerusalem. See Schürer, *History of the Jewish People*, 2:206–8.

37. In the account of the Council of Jerusalem, elders are always mentioned in conjunction with apostles (Acts 15:2, 4, 6, 22, 23; 16:4).

teaching" were worthy of "double honor" (1 Tim. 5:17). Deacons, which we will discuss below, were almost certainly chosen from the elder council, as were overseers or custodians of given congregations—*episkopoi*, in Greek; that is, "bishops." Paul instructs Titus to establish boards of elders in cities where there are believers and to choose bishops from among them (Titus 1:5). The Sanhedrin once again appears to have been a prototype, for the relationship between the bishop and the presbytery was comparable to the relationship between the high priest and the Sanhedrin. Both bishops and high priests were *primus inter pares* (first among equals) in relation to their ruling bodies.[38] In speaking of a church council, Ignatius even uses the same word for "council" that was used of the Jewish high council, calling it "the *synedrion* [Sanhedrin/council] of the bishop."[39] Thus a given member of the council of elders could be both an elder and the bishop, or an elder and a teacher, or an elder and a deacon. This may account for certain confusions of nomenclature in the New Testament regarding offices. For example, Philip is called a deacon in Acts 6:5, but in Acts 21:8, the same Philip (presumably) is called an evangelist.[40] First Peter assigns to bishop (2:25) and elder (5:1–5) the exact same function: to "shepherd the flock of God."

When the apostolic office wanned at the end of the first century, the boundaries between the emerging offices seem to have been somewhat fluid—though the council of elders was the preeminent office of authority. On the one hand, the council of elders perpetuated the authority of the apostles, and thus deserved equal honor and authority. Ignatius saw the office of the apostles

---

38. On the close association of the high priest and the elders of the Sanhedrin, see John 11:49 and especially Acts 23:1–5, where Paul mistakes the high priest for an ordinary elder. In *Church in the Roman Empire*, Ramsay correctly identifies the early Christian bishop as an individual presbyter with executive duties: "The word *episkopos* means overseer. Originally, when the deliberative council of elders resolved to perform some action, they would naturally direct one of their number to superintend it. This presbyter was an *episkopos* for the occasion. Any presbyter might be also an *episkopos*, and the terms were therefore applied to the same persons, and yet conveyed essentially different meanings. . . . Any presbyter might become an *episkopos* for an occasion, yet the latter term conveyed an idea of singleness and of executive authority which was wanting to the former" (367). Further, the bishop "was only a presbyter on whom certain duties had been imposed. . . . The *episkopos* was very far removed from the monarchical bishop of AD 170, and we find not a trace to suggest that he exercised any authority *ex officio* within the community" (368–69). Stewart, *Original Bishops*, 48, has proposed that the council of elders was a collective of bishops: "The relationship between the words *presbyteros* and *episkopos* is readily explained by taking *presbyteros* as a collective term for individual *episkopoi* gathered together." I am aware of no text from our era that employs *presbyteros* and *episkopoi* in the way Stewart proposes.

39. Ign. *Phld.* 8.

40. The Philip(s) of Acts 6:5 and 21:8 was (were) probably not Philip the apostle (Acts 1:13), however, for none of the Twelve appears to have been a Hellenistic Jew. On the question of Philip's identity, see Hengel, *Saint Peter*, 116–20.

fulfilled in the "presbyters of the church."[41] On the other hand, the authority of the council of elders was personified in the bishop, whose status now surpassed that of an ordinary elder.[42] In one of Ignatius's many literary gems, he reminds the church in Ephesus, "It is thus fitting for you to run in harmony with the mind of the bishop, as you are doing. For your council of elders, which is worthy of its name and worthy of God, is attuned to the bishop as strings to a lyre."[43]

The relationship between deacons and the council of elders in first-century churches is not as clear as that between the bishop and the council of elders. The relationship seems to be similar, however. The earliest mention of "bishops and deacons" is in Philippians 1:1, written in the early 50s. The discussion of the qualifications for bishops and deacons in 1 Timothy 3 suggests the roughly equivalent status of the two offices in the early church. The Didache, likewise, mentions bishops and deacons together, prescribing the same qualifications— "humble and not greedy and true and approved"—for both offices, since both bishops and deacons "carry forth the ministry of the prophets and teachers."[44] Ignatius regularly mentions bishops and deacons in tandem as well.[45]

Eating meals together was a hallmark of early Christianity, and the first deacons may have served food in such contexts (Acts 6). The duties of deacons very likely included "a strong economic element."[46] An important insight into the role and function of deacons is gained from looking at the history of the word "deacon," *diakonos*—which, until the New Testament, was not used in biblical and religious contexts. Jesus was the first exemplar of a new connotation of the term, and his posture as "deacon" created a new vocabulary for the church: "Who is greater, the one who reclines or the *one who serves*? Is it not the one who reclines? But I am in your midst as *one who serves* [Gk. *ho diakonōn*]" (Luke 22:27). The Greek word behind both uses of "serve" is *diakoneō*, from which "deacon" is derived. At the eucharistic table, Jesus consecrated bread and wine as his body and blood given for the salvation of the world. "That God divulges himself as God precisely in lowliness," concludes Eduard Schweizer, "means that his community must differentiate itself from the world by its willingness to take on lowliness."[47]

41. Ign. *Phld.* 5.1; Ign. *Trall.* 2.2; Ign. *Smyrn.* 8.1.

42. Ign. *Eph.* 2.2; 20.2; Ign. *Magn.* 2; Ign. *Trall.* 7.2.

43. Ign. *Eph.* 4.1.

44. Did. 15.1.

45. Ign. *Magn.* 13.1; Ign. *Trall.* 7.2; Ign. *Phld.* 4; 7.1; Ign. *Smyrn.* 12:2.

46. See the discussion of deacons in Stewart, *Original Bishops*, 113–19. The quotation is from p. 119.

47. On the secular associations of *diakonia* prior to Christianity, see Schweizer, *Gemeinde und Gemeindeordnung*, 154–64. The quotation is from p. 161 (my trans.).

To summarize the above, let us compare the offices of elder, deacon, and bishop with the offices of apostle, teacher, and prophet—as these offices appear to have functioned in the time between Jesus and Ignatius. Unlike the latter three offices, whose qualifications are listed nowhere in the New Testament or the Apostolic Fathers, qualifications for elders,[48] deacons,[49] and bishops[50] are manifold. This clarifies several things regarding the relationship of elders, deacons, and bishops to teaching offices in the early church. Unlike teachers, preachers, and prophets—whose calls were attributed to divine charism rather than to human appointment, and whose jurisdiction was "catholic" rather

48. Elders were chosen according to each church (Acts 14:23) or each city (Titus 1:5). According to Titus 1:5–6, an elder should be blameless, without a reputation of being undisciplined and debauched, married to one wife, and have faithful children. Polycarp's qualifications for the office of elder are more expansive: mercifulness; turning back the wayward; visiting the sick; not neglecting widows, orphans, or the poor; seeking what is honorable in God's eyes; avoiding anger, partiality, and unjust judgment; not being greedy; being slow to believe things spoken against others; and not being harsh in judgment—for all are sinners, and thus all are debtors (Pol. *Phil.* 6.1).

49. In 1 Tim. 3:8–13, qualifications for the office of deacon include seriousness, not being double-tongued, not indulging in wine, not being greedy for monetary gain, blamelessness, and adhering to the faith with a clear conscience. According to Polycarp, deacons should be blameless; servants of God rather than people; free from slander, insincerity, greed and love of money; self-controlled in all things; compassionate; diligent; walking according to the truth of the Lord; and servants of all (Pol. *Phil.* 5.1–2).

With regard to women deacons, the feminine form *diakonissa* emerges no earlier than the third century (see *PGL* 352). The masculine form *diakonos*, however, was used to refer to women who performed diaconal functions (e.g., Phoebe, in Rom. 16:1, is called a "*diakonos* of the church"). Evidence of women in official leadership capacities diminishes after the first Christian generation, however. See Stewart, *Original Bishops*, 290–91: "Beyond the first Christian generation, there is little evidence of women exercising leadership within Christian circles, except possibly in those settings in which the domestic basis of the church was still prominent, and in which there were single households." For an overall discussion of women in the life of the New Testament church, see ch. 8, pp. 142–44.

50. Qualifications for bishops are noted more frequently and fully. First Timothy 3:1–7 declares the office of bishop a "good work." It says that bishops are to be irreproachable, husbands of one wife, sober (with regard to alcohol), prudent, honorable, hospitable, learned, not bullies, gentle, peaceable, not lovers of money or dishonest gain, honorable heads of their households with obedient children, not inexperienced, and well regarded by people *outside* the church. The list of qualifications in Titus is shorter, but it adds that bishops should not be arrogant or inclined to anger (1:5–7). The New Testament sums up the role of bishops as being "stewards of God" (Titus 1:7) and "shepherds of the flock of God" (Acts 20:28; 1 Pet. 2:25). Bishops, according to Did. 15.1, should be humble, lacking avarice, and true and approved. According to Herm. Sim. 9.27.1–2, they should be hospitable, ready to receive servants of God gladly, protectors of widows and the poor, and promoters of holy conversation.

According to Breytenbach and Zimmermann, *Early Christianity in Lycaonia and Adjacent Areas*, in Galatia "the office of bishop in cities was given to well-educated men who influenced the administrative and theological development of the church" (596); presbyters were of respectable social standing as well (628); and deacons were present in both cities and villages, although "inscriptions reveal little about the office itself" (647). All three positions appear to have been raised up and approved by local communities (677).

than local—elders, deacons, and bishops needed to give evidence of suitability before being appointed to positions of authority in the church. The prerequisites are character traits rather than skill sets. Rather than enumerating specific responsibilities, the lists catalog ethical qualities and traits of character and disposition that equip persons for responsibilities in the various offices. The lists tell us *who* officers must be more than *what* they must do.[51]

Absent in *all* the lists of qualifications pertaining to elders, deacons, and bishops are characteristics pertaining to the offices of teaching, preaching, or prophecy. Paul, for instance, describes himself several times as a proclaimer (Gk. *kēryx*) of the gospel proclamation (i.e., the kerygma).[52] But being a *kēryx* appears on none of the lists of qualifications for being an elder, deacon, or bishop. In other words, the offices of elder, deacon, and bishop are distinctly different from those of teacher, preacher, and prophet. The former were defined primarily by administration and pastoral care, whereas the latter were defined primarily by preaching, evangelism, and mission. These two sets of offices were not redundant, nor were they in competition, nor did one set replace the other. They were complementary. The responsibility of apostles and teachers was not to look after a single church—nor even a particular series of churches (as it was for a bishop)—but rather, as the Shepherd of Hermas maintains, "to preach to the whole world, reverently and purely teaching the word of the Lord."[53] Warnings against false teachers and teachings appear repeatedly in the New Testament Epistles and the Apostolic Fathers, calling for sound and true proclamation to "contend for the faith once delivered to the saints" (Jude 3). By contrast, similar warnings with respect to false bishops, elders, and deacons are rare. These ruling offices were important, of course, but the Didache insightfully refers to them as "liturgists" of the ministry of the prophets and teachers,[54] whose kerygmatic proclamation makes known the saving mysteries of the faith.[55] The chief purpose of both the sacramental celebrations of the church and its ruling offices was and is to order and preserve the Christian community for the proper hearing and reception of the kerygma.

Monarchical Episcopate

By the time of Ignatius and Polycarp, at the turn of the second century, the authority of bishops surpassed that of deacons and extended beyond individual

---

51. In Herm. Sim. 9.27.2–3, by contrast, we see *duties*. A bishop "shelters those in need and the widows by their unceasing ministry."
52. 1 Cor. 1:17–21; 1 Tim. 2:7; 2 Tim. 1:11; 4:17; Titus 1:3.
53. Herm. Sim. 9.24.1; similarly, Herm. Sim. 9.15.4.
54. Did. 15.1.
55. See Rom. 3:21–28; 14:8–9; 1 Cor. 15; 2 Cor. 5; Gal. 2:20; Phil. 3:9–11.

churches to include clusters of churches. Monarchical episcopacy, or "monepis-copacy," refers to extending the authority of a bishop from one congregation to several congregations. The first two bishops known to have extended episcopal authority beyond their home churches were Ignatius and Polycarp.[56] In most cases, episcopal authority was amplified—and its amplification welcomed—as a means of defending the faith and the church from erroneous teachings and teachers.[57] The expanded episcopal profile is evident in Ignatius, who admonishes the church in Smyrna: "Flee from divisions as the beginning of evils. You must all follow the bishop as Jesus Christ followed the Father, and follow the council of elders as you would follow the apostles; respect also the deacons as God's commandment."[58] Note the alteration of the chain of authority here, which first extended from the Father to Jesus Christ, from Jesus Christ to the apostles, from the apostles to elders, and then from elders to bishops and deacons. With Ignatius, the offices of bishop and apostle are transposed, with the bishop becoming the direct heir of the Father and of Jesus Christ, and apostles becoming correlative with the council of elders. The bishop has risen in the chain of authority, no longer subordinate to the apostles but only to Jesus Christ himself.[59] Ignatius introduces an elevated concept of episcopal office.[60]

For Ignatius, bishops have assumed the role formerly filled by apostles.[61] Ignatius's new chain of succession required congregations to regard the bishop as they regarded the Lord,[62] for "the bishop is seated in the place

56. By the middle of the second century, monarchical episcopates are documented in Corinth, Athens, and Crete, and probably proconsular Asia. See Eusebius, *Hist. eccl.* 4.23; Lightfoot, *Philippians*, 214–17; Duchesne, *Early History*, 67. Stewart, *Original Bishops*, 290–95, denies that Ignatius practiced monarchical episcopacy by making the intriguing suggestion that Ignatius was imitating Paul's journey to Rome, and therefore extending the influence of the gospel—not the authority of the bishop—to churches en route.

57. Episcopal authority would rise to new levels of importance in the second century as a means of resisting the various strains of Gnosticism that were promoted by leaders of notoriety.

58. Ign. *Smyrn.* 8.1. The same lines of succession are repeated in Ign. *Trall.* 3.1 and Ign. *Magn.* 6.1.

59. Ign. *Trall.* 2.2; 7.1; 12.2; Ign. *Magn.* 6.1. This point is noted by Holmes, *Apostolic Fathers*, 168. On the other hand, Herm. Vis. 3.5.1 regards bishops, teachers, and deacons as subsidiaries of the apostles.

60. According to Koch, "The epistles of Ignatius reveal a theologian with a high concept of office who stands firmly in church tradition (any deviation in Christology—especially that related to the incarnation—is sharply opposed), whose diction is highly rhetorical and effectively metaphorical" (*Geschichte des Urchristentums*, 440, my trans.). Koch sees Ignatius's "high concept of office" as congruent with his understanding of and participation in church tradition.

61. Igna. *Trall.* 7.2; Ign. *Pol.* 6.1.

62. Ign. *Eph.* 6.1, "It is obvious, therefore, that we should regard the bishop as we regard the Lord himself." Stated otherwise, and more forcefully, "It is good to acknowledge God and the bishop. The one who honors the bishop has been honored by God; the one does something secretly without the bishop's knowledge serves the devil" (Ign. *Smyrn.* 9.1).

of God."[63] Consequently, to be subject to the bishop was to be subject to Jesus Christ.[64] Ignatius refers to the bishop as the Christian congregation in one person;[65] similarly, communion with a bishop is communion with his congregation.[66] Ignatius illustrates this point in his letter to Polycarp: in the middle of the letter, which ostensibly is a private letter to Polycarp, he addresses the congregation as a whole.[67] The bishop, obviously, was ordained not for his own vanity but to serve the entire congregation with "godly graciousness."[68] Ignatius's alteration of the hierarchy of authority, and particularly his emphasis on the bishop, marked a watershed in Christian ecclesiology. The preaching and mission emphasis of the apostles, teachers, and preachers had been superseded by the office of bishop as the guarantor of the *unity* of the church.[69] Ignatius's emphasis on unity again points to the role of the bishop in opposing division and heresy.[70] Later, in the apologists, and particularly in Irenaeus, the obligation of the bishop shifts from preserving the unity of the church to preserving the purity of the gospel and its faithful transmission.[71]

Finally, with regard to monarchical episcopacy, let us consider what would become the doctrine of the supremacy of the bishop of Rome (i.e., papal supremacy). Two texts in the Apostolic Fathers must be discounted that are sometimes cited as evidence for this doctrine.[72] Ignatius, as we have seen, famously elevates episcopal authority, but he does not assert the primacy of the Roman bishop, not

63. Ign. *Magn.* 6.1; similarly, Ign. *Trall.* 3.1.
64. Ign. *Trall.* 2.1; Ign. *Magn.* 13.2.
65. Ign. *Eph.* 1.3; Ign. *Trall.* 1.1.
66. Ign. *Eph.* 5.
67. A point noted by Ramsay, *Church in the Roman Empire*, 369.
68. Ign. *Phld.* 1.1–2.
69. Ign. *Eph.* 2–5, 20; Ign. *Magn.* 6, 13; Ign. *Trall.* 7; Ign. *Smyrn.* 8–9; and throughout Ign. *Phld.*
70. Moffett describes the role of eastern bishops as being more complementary: "The earliest Syrian histories of the church and the martyrologies reconstruct a succession of bishops from Addai to the time of Bardaisan and beyond, bishops who promoted missionary outreach, organized the true church, and protected the faith against heretics." *Christianity in Asia*, 1:59.
71. See Lightfoot, *Apostolic Fathers*, 1:396; Ramsay, *Church in the Roman Empire*, 370.
72. The first reads as follows: "It is disgraceful, dear friends, yes, utterly disgraceful and unworthy of your conduct in Christ, that it should be reported that the well-established and ancient church of the Corinthians, because of one or two persons, is rebelling against its presbyters. And this report has reached not only us but also those who differ from us, with the result that you heap blasphemies upon the name of the Lord because of your stupidity, and create danger for yourselves as well" (1 Clem. 47.6–7, Holmes trans.). The claim that Clement in Rome chastises the Corinthians on the basis of the preeminent status of the Roman church is neither asserted nor assumed in this text. The second text is the salutation of Ignatius's letter *To the Romans*, addressed to the church "which also presides in the place of the district of the Romans." This text speaks not to the status of the bishop but to the status of the church with respect to the city in which it resides. Ignatius affirms the church's authority in "the district of the Romans," not its authority as *ekklēsia katholikē* (see the note in Holmes, *Apostolic Fathers*, 225).

even when he writes to the church in Rome. Indeed, his letter to Rome addresses the community rather than its bishop and is on the subject of martyrdom rather than episcopacy. In the latter half of the second century, Irenaeus first asserts "the preeminent authority" of the Roman church on the basis of the martyrdoms of the apostles Peter and Paul in Rome.[73] Peter was remembered, accordingly, as the "rock" on which Christ promised to build his church (Matt. 16:18). This is the sole first-century text that might be used to justify the preeminence of the Roman bishopric, which Roman Catholicism regards as the successor to Peter's apostleship. However, I find no reference to Matthew 16:18 in the first two centuries of the Christian era used to justify the preeminence of the Roman bishop.[74] The Roman bishop rose to supremacy in the Western (Latin speaking) church, to be sure, but the supremacy was acknowledged later than the time period of our study and on grounds other than precedents or decrees originating from our time period. Developments within the Roman Empire itself provided the primary precedents for papal supremacy, for if the Roman emperor was *Pontifex Maximus* over the empire, the Roman bishop might be *Pontifex Maximus* over the church. When Constantine moved the capital of the empire from Rome to Constantinople in the fourth century, and, above all, when the Roman Empire collapsed in the fifth century, the mantle of the Roman emperors fell on the shoulders of the Roman bishops. Rome's preeminence was further fortified by its advocacy of positions in the first four ecumenical councils that emerged as "orthodox."[75] The primacy of the Roman episcopacy evolved over many centuries, although it was never accepted by Eastern (Orthodox) churches, and in the sixteenth century it was repudiated by Protestant churches. Papal infallibility was first officially promulgated at the First Vatican Council (1870), but it was moderated considerably by the Second Vatican Council (1963), which declared the "collegiality" of bishops and the pope in church government.[76]

Ordination

Let us conclude our inquiry into early church offices by considering the concept of ordination. We have seen that Jesus followed no precedent in including the

73. Irenaeus, *Haer.* 3.3.2. The Latin text of this passage is so corrupt that its translators include this disclaimer: "We are far from certain that [our] rendering is correct" (*ANF* 1:415).
74. There is no reference to Matt. 16:18 in the Apostolic Fathers, Justin Martyr, Irenaeus, Tatian, Clement of Alexandria, Theophilus, or Athenagoras. The first uses of the verse to justify the supremacy of the church of Rome and its bishop appear to be those of Tertullian (*Pud.* 21; *ANF* 4:99) and Hippolytus (*Holy Theoph.* 9; *ANF* 5:237), both dating no earlier than 200.
75. Nicaea, 325; Constantinople, 381; Ephesus, 431; Chalcedon, 451.
76. On Roman primacy, see Kidd, *Roman Primacy*; Lightfoot, *Apostolic Fathers*, 1:201–345; Pelikan, *Melody of Theology*, 209–12.

Twelve in his fellowship. No leader in Israel or Judaism gathered twelve assistants to accompany and succeed him as did Jesus. The Twelve followed and served Jesus on the sole basis of his personal authority. We have also seen that the early church discontinued Jesus's charismatic means of choosing leaders, except in the replacement of Judas by Matthias. Since Jesus established no protocols for the succession of offices, the early church innovated in its institutional formation on the basis of Jewish and Greco-Roman models. In the Roman Empire, magistrates and priests were installed in public office by a show of hands (Gk. *cheirotoneō*), or by casting lots, or by some combination of both. The Essene community at Qumran chose officials through "the voice of the many."[77] In the Old Testament, religious authority was conveyed via prophecy in some instances, but more frequently by human agency, such as pouring olive oil on the head of a priest (Lev. 21:10) or king (1 Sam. 10:1). Laying on of hands was another means of formal investiture, originally laid on the head of a sacrificial animal (Lev. 3:2) so that its death would vicariously benefit its patrons.[78] The practice of laying on hands was expanded as a means of consecrating Levites (Num. 8:5–13) and appointing successors, the most famous of whom was Joshua as successor to Moses.[79] This last practice influenced early Christian ordination.[80]

In the Old Testament, the hand often symbolizes God's presence and power, and it occasionally symbolizes the same in the New Testament.[81] The New Testament preserves scores of instances of laying on hands for the purposes of healing, performing miracles, blessing persons, bestowing God's Spirit, and restoring sinners. The early church expanded the practice of laying on hands as a formal means of installing officers in the church. The Greek word that signified election by vote of hands in the Greco-Roman world (*cheirotoneō*) appears twice in the New Testament with reference to ordination of church officers.[82] The premier instance in the New Testament of ordination by laying on hands occurs in Acts 6:1–7, where the office of deacons is established in Jerusalem.

Prayer, fasting, and laying on hands by the church in Antioch also commission Paul and Barnabas for the first mission journey (Acts 13:1–3). Paul and Barnabas, in turn, ordain elders in the same manner in churches that they found in the first mission (Acts 14:23). These early instances of laying hands on believers set them apart for specific services; the emphasis falls primarily

77. CD 10.4–6; 1QSa 1.13–17.
78. In addition to animal sacrifices (*m*. Men. 9:7–8; *m*. Kelim 1:8), the Mishnah prescribes laying hands on peace (*m*. Betzah 2:4; *m*. Hag. 2:2) and freewill (*m*. Tem. 3:4) offerings.
79. Num. 27:22–23; Deut. 34:8.
80. Regarding laying on of hands in the Old Testament, see Everett Ferguson, "Ordain, Ordination," *ABD* 5:37–40.
81. Luke 1:66; Acts 11:21.
82. Acts 14:23; 2 Cor. 8:19.

on the service or task to be performed rather than on the office itself. The greatest concentration of laying on hands for the purpose of ordination occurs in the Pastoral Letters, where the practice becomes a rite of the church for perpetuating its ministry. The apostle Paul acknowledges Timothy's gift of ministry (Gk. *charisma*), which Timothy received through prophecy and laying on of hands by the *presbyterion*, the council of elders (1 Tim. 4:14). Here for the first time in the New Testament, the council of elders assumes the role formerly performed by the apostles. Paul subsequently exhorts Timothy to "rekindle" the gift of ministry ratified by laying on hands (2 Tim. 1:6). The description of Timothy's ministry as *charisma* begins to shift the emphasis from the task or service to the office itself. *Charisma* also acknowledges the role of the Holy Spirit in the election and execution of the office. What is "handed on," however, is not an office but a ministry for which the office exists, a ministry whose supreme purpose is the faithful transmission of the gospel.[83]

We have seen that, apart from the twelve apostles, the offices of the church were not established by Christ but *emerged* to serve the practical needs of the church and its mission. In the first century, such offices were secondary to the charismatic offices of the Twelve, apostles, teachers, and prophets. Even in the second century, considerable fluidity persisted among bishops, elders, and deacons, although the authority and distinction of bishops steadily increased over that of the other two. The first description of a formal ordination ceremony comes from the hand of Hippolytus of Rome (the last Western church father to write in Greek) in the early third century. According to Hippolytus, bishops were chosen by their respective congregations, and they, assisted by presbyters, ordained members to ministries in the church by laying on hands (Gk. *cheirotonia*). An ordinand to a bishopric would celebrate the Eucharist immediately after his ordination. The essential elements in Hippolytus's account—formal appointment to church office; ordination by imposition of hands; and power of ordination residing in the bishop, apart from which ordination was rendered invalid—reappear in references to ordination ceremonies from the third century onward.[84]

---

83. See Schweizer, *Gemeinde und Gemeindeordnung*, 192–200, who emphasizes that the purpose of ordination was to promote the *faith* rather than to establish official structures. Apostolic authority cannot be transmitted, according to Schweizer, because it was grounded in a personal relationship with Christ, and its authority depended on such a relationship. "Continuity in the community of Jesus is an essential concern. It depends, however, on the succession of the *faithful*, among whom the gospel message is transmitted from one generation to the next. One scarcely comes to faith without a living witness who communicates the gospel message through his or her word or existence. There is no guarantee of the veracity of the gospel proclamation other than the Holy Spirit continually throwing its witnesses back to the apostolic witness in the New Testament" (200, my trans.).

84. See "*cheirotoneō*," *PGL* 1522–23.

12

From Sabbath to Sunday

Sabbath in Ancient Israel

The consecration of a day as sacred is unique in the world's religions. Nearly all religions revere sacred places and sacred objects, but no religion prior to Judaism sacralized time. Jews set aside a day of the week—and its name "Sabbath" (meaning "rest") defines its purpose. Jews celebrate Sabbath from Friday sundown until Saturday sundown. Islam follows Judaism in reserving a special day for worship (Friday rather than Saturday), but Muslims do not cease from work on Friday. The commandment to observe Sabbath is a fundamental characteristic of Judaism, identifying and setting Jews apart from other peoples. Another name for Jews might well be "Sabbatarians."

The oldest reference to Sabbath in the Old Testament probably occurs in Exodus 16, where Moses explains to the people, "'This is what the Lord commanded: "Tomorrow is to be a day of Sabbath rest, a holy Sabbath to the Lord." . . . Six days you are to gather [manna], but on the seventh day, the Sabbath, . . . no one is to go out.' So the people rested on the seventh day" (Exod. 16:23–30 passim). The essential elements of Sabbath are already present here: the references to "Sabbath" (Hb. *shabbat*) and "Sabbath feast" (Hb. *shabbaton*), the "sixth day" as a day of preparation, and the "seventh" (Sabbath) as a day of rest and feasting in accordance with the Lord's commandments.[1] These elements are formally codified

1. On Sabbath in the Old Testament, see Gerhard F. Hasel, "Sabbath," *ABD* 5:849–56.

in the two versions of the fourth commandment in Exodus 20:8–11 and Deuteronomy 5:12–15.

> Remember the Sabbath day, to keep it holy. Six days you shall labor, and do all your work, but the seventh day is a Sabbath to the LORD your God. On it you shall not do any work, you, or your son, or your daughter, your male servant, or your female servant, or your livestock, or the sojourner who is within your gates. For in six days the LORD made heaven and earth, the sea, and all that is in them, and rested on the seventh day. Therefore the LORD blessed the Sabbath day and made it holy. (Exod. 20:8–11 ESV)

The fourth is the longest of the Ten Commandments, and it is the only "Word," as Jews refer to each commandment, instituted by God prior to its decree through Moses at Sinai (Exod. 20:11). According to Genesis 2:2–3, after finishing the work of creation, God "rested" (Hb. *shabbat*) on the seventh day, blessed it, and declared it holy.[2] The fourth commandment defines Sabbath as a day of blessing and rest from labor, not only for one's immediate family but also for hired and slave laborers. Livestock, too, are accorded rest: indeed, the ox, mule, and draft animals are named *before* the human "sojourner who is within your gates." Even the land is accorded a fallow rest every seventh year (Exod. 23:10–11). The divine blessing of Sabbath to *all creation* links the fourth commandment to the first creation narrative of Genesis: human beings are made in the image of God, *imago Dei* (Gen. 1:26); and the fourth commandment calls them to the imitation of God, *imitatio Dei*, by resting from labor on the seventh day.

So essential was Sabbath rest in Israel that certain violations of it were punishable by death.[3] The object of the fourth commandment was not to instill dread, however, but to ensure the blessing and delight of Sabbath. Isaiah teaches that Sabbath belongs to the Lord God as a sign of the Sinai covenant, and to hold fast to Sabbath is to hold fast to God's covenant in toto (56:4–6). Sabbath keepers—including eunuchs and foreigners—weekly enjoy liberation from mundane pursuits and receive divine blessings (Isa. 56:2–8). "If you call the Sabbath a delight, . . . then you will find your joy in the LORD" (Isa. 58:13–14 NIV).

Sabbath in Second Temple Judaism

Beginning in the sixth century BC and extending into the early centuries of the Christian era, a number of factors conspired to alter this largely positive

2. Although the reference to Sabbath in Gen. 2:2–4 occurs in the canon before the Exod. 16 reference, it was almost certainly written later than the Exodus text.
3. Exod. 35:2; Num. 15:32–36.

understanding of Sabbath. The first and most important was the destruction of Jerusalem in 586 BC by Nebuchadnezzar, followed by fifty years of Babylonian captivity. Persia's defeat of the Babylonians in 539 allowed Jewish exiles to return to Jerusalem. An initial wave returned with Zerubbabel in 536, followed by a greater wave with Ezra seventy-five years later, in 458, and a third remnant with Nehemiah in 438. The returnees faced a daunting task. Reconstituting the old Israel was no longer possible, for the nucleus of Israelite life—the Jerusalem temple—had been destroyed and its priesthood eliminated. The Israelite monarchy had been terminated by the Babylonians, and *eretz Israel* (the land that had defined Israel since Abraham) was now Persian real estate. In a certain sense, the returning exiles were no longer even "Israelites," for the constitutive elements of Israel—temple, priesthood, king, nation, and land—were gone. The returnees were simply Jewish exiles whose existence was determined by a book, Torah, and a class of its interpreters, scribes. The exposition of Torah by scribes in weekly gatherings formed the basis of a third characteristic of postexilic Judaism: synagogues. Torah, scribes, and synagogues became the foundation on which the exiles erected a new religious synthesis in Israel.

Jesus's experience of Judaism four centuries later consisted primarily of these same elements—Torah, scribes, and synagogues. Postexilic Jews were largely agreed that assimilation with the surrounding nations had led to Israel's destruction and exile under Nebuchadnezzar. They further agreed that their tenuous toehold in Jerusalem and the twenty or so square miles around it depended on not repeating the mistake of assimilation. *Separation* from foreign and pagan influences, especially from intermarriage with foreign wives, occupied the frontal lobe of their ethnic consciousness.[4] Nehemiah's rebuilding of Jerusalem's walls and bolting of its gates was both practical and symbolic: it protected Jerusalem from foreign intruders, and it cloistered postexilic Judaism from a pluralistic environment (Neh. 13:19).

The rebuilding of the temple in 515 BC (i.e., the second temple) and the reconstitution of the priesthood did not essentially alter the above synthesis, especially for most Jews outside Jerusalem, whose experience of Judaism continued to be defined by the triangle of Torah, scribes, and synagogues. This triangle was strong enough to prevent the Seleucid king Antiochus IV's attempt to annihilate Judaism in 167 BC and remake Jerusalem as a Greek city-state. Against all odds, the Maccabees prevailed over the Seleucid onslaught and ruled Palestine until its annexation as the easternmost frontier of the Roman Empire by Pompey in 63 BC. The Jewish experience of Jesus and his

4. Ezra 9:1–4; 10:9–11.

followers was, for the most part, determined by the contours of the triangle, and its elements (Torah, scribes, and synagogues) were the sole vestiges of Judaism to survive the catastrophic destruction of Jerusalem in AD 70. The rabbinic schools that established themselves in Sepphoris and Tiberias following the Götterdämmerung of the First Revolt elevated synagogues, scribes, and, above all, Torah as the global arbiters of Judaism, which resulted in Sabbath playing an even more elevated role in Jewish life.

Old Testament laws generally set forth principles or moral values. Principles must be interpreted, however, in order to prescribe specific behaviors. The Mosaic law is a compendium not of moral ideals but of practical and achievable behaviors. It fell to the rabbinic scholars in Galilee to determine in all conceivable circumstances which behaviors accorded with a given principle. The result of this enormous project was the compilation of the Mishnah (Hb. for "repetition [of the law]"), published around AD 200 at the rabbinic schools in Galilee under the direction of Rabbi Judah the Prince.

The Mishnah consists of sixty-three chapters or "tractates," of which "Shabbat" is one of the longest and most detailed. The foundational principle of Shabbat is that Jews should forgo all unnecessary work on the Sabbath. But what constitutes "unnecessary work"? "Unnecessary" generally includes anything that is not an emergency or needed to preserve life. All foreseeable needs and labors—such as cooking, errands, handwork, going and coming, fetching and gathering—should be anticipated and prepared for in advance. Anything undone should remain so until after sundown on the Sabbath— unless, again, it is necessary to save or preserve a life. The Mishnah stipulates thirty-nine broad categories of Sabbath prohibitions. Some are obvious, such as sowing, plowing, sheering sheep, and weaving; others are less so, such as tying and untying knots, writing two letters, sewing two stiches, or lighting a fire.[5] Two thousand paces is the limit for Sabbath travel; a step farther is a journey.[6] Tasks that cannot be finished before Sabbath should not be begun; if unfinished, they must be suspended until the Sabbath is over. One should not go to a barber on Friday afternoon lest the haircut extend to the commencement of Sabbath at sundown.[7] One should not look in a mirror on Sabbath lest one be tempted to comb one's hair. A scribe should not pick up a pen on the Sabbath lest he add a jot or tittle to a text. A seamstress should not pick up a needle on Sabbath lest she sew on a button.[8]

5. *m*. Shabb. 7:2.
6. *m*. Eruv. 4:5.
7. *m*. Shabb. 1:2.
8. *m*. Shabb. 1:3.

Permissible tasks are those that cannot be suspended without causing suffering. Cows can be milked on the Sabbath, and infants can be nursed. Permissible tasks also include preventing foreseeable dangers. An oil lamp can be covered with a dish if it might scorch a rafter and set a dwelling on fire; and animal droppings can be covered to protect a child from being fouled.[9] If a fire breaks out on the Sabbath, a Torah scroll can be rescued from its flames, along with enough food for three meals.[10] Forestalling a problem is also regarded permissible work. If a rafter in a house breaks, for instance, it can be supported so that the break does not become worse.[11] But remedying a problem is not permissible work. A broken rafter cannot be repaired, nor can a broken leg be set.[12] If a roof or wall falls on someone, the individual can be pulled from the debris and, if alive, ministered to; but if the person is dead, the corpse must be left unattended until sundown. Not even the eyes can be closed.[13]

An episode from the First Revolt illustrates how seriously Jews adhered to such regulations. In *Jewish War*, Josephus records a speech of Herod Agrippa II imploring the rebel factions holding Jerusalem not to plunge the nation into war with Rome.[14] When Pompey invaded Palestine a little more than a century before, Agrippa reminds the rebels, the Jewish defenders of Jerusalem had chosen not to fight on the Sabbath, which allowed Pompey to press the siege and defeat them.[15] The present outcome will be no different, argues Agrippa. If the rebels refuse to fight on the Sabbath, Vespasian will savage Jerusalem; but if they fight, they will violate the fourth commandment and alienate themselves from the only God who can save them.[16] From beginning to end, Agrippa upholds the inviolability of Sabbath—even when the nation's destiny is at stake.[17]

Jesus and the Sabbath

The ministry of Jesus fell within this era of stringent Torah interpretation. The Mishnah, from which most of the foregoing examples are culled, is an

9. *m.* Shabb. 16:7.
10. *m.* Shabb. 16:1–2.
11. *m.* Shabb. 23:5.
12. *m.* Shabb. 22:6
13. *m.* Shabb. 23:5.
14. *J.W.* 2.345–402.
15. *J.W.* 1.146; *Ant.* 14.64–65.
16. *J.W.* 2.390–94.
17. Women disciples of Jesus exhibited similar Sabbath reverence by refraining from anointing his body in the tomb until after Sabbath (Mark 16:1; Luke 23:56).

encyclopedia of rabbinic *prescriptions* based on Torah *principles*. The Mishnah was not codified until a century and a half after Jesus, so we cannot assume that its massive detail was fully developed or observed during his ministry. The process was well underway during Jesus's lifetime, however, for the subjects and methods of some of his controversies with religious leaders are mirrored in the Mishnah.

Jesus was an observant Jew. He quoted the Old Testament as an authority for faith and life (Luke 4:17–21). The hem of his robe bore rabbinic tassels (Mark 5:27). He assumed a prophetic role (Luke 4:24) and spoke of himself as the fulfillment of prophecy (Luke 4:21). He restricted his ministry almost entirely to Jewish Galilee and Jerusalem rather than expanding into surrounding gentile regions. The four Gospels record his attendance at the major Jewish festivals in Jerusalem—which required of him, as it did of all Jewish pilgrims in Galilee, a 180-mile trek by foot to Jerusalem and back. Above all, Jesus regularly attended synagogue on the Sabbath (Luke 4:16) and preached in synagogues throughout Judea (Luke 4:44). The synagogue was the nucleus of the Jewish community, and it was a regular venue for Jesus's teaching.[18] Jesus consciously identified with Judaism and affirmed its essential observances.

According to the Gospels, many categories eventually covered in the Mishnah—including circumcision, tithes, mixing of unlike substances, idolatry, and temple offerings—played either no role in rabbinic controversies with Jesus or no role greater than they usually played in disputes between rabbis. On some issues, however, including elements of "the tradition of the elders" (Mark 7:5), the differences between Jesus and the rabbis were sharper. Fasting and bills of divorce are examples of such issues, as are the multitude of issues associated with cleanness versus uncleanness and food laws.

With regard to Sabbath, however, the conflict between Jesus and the rabbis came to its sharpest and most unreconcilable point. His repeated challenges to rabbinic Sabbath rulings open a window of insight into his judgment of the rabbinic project as a whole. Jesus criticized rabbinic rulings for shifting attention away from God to a maze of meritorious behaviors. Rabbinic interpretation of the fourth commandment, in particular, resulted in substituting legality for morality—or, in Jesus's words, "forsaking God's commandment while holding fast to human traditions" (Mark 7:8). Jesus occasionally cites texts from the Old Testament in support of his judgments, but he never—in contrast to the rabbinic norm—cites a rabbinic authority. Rather, he challenges rabbinic rulings on the basis of the divine authority resident within himself: "I tell you, something greater than the temple is here" (Matt. 12:6).

18. Mark 1:21; 6:2; Luke 4:16; 6:6; 13:10; John 6:59.

He was accused by scribes and Pharisees of picking grain (harvesting) on the Sabbath, a forbidden work.[19] More typical, however, were Jesus's violations of Sabbath by healing. He healed a man with a withered hand,[20] a man with an unclean spirit,[21] a woman bent double (Luke 13:10–17), a lame man at the Pool of Bethzatha,[22] and a blind man at the Pool of Siloam (John 9:1–34). His healing of a man with edema *in a Pharisee's house on the Sabbath* (Luke 14:1–6) makes it indisputably clear that Jesus's Sabbath violations were intentional.[23] None of these healings was necessary to save or preserve life; all would have achieved the same effect, at least physically speaking, had they been postponed until Sabbath was over. Indeed, had Jesus done so, the rabbis would have praised him. As performed, however, they saw his healings as impermissible exceptions to Sabbath observances.[24]

Jesus, however, did not regard Sabbath healings as impermissible exceptions. On the contrary, he regarded them as wholly in character with the divine intent for the Sabbath. "Is it not necessary," Jesus asked a synagogue ruler, "for this daughter of Abraham, whom Satan has bound for eighteen years, to be liberated from her bondage on the day of the Sabbath?" (Luke 13:16). "Is it right to do good on the Sabbath, or evil?" he asks (Mark 3:4).[25] His further declaration that "the Sabbath was made for humanity, not humanity for the Sabbath" (Mark 2:27) recovers the original intent of Sabbath—to affirm human life. The Sabbath is an island in time for *re*-creation, to promote human wholeness and thriving. *Healing* was thus a consummate fulfillment of the Sabbath. Jesus needed no external authority to justify Sabbath healing. The authority to judge Sabbath rightly was resident within himself as the Son of Man, "the Lord even of the Sabbath" (Mark 2:28). This declaration is a clear window into Jesus's self-consciousness as God's Son, for in making it he assumes the place of God, who instituted the Sabbath. Jesus is the rightful interpreter of Sabbath because he is the Lord of Sabbath.

The Early Church

One can take something of a grand tour through the Old Testament, intertestamental period, and subsequent rabbinic tradition by traveling the Sabbath

19. Matt. 12:1–8; Mark 2:23–28; Luke 6:1–5.
20. Matt. 12:9–14; Mark 3:1–6; Luke 6:6–11.
21. Mark 1:21–28; Luke 4:31–37.
22. John 5:2–9; see also 7:23.
23. The account of Jesus's Sabbath infractions in Luke 6:1–11 are clearly provocative, and John 5:16 expressly attributes Jewish persecution of Jesus to his Sabbath healings.
24. On the gravity of Sabbath violations, see Eduard Lohse, "*sabbaton*," *TWNT* 7:5.
25. The reference to doing "good" on the Sabbath may recall the opening of Genesis, where seven repetitions of the goodness of God's creation (1:4, 10, 12, 18, 21, 25, 31) lead to God's rest on the seventh day (2:2–3).

thoroughfare. With Jesus, however, the thoroughfare narrows to a path; and it disappears entirely with his followers. A concordance makes the revolutionary change immediately apparent. There are fifty-five references to Sabbath in the four Gospels and another ten in the Acts of the Apostles—a total of sixty-five references in the first five books of the New Testament. In the remainder of the New Testament, there are only three references to Sabbath.[26] The evidence in Acts is particularly illustrative. In the early chapters, Jesus followers identify closely with the temple. And even midway through Acts, the Pauline mission continues to identify, at least initially, with the synagogue. Paul regularly attends Sabbath services in synagogues as the first point of gospel proclamation and Christian mission. He even observes circumcision when it is expedient to do so (Acts 16:3). James the brother of Jesus, in his final word at the Council of Jerusalem, seems to assume that Christians were present "in synagogues every Sabbath" (15:21). Sabbath witness continues in synagogues on the second mission of Paul (and Silas and Timothy), at Philippi (16:12–13), Thessalonica (17:1–2), and Corinth (18:1–4). Thus the description in Acts of the Pauline witness in diaspora synagogues roughly parallels the descriptions in the Gospels of Jesus's witness in Galilean synagogues.

Acts hints at an alternative worship experiment or perhaps even practice among Jesus followers, however. Near the end of the third mission, perhaps in the year 57, Luke records a rendezvous of Paul with seven fellow workers in Troas, not far from the ancient site of Troy on the west coast of Roman Asia (modern Turkey). Luke identifies the seven as Sopater from Berea, Aristarchus and Secundus from Thessalonica, Gaius and Timothy from Derbe, and Tychicus and Trophimus from the province of Asia (Acts 20:4–5). Paul likely knew these men from previous mission journeys, for they all came from places where he had evangelized. Six of the names are Greek; the seventh, Secundus, is Latin (Roman). Jews, of course, could bear Greek or Latin names. Aristarchus and Timothy appear to have been Jewish,[27] but the remainder were likely gentiles. Luke writes, "On the first day of the week the group came together [at Troas] to break bread" (Acts 20:7). In the New Testament, "the first day of the week" denotes Sunday, not Sabbath.[28] Breaking of bread is specifically Christian, suggesting an *agapē* feast, or even Eucharist. This understated account appears to describe the first-known Sunday worship in

---

26. 1 Cor. 16:2; Col. 2:16; Heb. 4:9.

27. For Aristarchus, see Col 4:10–11; for Timothy, Acts 16:1–3.

28. "The first day of the week" (Gk. *mia sabbatōn/sabbatou*) occurs eight times in the New Testament (Matt. 28:1; Mark 16:2, 9; Luke 24:1; John 20:1, 19; Acts 20:7; 1 Cor. 16:2). The first six refer explicitly to Jesus's resurrection on Sunday, and Sunday is also the intended sense of the last two.

the Christian tradition, in Troas in the late 50s, celebrated by Greek-gentile believers and Greek-Jewish believers.[29] They worship on Sunday. The worship is narrated in terms reminiscent of the Last Supper. Yet no element of the worship recalls the Sabbath. That Luke reports the event without any indication of its novelty may even indicate that it was not the first Sunday worship experience of Jesus followers.

The exact process by which the early church shifted from Saturday to Sunday worship is not preserved in the New Testament or in other early Christian sources. Only isolated steps in the process can be detected. To begin with, it is important to recall that the designation of a regular day of the week for worship, whether Sabbath or Sunday, was unique in the first century—when sacrifices, reverence, and prayers were accorded the Greco-Roman pantheon only occasionally. Tentative references to Sunday worship among Jesus followers may be discernible in the occasional use of "days" in the New Testament. "You observe days and months and seasons and years" (Gal. 4:10), writes Paul around the year 50. Later, in perhaps the year 57, he again writes, "Some consider one day more sacred than another; others consider every day alike. Everyone should be fully convinced in their own mind. Those who regard one day as special do so to the Lord" (Rom. 14:5–6). Then around the year 60, he explicitly admonishes, "Do not let anyone judge you by what you eat or drink, or with regard to a religious festival, a new moon celebration, or a Sabbath day. These things are a shadow of things to come, but the substance is of Christ" (Col. 2:16–17). This text speaks of Sabbath as a "shadow" of a substantial "body" (Gk. *sōma*)—as something with no independent significance apart from its relation to Christ. These sporadic references to "days" may allude to controversies among Jesus followers regarding the proper day of worship. The ambiguity of the references and the tolerant tone suggest that church leaders left Christian communions to judge the matter independently. In this early period, no more than twenty years after Jesus's death, the question of whether to worship on the Sabbath or the Lord's Day seems to have been a matter of *adiaphora* (one on which believers could differ without breaking fellowship with one another) rather than a matter of *diapheronta* (one on which they could not differ without breaking fellowship).

The gravitational pull toward Sunday worship continued to gain strength and adherents, however. In the mid-50s, Paul instructs the Corinthians to

29. See Williams, *Acts of the Apostles*, 140; Larkin, *Acts*, 288–89; Hengel, *Four Gospels and the One Gospel*, 119, 281. The judgment of Keener, *Acts*, 3:2964–68, that Acts 20:7 does not describe a Sunday worship event disregards the significance of the "first day of the week" and the breaking of bread, both of which typically indicate a Sunday worship gathering of early Christians.

present their individual financial offerings "on the first day of the week" (1 Cor. 16:2).[30] "The first day of the week," as noted above, refers to Sunday. The resolve of Jesus to reinterpret Sabbath with reference to his person and mission was transmitted to his followers. The seer John reports, for example, that his apocalyptic vision occurred "on the Lord's Day" (Rev. 1:10). The Greek word for "Lord's" or "belonging to the Lord," *kyriakos*, is rare in the New Testament—occurring only in Revelation 1:10, with reference to the Lord's Day (Sunday), and in 1 Corinthians 11:20, with reference to the Lord's Eucharist. Both references appear to be adaptations of the earliest christological confession, "Jesus is Lord"[31]—and as such, they claim the day and feast that "belong" to Jesus.[32] The reference to Sunday as "the Lord's Day" rather than "the Lord's *Sabbath*" is especially important, for it defines the Christian holy day no longer in terms of cessation from work, as in the fourth commandment, but solely with reference to Jesus.

With regard to the issue of Sabbath, the Council of Jerusalem is, once again, significant. Meeting in the late 40s, the council considered the essential elements that gentile Christian converts needed to observe in order to preserve rather than imperil their fragile consensus with Jewish Christians. It required new converts to refrain from eating meat offered to idols, from consuming blood or eating flesh that had been strangled rather than slaughtered, and from sexual immorality (Acts 15:20, 29). Three of the requirements imposed on gentile Christians concern unclean food, and the fourth concerns unclean sexual behaviors. Remarkably, the two most defining elements of Judaism—circumcision and Sabbath—are not included in the requirements. Despite the importance of these two practices to the Pharisaic wing of the early church, the council made no attempt to impose either circumcision or Sabbath observance on gentile Christians. Rather, it advanced a minimalist and pragmatic program of eliminating the most offensive behaviors of gentile believers that would rend the fellowship of Jews and gentiles in the church.

Exactly how long and in what regions Jesus followers continued their inherited observance of Sabbath is unknown. At some point, however, like ice that shrinks as the temperature rises until it vanishes, the observance of Sabbath among Jesus followers decreased until it yielded altogether to Sunday worship.

---

30. In light of the above discussion, the skepticism of Meeks, *First Urban Christians*, 143, that the directive in 1 Cor. 16:2 "offers no proof that the assembly was also on 'the first day of every week'" is unwarranted.

31. For "Jesus is Lord" (Gk. *Kyrios Iēsous*), see Mark 16:19; 1 Cor. 8:6; 11:23; 12:3; Phil. 2:11; 2 Thess. 2:8.

32. On *kyriakos* as a synonym for "of the Lord (Jesus)," see Bauckham, *Christian World*, 358. Bauckham correctly rejects the assertion of Werner Foerster, "*kyriakos*," *TWNT* 3:1095–96, that the two expressions are "indirectly related" rather than synonymous.

The transition appears to have been remarkably unclimactic. No council was convened to decide the matter. No "Sabbath sect" is known to have broken off from the emerging church in protest of Sunday worship. No formal discussion of the matter is preserved in all early Christian literature.[33] Even the Ebionite sect—Jewish believers who retained stronger allegiance to Jewish traditions than did mainstream Christians—forsook Sabbath observance and instead practiced "commemoration of the Savior's resurrection" on Sunday.[34]

It would not surprise us to find evidence of early Christian communion(s) reverting to Sabbath observance from Sunday worship. The Epistle to the Hebrews—which was written to dissuade Christians from reverting to Judaism to escape Roman recriminations from which Jews were exempt—would be a likely place to find such evidence. However, the lone reference to Sabbath in Hebrews (v. 4:9) offers no evidence that Sabbath played a role in the predicament addressed in the epistle. The Didache, an early manual on the Christian life that is strongly influenced by Judaism, is equally silent on the matter. However and whenever the early church shifted its day of worship from Saturday to Sunday, our literary evidence represents the transition as a done deal. The Didache enjoins believers, in words reminiscent of Acts 20:7, "Come together on the Lord's Day, break bread and give thanks after first confessing your sins."[35] The Greek word for "Lord's" in "Lord's Day" is the same *kyriakos* seen in 1 Corinthians 11:20 and Revelation 1:10 with reference to Sunday worship. The Lord's Day consists of believers gathering publicly, breaking bread and giving thanks, and confessing their sins. "Breaking bread and giving thanks" are syntactically related in Greek, suggesting a single event. The word for "give thanks" (Gk. *eucharisteō*) is the word by which the Lord's Supper would be known in early Christianity: "Eucharist." The Didache—probably the earliest text in the Apostolic Fathers—thus describes a Christian Sunday worship event untethered from the Jewish Sabbath.[36]

"The Lord's Day" is also common in the letters of Ignatius. Writing to the Magnesians, Ignatius describes the Christian experience as coming to

---

33. The Gospel of Thomas is the sole early "Christian" text that warns against scuttling Sabbath: "If you do not keep the Sabbath as Sabbath, you will not see the Father" (*log.* 27). Eusebius, however, solemnly reminds his contemporaries that the Gospel of Thomas was recognized by "none of the succession of the orthodox" and held no authority for early Christians. The canonical tradition going back to Origen (d. 254) and his teacher Ammonius Saccas (d. 242) considered Thomas heretical (*Hist. eccl.* 3.25.6).

34. Eusebius, *Hist. eccl.* 3.27.4–5. For further consideration of Sabbath worship in various Jewish-Christian sects, see Dunn, *Neither Jew nor Greek*, 578–80; Eduard Lohse, "*sabbaton*," *TWNT* 7:33–34.

35. Did. 14.1.

36. Did. 14.1.

"newness of hope, no longer sabbatizing but living according to the Lord's Day, on which our life also arose through him and his death."[37] Ignatius sharply distinguishes the Lord's Day from the Sabbath, referring pejoratively to the latter as "*sabbatizing*." Christian Sunday worship was not simply the Jewish Sabbath worship delayed twenty-four hours. It was a fundamentally different event, no longer defined primarily by prohibitions but by the resurrection of Jesus Christ, "on which our life also arose through him and his death."[38] The judgment on Sabbath in the Epistle of Barnabas is sharper and more polemical. For Barnabas, Sabbath is an abortive Judaistic interpretation of the old covenant, a covenant that Jews forfeited because of their sins. The breaking of the tablets of the Ten Commandments by Moses symbolizes God's breaking of his covenant with the Jews, a covenant that now belongs exclusively to Christians.[39] Citing Isaiah 1:13 (LXX), "I cannot endure your new moons and Sabbaths," Barnabas declares that, in the resurrection of Jesus Christ, God nullified and superseded the Jewish Sabbath by the creation of "an eighth day, on which Jesus rose from the dead, appeared, and ascended into heaven."[40]

The reference to an "eighth day" rewards further consideration. Unlike the numbers three, seven, and twelve, eight is not typically symbolic in Scripture. References to eight, however, are occasionally associated with the resurrection of Jesus. Three references in John imply that Jesus was resurrected on the eighth day.[41] Luke 9:28 associates the eighth day with the transfiguration of Jesus, which prefigures his resurrection. The eight members of Noah's family rescued from the flood (Gen. 7:13) are referred to in 1 Peter 3:20–21 as prototypes of salvation to new life through baptism.[42] The theological association of eight with resurrection and new creation may have influenced the material culture of early Christianity. An architectural feature original to ancient Christianity was octagonal sacred structures. Two concentric octagonal sanctuaries were constructed no later than the fifth century over what was ostensibly the house of Peter in Capernaum, which had been venerated as a holy space from the end of the first century. In the Constantinian era, the octagon determined the structure of some of Christianity's most renowned

37. Ign. *Magn.* 9.1.

38. For a full note on Ign. *Magn.* 9.1, see Bauckham, *Christian World*, 363–64.

39. Barn. 4.6–8; 6.19; 14.5. Barn. 14.6–9 sees the promises of God in Isa. 42:6–7; 49:6–7; and 61:1–2 fulfilled in Jesus Christ.

40. Barn. 15.8–9.

41. John 20:1, 19, 26.

42. For later patristic uses of the eighth day with reference to the resurrection of Jesus Christ, see Justin, *Dial.* 41.4; 138.1; Origen, *Sel. Ps.* 118.1; Gregory of Nyssa, *Ep.* 25 (*To Amphilochius*) 3.6.

churches.[43] More frequently, it determined the shape of baptismal fonts, altars, and mensas. The octagonal shape of Islam's second holiest site, the Dome of the Rock in Jerusalem (completed in 691–92), was patterned after the octagonal rotunda of the Church of the Holy Sepulchre.[44]

Eusebius sums up Sunday worship services in the postapostolic era using the word *kyriakos*, the same Greek word we have already seen used for "the Lord's Day." In one text, he refers to the Lord's Day as "holy," a day in which letters from Clement, bishop of Rome, were read to the gathering.[45] In two other texts, he links the Lord's Day expressly to the mystery of the Savior's resurrection from the dead.[46]

A singular insight into early Sunday worship is offered not by a Christian but by a Roman persecutor of Christians, Pliny the Younger.[47] Pliny was a Roman governor of Bithynia (modern north-central Turkey), one of the areas to which 1 Peter was addressed (1 Pet. 1:1). Writing in Latin in approximately the year 113, Pliny solicits advice from the emperor Trajan on dealing with a religious sect that he identifies as "Christians." A Christian presence, according to Pliny, had existed in Bithynia for at least twenty years before his arrival there as governor. By his day, Christians numbered "all ages and every rank, and even both sexes," including women officials called "deaconesses." The Christian community in Bithynia was obviously numerous, diverse, and well organized. Its influence in both the urban areas and the countryside was considerable. Indeed, from a Roman perspective the Christian influence was deleterious, for Roman temples were "deserted" and income from religious sacrifices was declining. Pliny writes to Trajan on the basis of both his own interrogations of Christians and what he has heard from anonymous informants. Such informants, in fact, are further evidence of the significant roots of Christianity in the region. Pliny describes Christians as "regularly assembling on a fixed day [*stato die*] before sunrise and singing a hymn to Christ as to God, and binding themselves by an oath [*sacramentum*]" not to steal, rob, commit adultery,

---

43. The rotunda of the Church of the Holy Sepulchre in Jerusalem is octagonal, as is the apse of the Church of the Nativity in Bethlehem. Churches in Caesarea Maritima and Antioch are also octagonal.

44. See Everett Ferguson, "Octagon," *EEECAA* 2:241–42; Murphy-O'Connor, *Holy Land*, 198–205, 217–21.

45. *Hist. eccl.* 4.23.11.

46. *Hist. eccl.* 3.27.5; 5.23.2.

47. *Ep. Tra.* 10.96. Pliny's letter to Trajan is also referred to in Eusebius, *Hist. eccl.* 3.33.1. A full exegesis of Pliny's letter appears in Koch, *Geschichte des Urchristentums*, 521–28. For Pliny's letter both in Latin and in English translation, see Gwatkin, *Selections from Early Writers*, 26–31. For excellent discussions of the letter, see Hurtado, *Destroyer of the Gods*, 22–26; Fox, *Classical World*, 547–54; and esp. Wilken, *Christians as the Romans Saw Them*, 1–30.

break their word, or deny deposits. The reference to an "oath" and the list of proscriptions may suggest the influence of the Ten Commandments in the life of the Christian community in Bithynia. Pliny's first detail, however, is of interest for our present purposes, that Christians were in the habit of meeting early on a fixed day of the week. He does not identify the day as Sunday, but the only other "association" that met on a fixed day of the week was the Jews, and they met on Saturday. Jews would not have sung a hymn to Jesus Christ as to God, nor would they have self-identified as Christians. Pliny's reference can only refer to Christian Sunday worship. Indeed, from his perspective, Sunday worship was Christians' chief public identifier.

By the early second century, Sunday had established itself among Christians as the holy day of worship.[48] "Sabbath" was abandoned in favor of "the Lord's Day" as the proper reference to Sunday. Christians retained references to Passover and Pentecost because these celebrations and their dates were received relatively unaltered from the Old Testament. Sunday, by contrast, was an entirely new creation and thus required a new name and day.[49] The earliest official declaration of Sunday as the church's holy day appears in a decree of Pope Sixtus (r. ca. 116–ca. 126) that Easter was to be celebrated on Sunday.[50] From what we have seen, however, it is clear that Sixtus's decree did not introduce Sunday as the Christian holy day but merely *confirmed* it as such.[51]

Why the Early Church Adopted Sunday

The preeminent role that Sabbath played in the Old Testament and subsequent Judaism would seem to have ordained it for a similar role in Christianity.

---

48. Zahn, *Skizzen*, 180, emphasizes how early and thoroughly Sunday gained traction in church: "The Sunday celebration must have become generally accepted quite early. The Christian writers from the beginning of the second century onward speak of the Christian custom [of Sunday worship] as a common custom" (my trans.). Bauckham places the supremacy of Sunday worship among Christians in Roman Asia (what is now western Turkey) even earlier: "The first day of the week was the Christian day of regular corporate worship in the churches of Asia at the end of the first century" (*Christian World*, 370).

49. Zahn, *Skizzen*, 183.

50. Bacchiocchi, *From Sabbath to Sunday*, 49–53.

51. A final reference to "Sabbath" from our era (although perhaps slightly later than others cited in this chapter) comes from the Martyrdom of Polycarp (8.1; 21), which twice testifies that Polycarp was martyred on "a great Sabbath." The day and month of Polycarp's martyrdom equate to February 22 (or perhaps 23), and the year (though not given) is probably 156 (see Holmes, *Apostolic Fathers*, 301–2). "Great Sabbath" appears to be another allusion in Mart. Pol., of which there are many, comparing the martyrdom of Polycarp to the passion of Jesus (e.g., John 19:31). Lightfoot, *Apostolic Fathers*, 1:709–13, argues that "great Sabbath" is a metonym for the Jewish festival of Purim that also coincided in 156 with the great anniversary of Caesar worship in Roman Asia. The martyrdom of Polycarp thus afforded Jews and pagans the opportunity of celebrating two disparate festivals at the same time. Lightfoot's conclusion is followed by Fox, *Pagans and Christians*, 486–87.

Jesus did not command his followers to abandon Sabbath, and his ministry provided no apparent precedent or reason for the early church to do so. The early church retained pagan names for other weekdays, after all, which makes its discarding of "Sabbath" all the more surprising. Equally surprising is that the change in name, day, and form of observance took place without major disruption or division in the church—as occurred, for example, in the fourth-century controversy over the date on which to celebrate Easter.[52] Any one of these factors—and certainly all of them together—would have made a strong case for the retention of Sabbath by the early church.

Why then did the early church abandon such a key element in its collective inheritance with Judaism? Sociological factors may have played roles in some parts of the church. Gentile Christians, as we have noted, may have separated from the Jewish synagogue following the First Revolt in order to avoid the *fiscus Judaicus*.[53] Additionally, it has been suggested that gentile Christians abandoned Sabbath in order to accommodate themselves to their Hellenistic context; Justin Martyr's reference to Sunday as "the Day of the Sun" has been cited as evidence of such accommodation.[54] I find it wholly improbable that either he or early Christianity in general abandoned Sabbath as a concession to gentile cults that worshiped the sun.[55] The above factors, either alone or combined, could scarcely have uprooted the deep Sabbath precedent that the church inherited from Torah and synagogue.

Despite the weight of tradition against it, however, the early church took the road less traveled: it forsook Sabbath and embraced Sunday. It did so neither arbitrarily nor from sociological accommodation, but from theological conviction. The old wineskin of Sabbath was incapable of accommodating the new wine of Sunday. For one, Sunday was believed to commemorate the completion of creation (Gen. 2:2–3).[56] But most importantly, Sunday was the day of Jesus's

52. Zahn observes, "When one considers the significance that the Sabbath held for Jewish life, at the very least one would suppose that, rather than observing a different day of the week, early Christians would have accentuated Sabbath observance. Sabbath was a strong bond of fellowship that united early Christians with God's gathered people in Israel; and in keeping Sabbath holy, Christians adhered not only to the example of God's people but also to the example of Jesus himself." *Skizzen*, 169 (my trans.).

53. On the *fiscus Judaicus*, see ch. 6, pp. 105–6. Both Zahn, *Skizzen*, 169, and Geraty, "From Sabbath to Sunday," 257, find it difficult to imagine that the early church introduced a new day of worship prior to the Roman destruction of Jerusalem in 70. However, we have noted evidence in Acts 20 of a movement to Sunday worship, especially in the diaspora, prior to the First Revolt (see above, pp. 214–15).

54. Justin, *1 Apol.* 67: "on the Sun's day."

55. On various sociological factors that may have influenced the early church to abandon Sabbath in favor of Sunday, see Geraty, "From Sabbath to Sunday," 258–59.

56. Mark 2:27–28; Barn. 15.3; Justin, *1 Apol.* 67.

resurrection from the dead. The commemoration of the resurrection, especially by means of the Eucharist,[57] established Sunday as a recurring, weekly Easter celebration. Like Easter, Sunday was not a day of fasting, prohibitions, and abstentions but one of witness, commemoration, and celebration—the primary manifestations of which were the celebration of the Lord's Supper and prayer.[58]

Our earliest and fullest description of a Lord's Day celebration comes from the second-century apologist Justin Martyr, who addressed his *First Apology* to the Roman emperor Antoninus Pius (r. 138–61).[59] Those who live in cities or in the country, he writes, gather in one place and read memoirs of the apostles or prophets. The leader then instructs and exhorts the gathering to imitate the good commended in the readings. Following the homily, the congregation stands for prayer, after which thanks is given for bread, wine, and water, which are shared by the gathering. A "thank offering" is distributed by deacons to those unable to attend. Those who are financially able and willing give money as they see fit, which is collected and deposited with the leader of the community for distribution to orphans, widows, sick, needy, prisoners, and strangers in their midst. All this occurs on Sunday, concludes Justin, "because it is the first day on which God, having wrought a change in the darkness and matter, made the world; and Jesus Christ our Saviour on the same day rose from the dead."[60] Justin's description concludes with the two elements that defined Sunday worship throughout early Christianity—a commemoration of the creation of the world and of the resurrection of Jesus Christ.

From a Sabbath perspective, what is most striking about Justin's Sunday description is the absence of any reference to cessation from work. In fact, cessation from work is absent from all references to Sunday worship in the New Testament and Apostolic Fathers. We need not conclude from this that rest and cessation from work played no role in early Christian Sunday observances. Given their importance in Judaism and the close relation of the early church to Judaism, it would be surprising if cessation from work vanished from the early Sunday observances.[61] Indeed, by late antiquity, the theme of

---

57. Ign. *Magn.* 9.1; Barn. 15.9; Eusebius, *Hist. eccl.* 3.27.5; 5.23.2.

58. Perhaps because Sunday was a day of celebration, prayer was observed while standing. On early Christian Sunday celebrations, see Zahn, *Skizzen*, 184–85.

59. The dedication of the apology to Antoninus Pius was strategic, for, as Eusebius reminds readers in *Hist. eccl.* 5.1–4, Christian martyrdoms spiked under the reign of Antoninus. (The most celebrated martyr of the early church, Polycarp, was put to death at this time.) One purpose of Justin's comprehensive description of the Lord's Day was to allay suspicion that Sunday gatherings posed a threat to the Roman Empire.

60. *1 Apol.* 67 (ANF 1:186).

61. The "Sabbath rest" enjoined of believers in Heb. 4:1–11 is not a reference to cessation from work but, rather, a metaphor for salvation. For the author of Hebrews, forsaking

rest reasserts itself in Christian Sunday celebrations, and it has continued to do so in varying degrees and forms to the modern era.[62]

To what degree rest and cessation from labor were retained in the Sunday celebrations of the early church is impossible to say for certain. What can be said for certain is that no text in the New Testament or Apostolic Fathers defines Sunday with reference to the fourth commandment or cessation from work. Sunday is never called the "Christian Sabbath." Sunday, rather, is observed and celebrated as the day of Jesus's resurrection from the dead on the first day of the week. It is truly and absolutely "the Lord's Day." So important was the first day of the week that it was associated with the renewal of creation on "the eighth day." The decisive influence that shifted the church's holy day from Sabbath to Sunday was Christology. The resurrection of Jesus from the dead was so momentous that it required of the church a new understanding of time. The church now lived in the new eschatological era—one not of death but of life, not of decay but of resurrection. The resurrection of Jesus inaugurated the "last days," the penultimate era of history immediately prior to the final consummation of all history—the return of Jesus Christ in judgment and glory. The dawn of this new era is celebrated by Sunday worship. Sunday witness to the resurrection of Christ became virtually inviolable among Christians. As Pliny wrote to Trajan, Christians regarded Sunday worship as a *public* expression of faith, one that they were committed to even when it exposed them to the potential of capital punishment by the empire. Sunday was "the Lord's Day"—a celebration of the benefits of Jesus's death and resurrection, of the blessings of Christian fellowship (especially common meals), and of the new world inaugurated by salvation in his name.

Christianity for Judaism is a "disobedience" that forfeits "Sabbath rest"—that is, salvation: "So then, there remains a Sabbath rest for the people of God, for whoever has entered God's rest has also rested from his works as God did from his. Let us therefore strive to enter that rest, so that no one may fall by the same sort of disobedience" (4:9–11).

62. For discussions of Sabbath and Sunday in the second, third, and fourth centuries, see Bauckham, *Christian World*, 385–433.

13

From "Way" to "Christian"

The First Names

Early attempts at naming the Christian movement proved elusive. This was as true for the mission of Jesus as it was for his later followers. According to the Gospels, the most common conjecture about the identity of Jesus was that he was a figure returned from the past: either John the Baptist or Elijah or one of the prophets. These opinions were shared by disciples and non-disciples alike, even by Herod Antipas, an arch-opponent of Jesus.[1] That opponents and advocates were united in this judgment indicates, surprisingly perhaps, that being a follower of Jesus did not necessarily give one an inside track in understanding his identity.

The terminology that Jesus used for himself was no less puzzling. He refused to claim leading Old Testament titles such as "king" or "Messiah,"[2] although he allowed the title of "prophet."[3] His preferred self-designation was "Son of Man," an Old Testament title that was both uncommon and poorly understood. In the sense that he often used it of himself—indicating a divine figure who would come on the clouds of heaven to receive dominion over the earth—it occurs only once in the Old Testament (Dan. 7:13–14). When crowds pressed Jesus if he was the promised Messiah of Israel, he employed the Son of Man title in response: "The Son of Man must be lifted

1. Matt. 16:14; Mark 6:14–15; 8:28; Luke 9:7–8; 9:19.
2. Matt. 26:63–64; Mark 15:2; John 6:15.
3. Luke 4:24; 11:32.

up," he replied—to which the crowds inquired in perplexity, "Who is this Son of Man?" (John 12:34).

The preeminent twentieth-century New Testament scholar Eduard Schweizer believed that Jesus's avoidance and even subversion of common messianic imagery and titles in first-century Judaism was an all-important first step in understanding his person and mission. Schweizer calls Jesus "the man who fits no formula."[4] What was true of the master was also true of his disciples, for the first generation of Jesus followers developed its distinctive communal life and missionary program without a brand name. Early believers consequently displayed freedom and originality in their self-designations. The earliest was probably "disciples," a corollary of the designation of Jesus as "the Teacher." "Nazarenes" and "Galileans" were also early names, both identifying the geographical location of Jesus's followers. Other descriptions appear, often as metaphors or analogies: "God's people," "Israel in the Spirit," "Seed of Abraham," "Chosen People" or "Elect," "Twelve Tribes," and "Servants of God." Many of these did not survive, but they attest to the importance of Israel's story for the self-understanding of Jesus followers.[5]

Four designations emerge with increasing frequency in the New Testament: "disciples" (Gk. *mathētai*), "believers" (Gk. *pisteuontes*), "brothers" (Gk. *adelphoi*), and "saints" (Gk. *hagioi*). The first two occur with reference to followers during Jesus's earthly ministry. "Disciples" derives from the Greek word meaning "learners," "students," or "apprentices," and it occurs frequently in all four Gospels and Acts but nowhere else in the New Testament. In the Gospels, disciples do not choose Jesus; Jesus chooses them. The term binds them closely to the call and mission of Jesus. In Acts, "disciples" refers to the community that derived from Jesus's apostles and first adherents. "Believers" occurs occasionally throughout the New Testament, but the term proliferates in the Gospel and First Epistle of John as the preferred designation of Jesus followers. The Greek noun *pistis* (faith, belief) never occurs in the Gospel of John, but the verb *pisteuō* (to believe) occurs nearly a hundred times, accentuating the importance of active commitment to the person and proclamation of Jesus.

---

4. Schweizer, *Jesus*, ch. 2. In his intellectual autobiography, *Jesus Christ: The Man from Nazareth and the Exalted Lord*, Schweizer writes, "The title, 'Jesus: The Man Who Fits No Formula,' became, for my understanding of Jesus and the further development of this understanding, perhaps the most important part [of the book]" (86).

5. On these early names, see Harnack, *Mission and Expansion*, 399–418, including his comment that "[The names] show how the new community felt itself to be heir to all the promises and privileges of the Jewish nation" (403).

"Brothers" and "saints" appear in the New Testament with reference to the post-resurrection community of Jesus followers. "Brothers" derives from the family unit, which was constitutive of Jewish life, and defines belonging in Christian communities in terms of a genetic bond, a sibling relationship. The grammatically masculine "brothers" is not gender-specific; it includes men, women, and children. The Gospels do not call Jesus's disciples brothers. Only in the book of Acts and, especially, the Pauline Epistles (where it occurs more than 130 times) does "brothers" become a standard term of reference for Jesus followers. The concept derives from Jesus, however, who teaches his disciples that whoever loves father or mother, son or daughter more than him is unworthy to follow him (Matt. 10:37). Indeed, whoever does the will of God is his brother, sister, and mother (Mark 3:35).

"Saints," by contrast, derives from the cultic life of Israel. The holy God sanctified the divine dwelling place in the temple and, above all, in the people called by the divine name. "I am the Lord your God; consecrate yourselves and be holy, because I am holy" (Lev. 11:44 NIV). The early church appropriated this commandment and applied it to believers in Jesus Christ (1 Pet. 1:16), because Jesus "loved the church and gave himself up for it, to make it holy, cleansing it by the washing of the water in the word" (Eph. 5:25–26). The Greek word *hagios* (holy, sacred) is at the root of the designation for Christians themselves—*hagioi* (saints, holy ones). This term appears throughout the New Testament, but it proliferates in the Pauline Epistles and in Revelation. The gospel causes a tectonic shift in the concept of human community, for the body of Christ is defined not by familial, geographic, racial, gender, ethnic, or linguistic boundaries. "Saints" come from every nation, tribe, people, and tongue; any "who call upon the name of our Lord Jesus Christ in every place" may be numbered among them (1 Cor. 1:2).[6]

The Way

The earliest semiformal designation for Jesus followers is "the Way" (Gk. *ho hodos*). Used by both believers and nonbelievers, "the Way" first appears in the New Testament with reference to Saul's journey to Damascus in search "of members of the Way, both men and women, to seize them and bring them to Jerusalem" (Acts 9:2). In distant Corinth, Apollos proclaims "the Way of the Lord" (18:25, 26). And in Ephesus, the Way is impugned in the Jewish synagogue, causing Paul to withdraw and form his own community of

6. Rev. 5:9; 7:9; 10:11; 11:9; 13:7; 14:6; 17:15. See also Otto Procksch, "*hagios*," *TWNT* 1:107–9.

instruction in the lecture hall of Tyrannus (19:9). The silversmith Demetrius later foments a riot in Ephesus because of the Way (19:23–41). Also in Acts, when Paul is arrested in the temple in Jerusalem, he speaks to the crowd in Hebrew, confessing that he himself had also once persecuted members of the Way (22:4). Following Paul's arrest, the Roman prefect Felix expresses interest in learning more about the Way (24:22, 24). These references attest to the scope and versatility of "the Way" as a designation for Jesus followers by the mid-first century.

Ironically, the book of Acts—which is the only New Testament document to refer to Jesus followers, collectively, as "the Way"—does not explain the epithet. We do not know for certain why the early church chose the designation, but it likely derived from Jewish tradition. According to the prophet Jeremiah, God promised to make of his people "one heart and one way."[7] The Gospel of John records Jesus taking "the way" as a self-designation: "I am the way, the truth, and the life" (John 14:6). Jesus followers characterize his kingdom variously as "the way of truth" (2 Pet. 2:2); "the way of righteousness" (2 Pet. 2:21); "the way of salvation" (Acts 16:17); or, all-inclusively, "the way(s) of the Lord" (Acts 13:10; 18:25). "The Way" is an all-encompassing metaphor for both Christ and the gospel.[8] A *way* is more than thoughts and words. It also includes acting, moving toward a goal. An entire division of Jewish law, halakah (from the Hb. *halak*, "to walk") prescribes ethical behaviors—"manner of life" and "lifestyles." The Psalms and Proverbs emphasize the godly way of wisdom as opposed to the way of folly, a concern that characterizes the Dead Sea Scrolls as well.[9] When Paul refers to love as a "more excellent way" (1 Cor. 12:31), he thinks and speaks similarly. Jesus followers thus present themselves as living examples of a *way* to be the people of Israel.[10]

"The Way" was the most important name for early Jesus followers, but it was not the only name. Another, though less frequent, was "sect." The word for "sect" (Gk. *hairesis*) is applied to the Way in Acts 24:14, and Jesus followers are elsewhere called "the sect of the Nazarenes" (Acts 24:5) or simply "*this* sect" (Acts 28:22). In the first century, "sect" was less pejorative than it is in modern parlance. Josephus uses the term—without disparagement—of Sadducees, Pharisees, and Essenes, speaking of them as three Jewish schools or divisions.[11] The book of Acts refers to Sadducees (5:17) and Pharisees (15:5) as sects; the latter, according to the apostle Paul, is "the most exact-

---

7. Jer. 32:38–39. The LXX version reads "another heart and another way."
8. Wilhelm Michaelis, "*hodos*," *TWNT* 5:93–94.
9. See 1QS 9.17–18, 21; 10.21; CD 1.13; 2.6.
10. So Dunn, "From the Crucifixion," 27–29.
11. *J.W.* 2.119–166; *Ant.* 18.11–15.

ing sect of our religion" (26:5). Uses of "sect" for Jesus followers are also non-pejorative.[12] When the apostle Paul arrives in Rome in chains and meets with Jewish leaders, they inform him that they have "not received any letters from Judea" about him and that none of their people have "reported or said anything bad" about him; but they want to hear what his views are—"for," they say, "people everywhere are talking against this sect" (28:21–22). "Sect" is used here much as Second Temple Jews referred to different "schools" or "groups." The epithet could be used pejoratively, however. When Paul is charged by antagonists in the Sanhedrin as "a ringleader of the sect of the Nazarenes" (24:5), both "sect" and "ringleader" connote public menace and insurrection.

A less common epithet for a Jesus follower is "Nazarene," as just noted in "the sect of the Nazarenes" (Acts 24:5). Jesus is identified as a Nazarene a dozen times in the four Gospels,[13] and half that number again in the book of Acts.[14] "Nazarene" is not a major christological title, but it identifies Jesus as a Galilean, from Nazareth, and his disciples as those who share his Galilean roots.[15] A final epithet for Jesus followers, *deisidaimonia* in Greek, which might be translated "respectable religion," occurs only once in the New Testament (Acts 25:19).[16] *Deisidaimonia* refers to religion within the tolerances of the Roman ideal of public order and the Greek ideal of moderation, thus religion that is not *superstitio* but balanced and controlled.

Let me make two summary comments about these early titles and epithets. First, the foregoing terms all begin to wane, and in some cases disappear, in the latter half of the first century. Already in the New Testament Epistles and Apostolic Fathers, "sect" refers no longer to a school of thought but to a heresy opposed to Christian teaching.[17] "Nazarene" occurs occasionally in the early patristic period as a circumlocution for "Christian," but usually as a more familiar, even intimate, reference to the Christian movement.[18] "The Way" also diminishes, but it does not disappear. The Didache uses it in the

12. Acts 24:5, 14; 28:22.

13. *Nazarēnos*: Mark 1:24; 10:47; 14:67; 16:6; Luke 4:34; 24:19. *Nazōraios*: Matt. 2:23; 26:71; Luke 18:37; John 18:5, 7; 19:19.

14. *Nazōraios*: Acts 2:22; 3:6; 4:10; 6:14; 22:8; 26:9.

15. It is possible that "Nazarene" bears some relation to Samson, who in the Codex Alexandrinus LXX text of Judg. 16:17 is called *naziraios theou*, "Nazirite of God," i.e., one consecrated or devoted to God, whereas in the Vaticanus text of the same passage, the title reads *hagios theou*, "holy one of God." If "Nazarene" is related to the Nazirite vow and Samson, then for both Jesus and his followers it would refer to Jesus's particular relationship to God as well as to the town of Nazareth. See Schweizer, *Neotestamentica*, 51–55.

16. See BDAG 216.

17. See 1 Cor. 11:19; Gal. 5:20; 2 Pet. 2:1.

18. See *PGL* 896–97.

opening description of the Christian faith as the "way of life," as opposed to the "way of death." The way of life is summarized by the two greatest commandments—to love God and to love neighbor—and by the "silver rule" (not to do to others what one does not want done to oneself). The Didache defines the way largely in terms of ethical behaviors, which is reinforced by frequent use of the Greek verb *hodēgeō*, meaning "lead" or "guide." The exhortation on the "two ways" at the end of the Epistle of Barnabas repeats the same theme. In the postapostolic era, "way" designates various virtues and vices more often than it designates the Christian faith itself.[19] "The way" thus retains a descriptive function in early Christianity, but it ceases to function as a name for the Christian movement, as it does in the book of Acts.

Second, and more important, the growth and development of Christianity was not impeded by lack of a formal name. The body of belief and believers that the foregoing terms denote became increasingly defined and identifiable even before it was known by a proper name. A broad range of essential tenets—including identification with the name and person of Jesus, bearing witness to Jesus, regular gatherings, sharing common meals, acts of mercy, missionary preaching and teaching, and willingness to suffer persecution—characterized the early church before it became known as "Christian."[20]

Christians

Following the persecution of Stephen, Jesus followers in Jerusalem fled north to Phoenicia and Cyprus, and finally to Antioch, where they were first called "Christians" (Acts 11:26). Stephen was probably martyred in the year 33, so

19. Thus the allegory in Herm. Vis. 3.7.1 is constructed on the motif of stones rolling off the right way and onto a rough, untracked way. "The way" here no longer refers to the faith—*the* Way—but to the virtue of steadfastness. Similarly, we hear of the "way of righteousness" as the straight and godly way that leads to the Lord (Herm. Mand. 6.1.4–5)—"the way of truth" (1 Clem. 35.5), "the way of righteousness" (Barn. 1.4), "the way of the just" (2 Clem. 5.7), "the straight way" (2 Clem. 7.3). Ignatius speaks of love as the way leading to God, on which believers are "fellow-travelers" (Ign. *Rom.* 9.1–2). These uses abandon "way" as a substantive for Christianity in favor of its function in the Old Testament wisdom literature, especially Proverbs, as a way of speaking about particular virtues and vices (e.g., Prov. 15:10, 24). For similar uses of "the way," see *PGL* 936.

20. In "Beyond the Jewish People," 183–203, Dunn writes that referential terms for the early Christian movement are not satisfactory because "the situation described was so diverse and fluid" and because the "movement [which we know as Christian] whose defining distinctives were or may still have been taking shape had, in a real sense, not yet been born" (p. 185). I do not share Dunn's judgment in this matter. The kerygma of the early church stands in a faithful continuum with the gospel proclaimed by Jesus. Dunn's description of "embryonic Christianity" seems to testify to this continuity, in fact, for an embryo does not change its DNA. Nor did the Christian faith change its theological DNA in the transition from Jesus movement to Christian church.

the dispersion of Jesus followers to Antioch and their being called Christians there must have occurred no later than the midthirties. Luke does not say who first called believers "Christians,"[21] although he introduces the new name at the conclusion of Paul and Barnabas's yearlong ministry in Antioch, which may suggest that "Christian" was related to the influence of those two apostles. At any rate, "Christians" forms the climax of his account of the advance of the gospel in Antioch. Luke prepares for this climax by informing readers that Christian evangelists in Antioch broke with the custom of proclaiming the gospel only to Jews by proclaiming it also to "Hellenists" (Acts 11:20). Luke uses "Hellenists" in Acts 6:1 and 9:29 as a reference to Greek-speaking *Jews*, but in 11:20 the term must refer to *gentiles*, for the proclamation of the gospel to Greek-speaking Jews was already accepted in Jerusalem and would have been unremarkable in Antioch, where most Jews were Greek speaking.[22] "The hand of the Lord was with" the outreach in Antioch (Acts 11:21), and a great many became Christians. Church leaders in Jerusalem dispatched Barnabas to investigate the situation in Antioch. Barnabas summoned Saul from Tarsus, and both went to Antioch, where they ministered for a year. The growth of the church in Antioch, due to the influx of gentiles, is crowned by Luke's announcement of Jesus followers being named "Christians."

The new name did not immediately terminate other nomenclature, especially within the community itself. "Disciples," "believers," "brothers," "saints," "way," "sect," and "Nazarenes" continued in intramural communications of the early church alongside the growing use of "Christian" as a public epithet. In extramural communication outside Jerusalem and Judea, however, "Christian" increasingly supplanted earlier references to the new faith. In extant literature from our era—the New Testament, the Apostolic Fathers, and Greek and Roman writings—"Christian" becomes a default name for the new movement, for this "third way" or "third race" (as it was sometimes described), signifying its autonomy as a community and system of belief distinct from Judaism as well as from Greco-Roman religion and custom.[23]

Virtually all occurrences of "Christian" in our relevant sources underscore this point. Following the introduction of the name in Acts 11, "Christian" appears only once again in Acts, and then from an unbeliever. At Paul's trial

21. Harnack, *Mission and Expansion*, 411, suggests that Roman magistrates in Antioch coined the term and that Luke was mum on the subject because "the pagan origin of the name was already felt by him to be a drawback." Harnack's hypothesis is possible, but it is based on conjecture rather than textual evidence. It seems equally plausible that the origin of the name was lost in the flurry of unknown and unnamed evangelists converging on Antioch, or, as I suggest, that it arose in relation to the mission of Paul and Barnabas in Antioch.

22. See Hengel, *Between Jesus and Paul*, 8–9; Keener, *Acts*, 2:1840–42.

23. On "third way" or "third race," see ch. 6, pp. 151–52.

before Herod Agrippa II (in Caesarea in the year 58), Agrippa chides Paul for trying to make him a Christian (Acts 26:28). That Agrippa identified Paul's witness as "Christian" attests to the currency of the name twenty years after its introduction in Antioch. Both Tacitus and Suetonius identify victims of Nero's persecution in Rome in the year 64 as "Christians," indicating that the epithet was current in Rome just as it was in the eastern Mediterranean. A third and final use of "Christian" in the New Testament also occurs with reference to suffering—which, in the early years of the faith, was not infrequently the consequence of Christian witness. "Let not one who suffers as a Christian be ashamed, but let him glorify God in this name," exhorts 1 Peter 4:16. These various strains of evidence, from sources Christian and non-Christian and from places as distant from one another as Jerusalem and Rome, attest that the name "Christian" identified Jesus followers from the early 40s onward.

The Apostolic Fathers admonish readers not to allow the name "Christian" to become a substitute for Christian behavior. The admonition itself implies that, by the late first century, "Christian" had achieved a degree of currency—as had its misuse. The Didache applies a similar admonition to traveling evangelists not to overstay their welcome. If evangelists stay more than two or three days, let them practice a trade rather than remain idle and presume on the hospitality of the church. Idleness is not Christian living. In a play on words, the Didache says a freeloader is not a Christian but a *Christemporos*, a "trafficker in Christ."[24] Ignatius issues a similar warning to his readers in Magnesia (modern western Turkey): "We should not simply be known as Christians, but really *be* Christians."[25] Indeed, and more personally, Ignatius exhorts the Romans to pray that, in his impending martyrdom, he "may not simply be called a Christian, but actually prove to be one."[26]

At the beginning of the second century, three Roman historians, all writing within ten years of one another, employ the term "Christian." Pliny the Younger, writing to the Emperor Trajan from Bithynia (modern central Turkey) around the year 110, asks for advice concerning a "degenerate and unrestrained superstition" (*superstitionem pravam et immodicam*) that he repeatedly refers to as "Christian."[27] In his response, Trajan, who also refers to Jesus followers as "Christians," counsels Pliny in a course of moderation: to punish proven Christian individuals, but not to persecute Christians en masse.[28] The Roman historian Tacitus, writing about the year 115, also refers to Jesus followers

24. Did. 12.3–5.
25. Ign. *Magn.* 4.
26. Ign. *Rom.* 3.2.
27. Pliny, *Ep. Tra.* 10.96.
28. Pliny, *Ep. Tra.* 10.97.

as "Christians." Reporting on the Neronian persecution of 64, he says that Nero, attempting "to scotch the rumor [that he himself had set Rome afire], substituted as culprits and punished with the utmost refinements of cruelty, a class of people loathed for their vices, whom the crowd styled Christians."[29] Like Pliny, Tacitus thinks of the Christian faith as "a pernicious superstition" (*exitiabilis superstitio*). Around the year 120, regarding the same Neronian persecution, Suetonius writes, "Punishment was inflicted on the Christians, a class of people practicing a new and evil superstition" (*genus hominum superstitionis novae ac maleficae*).[30] All three writers characterize the Christian movement as a *superstitio*, whose adherents were numerous enough to be termed a "class" or "race."

The label *superstitio* deserves a word of consideration. The Roman world was inherently conservative. Rustlings of sedition under the cloak of a religion that was not sanctioned by the state were danger signals for Roman authorities. Judaism was the sole religion that Rome allowed to exist outside its conventional boundaries. As long as Jesus followers remained a sect within Judaism, they enjoyed the privilege of conscientious objection from Roman state religion. But by the year 64, in Rome, "Christian" connoted something other than Judaism. It was a *superstitio*, a belief perceived to pose a threat both to Roman order and decorum and to the Greek ideal of moderation. It aroused suspicions in ancients similar to the suspicions that "fanatics" or "terrorists" arouse in moderns. A *superstitio* was perceived to be politically subversive, a peril to the state. Thus simply to be a Christian—regardless of what one *did* as a Christian—was sufficient cause for punishment, even capital punishment.[31] When Christians came to constitute a *genus*, an entire "class" or "race" (in the words of Pliny, Tacitus, and Suetonius), their presence caused alarm among Roman officials. It is worth recalling that the Jewish historian Josephus did not regard Jesus followers as a menace (as did Pliny, Tacitus, and Suetonius). Writing only a decade before the three Roman historians, Josephus mentions three members of the Jesus movement—Jesus himself, John the Baptist, and James the brother of the Lord—without reference to "race" or "superstition."[32] For Romans, by contrast, the rising tide of the Christian *superstitio* crested in the middle of the second century at the trial of Polycarp, where Roman phobias of Christian *superstitio* determined the outcome of the "trial" from the outset. When the eighty-six-year-old bishop of Smyrna

29. Tacitus, *Ann.* 15.44 (LCL).
30. Suetonius, *Nero* 16.
31. On Roman anxiety over the rise of Christianity, see Nock, *Conversion*, 227–28.
32. For Jesus, see Josephus, *Ant.* 18.63–64; John the Baptist, *Ant.* 18.116–19; James the brother of Jesus, *Ant.* 20.200.

confessed, "I am a Christian,"[33] he was lumped with the "race (Gk. *genos*) of Christians."[34] Indeed, he was proclaimed "the father of Christians."[35] "Away with the atheists," cried the crowds.[36] "Atheists" referred to those who did not venerate the state-sanctioned gods and cults. Polycarp was first burned at the stake and then, still alive, stabbed to death.[37]

Christianity

As we have seen, Jesus followers were first called Christians in Antioch. Antioch is also where Ignatius, who was either Antioch's second or third bishop,[38] first christened the Jesus movement with the name by which it has been known ever since: "Christianity." In his epistle *To the Trallians*, Ignatius's reflections on his role as bishop and his impending martyrdom in Rome cause him to consider the nature of the Christian movement. "Partake only of Christian food," he writes, speaking metaphorically of the Christian movement, "and keep away from every alien plant, which is heresy."[39] We noted earlier that the Greek word *hairesis* (sect) originally designated various schools of thought within Judaism, including that of the Jesus followers. Here, however, Ignatius employs *hairesis* with its acquired, negative sense of a cancer in an otherwise healthy organism, and the English word that derives from this sense is "heresy." For Ignatius, the healthy organism is a "plant," and his word for the healthy plant is "Christianity."

Ignatius first introduces the term for the whole organism in his epistle *To the Magnesians*. "Therefore, since we have become [Christ's] disciples, let us learn to live in accordance with Christianity. For whoever is called by any other name than this is not of God."[40] Ignatius distinguishes Jesus followers from Judaism by the same term. "It is improper to profess Jesus Christ and practice Judaism," he declares, "for Christianity did not believe in Judaism, but Judaism in Christianity."[41] And again in his epistle *To the Philadelphians*:

33. Mart. Pol. 10.1; 12.1.
34. Mart. Pol. 3.2.
35. Mart. Pol. 12.2.
36. Mart. Pol. 32.
37. The apocryphal Acts of Paul and Thecla, composed in either the second or third century, appears to have used the Martyrdom of Polycarp (which was widely read and revered from the mid-second century onward) as a template for a supposed trial of Paul at Iconium. "Away with the sorcerer!" Paul's persecutors cry, just as the crowd cried of Polycarp. The charges brought against Paul—"corrupting" society and claiming to be a "Christian"—likewise echo those brought against Polycarp. Acts Paul Thec. 15–16, in *NTApoc* 2:241.
38. Second, according to Origen; third, according to Eusebius.
39. Ign. *Trall.* 6.1.
40. Ign. *Magn.* 10.1.
41. Ign. *Magn.* 10.3.

"It is better to hear about Christianity from a man who is circumcised than about Judaism from one who is not."[42] For Ignatius, a Jewish convert to Christianity can properly proclaim Christianity as the fulfillment of Judaism; but the reverse claim, made by an uncircumcised Godfearer, for example, who proclaims Judaism as God's ultimate revelation, must be refuted.[43] Ignatius here broaches the concept of "recapitulation" that would be formally introduced later by the apologists and church fathers and that continues to play a role in Christian theology to this day—namely, that the essence of Judaism, and indeed of all human spiritual longings, has been fulfilled or "summed up" in the gospel of Jesus Christ.[44] It is worth noting that Ignatius does not maintain the uniqueness or superiority of Christianity in ethnic terms. The essential divide between Judaism and Christianity is not between Jew and gentile but between old and new (i.e., the "new yeast [of Christianity], which is Jesus Christ").[45] For Ignatius, Christianity is the terminal point on a trajectory that began in Judaism and reached its goal, its fulfillment, in the person and work of Jesus Christ.

We conclude our pilgrimage from "Way" to "Christian" with two comments about the nature of Christianity as Ignatius understood it. First, in the eyes of Ignatius, Christianity is birthed from the womb of Israel; as such, Jews have a privileged understanding of Christianity. Judaism is the penultimate point on the history-of-salvation trajectory. The history of Jews therefore prepares and predisposes them for Christianity. Second, Ignatius understands Christianity as a state of maturity and independence apart from Judaism. In coining the word "Christianity," he no longer focuses on the particular adherents of the movement but on the movement itself. "Christianity" is a self-reflective epithet for a "race" (to use a category introduced by early Christians themselves), whose substantive nature and doctrines are distinct both from Judaism and from Greco-Roman culture. Ignatius thus introduces Christianity as a distinct alternative to these other two "races." So distinctive

---

42. Ign. *Phil.* 6.1. The same argument appears in Ign. *Magn.* 10.2–3.

43. The reference to a circumcised man proclaiming Christianity refers to the propriety of a Jew proclaiming the fulfillment of Judaism in Christianity. An uncircumcised man preaching Judaism may refer to gentile "Godfearers" who wished to retain Jewish observances regarding food laws and Sabbath practices, like many Jewish Christians, yet refrain from circumcision. In this and in all references to Judaism, Ignatius regards Christianity to have superseded Judaism. For more on this, see Lightfoot, *Apostolic Fathers*, 2:263–64; Reed and Vuong, "Christianity in Antioch," 118–19.

44. The word "recapitulation" (from Gk. *anakephalaioō*) occurs in the New Testament only in Rom. 13:9 and Eph. 1:10. But the doctrine that Jesus Christ "sums up" or consummates the prior initiatives of God in human history, especially in Judaism but also in other religions, is developed first by Irenaeus (*Haer.* 3.21.10; 3.22.3; 4.40.3) and later by Augustine (*Civ.* 7.32–33).

45. Ign. *Magn.* 10.2.

is Christianity that it subverts the scale of values by which races are otherwise measured. "Christianity is greatest," testifies Ignatius shortly before his
martyrdom in Rome, "when it is hated by the world."[46] Polycarp concurs. He
volunteers to expound the doctrines of the new faith to his accusers shortly
before his martyrdom: "I am a Christian. If you wish to learn the doctrine
[*logos*] of Christianity, give me a day and hear what I have to say."[47] Both
Ignatius and Polycarp are clear that Christianity is a new faith, a third race.
Its proper understanding cannot rest on proclamation and persuasion alone;
it requires genuine witness. The Greek word for "witness," *martyreō*, is the
root of the English word *martyr*. For both Ignatius and Polycarp, Christian
witness led, ultimately, to martyrdom.

---

46. Ign. *Rom.* 3.3.
47. Mart. Pol. 10.1.

14

From Scroll to Codex

A Momentous Change

A mosaic in the Berlin Cathedral provides an apropos introduction to this chapter. Midway up its immense interior, at perhaps the 150-foot point, the pendentives of the cathedral are emblazoned with mosaics of the Four Evangelists. The evangelists are a conventional motif in ecclesiastical iconography, but the depiction of the Second Evangelist in the Berlin Cathedral is quite unconventional. In it, the evangelist is copying from a scroll into a codex (a bound book). This final chapter addresses the transition from scroll to codex, for the medium of the codex constituted a "momentous change" in information technology in ancient Mediterranean culture and played a unique role in the formation of the New Testament canon.[1]

No religious tradition in human history lays greater emphasis on words than does the Judeo-Christian tradition. The Hebrew tradition attributes the creation of the cosmos and everything in it to divine speech (Gen. 1), and the "Ten Words," as Jews refer to the Ten Commandments, apply the same speech to the divine ordering of human life.[2] Words are even more important in Christianity, which confesses Jesus Christ as the very Word of God who "became flesh" (John 1:14). The practical importance of words

---

1. Parker, *New Testament Manuscripts*, 13, speaks of the "momentous change" that the transition from scroll to codex constituted in the Mediterranean world. Reynolds and Wilson, *Scribes and Scholars*, 34, refer to this transition as one of "utmost significance."
2. Exod. 20:1–17; Deut. 5:1–21.

was also furthered in early Christianity by the fact that, unlike Jews (at that time), the first followers of Jesus had no altars or priests or sacrifices through which their faith was symbolized and transmitted to the faithful. Words were the chief, and virtually the only, medium by which Christian identity was articulated and disseminated.[3] The Epistle to the Colossians exhorts believers, "Let the word of God dwell within you richly, teaching and admonishing yourselves in all wisdom by psalms, hymns, and spiritual songs, singing in grace in your hearts to God" (3:16). We have seen how the gospel was introduced to the ancient world via the kerygma (that is, oral proclamation summaries). Soon thereafter, the kerygma was also transmitted through the occasional letters of early Christians—through those of the apostle Paul, above all, but also through those of Peter, John, James, Clement, Ignatius, and the unknown authors of the Epistle to the Hebrews, the Didache, Second Clement, the Epistle to Diognetus, and many others. In the latter half of the first century, the kerygma was famously transmitted through a new literary genre unique to Christians: Gospels. The enduring significance of the *word* is expressed in the final vision of the seer John in Revelation, where the Lamb, who is the Word of God, replaces the temple in the new Jerusalem (Rev. 21:22).

Like the mosaic of the Second Evangelist in the Berlin Cathedral, the early church received its sacred texts from Judaism in the form of scrolls, but it produced and transmitted its own texts in the form of books. The early manuscript book form—in which individual pages, with writing on both sides, are bound together along one of the edges—is known as the "codex" (pl. codices). The transition from scroll to codex is attested in the Greek New Testament in the use of two different words that occur roughly the same number of times: *biblos*, which denotes a codex or book,[4] and *biblion*, which denotes a scroll.[5] As with many words, however, early writers use *biblos* and *biblion* more broadly and interchangeably than their formal lexical definitions might suggest, and this complicates rather than clarifies our task of tracing the transition from scrolls to codices. Both Josephus and Philo, for instance, use *biblos* countless times to refer to the Torah and various other texts of the Old Testament, which we know circulated only in scroll format.[6] Writers in the

---

3. Barclay, *Pauline Churches*, 25–26.
4. Matt. 1:1; Mark 12:26; Luke 3:4; 20:42; Acts 1:20; 7:42; 19:19; Phil. 4:3; Rev. 3:5; 20:15.
5. Matt. 19:7; Mark 10:4; Luke 4:17, 20; John 20:30; 21:25; Gal. 3:10; 2 Tim. 4:13; Heb. 9:19; 10:7. *Biblion* occurs twenty-three times in the book of Revelation (see 6:14, "like a *biblion* [scroll] being rolled up"). For lexical definitions of both terms, see BDAG 176.
6. Gottlob Schrenk, "*biblos, biblion*," *TWNT* 1:614–15.

early patristic period also employ *biblos* and *biblion* interchangeably.[7] The contexts in which the two words occur are thus often more important than their lexical denotations in determining their meaning.

Even in context, however, the meaning is not always certain, for only in a few instances are the details specific enough to help us. Luke 4, fortunately, is a text where denotation and connotation agree: Jesus "unrolled the *biblion*" of the prophet Isaiah in order to preach from it in the synagogue of Nazareth (v. 17), and when he was finished reading, "he rolled up the *biblion*, handed it to the attendant, and sat down" (v. 20). Here *biblion*, true to its lexical definition, means "scroll." Revelation 5:1 probably refers to a scroll as well: "I saw at the right hand of the one seated on the throne a *biblion* written on the front and back, sealed with seven seals." Scrolls normally had writing only on the front side, facing the reader, but they would occasionally have writing on both the front and the back (e.g., Ezek. 2:10). The Greek technical term for a scroll with writing on both front and back was *opisthographos* (written on the back).[8] If scrolls contained important or official information, they were often, as here, "sealed" (e.g., 1 Kings 21:8). It was difficult to seal a codex similarly, and, not surprisingly, after codices replaced scrolls in the apostolic era, the use of "seal" in this regard seldom occurred.[9] Thus, Revelation 5:1 probably intends a scroll with writing on front and back, an *opisthographos*.

Other references from the New Testament and post–New Testament eras are best understood as codices. In 2 Timothy 4:13, Paul beseeches Timothy from prison to come to him before winter, bringing "the *biblia* [pl. from *biblion*], especially the *membranas*." *Membranas* may refer to books here—that is, Paul asks for both the scrolls and the books.[10] *Membranas* were early alternatives to scrolls, consisting of wax-coated boards fastened together with a thong or clasp. Later generations of *membranas* replaced the boards with parchment leaves that were stitched together. In the first and second centuries, such parchment notebooks were widely used for letters, school exercises, notes of various kinds, and shorter casual documents.[11] They were simply called *membranas*, "parchments," similar perhaps to the modern use of "paperbacks" to refer to cheaper and less durable books. Paul asks Timothy

---

7. *PGL* 296–97.

8. *LSJ* 1238; Lohmeyer, *Offenbarung*, 53; Caird, *Revelation*, 72.

9. On the use of scroll seals in the ancient world and Judaism, see Gottfried Fitzer, "*sphragis, sphragizō*," *TWNT* 7:939–54.

10. The Greek wording of the verse, however, allows *membranas* also to be understood as a specific kind of scroll (i.e., the kind made of leather). For a full note arguing for *membranas* as meaning books, see Hengel, *Four Gospels and the One Gospel*, 281–82, 484n.

11. See Reynolds and Wilson, *Scribes and Scholars*, 34.

to bring "especially the parchments." His desire for the parchments may even indicate his preference for them as a form of written communication.[12]

Further references to codices occur in the Apostolic Fathers. Polycarp, writing probably in the early second century, commends the Philippians for being well trained in "Sacred Scriptures."[13] In his commendation, Polycarp twice quotes a text that we know as Ephesians 4:26. These "Sacred Scriptures," as he refers to them, would later be included in the corpus of New Testament Scriptures. Since we have no evidence of New Testament texts circulating as scrolls, we may assume that Polycarp's reference is to Scriptures in codex form. Polycarp further informs his readers that he is appending the letters of Ignatius and certain other documents in his possession to his letter (*To the Philippians* 13). The reference to appending material almost certainly implies a codex. A scroll was a length of papyrus[14] or parchment[15] with sticks attached at both ends; the sticks were held one in each hand for scrolling horizontally. Scrolls were normally about ten inches in height and could be of any length, although a scroll longer than about thirty feet became too heavy and unmanageable to be useful. Once the papyrus or parchment had been cut and affixed to end sticks, its length could not be increased. One could copy text in blank space at the end of a scroll, but one could not append letters to a scroll. A codex, on the other hand, was a stack of papyrus or parchment leaves that was affixed on one edge, to which additional leaves could be added to expand its size. When Polycarp speaks of appending the letters of Ignatius and other materials in his possession to his own letter, he refers to a codex.[16]

A similar picture emerges in the Shepherd of Hermas, the longest text in the Apostolic Fathers, which recounts a series of allegorical visions that reflect the state of Christianity in early second-century Rome. Early in the Shepherd, a "small book" (*biblidion*) is given to Hermas by a lady (who symbolizes the church). The lady "snatched it from his hand" in order to augment it with further words.[17] A book small enough to be held in one hand, to which additional material could be appended, and that is bequeathed by the church

12. McCormick, "Birth of the Codex," 155, suggests that "the author of 2 Timothy expected his audience to identify writings in the novel format [*membranas*] with St. Paul."

13. Pol. *Phil*. 12.1. On the date of the epistle, see Holmes, *Apostolic Fathers*, 275–76, and the sources cited there.

14. Papyrus was produced by splaying the stems of papyrus plants and cross-hatching and pressing the wet sides together, which, when dried, resulted in durable, paperlike writing material.

15. Parchment is a high-quality writing material made of animal hides (usually of sheep or goats) scraped clean of hair.

16. On the making and materials of scrolls, see Parker, *New Testament Manuscripts*, 13–14.

17. Herm. Vis. 2.1.4; 2.4.1–3.

(which by the second century was circulating its Scriptures only in codex form) implies a codex rather than a scroll.

Why Early Christians Preferred Codices

The foregoing survey considers all relevant evidence in the New Testament and Apostolic Fathers concerning the use of scrolls and codices in early Christianity. Although the evidence is not decisive, a preference for codices over scrolls seems evident in these early Christian writings. When we expand the survey to include all extant Hebrew and Greek manuscripts, however, a decisive picture emerges: virtually all extant ancient Jewish texts from the era under consideration exist as scrolls, and virtually all extant Christian texts from the same era exist as codices. In fact, in the words of Larry Hurtado, "About 95 percent of extant second-century AD non-Christian copies of literary texts are bookrolls, and about 5 percent are codices. But at least 75 percent of all second-century AD Christian manuscripts of any text are codices."[18]

In order to understand this distinct difference, let us first consider the Jewish preference for scrolls. The Dead Sea Scrolls at Qumran confirm with cast-iron certainty that the Old Testament and other ancient Jewish texts were written and disseminated in scroll form. The Essene community occupied the Qumran plateau on the northwest shore of the Dead Sea for roughly two centuries (ca. 130 BC to AD 70), during which time it produced and copied hundreds of Jewish texts. The Essenes "display[ed] an extraordinary interest in the writings of the ancients, singling out in particular those which made for the welfare of soul and body," declares Josephus.[19] Anticipating the Roman assault on Qumran following the destruction of Jerusalem in the First Revolt, the Essenes hid their library of scrolls in caves in the vicinity of their settlement.[20] There the scrolls remained untouched until their chance discovery in the late 1940s, when eleven caves around Qumran yielded nine hundred different Hebrew texts, two hundred of which were Old Testament texts. The remaining texts were related to the sectarian interests and practices of the Essenes themselves. The largest trove of documents was discovered in Cave 4, which contained some forty thousand scroll fragments. All the texts relate either to the Old Testament or to the customs and practices of the Essenes as a Jewish sect. No copies of New Testament documents appear in

18. Hurtado, *Destroyer of the Gods*, 134. Hurtado's judgment is based on research in the Leuven Database of Ancient Books.
19. *J.W.* 2.136 (LCL).
20. On the First Jewish Revolt, see ch. 7, pp. 103–6.

the Scrolls, nor do references to Jesus or any other New Testament figures or to specifically Christian doctrines. Most important for our present purposes, however, is that all Dead Sea Scrolls were written and preserved in scroll form.

The scroll was more than simply a preferred form for Jewish texts. Rather, as we discussed in chapter 4, the scroll enjoyed orthodox status; it was considered the *correct* format for the production, preservation, and dissemination of sacred Hebrew texts.[21] In order to qualify as a legitimate liturgical document in Judaism, a Torah text had to be written in Hebrew, in ink, and on a scroll.[22] The Hebrew content of the Jewish Scriptures was so wedded to the form of the scroll that Hebrew texts were generally not produced in codex form until the seventh century AD.[23]

Extant manuscripts of the New Testament and subsequent Christian writings, by contrast, are almost without exception preserved in book form. We do not know when the codex was invented, but the earliest reference in Judeo-Christian literature to something resembling it is the Hebrew word *'iggeret*, which appears a half-dozen times in 2 Chronicles, Nehemiah, and Esther.[24] An *'iggeret* was a letter written on "a special kind of tablet"[25] that Jews may have acquired during the exile, for each of the Old Testament documents in which *'iggeret* occurs is postexilic (i.e., post-500 BC). It is not certain that the codex descended from the *'iggeret*, but it is certain that the codex became the dominant form of written communication among Christians.

A survey of ancient Greek manuscripts reveals how indissolubly the Christian faith was yoked to the codex. There are some seven thousand extant Greek manuscript witnesses to the text of the Greek New Testament. Some of these manuscripts—Codex Sinaiticus or Codex Alexandrinus, for example—preserve the entire New Testament, but the vast majority preserve only portions or fragments of it. The earliest fragment of a canonical New Testament text is $\mathfrak{P}^{52}$, which preserves John 18:31–33 and 35–38, and it dates to about 135. The latest manuscripts and fragments date to the Renaissance. These New Testament texts "are almost without exception preserved in the manuscript form called the codex," states textual scholar D. C. Parker.[26] Indeed, of the thousands of extant witnesses to the text of the New Testament, all but

---

21. See ch. 4, pp. 71–72.
22. "[The Holy Scriptures (scrolls)] render the hand unclean only if they are written in the Assyrian [Hebrew] character, on leather, and in ink" (*m.* Yad. 4:5). Hebrew script, leather material, and ink medium were essential to qualify a Jewish text for public reading in a religious context. For discussion of this teaching, see Alexander, "Parting of the Ways," 12–13.
23. From an exhibition on the Hebrew scroll at the British Museum, 2016.
24. 2 Chron. 30:1; Neh. 2:7–9; 6:17, 19; Esther 9:29.
25. *HALOT* 1:11.
26. Parker, *New Testament Manuscripts*, 13.

three are in codex form.[27] The first word of the Greek New Testament, *biblos* (Matt. 1:1), designates a codex. The early church adopted the codex format so completely that *all* its texts, including the Septuagint, Josephus, and Philo (all three of which were copied and disseminated by Christian scribes) were transmitted in book form.[28]

The codex was also the format of choice for heterodox and heretical forms of Christianity. In 1945, two years before the discovery of the Dead Sea Scrolls, fifty-two Coptic texts bound in twelve separate volumes (plus eight leaves from a thirteenth volume) were recovered from the caves at Nag Hammadi, in the Nile River valley of Egypt. We do not know exactly when the Nag Hammadi codices were produced, but we know they were buried around the year 400 and, like the Dead Sea Scrolls, lay undisturbed for nearly two millennia. The Nag Hammadi texts are distinctly Gnostic and thus represent a heterodox expression of Christianity that was not embraced by the Christian tradition preserved in the New Testament and Apostolic Fathers. The particular relevance of the Nag Hammadi discovery for our discussion is that all fifty-two tractates were bound as codices. The production of the Nag Hammadi library in book form is revealing—for, as we have seen, Christian texts were virtually the only texts to be produced as codices until well into the second century. As a heterodox form of Christianity, the essential tenets of which were more indebted to Neoplatonism than to the New Testament, the Nag Hammadi community may have copied and disseminated its texts in codex form in order to conform to and gain acceptance within orthodox Christianity.[29]

The codex was the most revolutionary information technology that the world had seen. In the 80s of the first century, the Latin poet Martial, author of *Epigrams*, praised the "compactness" of the codex over the size and unwieldiness of the scroll. A Torah scroll required a large lectern on which to place it, like the hefty Torah stone recently discovered at the Magdala synagogue, on the west shore of the Sea of Galilee. Unlike a scroll, however, a codex could be held "in a single hand," as Martial acclaimed.[30] And there were further advantages. As one read a scroll written in a Semitic language, the right hand had to hold an increasingly large coil, which then had to be

---

27. The twenty-five-page Appendix I of Nestle-Aland[28] (pp. 792–819) preserves a complete list of Greek and Latin manuscript witnesses to the text of the New Testament, all of which are in codex form. In addition, "all of the papyri are in codex form, except for $\mathfrak{P}^{13}$, $\mathfrak{P}^{18}$, and $\mathfrak{P}^{43}$ (?)." Metzger, *Text of the New Testament*, 247.

28. See Kraft and Luijendijk, "Christianity's Rise," 183.

29. For a discussion of the contents of the Nag Hammadi library and its discovery, see *NHL* 1–25.

30. On Martial, see Reynolds and Wilson, *Scribes and Scholars*, 34–35; Parker, *New Testament Manuscripts*, 14–15.

rewound in the opposite direction before the scroll could be read again. A codex, however, could be opened and closed at any place, and its numbered pages afforded faster and easier access to information. A codex was also more capacious than a scroll since its pages were written on both sides. Its smaller size and lighter weight made it more portable than a scroll. As noted above, a codex could be expanded in size by appending additional pages, and lists of contents could be added along with new material, safeguarding the contents against illicit interpolations or additions. This latter aspect was especially advantageous when a codex contained documents considered authoritative and sacred. "No other philosophical or religious group of the time," writes Larry Hurtado, "exhibits an appropriation of the letterform" as seriously as did ancient Christian writers.[31] The codex played a particularly important role in disseminating such letters, whether as singular documents or as collections. So versatile was the codex that occasionally all New Testament documents were combined in a single codex. Whereas it would require multiple scrolls to reproduce the contents of the entire New Testament, a single codex—as both Codex Sinaiticus and Codex Alexandrinus demonstrate—could accommodate the entire New Testament between two covers. In sum, the codex reproduced information more manageably (and perhaps more cheaply) than did the scroll, providing Christian missionaries with an accessible, durable, and portable information vehicle for the written gospel.[32]

The British paleographer T. C. Skeat, whose studies of ancient texts achieve the highest standards of excellence, writes that "within a very short space of time [the papyrus codex] won acceptance as the only possible format for the Christian Scriptures."[33] C. H. Roberts corroborates Skeat's conclusion, stating that non-Christian literature very rarely occurs in codex form before the year 200, and only gradually thereafter, whereas 99 percent of Christian biblical fragments that were written in Egypt prior to that time appear in codices.[34] This implies that the Christian preference for the book form exceeded mere utility. Larry Hurtado rightly argues that Christians elected the codex as a distinguishing mark of their texts in the Roman world.

> Given the prominence of the bookroll for literary texts generally in the Roman era, early Christians must have been well aware that in preferring the codex they were at odds with the large book culture of the time. The bookroll was the prestige bookform of the day, and so, if Christians wanted to commend

31. Hurtado, *Destroyer of the Gods*, 121.
32. See Reynolds and Wilson, *Scribes and Scholars*, 35.
33. Skeat, "Early Christian Book-Production," 72.
34. Skeat, "Early Christian Book-Production," 69.

their texts to the wider culture, especially the texts that they read as scripture, it would seem an odd and counterintuitive choice to prefer the codex bookform for these texts. Indeed, it would seem like a deliberately countercultural move. . . . It certainly had the effect of distinguishing early Christian books physically, especially Christian copies of their sacred books.[35]

The codex afforded literary innovations helpful to Christian teaching and preaching. Early Christian manuscripts display an ingenious system, first introduced in Codex Alexandrinus (fifth century), for the comparative analysis of the four Gospels. In the early third century, Ammonius Saccas (175–242) divided each Gospel into numbered units (355 in Matthew, 233 in Mark, 342 in Luke, and 232 in John), on the basis of which he produced ten tables or "canons" that compared the numbered units in one Gospel with similar units in one, two, or all three of the other Gospels. The system was further perfected by Eusebius in the fourth century and became known as the "Eusebian Canons." The Canons would be virtually impossible to apply if the Gospels were written in scroll format. In codex format, however, the Canons afforded early Christians—and scholars still today—a sophisticated and effective means of Gospel analysis.[36]

A second innovation in early Christian codices may have been inspired by the Jewish Scriptures. The personal name of God in the Hebrew Old Testament consists of four consonants, YHWH (called the tetragrammaton), and no vowels—and is therefore unpronounceable. This is intentional, for if one cannot pronounce the word, one cannot take the word in vain—and thus violate the third commandment.[37] Already in the earliest Greek Christian manuscripts, we find something analogous with regard to the name of God, which is additionally extended to a select group of names and terms that are not contracted in Jewish (or pagan) writings. The four most common Christian "sacred names," *nomina sacra*, as they are called, are the Greek words for "God," "Lord," "Christ," and "Jesus," each of which is abbreviated to the first and last letters and placed beneath a horizontal line. By the Byzantine era, the number of *nomina sacra* had increased to some twenty words.[38] In time, Jews adopted the custom of *nomina sacra* from Christians, although with less frequency and for fewer words.[39] Unlike the tetragrammaton, however,

35. Hurtado, *Destroyer of the Gods*, 135–36. For a condensed version of Hurtado's treatment of scrolls and codices in early Christianity, see Hurtado, "Early Christian Dilemma," 54, 56, 66.

36. See Edwards, "Hermeneutical Significance of Chapter Divisions."

37. Exod. 20:7; Deut. 5:11.

38. For example: Spirit, mother, Savior, heaven, Son, Father, man, cross, David, Israel, Jerusalem, Theotokos, and names of apostles (esp. John, Peter, and Paul).

39. See Edwards, "*Nomen Sacrum* in the Sardis Synagogue"; Hengel, *Four Gospels and the One Gospel*, 280, 479n.

which was written unconventionally because it was considered too significant to be pronounced, *nomina sacra* were written unconventionally in order to accentuate their pronunciation. *Nomina sacra* identified the load-bearing vocabulary, both devotional and theological, of the new Christian faith, signaling its unique eschatological character. Along with the unprecedented shift in the Christian holy day from Sabbath to Sunday, and the use of the codex rather than the scroll, *nomina sacra* witnessed to the uniqueness and autonomy of the nascent church from the Jewish synagogue.[40]

The Codex and the New Testament Canon

Justin Martyr describes a Sunday worship service consisting of reading "the memoirs of the apostles and the writings of the prophets," praying, and celebrating a thanksgiving service of bread and wine (the Eucharist).[41] Like the Hebrew and Greek versions of the Old Testament, Justin groups "the writings of the prophets" with the historical books (Joshua through 2 Kings). That the Old Testament remained a staple in early Christian worship is no surprise, for the New Testament (especially the Gospels, Romans, Galatians, and Hebrews) and the Apostolic Fathers (especially 1–2 Clement and Barnabas) quote extensively from the Old Testament. Had the Old Testament not been read regularly in worship, early Christians could not have understood the gospel, which presupposes the Old Testament so thoroughly. A book receptacle was required for "the memoirs of the apostles and the writings of the prophets" that were regularly read in public worship. A mosaic in the fifth-century Mausoleum of Galla Placidia in Ravenna, Italy, depicts such a receptacle in detail. The receptacle, technically known as a *scrinium*, was an early Christian book chest modeled on a synagogue Torah shrine. The Galla Placidia mosaic depicts the book chest with opened doors, displaying four thick codices: the Gospels of Mark and Luke on the top shelf, and Matthew and John on the bottom shelf.[42]

A brief overview of the literary productivity of the early church by the year 100 aids our understanding of the importance of such book chests. At the end of the first century, rabbinic scholars were in the process of determining the contents and limits of the three main divisions of the Jewish Scriptures—Torah, Prophets, and Writings. One purpose of the process was to safeguard the integrity of the

---

40. Hengel, *Four Gospels and the One Gospel*, 119.

41. Justin, *1 Apol.* 67 (*ANF* 1:186). See also ch. 12 above, p. 222.

42. For a photograph and description of the book-chest mosaic, see Lowden, *Early Christian and Byzantine Art*, 109. See also Helmut Buschhausen, "Box," *EEECAA* 1:210; *EEECAA* vol. 3, plate 13.

Jewish textual tradition from the inclusion of Christian texts, which the rabbis regarded as heretical. Traces of a similar process are also evident in Christianity around the same time. The reference to a collection of Pauline letters in 2 Peter 3:15–16 assumes their received status in Christian circles. Likewise, Polycarp's reference to "the Sacred Scriptures" in the early second century[43] and Justin's mention of "the memoirs of the apostles and the writings of the prophets" in the mid-second century are evidence of the growing authority of a core body of documents in Jerusalem, Asia Minor, and Rome. This winnowing process was neither formal nor final nor superintended by church officials. It was influenced, rather, by the same essential criteria that had been operative from the outset of the Christian movement—namely, the primacy of the words of Jesus and the testimony of the apostles. Justin's reference to "the memoirs of the apostles" assumes and asserts these criteria. The Greek word for "memoirs," *hypomnēmata*, meaning "recollections" or "testimonies," locates the guideline in the functional authority of the apostolic witness to Jesus's teaching and acts.[44]

Justin was a witness to, rather than an inventor of, this functional authority. The writings that were eventually included in what became the New Testament presuppose a similar authority that was operative in the Jewish scriptural tradition before them. The vast majority of quotations in the New Testament come from the thirty-nine books that now make up the Old Testament (these quotations usually follow the Septuagint more closely than the Hebrew). The deuterocanonical books (Apocrypha) are quoted much less frequently, and the Pseudepigrapha even less.[45] This is clear evidence of the functional authority of the Old Testament (especially in the Septuagint translation) for New Testament writers, and of these writers' profound knowledge of it and commitment to it. Similarly, a vast majority of quotations in the Apostolic Fathers are from texts that would later compose the New Testament canon, although the fathers are even more closely bound to these texts than the New Testament writers are to the Septuagint. Within the roughly fifteen documents that make up the Apostolic Fathers (composed between the years 75 and 150), nearly every document that would later be included in the New Testament canon is referred to as an authority (only Philemon and 2 John do not appear). In the entire corpus of the fathers, there are only six references to texts that do not belong to either the Septuagint or the body of texts that would eventually

43. Pol. *Phil.* 12.1.
44. Hurtado, *Destroyer of the Gods*, 115.
45. Appendix III of *Nestle-Aland*[28] is a comprehensive list of citations and allusions appearing in the Greek New Testament. The appendix has sixty-three columns of quotations from the thirty-nine books of the canonical Old Testament. Compare that to its eleven and seven columns of quotations, respectively, from the Apocrypha and Pseudepigrapha.

compose the New Testament.[46] This means that most of the documents that
would be declared canonical by the church in the fourth century were, already
in the early second century, widely accepted as authoritative tradition. It was
this authoritative tradition that Justin refers to as "the memoirs of the apostles
and the prophets." By the first half of the second century, in other words, the
Apostolic Fathers were, with very few exceptions, appropriating a corpus of
texts that would, in the fourth century, be acknowledged as "canonical," and
that we today recognize as the Old and New Testaments.

With this in mind, we may return to the significance of the *scrinium*, the
book chest depicted in the mosaic of Galla Placidia. Similar to the holy place
of the temple (which was furnished with table and lampstand) and to the
Torah shrines in synagogues, early churches were furnished with a book chest
containing "the memoirs of the apostles and the writings of the prophets" for
the aid of lectors and preachers. The Gospels of the Galla Placidia mosaic are
the same four that emerged as canonical in Christianity. The lion, ox, man,
and eagle of Revelation 4:7 appear in the same order and number as their
corresponding Gospels in the Galla Placidia *scrinum* mosaic—Mark, Luke,
Matthew, and John. The four creatures, with eyes all around, are the all-seeing
witnesses to the incarnate Word in John's community in Asia Minor at the end
of the first century. The *scrinium* of the early church was thus an important
early step in the acknowledgment of the authority of the four Gospels in the
church and their eventual canonization.[47]

In conclusion, the material form of the codex became as fundamental for
Christian texts as the material form of the scroll was and is for Jewish religious
and liturgical texts. The practicality of the codex was demonstrably superior to
that of the scroll, but this alone did not account for its near exclusive preference
by the church. The codex became the signature material form with which Christians chose to identify. The codex afforded the church a unique format with which
it could employ a system of comparative analysis of the four Gospels (known as
the Eusebian Canons). And Christian codices were distinguished by some two
dozen *nomina sacra* that signified, by means of a unique shorthand, vocabulary
sacred to Christians. Finally, the book chests in which Christian codices were
gathered and preserved for use in worship spaces not only distinguish the documents that the early church deemed essential for its corporate life but also attest
to the initial steps of the Christian church in determining its canon of Scriptures.

---

46. First Enoch is cited twice, 2 Baruch once, 4 Ezra twice, and the Gospel of Thomas once.
For a complete list of texts cited or alluded to in the Apostolic Fathers, see Holmes, *Apostolic
Fathers*, 791–98.

47. On the significance of the Christian book chest, see Hengel, *Four Gospels and the One
Gospel*, 116–18.

Conclusion

New Wine in New Wineskins

The transitions from the Jesus movement to the Christian church that we have traced in this book were largely accomplished between the death of Jesus and the death of Ignatius of Antioch. These seventy-five years witnessed the greatest and most formative changes in the history of Christianity. The changes did not happen either simultaneously or sequentially, and they were not the result of a centralized plan of any person or party in the early church. Like the various plant and animal life forms that are attracted to and nourished by a water source, the changes were organic responses of the early church to its conviction of the preeminence of Jesus Christ and the mission consciousness (which necessarily resulted from the preeminence of Christ) to proclaim the gospel to all nations.[1] Not only did the changes occur in a remarkably brief time span, but they were the greater because they were accomplished

- not when the church enjoyed power but when it was largely powerless and was beset by obstacles and opposition from many quarters;
- not when the church was driven by an overarching and uniting architectural vision but when it was a disparate movement in various lands and languages of the ancient world; and
- not when the church enjoyed a single formative leader but when it was a grassroots movement of charismatic and itinerant missionaries, preachers, and pastors.

1. Matt 28:19–20; Acts 1:8.

Christianity was born at a time when two great luminaries dominated the ancient world: the Roman Empire and the Jewish religious and cultural tradition. Both luminaries influenced the church's development, but the latter far outshone the former in lighting the way for earliest Christianity. Jesus was born and reared as a son of Israel, as were his early disciples and followers and the people to whom he ministered in Galilee and Jerusalem. The living water of Jesus's ministry had its wellsprings in the Old Testament witness to Israel, including his all-important gentile ministry, which was foundational for the eventual separation of Jesus followers from Judaism. Even though Jesus followers diverged from the synagogue on the issue of the full inclusion of gentiles, and further distinguished themselves with their confession of Jesus as Israel's long-awaited Messiah, they did not cease to think of themselves as due heirs of God's promises to Israel. The early church parted ways with Judaism, but it did not part ways with the foundational story of the Old Testament, which determined its theological genetic code. A full century into the Christian movement, Justin Martyr rebuked Jews for persecuting Christians and, in the next breath, extolled the Jewish Scriptures for preparing the way for Jesus "our Christ."[2] Following the First Revolt, Jewish academies in Galilee attempted to reconstruct Judaism on the basis of a meticulous interpretation of Old Testament law. At the same time, early Christianity increasingly identified its story with the Old Testament prophets, above all with the messianic hope and inauguration of a new covenant, which it saw fulfilled in the life, death, and resurrection of Jesus.

The success of Christianity thus did not consist in moving away from its inheritance in Israel but, rather, in extending its inheritance to include the gentile world as well. The success was due to many factors; one of the most important (but least recognized) was the extent of time it took. The crowning event we normally associate with the "success" of Christianity was its adoption by the Roman Empire in the fourth century, but a full three centuries transpired between the death and resurrection of Jesus and that event. In that long interlude, Christianity remained largely in the shadow of the greater Roman and Jewish luminaries, growing and preparing itself for survival. The scarcity of attention it received in those shadow centuries testifies to the fact that neither Rome nor Judaism thought it very significant or likely to survive.

The fact that Christianity survived is, of course, remarkable. But it did more than survive. It also adapted. Something in its heart and essence required such adaptations, or Christianity would not have remained Christianity. From

2. *1 Apol.* 31.5–6.

its very inception, "the Way" displayed a genius of *incorporating* itself in a variety of institutional forms that attracted a growing number of believers, in fulfillment of its universal mission. In its first seventy-five years, the church showed itself capable of greater change than either Judaism or Rome was capable of, yet it remained characterized throughout by the unchanging constant of the gospel. The gospel reached a wider array of first-century society, worked its way into more diverse social strata, than did the teachings and dogmas of any other association or cult or even the politics of the Roman Empire itself; and it did so without compromising or sacrificing its essence. The genius of early Christianity in this respect was its ability to be adaptive without becoming captive. It has frequently been said that "the church must change in order to remain the same."[3] This is a seminal insight, although it mistakes the church as the constant. The true constant is the gospel, the kerygma rather than the church.[4] As we have seen in the course of our study, with the exception of the gentile question, early sources reflect very little on Christianity's cataclysmic changes in its first seventy-five years. This was due to the fact that, for early Christians, the *unseen* reality, "the faith once delivered to the saints" (Jude 3), was the formative reality, and thus the reality of ultimate importance. Eusebius attests to this formative reality in saying that the church flourished because "it ever held to the same points in the same ways."[5]

The kerygma is the straightforward story of salvation that begins with the promises of God in Israel and culminates in the life, death, and resurrection of Jesus. No figure in the Greco-Roman world, and no figure in the history of Israel, influenced either the pagan or Jewish worlds anywhere nearly as completely as Jesus Christ influenced the "third race" of Christians. This conclusion is not a denigration of ancient pagan or Jewish leaders; it is merely a recognition that Christians made claims about Jesus that Romans and Jews never made of even their most revered leaders—indeed, claims that no other religion has made of its founder. The kerygma itself could be boiled down to two words: *kyrios Iēsous*, "Jesus is Lord" (the earliest known formula of Christianity). Without Jesus Christ, there would have been no "third race" of Christians. Even if a similar "race" had arisen, following any messiah other

3. This saying, frequently quoted by modern theologians, including Pope Benedict XVI, was been variously attributed to the Orthodox theologian Alexander Schmemann or, earlier, to the Catholic theologian John Henry Newman.

4. "The guiding line [of a history of earliest Christianity]," Hengel writes, "is, in my opinion, the *development of Christology* and only in the second place the growth of church organization. Faith, not social structure, was the propelling power." *Studien zum Urchristentum*, 309–10 (my trans.; italics original).

5. *Hist. eccl.* 4.7.13–14 (LCL).

than *kyrios Iēsous*, it would have been absorbed into Judaism, or it would have perished—as did many variants of Christianity in the early centuries. Jesus Christ is Christianity, and Christianity is Jesus Christ; and when Christianity becomes anything other than Jesus Christ, it ceases being. In the succeeding centuries, and not least today, when Christianity has been or is reduced to mere moral principles or moral values, or when it is made a "spiritual" component of an overarching ideological or political program, or when it is used as a force for domination, as something coercive, then its defamation results in its denial.

A century after the death of Jesus, his followers—including Papias and Irenaeus—proudly traced the lineage of their teachers and their teachers' teachers back to the apostles and to Jesus himself. Still later, Eusebius began his massive *Ecclesiastical History* with the declaration that, as the preexistent and divine Logos, Jesus Christ is the manifestation of the one, holy, and sovereign God of Israel.[6] Here again, the kerygma of the church extended the story of Israel beyond Israel to the world. The early Christian confession that "Jesus is Lord" globalized the monotheism of provincial Israel. The genius of the paradox of adaptivity without captivity is again apparent. Christianity embraces everything without becoming everything. It goes to the ends of the earth without becoming rootless. It thrives within complexity and multiplicity, yet its core message remains ever simple: there is one by whom all things were made, in whom they exist, and for whom they are destined; and his name is above every other name—Jesus Christ (Phil. 2:9). All things have been summed up in Christ (Eph. 1:10).

The ability of the first Jesus followers to encapsulate the story of salvation in a clear and concise summary put a public face on the gospel that distinguished it from sequestered Judaism, secretive mystery cults, and predictably conventional Roman religion. The public face of the gospel was the church, and the peculiarity of the church was the result of the particularity of Jesus Christ. Jesus Christ is the new wine, and the church is the new wineskin. The wine does not conform to the wineskin; the supple wineskin, rather, expands to accommodate the wine. The church embodies the gospel only by conforming to it. The early church, like the synagogue, became the mobile embodiment of the faith proclaimed, taking root wherever believers heard and received the gospel. But the suppleness of the church exceeded that of the synagogue, for the church included—as equals!—believers who were not so included in synagogues: uncircumcised gentiles, the "impure" and "unclean," women, slaves, and other outcasts. The church bore witness to

6. *Hist. eccl.* 1.1–4.

the gospel not only by proclamation, mission, and catechesis but also, and equally, by a commitment to *lived faith*. For Greco-Roman cults, morality was suggestive and relative, depending on the various cults and deities revered. For Christianity, moral integrity consisted in the transformation of behavior and character in accordance with the image of Christ, and such transformation—like faith itself—was unconditional. This transformation was signified by *conversion*, which called believers not simply to include the Christian Way as one way among others in their lives but to embrace it wholly, to become so wholly embraced by it that all other "ways" were forsaken.

Lived faith was the truest reflection of the way of Jesus. Lived faith expressed itself in communities of called-out believers that gathered weekly for Sunday worship. Christian communities were characterized by social egalitarianism of men, women, children, and slaves (Gal. 3:26), hospitality to outsiders (Heb 13:2), and common meals, including the Eucharist (Acts 2:42). The gospel joined believers into a family that superseded families determined by biology, sociology, or polity. The new family was characterized by an ethos of mercy, and mercy—although it also characterizes the Old Testament, especially the Psalms—was absent from Greco-Roman religious expressions. Mercy was demonstrated in caring for widows and orphans, for the needy and poor, as enjoined by Jesus himself (Matt. 25:31–46). The exceptional role that women enjoyed in the early church, and the mercy—although unfortunately not the liberation—shown to slaves, equally signified the lived faith of early Christianity.

The most peculiar aspect of the early church was its missional consciousness. And a unique facet of that consciousness was its literary productivity—which, in less than a century, produced the New Testament and the writings of the Apostolic Fathers. These texts filled a vacuum left by a plummet in secular Greek literary output in the first century. And in the following centuries, the thousands of pages of Christian writings from the apologists and church fathers overtook the then-revived pagan Greek literature. The most distinctive achievement of the church's missional consciousness was, of course, its geographical expansion. Within the first century, this sense of mission propelled the gospel "to the limits of the west" (a possible reference to Spain);[7] all across the southern coast of the Mediterranean Sea, in North Africa; and east all the way to India, and perhaps farther. Even the meteoric conquest of Alexander the Great did not equal the extent of early Christian expansion, which was without parallel in the ancient world.

7. 1 Clem. 5.7; Rom. 15:24.

The particularity of Jesus Christ and the peculiarity of the Christian church wrought something new in the world that is still present today. The "third race" of the first century has grown into a worldwide community of Jesus followers in the twenty-first century. And yet, perhaps more than in any intervening era, the church today (even in the astounding variety of its manifestations around the globe) stands in a position analogous to the church in the first century. The first century required Jesus followers to define and propagate the gospel in a culture defined primarily by the pagentry, pantheon, and power of Rome; the twenty-first century requires Jesus followers, certainly in the West, to define and propagate the gospel in a culture of pervasive materialism and secularism, the chief hallmarks of which are personal pleasure and prosperity.

In every age, the church must learn from the past, as the first Christians themselves learned from Israel, in order rightly to hear the word of God for its own day. I close with an inimitable testimony from the past that witnesses to the major developments in Christianity that we have considered in this book, and that also may be a prophetic word to the church today, from the Apology of Aristides. Writing in the early second century, Aristides, an Athenian philosopher, celebrates in his day what Jesus followers also celebrate in ours: the particularity of Christology and the peculiarity of the church.

> Christians trace their origin from the Lord Jesus Christ who is acknowledged by the Holy Spirit to be the son of the most high God, who came down from heaven for the salvation of humanity. Being born of a pure virgin, unbegotten and immaculate, Christ assumed flesh and revealed himself among people that he might recall them to himself from their wanderings after many gods. After accomplishing his new order, by a voluntary choice he tasted death on the cross. After three days he came to life again and ascended into heaven.
>
> He had twelve disciples, who after his ascension went forth into the provinces of the whole world and declared his greatness. His followers have the commands of the Lord Jesus Christ himself graven on their hearts; and they observe them, looking forward to the resurrection of the dead and life in the world to come. They do not commit adultery or fornication, nor bear false witness, nor covet the things of others; they honor father and mother, and love their neighbors; they judge justly, and they never do to others what they would not wish to happen to themselves; they appeal to those who injure them, and try to win them as friends; they are eager to do good to their enemies; they are gentle and easily reconciled; they abstain from all unlawful conversation and from all impurity; they despise not the widow, nor oppress the orphan; and whoever has, gives ungrudgingly for the maintenance of the one who has not. If they see a stranger, they take him under their roof, and rejoice over him as over a true brother, for they call themselves brethren not after the flesh but after

the spirit. They are ready to sacrifice their lives for the sake of Christ, for they observe his commandments without swerving, and live holy and just lives, as the Lord God appointed for them. Truly then, this is the way of the truth that leads those who travel therein to the everlasting kingdom promised through Christ in the life to come.[8]

---

8. Aristides, *Apol.* 15–16 (*ANF* alt.). See D. M. Kay, "The Apology of Aristides the Philosopher," *ANF* 10:257–79. For an account of the discovery of the apology at the Monastery of St. Catherine in 1889 by J. Rendel Harris, see Soskice, *Sisters of Sinai*, 101. For a discussion of its content, see Quasten, *Patrology*, 1:191–95. Regarding its date, the apology was addressed either to emperor Hadrian (r. 117–138) (so Eusebius, *Hist. eccl.* 4.3.3; Jerome, *Vir. ill.* 20; D. M. Kay, *ANF* 10:261) or, more probably, to emperor Antoninus Pius, in the early years of his reign (138–47) (so Harnack, *Geschichte der altchristlichen Literatur*, vol. 1, part 1, 96–99; Metzger, *Canon*, 127–28).

Bibliography

Aland, Kurt. *Did the Early Church Baptize Infants?* Translated by G. R. Beasley-Murray. Eugene, OR: Wipf & Stock, 2004.

Alexander, Philip S. "'The Parting of the Ways' from the Perspective of Rabbinic Judaism." In *Jews and Christians: The Parting of the Ways, A.D. 70 to 135*, edited by James D. G. Dunn, 1–25. Grand Rapids: Eerdmans, 1999.

Bacchiocchi, Samuele. *From Sabbath to Sunday: A Historical Investigation of the Rise of Sunday Observance in Early Christianity*. Rome: Pontifical Gregorian University, 1977.

Bainton, Roland H., *Early Christianity*. New York: D. van Nostrand, 1960.

Barclay, John M. G. *Pauline Churches and Diaspora Jews*. Grand Rapids: Eerdmans, 2016.

Barrett, C. K. *The New Testament Background: Selected Documents*. New York: Harper & Row, 1961.

Bauckham, Richard. *The Christian World around the New Testament*. Grand Rapids: Baker Academic, 2017.

Bauer, Martin. *Anfänge der Christenheit: Von Jesus von Nazareth zur frühchristlichen Kirche*. 6th ed. Berlin: Evangelische Verlagsanstalt, 1981.

Bauer, Walter. *Orthodoxy and Heresy in Earliest Christianity*. 2nd ed. Edited by Robert A. Kraft and Gerhard Krodel. Philadelphia: Fortress, 1971.

———. *Rechtgläubigkeit und Ketzerei im ältesten Christentum*. 2nd ed. Edited by Georg Strecker and Gerhard Ebeling. BHT 10. Tübingen: Mohr Siebeck, 1964.

Beard, Mary. *SPQR: A History of Ancient Rome*. New York: Liveright, 2015.

Beasley-Murray, G. R. *Baptism in the New Testament*. Grand Rapids: Eerdmans, 1962.

Berger, Klaus. *Die Urchristen: Gründerjahre einer Weltreligion*. Munich: Pattloch, 2008.

Berthelot, Katell. "The Paradoxical Similarities between the Jews and the Roman Other." In *Perceiving the Other in Ancient Judaism and Early Christianity*, edited by M. Siegal, W. Grünstäudl, and M. Thiessen, 95–109. WUNT 394. Tübingen: Mohr Siebeck, 2017.

Bickerman, Elias. *The Jews in the Greek Age*. Cambridge, MA: Harvard University Press, 1988.

Boatswain, Tim, and Colin Nicolson. *A Traveller's History of Greece*. 5th ed. New York: Interlink Books, 2004.

Bockmuehl, Markus. *Simon Peter in Scripture and Memory: The New Testament Apostle in the Early Church*. Grand Rapids: Baker Academic, 2012.

Boughton, L. C. "'Being Shed for You/ Many': Time-Sense and Consequences in the Synoptic Cup Citations." *Tyndale Bulletin* 48 (1997): 249–270.

Boulton, Matthew Meyer. "Supersession or Subsession? Exodus Typology, the Christian Eucharist and the Jewish Passover Meal." *SJT* 66, no. 1 (2013): 18–29.

Bourke, Stephen. "The Christian Flight to Pella: True or Tale?" *BAR* 39, no. 3 (2013): 30–39, 70–71.

Boyarin, Daniel. "The Parables of Enoch and the Foundation of the Rabbinic Sect: A Hypothesis." In *"The Words of a Wise Man's Mouth Are Gracious" (Qoh 10,12): Festschrift for Günter Stemberger on the Occasion of His 65th Birthday*, edited by Mauro Perani, 53–72. Berlin: de Gruyter, 2005.

Breytenbach, Cilliers, and Christiane Zimmermann. *Early Christianity in Lycaonia and Adjacent Areas: From Paul to Amphilochius of Iconium*. Early Christianity in Asia Minor 2. Ancient Judaism and Early Christianity 101. Leiden and Boston: Brill, 2018.

Brock, Sebastian. *An Introduction to Syriac Studies*. 2nd ed. Gorgias Handbooks 4. Piscataway, NJ: Gorgias, 2006.

Brown, Peter. *The Body and Society: Men, Women, and Sexual Renunciation in Early Christianity*. New York: Columbia University Press, 1988.

Bruce, F. F. *Peter, Stephen, James, and John: Studies in Early Non-Pauline Christianity*. Grand Rapids: Eerdmans, 1979.

Burkitt, F. Crawford. *Early Eastern Christianity: St. Margaret's Lectures 1904 on the Syriac-Speaking Church*. London: John Murray, 1904.

Butterworth, G. W. "Appendix on the Greek Mysteries." In *Clement of Alexandria*, edited by G. W. Butterworth, 379–90. LCL 92. Cambridge, MA: Harvard University Press. First published 1919.

Caird, G. B. *A Commentary on the Revelation of St. John the Divine*. HNTC. New York: Harper & Row, 1966.

Chadwick, Henry. *The Early Church*. Penguin History of the Church 1. Baltimore: Penguin Books, 1967.

Chester, Andrew. "The Parting of the Ways: Eschatology and Messianic Hope." In *Jews and Christians: The Parting of the Ways, A.D. 70 to 135*, edited by James D. G. Dunn, 239–314. Grand Rapids: Eerdmans, 1999.

Chilton, Bruce. "The Godfearers: From the Gospels to Aphrodisias." In *Partings: How Judaism and Christianity Became Two*, edited by Hershel Shanks, 55–71. Washington, DC: Biblical Archaeology Society, 2013.

Choat, Malcolm, Jitse Dijkstra, Christopher Haas, and William Tabbernee. "The World of the Nile." In *Early Christianity in Contexts: An Exploration across Cultures and Continents*, edited by William Tabbernee, 181–222. Grand Rapids: Baker Academic, 2014.

Cochrane, Charles Norris. *Christianity and Classical Culture: A Study of Thought and Action from Augustus to Augustine*. New York: Oxford University Press, 1957.

Cohen, Shaye. "In Between: Jewish-Christians and the Curse of the Heretics." In *Partings: How Judaism and Christianity Became Two*, edited by Hershel Shanks, 207–36. Washington, DC: Biblical Archaeology Society, 2013.

Cullmann, Oscar. *The Christology of the New Testament*. Translated by Shirley Guthrie and Charles Hall. Philadelphia: Westminster, 1963.

Cureton, William, trans. and ed. *Ancient Syriac Documents*. Amsterdam: Oriental Press, 1967. First published, London: Williams & Norgate, 1864.

Dalman, Gustaf. *Jesus Christ in the Talmud, Midrash, Zohar, and the Liturgy of the Synagogue*. Cambridge: Deighton, Bell, & Co., 1893.

Danby, Herbert. *The Mishnah*. Oxford: Oxford University Press, 1977.

Davies, J. G. *The Early Christian Church*. Garden City, NY: Doubleday Anchor Books, 1967.

Deissmann, Adolf. *Light from the Ancient East*. Translated by Lionel Strachen. Grand Rapids: Baker, 1978.

Doering, Lutz. *Ancient Jewish Letters and the Beginnings of Christian Epistolography*. WUNT 298. Tübingen: Mohr Siebeck, 2012.

Duchesne, Louis. *Early History of the Christian Church: From Its Foundations to the End of the Third Century*. Translated from the 4th French ed. New York: Longmans, Green, 1909.

Duff, Paul B. *Jesus Followers in the Roman Empire*. Grand Rapids: Eerdmans, 2017.

Dunn, James D. G. "From the Crucifixion to the End of the First Century." In *Partings: How Judaism and Christianity Became Two*, edited by Hershel Shanks, 27–53. Washington, DC: Biblical Archaeology Society, 2013.

———. *Neither Jew nor Greek: A Contested Identity*. Christianity in the Making 3. Grand Rapids: Eerdmans, 2015.

———. "Why and How Did Embryonic Christianity Expand beyond the Jewish People?" In *The Rise and Expansion of Christianity in the First Three Centuries of the Common Era*, edited by Clare K. Rothschild and Jens Schröter, 183–204. WUNT 301. Tübingen: Mohr Siebeck, 2013.

Edwards, James R. "Archaeology Gives New Reality to Paul's Ephesus Riot." *BAR* 42, no. 4 (2016): 24–32, 62.

———. *Between the Swastika and the Sickle: The Life, Disappearance, and Execution of Ernst Lohmeyer*. Grand Rapids: Eerdmans, 2019.

———. "Galatians 5:12: Circumcision, the Mother Goddess, and the Scandal of the Cross." *Novum Testamentum* 53 (2011): 319–37.

———. *The Gospel according to Luke*. PNTC. Grand Rapids: Eerdmans, 2015.

———. *The Hebrew Gospel and the Development of the Synoptic Tradition*. Grand Rapids: Eerdmans, 2009.

———. "The Hermeneutical Significance of Chapter Divisions in Ancient Gospel Manuscripts." *NTS* 56, no. 3 (2010): 413–26.

———. *Is Jesus the Only Savior?* Grand Rapids: Eerdmans, 2005.

———. "A *Nomen Sacrum* in the Sardis Synagogue." *JBL* 128, no. 4 (2009): 813–21.

———. "'Public Theology' in Luke-Acts: The Witness of the Gospel to Powers and Authorities." *New Testament Studies* 62, no. 2 (2016): 227–52.

———. "The Rider on the White Horse, the Thigh Inscription, and Apollo: Revelation 19:16." *JBL* 137, no. 2 (2018): 519–36.

———. *Romans*. NIBCNT 6. Peabody, MA: Hendrickson, 1992.

———. "The Servant of the Lord and the Gospel of Mark." In *Biblical Interpretation in Early Christian Gospels*. Vol. 1, *The Gospel of Mark*, edited by Thomas R. Hatina, 49–63. LNTS 304. London: T&T Clark, 2006.

———. "The Son of God: Its Antecedents in Judaism and Hellenism and Its Use in the Earliest Gospel." PhD diss., Fuller Theological Seminary, 1978.

Ehrman, Bart D. *Jesus, Interrupted: Revealing the Hidden Contradictions in the Bible (and Why We Don't Know about Them)*. New York: HarperCollins, 2009.

Eusebius. *Ecclesiastical History*. Vol. 1, translated by Kirsopp Lake. LCL 153. Cambridge, MA: Harvard University Press, 1926.

Evans, Craig A. *From Jesus to the Church: The First Christian Generation*. Louisville: Westminster John Knox, 2014.

Fox, Robin Lane. *The Classical World: An Epic History from Homer to Hadrian*. New York: Basic Books, 2006.

———. *Pagans and Christians*. New York: Knopf, 1989.

Frankopan, Peter. *The Silk Roads: A New History of the World*. New York: Vintage Books, 2017.

Fredriksen, Paula. "Did Jesus Oppose the Purity Laws?" *BRev* 11, no. 3 (1995): 18–25, 42–45.

———. *When Christians Were Jews: The First Generation*. New Haven: Yale University Press, 2018.

Frend, W. H. C. *The Rise of Christianity*. Philadelphia: Fortress, 1984.

Freyne, Seán. *The Jesus Movement and Its Expansion: Meaning and Mission*. Grand Rapids: Eerdmans, 2014.

Froehlich, Karlfried, trans. and ed. *Biblical Interpretation in the Early Church*. Sources of Early Christian Thought. Philadelphia: Fortress, 1984.

García Martínez, F. "Messianische Erwartungen in den Qumranschriften." In *Der Messias*, 171–208. *JBTh* 8. Göttingen: Vandenhoeck & Reprecht, 1993.

Geraty, Lawrence. "From Sabbath to Sunday: Why, How and When?" In *Partings: How Judaism and Christianity Became Two*, edited by Hershel Shanks, 255–68. Washington, DC: Biblical Archaeology Society, 2013.

Gingras, George E. *Egeria: Diary of a Pilgrimage*. Ancient Christian Writers 38. New York: Newman, 1970.

Goguel, Maurice. *The Birth of Christianity*. Translated by H. C. Snape. London: George Allen & Unwin, 1953.

Goldsworthy, Adrian. *Pax Romana: War, Peace and Conquest in the Roman World*. New Haven: Yale University Press, 2016.

Goodman, Martin. "Diaspora Reactions to the Destruction of the Temple." In *Jews and Christians: The Parting of the Ways, A.D. 70 to 135*, edited by James D. G. Dunn, 27–38. Grand Rapids: Eerdmans, 1999.

Goppelt, Leonard. *Apostolic and Post-Apostolic Times*. Translated by Robert A. Guelich. Grand Rapids: Baker, 1970.

Grant, Frederick C. *Roman Hellenism and the New Testament*. New York: Scribner's Sons, 1962.

Grant, Robert M. *After the New Testament*. Philadelphia: Fortress, 1967.

———. *Gnosticism and Early Christianity*. New York: Columbia University Press, 1959.

Grillmeier, Aloys, SJ. *Christ in Christian Tradition: From the Apostolic Age to Chalcedon (451)*. New York: Sheed & Ward, 1965.

Guder, Darrell L. *Be My Witnesses: The Church's Mission, Message, and Messengers*. Grand Rapids: Eerdmans, 1985.

———. *The Incarnation and the Church's Witness*. Eugene, OR: Wipf & Stock, 1999.

Gwatkin, Henry Melvill. *Selections from Early Writers Illustrative of Church History to the Time of Constantine*. London: Macmillan, 1911.

Haas, Christopher. "The Caucasus." In *Early Christianity in Contexts: An Exploration across Cultures and Continents*, edited by William Tabbernee, 111–44. Grand Rapids: Baker Academic, 2014.

Halton, Thomas P., trans. *Saint Jerome: On Illustrious Men*. Fathers of the Church 100. Washington, DC: Catholic University Press of America, 1999.

Harnack, Adolf. *Geschichte der altchristlichen Literatur bis Eusebius*. 2nd ed. 4 vols. Leipzig: Hinrichs, 1958.

———. *The Mission and Expansion of Christianity in the First Three Centuries*. Translated by James Moffatt. New York: Harper Torchbooks, 1962.

———. *Die Mission und Ausbreitung des Christentums in den ersten drei Jahrhunderten*. 4th ed. 2 vols. Leipzig: Hinrichs, 1924.

Hartog, Paul A., ed. *Orthodoxy and Heresy in Early Christian Contexts: Reconsidering the Bauer Thesis*. Eugene, OR: Pickwick, 2015.

Harvey, Paul, ed. *The Oxford Companion to Classical Literature*. Oxford: Clarendon, 1966.

Harvey, Susan Ashbrook. "Antioch and Christianity." In *Antioch: The Lost Ancient City*, edited by Christine Kondoleon, 39–48. Princeton: Princeton University Press, 2000.

Hatch, Edwin. *The Influence of Greek Ideas on Christianity*. New York: Harper Torchbooks, 1957.

Hellholm, David, Tor Vegge, Øyvind Nor-derval, and Christer Hellholm, eds. *Ablution, Initiation, and Baptism: Late Antiquity, Early Judaism, and Early Christianity*. 3 vols. BZNW 176. Berlin: de Gruyter, 2011.

Hengel, Martin. *Acts and the History of Earliest Christianity*. Translated by John Bowden. Philadelphia: Fortress, 1979.

———. *Between Jesus and Paul*. London: SCM, 1983.

———. *The Four Gospels and the One Gospel of Jesus Christ*. Translated by John Bowden. Harrisburg, PA: Trinity Press International, 2000.

———. *Paulus und Jakobus*. Vol. 3 of *Kleine Schriften*. Tübingen: Mohr Siebeck, 2002.

———. *Saint Peter: The Underestimated Apostle*. Translated by Thomas Trapp. Grand Rapids: Eerdmans, 2010.

———. "The Septuagint as a Collection of Writings Claimed by Christians." In *Jews and Christians: The Parting of the Ways, A.D. 70 to 135*, edited by James D. G. Dunn, 39–83. Grand Rapids: Eerdmans, 1999.

———. *The Septuagint as Christian Scripture: Its Prehistory and the Problem of Its Canon*. Translated by Mark E. Biddle. Grand Rapids: Baker Academic, 2002.

———. *Studien zum Urchristentum*. Vol. 6 of *Kleine Schriften*, edited by Claus-Jürgen Thornton. WUNT 234. Tübingen: Mohr Siebeck, 2008.

———. *Theologische, historische und biographische Skizzen*. Vol. 7 of *Kleine Schriften*, edited by Claus-Jürgen Thornton and Jörg Frey. WUNT 253. Tübingen: Mohr Siebeck, 2010.

Hertel, Katharina, and Martin-Luther-Gymnasium, eds. *Gratwanderungen—Das "Entjudungsinstitut" in Eisenach: Eine Dokumentation zur Ausstellung des Martin-Luther-Gymnasiums Eisenach*. Weimar/Eisenach: Wartburg Verlag, 2013.

Hock, Ronald F. *The Social Context of Paul's Ministry: Tentmaking and Apostleship*. Philadelphia: Fortress, 1980.

Hofius, Otfried. "Ist Jesus der Messias? Thesen." In *Der Messias*, 103–29. *JBTh* 8. Göttingen: Vandenhoeck & Reprecht, 1993.

Holmes, Michael W., ed. and trans. *The Apostolic Fathers: Greek Texts and English Translations*. 3rd ed. Grand Rapids: Baker Academic, 2007.

Horbury, William. "Jewish-Christian Relations in Barnabas and Justin Martyr." In *Jews and Christians: The Parting of the Ways, A.D. 70 to 135*, edited by James D. G. Dunn, 315–46. Grand Rapids: Eerdmans, 1999.

Horn, Cornelia, Samuel N. C. Lieu, and Robert R. Phenix Jr. "Beyond the Eastern Frontier." In *Early Christianity in Contexts: An Exploration across Cultures and Continents*, edited by William Tabbernee, 63–109. Grand Rapids: Baker Academic, 2014.

Hurtado, Larry W. *Destroyer of the Gods: Early Christian Distinctiveness in the Roman World*. Waco: Baylor University Press, 2017.

———. "Early Christian Dilemma: Codex or Scroll?" *BAR* 44, no. 6 (2018): 54–56, 66.

Jeremias, Joachim. *The Eucharistic Words of Jesus*. Translated by Norman Perrin. Philadelphia: Fortress, 1977.

———. *Infant Baptism in the First Four Centuries*. Translated by David Cairns. Eugene, OR: Wipf & Stock, 2004.

Johnson, Luke Timothy. *Among the Gentiles: Greco-Roman Religion and Christianity*. AYBRL. New Haven: Yale University Press, 2009.

Josephus, Flavius. *Jewish Antiquities*. Translated by H. St. J. Thackeray et al. 9 vols. LCL. Cambridge, MA: Harvard University Press, 1930–65.

———. *The Jewish War*. Translated by H. St. J. Thackeray. 3 vols. LCL. Cambridge: Harvard University Press, 1927–28.

———. *The Life. Against Apion*. Translated by H. St. J. Thackeray. LCL. Cambridge: Harvard University Press, 1926.

Karaman, Elif Hilal. *Ephesian Women in Greco-Roman and Early Christian Perspective*. WUNT 474. Tübingen: Mohr Siebeck, 2018.

Keener, Craig S. *Acts: An Exegetical Commentary*. 4 vols. Grand Rapids: Baker Academic, 2012–15.

Kelly, J. N. D. *Early Christian Doctrines*. 2nd ed. New York: Harper & Row, 1960.

Kidd, B. J. *The Roman Primacy to A.D. 461*. London: SPCK, 1936.

Klauck, Hans-Josef. *The Religious Context of Early Christianity: A Guide to Graeco-Roman Religions*. Translated by Brian McNeil. Minneapolis: Fortress, 2003.

Kleinknecht, Hermann. *Pantheion: Religiöse Texts des Griechentums*. Tübingen: Mohr Siebeck, 1959.

Koch, Dietrich-Alex. *Geschichte des Urchristentums: Ein Lehrbuch*. Göttingen: Vandenhoeck & Ruprecht, 2013.

Komroff, Manuel, ed. *The Travels of Marco Polo*. New York: Modern Library, 1953.

Kondoleon, Christine, ed. *Antioch: The Lost Ancient City*. Princeton: Princeton University Press, 2000.

Kraft, Robert A., and AnneMarie Luijendijk. "Christianity's Rise after Judaism's Demise in Early Egypt." In *Partings: How Judaism and Christianity Became Two*, edited by Hershel Shanks, 179–85. Washington, DC: Biblical Archaeology Society, 2013.

Kruger, Michael. *The Question of Canon: Challenging the Status Quo in the New Testament Debate*. Downer's Grove, IL: InterVarsity Press, 2013.

Lake, Kirsopp, trans. *The Apostolic Fathers*. 2 vols. LCL. Cambridge: Harvard University Press, 1970–75.

———. "Introduction." In Eusebius, *Ecclesiastical History*. Vol. 1, translated by Kirsopp Lake. LCL 153. Cambridge, MA: Harvard University Press, 1926.

Larkin, William J., Jr. *Acts*. IVPNTC 5. Downers Grove, IL: InterVarsity, 1995.

Lewis, Naphtali, Yigael Yadin, and Jonas C. Greenfield, eds. *Greek Papyri; Aramaic and Nabatean Signatures and Subscriptions*. Vol. 2 of *The Documents from the Bar Kokhba Period in the Cave of Letters*. Judean Desert Studies. Jerusalem: Israel Exploration Society, 1989.

Lietzmann, Hans. *Geschichte der Alten Kirche*. Foreword by Christoph Markschies. Berlin: Walter de Gruyter, 1999.

———. *A History of the Early Church*. Translated by Bertram Lee Woolf. 4 vols. Cleveland: Meridian Books, 1961.

———. *Mass and Lord's Supper: A Study in the History of the Liturgy*. Translated by Dorothea H. G. Reeve. Introduction and Supplementary Essay by Robert Douglas Richardson. Leiden: Brill, 1953–79.

Lieu, Samuel N. C., and Ken Parry. "Deep into Asia." In *Early Christianity in Contexts: An Exploration across Cultures and Continents*, edited by William Tabbernee, 143–80. Grand Rapids: Baker Academic, 2014.

Lightfoot, J. B. *The Apostolic Fathers*. 2nd ed. 5 vols. Grand Rapids: Baker, 1981.

———. *Saint Paul's Epistle to the Philippians*. Rev. ed. Grand Rapids: Zondervan, 1953.

Lohmeyer, Ernst. *Die Briefe an die Philipper, Kolosser und an Philemon*. KEK. Göttingen: Vandenhoeck & Ruprecht, 1961.

———. *Christuskult und Kaiserkult*. Tübingen: Mohr Siebeck, 1919.

———. *Galiläa und Jerusalem*. FRLANT 52. Göttingen: Vandenhoeck & Ruprecht, 1936.

———. *Die Offenbarung des Johannes*. 2nd ed. HNT 16. Tübingen: Mohr Siebeck, 1953.

———. *Soziale Fragen im Urchristentum*. Darmstadt: Wissenschaftliche Buchgesellschaft, 1973.

Lowden, John. *Early Christian and Byzantine Art*. London: Phaidon, 2003.

Luke, Trevor S. *Ushering in a New Republic: Theologies of Arrival at Rome in the First Century BCE*. Ann Arbor, MI: University of Michigan Press, 2014.

Maas, Michael. "People and Identity in Roman Antioch." In *Antioch: The Lost Ancient City*, edited by Christine

Kondoleon, 13–22. Princeton: Princeton University Press, 2000.

MacMullen, Ramsay. *Christianizing the Roman Empire (A.D. 100–400).* New Haven: Yale University Press, 1984.

MacMullen, Ramsay, and Eugene N. Lane, eds. *Paganism and Christianity, 100–425 C.E.: A Sourcebook.* Minneapolis: Fortress, 1992.

Maier, Harry O. *New Testament Christianity in the Roman World.* Essentials of Biblical Studies. New York: Oxford University Press, 2019.

McCormick, Michael. "The Birth of the Codex and the Apostolic Life-Style." *Scriptorium* 39, no. 1 (1985): 150–58.

McGinn, Sheila E. *The Jesus Movement and the World of the Early Church.* Winona, MN: Anselm Academic, 2014.

McGowan, Andrew Brian. "'Is There a Liturgical Text in This Gospel?': The Institution Narratives and Their Early Interpretive Communities." *JBL* 118, no. 1 (1999): 73–87.

Meeks, Wayne A. *The First Urban Christians: The Social World of the Apostle Paul.* 2nd ed. New Haven: Yale University Press, 2003.

Merdinger, Jane. "Roman North Africa." In *Early Christianity in Contexts: An Exploration across Cultures and Continents,* edited by William Tabbernee, 223–60. Grand Rapids: Baker Academic, 2014.

Metzger, Bruce M. *The Canon of the New Testament: Its Origin, Development, and Significance.* Oxford: Clarendon, 1997.

———. *The Early Versions of the New Testament: Their Origin, Transmission, and Limitations.* Oxford: Clarendon, 1977.

———. *Historical and Literary Studies: Pagan, Jewish, and Christian.* Grand Rapids: Eerdmans, 1968.

———. *The Text of the New Testament: Its Transmission, Corruption, and Restoration.* New York: Oxford University Press, 1964.

Meyers, Eric M. "Living Side by Side in Galilee." In *Partings: How Judaism and Christianity Became Two,* edited by Hershel Shanks, 133–50. Washington, DC: Biblical Archaeology Society, 2013.

Meyers, Eric M., and Mark A. Chancey. *Alexander to Constantine: Archaeology of the Land of the Bible.* AYBRL 3. New Haven: Yale University Press, 2012.

Milik, J. T. *Ten Years of Discovery in the Wilderness of Judea.* Translated by John Strugnell. SBT 26. Naperville, IL: Allenson, 1959.

Moffett, Samuel Hugh. *A History of Christianity in Asia.* Vol. 1, *Beginnings to 1500.* San Francisco: HarperSanFrancisco, 1992.

Moo, Douglas. *The Epistle to the Romans.* NICNT. Grand Rapids: Eerdmans, 1996.

Moore, George Foot. *Judaism in the First Centuries of the Christian Era.* 2 vols. New York: Schocken Books, 1971.

Moussaieff, Shlomo. "The New Cleopatra and the Jewish Tax." *BAR* 36, no. 1 (2010). 47–49.

Murphy-O'Connor, Jerome. "Fishers of Fish, Fishers of Men: What We Know of the First Disciples from Their Profession." *BRev* 15, no. 3 (1999): 22–28.

———. *The Holy Land: An Oxford Archaeological Guide from Earliest Times to 1700.* 4th ed. Oxford Archaeological Guides. New York: Oxford University Press, 1998.

Nock, Arthur Darby. *Conversion: The Old and New in Religion from Alexander the Great to Augustine of Hippo.* London: Oxford University Press, 1933.

———. *Early Gentile Christianity and Its Hellenistic Background.* New York: Harper Torchbooks, 1964.

Nun, Mendel. "Ports of Galilee." *BAR* 25, no. 4 (1999): 18–31.

Paget, James Carleton. "Hellenistic and Early Roman Period Jewish Missionary Efforts in the Diaspora." In *The Rise and Expansion of Christianity in the First Three Centuries of the Common Era,* edited by Clare K. Rothschild and Jens Schröter, 11–60. WUNT 301. Tübingen: Mohr Siebeck, 2013.

Parker, D. C. *An Introduction to the New Testament Manuscripts and Their Texts.* Cambridge: Cambridge University Press, 2008.

Pelikan, Jaroslav. *The Christian Tradition: A History of the Development of Doctrine.* Vol. 1, *The Emergence of the Catholic Tradition (100–600).* Chicago: University of Chicago Press, 1971.

———. *The Melody of Theology: A Philosophical Dictionary.* Cambridge, MA: Harvard University Press, 1988.

Poirier, John C. "Purity beyond the Temple in the Second Temple Era." *JBL* 122, no. 2 (2003): 247–65.

Pratscher, William, ed. *The Apostolic Fathers: An Introduction.* Waco: Baylor University Press, 2010.

Quasten, Johannes. *Patrology.* 4 vols. Westminster, MD: Christian Classics, 1993–94.

Rabenau, Konrad von, ed. *Latinitas christiana: Ein lateinisches Lesebuch mit Texten aus der Geschichte der christlichen Kirchen.* Vol. 1. Berlin: Evangelische Verlagsanstalt, 1978.

Rabin, Chaim. "Hebrew and Aramaic in the First Century." In *The Jewish People in the First Century: Historical Geography, Political History, Social, Cultural and Religious Life and Institutions*, edited by S. Safrai and M. Stern, 1007–39. Vol. 2. CRINT. Philadelphia: Fortress, 1976.

Rahlfs, Alfred. "History of the Septuagint Text." In *Septuaginta*, xxii–xxxi. 8th ed. Stuttgart: Würtembergische Bibelanstalt, 1965.

Ramsay, William M. *The Church in the Roman Empire before A.D. 170.* Grand Rapids: Baker, 1979. First published, London: Hodder & Stoughton, 1893.

Reed, Annette Yoshiko, and Lily Vuong. "Christianity in Antioch: Partings in Roman Syria." In *Partings: How Judaism and Christianity Became Two*, edited by Hershel Shanks, 105–32. Washington, DC: Biblical Archaeology Society, 2013.

Reynolds, J. M., and R. F. Tannenbaum. *Jews and Godfearers at Aphrodisias.* Cambridge: Cambridge University Press, 1987.

Reynolds, L. D., and N. G. Wilson. *Scribes and Scholars: A Guide to the Transmission of Greek and Latin Literature.* 3rd ed. Oxford: Clarendon, 1991.

Richardson, Peter. *Herod: King of the Jews and Friend of the Romans.* Columbia, SC: University of South Carolina Press, 1996.

Robinson, Thomas A. *Who Were the First Urban Christians? Dismantling the Urban Thesis.* New York: Oxford University Press, 2017.

Sanders, E. P. *Judaism: Practice and Belief, 63 BCE–66 CE.* Philadelphia: Trinity Press International, 1992.

Sanneh, Lamin. *Translating the Message: The Missionary Impact on Culture.* 2nd ed. Maryknoll, NY: Orbis Books, 2009.

Schäfer, Peter. *The Jewish Jesus: How Judaism and Christianity Shaped Each Other.* Princeton: Princeton University Press, 2012.

Schlatter, Adolf. *Der Evangelist Matthäus: Seine Sprache, sein Ziel, seine Selbständigkeit.* Stuttgart: Calwer, 1948.

———. *Die Kirche Jerusalems vom Jahre 70–130.* Gütersloh: G. Bertelsmann, 1898.

Schlichting, Günter. *Ein jüdisches Leben Jesu.* WUNT 24. Tübingen: Mohr Siebeck, 1982.

Schröter, Jens. "'Harnack Revisited': Die Entstehung und Ausbreitung des Christentums in den ersten drei Jahrhunderten." In *The Rise and Expansion of Christianity in the First Three Centuries of the Common Era*, edited by Clare K. Rothschild and Jens Schröter, 487–99. WUNT 301. Tübingen: Mohr Siebeck, 2013.

Schürer, Emil. *The History of the Jewish People in the Age of Jesus Christ (175 B.C.–A.D. 135).* Translated, revised, and edited by Geza Vermes, Fergus Millar, Pamela Vermes, and Matthew Black. 4 vols. Edinburgh: T&T Clark, 1973.

Schweizer, Eduard. *Gemeinde und Gemeindeordnung im Neuen Testament.*

2nd ed. ATANT 35. Zurich: Zwingli, 1962.

———. *The Good News according to Mark*. Translated by Donald H. Madvig. Atlanta: John Knox, 1970.

———. *Jesus*. Translated by David Green. Atlanta: John Knox, 1971.

———. *Jesus Christ: The Man from Nazareth and the Exalted Lord*. The 1984 Sizemore Lectures in Biblical Studies at Midwestern Baptist Theological Seminary. Edited by Hulitt Gloer. Macon, GA: Mercer University Press, 1987.

———. *The Lord's Supper according to the New Testament*. Translated by James M. Davis. Philadelphia: Fortress, 1967.

———. *Neotestamentica: Deutsche und Englische Aufsätze 1951–1963*. Zurich: Zwingli, 1963.

Segal, Alan F. *Rebecca's Children: Judaism and Christianity in the Roman World*. Cambridge, MA: Harvard University Press, 1986.

Sittser, Gerald L. *Resilient Faith: How the Early Christian "Third Way" Changed the World*. Grand Rapids: Brazos, 2019.

Skeat, T. C. "Early Christian Book-Production: Papyri and Manuscripts." In *The Cambridge History of the Bible*. Vol. 2, *The West from the Fathers to the Reformation*, edited by G. W. H. Lampe, 54–79. Cambridge: Cambridge University Press, 1976.

Smith, Dennis. "Dinner with Jesus and Paul." *BRev* 20, no. 4 (2004): 30–39.

Soskice, Janet. *The Sisters of Sinai: How Two Lady Adventurers Discovered the Hidden Gospels*. New York: Vintage, 2010.

Speake, Graham. *A History of the Athonite Commonwealth: The Spiritual and Cultural Diaspora of Mount Athos*. Cambridge: Cambridge University Press, 2018.

Stark, Rodney. *The Rise of Christianity: A Sociologist Reconsiders History*. Princeton: Princeton University Press, 1996.

Stegemann, Ekkehard W., and Wolfgang Stegemann. *The Jesus Movemen: A Social History of Its First Century*. Translated by O. C. Dean Jr. Minneapolis: Fortress, 1999.

Stevenson, J. *A New Eusebius: Documents Illustrative of the History of the Church to A.D. 337*. London: SPCK, 1963.

Stewart, Alistair C. *The Original Bishops: Office and Order of the First Christian Communities*. Grand Rapids: Baker Academic, 2014.

Stuhlmacher, Peter. "The Understanding of Christ in the Pauline School: A Sketch." In *Jews and Christians: The Parting of the Ways, A.D. 70 to 135*, edited by James D. G. Dunn, 159–76. Grand Rapids: Eerdmans, 1999.

Suetonius. *Lives of the Caesars*. Vol. 1, *Julius. Augustus. Tiberius. Gaius. Caligula*, translated by J. C. Rolfe. LCL 31. Cambridge, MA: Harvard University Press, 1914.

Tacitus. *Annals*. Vol. 4, *Books 4–6, 11–12*, translated by John Jackson. LCL 312. Cambridge, MA: Harvard University Press, 1937.

———. *Annals*. Vol. 5, *Books 13–16*, translated by John Jackson. LCL 322. Cambridge, MA: Harvard University Press, 1937.

Taylor, Joan. "Parting in Palestine." In *Partings: How Judaism and Christianity Became Two*, edited by Hershel Shanks, 87–104. Washington, DC: Biblical Archaeology Society, 2013.

Tixeront, L. J. *Les origines de l'église d'Édesse et la légend d'Abgar*. Paris: Maisonneuve et Ch. Leclerc, 1888.

Treu, Kurt. "Die Bedeutung des Griechischen für die Juden im Römischen Reich." *Kairos* 15 (1973): 123–44.

Trumler, Gerhard. *Athos: The Garden of the Virgin*. Athens: Adam Editions, 1999.

Tzaferis, Vassilios. "Inscribed 'To God Jesus Christ.'" *BAR* 33, no. 2 (2007): 38–49.

van der Toorn, Karel. "Egyptian Papyrus Sheds New Light on Jewish History." *BAR* 44, no. 4 (2018): 32–39, 66–70.

von Campenhausen, Hans Freiherr. *Aus der Frühzeit des Christentums: Studien zur Kirchengeschichte des ersten und zweiten Jahrhunderts.* Tübingen: Mohr Siebeck, 1963.

———. *Die Entstehung der christlichen Bibel.* BHT 39. Tübingen: Mohr Siebeck, 1968.

———. *Urchristliches und Altkirchliches: Vorträge und Aufsätze.* Tübingen: Mohr Siebeck, 1979.

Wander, Bernd. *Gottesfürchtige und Sympathisanten: Studien zum heidnischen Umfeld von Diasporasynagogen.* WUNT 104. Tübingen: Mohr Siebeck, 1998.

Wardle, Timothy. "Pillars, Foundations, and Stones: Individual Believers as Constituent Parts of the Early Christian Communal Temple." In *Sacrifice, Cult, and Atonement in Early Judaism and Christianity: Constituents and Critique,* ed. Henrietta L. Wiley and Christian A. Eberhardt, 289–309. Resources for Biblical Study 85. Atlanta: SBL Press, 2017.

Watson, Pamela. "The Christian Flight to Pella? The Archaeological Picture." In *Partings: How Judaism and Christianity Became Two,* edited by Hershel Shanks, 73–86. Washington, DC: Biblical Archaeology Society, 2013.

Wehr, Lothar. *Arznei der Unsterblichkeit: Die Eucharistie bei Ignatius von Antiochien und im Johannesevangelium.* NTAbh 8. Münster: Aschendorff, 1987.

Wilken, Robert Louis. *The Christians as the Romans Saw Them.* 2nd ed. New Haven: Yale University Press, 2003.

Wilkinson, John, trans. *Egeria's Travels.* 3rd ed. Oxford: Aris & Phillips, 2006.

Williams, Margaret H. "Jews and Christians at Rome: An Early Parting of the Ways." In *Partings: How Judaism and Christianity Became Two,* edited by Hershel Shanks, 151–78. Washington, DC: Biblical Archaeology Society, 2013.

Williams, R. R. *Acts of the Apostles: "Nothing Can Stop the Gospel."* TBC. London: SCM, 1965.

Wilson, Mark. *Biblical Turkey: A Guide to the Jewish and Christian Sites of Asia Minor.* Istanbul: Yayinlari, 2010.

Winter, Bruce W. *Divine Honours for the Caesars: The First Christians' Responses.* Grand Rapids: Eerdmans, 2015.

Wise, Michael O. *Language and Literacy in Roman Judaea: A Study of the Bar Kokhba Documents.* AYBRL. New Haven: Yale University Press, 2015.

Wright, N. T. *Paul and the Faithfulness of God.* Minneapolis: Fortress, 2013.

Zahn, Theodor. *Geschichte des Neutestamentlichen Kanons.* 3 vols. Erlangen: Deichert, 1888.

———. *Ignatius von Antiochien.* Gotha: Perthes, 1873.

———. *Skizzen aus dem Leben der Alten Kirche.* 2nd ed. Erlangen: Deichert, 1898.

Scripture Index

Ancient Writings Index

Subject Index